CONTENTS

I am standing on the Pont des Arts in Paris. On one side of the Seine is the harmonious, reasonable façade of the Institute of France, built as a college in about 1670. On the other bank is the Louvre, built continuously from the Middle Ages to the nineteenth century : classical architecture at its most splendid and assured. Just visible upstream is the Cathedral of Notre-Dame — not perhaps the most lovable of cathedrals, but the most rigorously intellectual façade in the whole of Gothic art. The houses that line the banks of the river are also a humane and reasonable solution of what town architecture should be...

Kenneth Clark : Civilisation.
John Murray (Publishers) Ltd/BBC Publications/Harper and Row Ltd

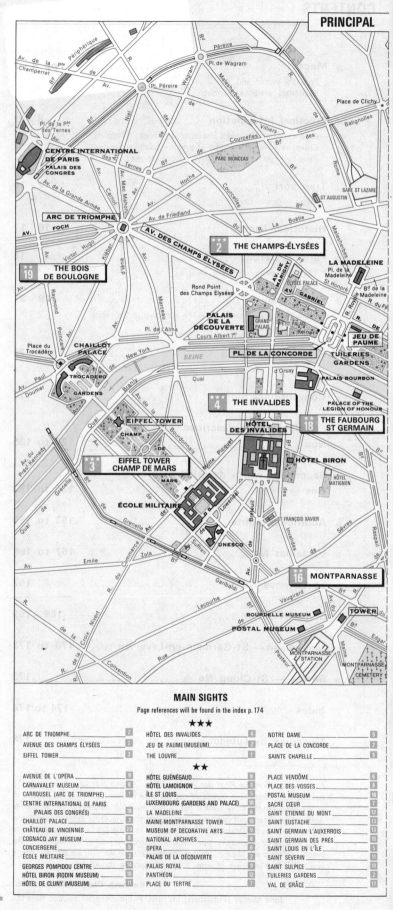

MAIN SIGHTS

Page references will be found in the index p. 174

★★★

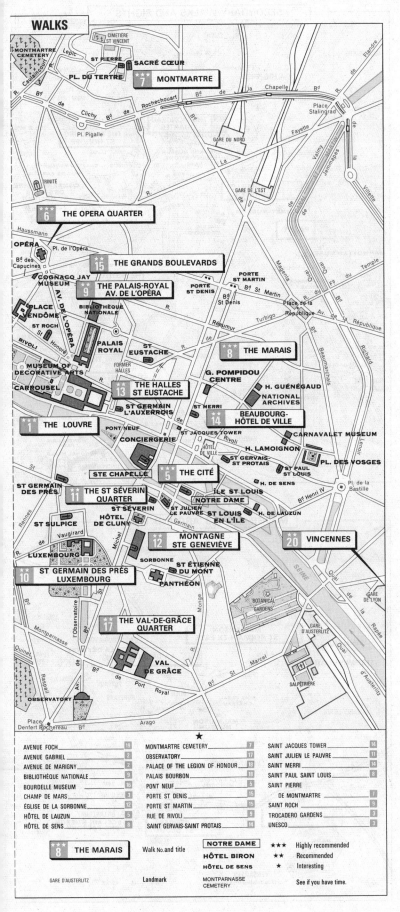

WALKS

MONTMARTRE CEMETERY

CIMETIÈRE ST ST VINCENT

ST PIERRE

SACRÉ CŒUR

PL. DU TERTRE

★★★
7 MONTMARTRE

Pl. Pigalle

GARE DU NORD

TRINITÉ

GARE DE L'EST

Place Stalingrad

★★★
6 THE OPERA QUARTER

OPÉRA

Pl. de l'Opéra

Bd des Capucines

★★
15 THE GRANDS BOULEVARDS

COGNACQ JAY MUSEUM

PORTE ST MARTIN

★★
9 THE PALAIS-ROYAL AV. DE L'OPÉRA

PORTE ST DENIS

St Martin

St Denis

PLACE VENDÔME

BIBLIOTHÈQUE NATIONALE

Place de la République

ST ROCH

PALAIS ROYAL

ST EUSTACHE

MUSEUM OF DECORATIVE ARTS

FORMER HALLES

G. POMPIDOU CENTRE

★★
8 THE MARAIS

CARROUSEL

★★
13 THE HALLES ST EUSTACHE

H. GUÉNÉGAUD

NATIONAL ARCHIVES

ST GERMAIN L'AUXERROIS

ST MERRI

★★
14 BEAUBOURG-HÔTEL DE VILLE

CARNAVALET MUSEUM

★★★
1 THE LOUVRE

PONT NEUF

CONCIERGERIE

ST JACQUES TOWER

H. LAMOIGNON

PL. DES VOSGES

HÔTEL DE VILLE

ST GERVAIS-ST PROTAIS

ST PAUL ST LOUIS

H. DE SENS

★★★
5 THE CITÉ

★★
11 THE ST SÉVERIN QUARTER

ST GERMAIN DES PRÉS

ÎLE ST LOUIS

NOTRE DAME

Pl. de la Bastille

ST SÉVERIN

ST JULIEN LE PAUVRE

ST LOUIS EN L'ÎLE

H. DE LAUZUN

ST SULPICE

HÔTEL DE CLUNY

★★
12 MONTAGNE STE GENEVIÈVE

★★
20 VINCENNES

LUXEMBOURG

SORBONNE

ST ÉTIENNE DU MONT

★★★
10 ST GERMAIN DES PRÉS LUXEMBOURG

PANTHÉON

BOTANICAL GARDENS

GARE D'AUSTERLITZ

GARE DE LYON

★★
17 THE VAL-DE-GRÂCE QUARTER

VAL DE GRÂCE

SALPÊTRIÈRE

OBSERVATORY

Place Denfert Rocherau

★

★★★
8 THE MARAIS

Walk No. and title

NOTRE DAME
HÔTEL BIRON
HÔTEL DE SENS

★★★ Highly recommended
★★ Recommended
★ Interesting

GARE D'AUSTERLITZ

Landmark

MONTPARNASSE CEMETERY

See if you have time.

5

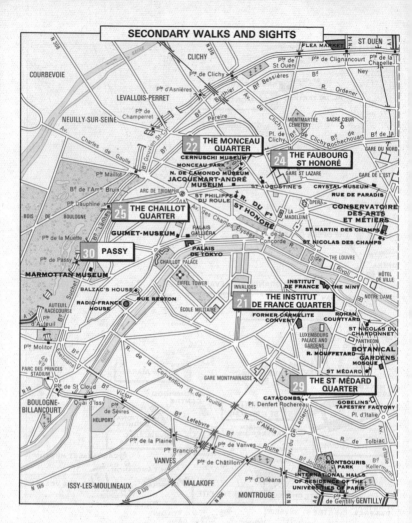

SECONDARY WALKS AND SIGHTS

COURBEVOIE

CLICHY

FLEA MARKET ST OUEN

Pte de St Ouen Pte de Clignancourt Pte de la Chapelle

LEVALLOIS-PERRET

Pte d'Asnières Berthier Av. de Clichy Bd Bessières Ney

R. Ordener

NEUILLY-SUR-SEINE

Pte de Champerret Pereire Montmartre Cemetery Sacré Cœur

Pl. de Clichy Bd de Rochechouart Bd de la

Charles de Gaulle Bd Gouvion St-Cyr

22 THE MONCEAU QUARTER

CERNUSCHI MUSEUM
MONCEAU PARK
N. DE CAMONDO MUSEUM
JACQUEMART-ANDRÉ MUSEUM

24 THE FAUBOURG ST HONORÉ

GARE ST LAZARE GARE DE L'EST

GARE DU NORD

Pte Maillot ARC DE TRIOMPHE
Bd de l'Amal Bruix

ST AUGUSTINE'S CRYSTAL MUSEUM RUE DE PARADIS

ST PHILIPPE DU ROULE R. DU F.

25 THE CHAILLOT QUARTER

Pte Dauphine

BOIS DE BOULOGNE

Bd Lannes

ARC DE TRIOMPHE
Av. des Champs Élysées

ST HONORÉ OPÉRA CONSERVATOIRE DES ARTS ET MÉTIERS

LA MADELEINE ST MARTIN DES CHAMPS
ST NICOLAS DES CHAMPS

Pte de la Muette

GUIMET-MUSEUM PALAIS GALLIERA

Pl. de la Concorde THE LOUVRE Rivoli HÔTEL DE VILLE

30 PASSY

Pte de Passy

Suchet PALAIS DE TOKYO CHAILLOT PALACE

INSTITUT DE FRANCE THE MINT NOTRE DAME

MARMOTTAN MUSEUM

EIFFEL TOWER

INVALIDES

21 THE INSTITUT DE FRANCE QUARTER

ROHAN COURTYARD

AUTEUIL RACECOURSE

BALZAC'S HOUSE RUE BERTON
RADIO-FRANCE HOUSE

ÉCOLE MILITAIRE

FORMER CARMELITE CONVENT

ST NICOLAS DU CHARDONNET
PANTHEON

Pte d'Auteuil

LUXEMBOURG PALACE AND GARDENS

BOTANICAL GARDENS MOSQUE

Pte Molitor

R. de la Convention R. de Vaugirard

R. MOUFFETARD

GARE MONTPARNASSE ST MÉDARD

PARC DES PRINCES STADIUM

Pte de St Cloud Bd Victor Quai d'Issy de Sèvres HELIPORT

R. de Vouillé

29 THE ST MÉDARD QUARTER

CATACOMBS
Pl. Denfert Rochereau

GOBELINS' TAPESTRY FACTORY

Pl. d'Italie

BOULOGNE-BILLANCOURT

Bd Lefebvre R. d'Alésia Av. du Gal Leclerc R. de Tolbiac

Pte de la Plaine Pte de Vanves Brune Bd Jourdan Bd Kellermann

VANVES Pte de Châtillon

MONTSOURIS PARK

Pte d'Orléans

INTERNATIONAL HALLS OF RESIDENCE OF THE UNIVERSITIES OF PARIS

ISSY-LES-MOULINEAUX MALAKOFF MONTROUGE Pte de Gentilly GENTILLY

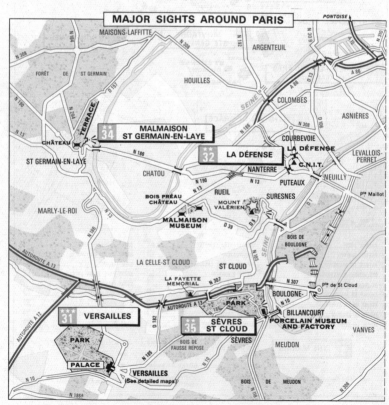

MAJOR SIGHTS AROUND PARIS

PONTOISE

MAISONS-LAFFITTE

ARGENTEUIL

FORÊT DE ST GERMAIN

HOUILLES

COLOMBES

ASNIÈRES

ST GERMAIN-EN-LAYE

TERRACE.

34 MALMAISON ST GERMAIN-EN-LAYE

CHÂTEAU

CHATOU

COURBEVOIE LA DÉFENSE LEVALLOIS-PERRET

32 LA DÉFENSE

C.N.I.T.

NANTERRE PUTEAUX NEUILLY

Pte Maillot

BOIS PRÉAU CHÂTEAU

RUEIL SURESNES

MARLY-LE-ROI

MALMAISON MUSEUM

MOUNT VALÉRIEN

BOIS DE BOULOGNE

LA CELLE-ST CLOUD

ST CLOUD

LA FAYETTE MEMORIAL

Pte de St Cloud

BOULOGNE-BILLANCOURT

31 VERSAILLES

PARK

AUTOROUTE A 13

PARK

35 SÈVRES ST CLOUD

PORCELAIN MUSEUM AND FACTORY

VANVES

PALACE

BOIS DE FAUSSE REPOSE

SÈVRES

MEUDON

VERSAILLES
(See detailed maps)

BOIS DE MEUDON

6

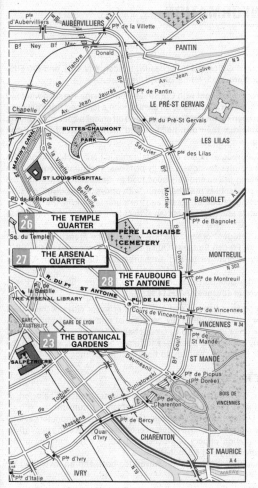

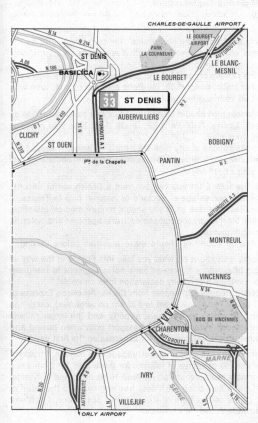

MICHELIN awaits you at
46 Avenue de Breteuil, 7e,
℡ 539.25.00.

In the reception and sales office,
Mondays to Fridays 9 am to
noon and 1 to 4.30 pm,
staff will provide you with
information
on tourist attractions,
hotel accommodation
(no reservation facilities),
and show you the full range of

Michelin maps

Michelin red annual Hotel and
Restaurant Guides

Michelin Green Tourist Guides
in English and French

and will sell you what you
require on the spot.

■

MICHELIN publications
for your stay in Paris

PARIS and environs
Hotels and Restaurants
(red annual leaflet —
extract from the Guide FRANCE)
Plan de PARIS ⑩
scale 1/10 000
PARIS Index et Plan ⑪
practical information,
useful addresses
street index
transports (métro, bus, car)

Map ⑩① **Outskirts of
PARIS**
to cross Paris rapidly
to find your way in the suburbs
to avoid Sunday evening bottlenecks

Green Guide PARIS
if the copy you are
reading now is not your own
or the latest edition!

■

Michelin maps to get you to
Paris

Map ⑨⑧⑨ Main Roads of France
or

Map ⑨①⑥ Main Roads of France
(printed both sides of a half-
size sheet for convenience)

Map ⑨⑨⑧ Main Roads of
Northern France
(all scale 1/1 000 000)

PRACTICAL INFORMATION

BEFORE LEAVING

The French Government Tourist Office at 178 Piccadilly, London WIV OAL and 610 Fifth Avenue New York, ☎ 757-1125 will provide information and literature.

When to go. — In winter the streets are bright with Christmas illuminations, the shop windows brilliant; in summer you can sit beneath the trees or an awning with a long cool drink between seeing the sights or idle away an evening on a café terrace, or go on an open boat on the Seine; in the autumn Parisians are back from their own holidays and there's an air of energy and bustle; and Paris in the spring...

Where to stay. — There are hundreds of hotels and restaurants in Paris. Hotels range from the sumptuous with millionaires' suites to modest family *pensions;* restaurants equally can provide luxurious fare at frightening prices and very good food at reasonable cost — and the great advantage with French restaurants is that the menu, with prices, is displayed outside. For a comprehensive list including prices of hotels and restaurants look in the Michelin Leaflet Paris and environs — Hotels and Restaurants (an extract from the Michelin Red Guide France).

There are several youth and student organizations — apply to the French Government Tourist Office *(address above),* the French Embassy Office 22 Wilton Crescent, London SW1, or the Central Bureau for Educational Visits and Exchanges, 44 Baker Street, London W1 M2HJ.

There is a camping site in the Bois de Boulogne (Allée du Bord de l'Eau, 75016 Paris; *open all the year round).* Apply well in advance. ☎ 506.14.98.

How to get there. — You can go from London and several other major cities in the United Kingdom directly by scheduled national airlines, by commercial and package tour flights, possibly with a rail or coach link-up or you can go by cross-channel ferry or by hovercraft and or by car or train. Enquire at any good travel agent — and remember, if you are going in the holiday season or at Christmas, Easter or Whitsun, to book well in advance.

CUSTOMS AND OTHER FORMALITIES

Papers and other documents. — A valid British Passport or other national passport or British Visitor's Passport is all that is required in the way of personal documents.

For the car a UK Driving Licence, an International Driving Licence, and International Insurance Certificate if you have a comprehensive insurance, otherwise your own policy gives you third party cover, car registration papers (log-book) and GB or other national plates (measuring not less than 6.9 inches long and 4.5 inches deep).

Caravan owners must, in addition, produce the caravan log-book and an inventory, for customs clearance.

Assistance provided by the Motoring Organizations. — The AA, RAC and Routiers (354 Fulham Road, London SW10) run accident insurance and breakdown service schemes for their members.

Hiring a car. — There are agents at airports, the air terminal, railway stations and on the main streets. Hotels, travel agents, etc. will put you in touch. You require an International Driving Licence.

There are restricted and paying parking zones (blue and grey zones) — beware where you leave your car! In an effort to clear traffic congestion, the Paris police are strict, even with tourists. Mistakes are costly and, of course, time wasting.

Post and Telephone. — *Poste restante* mail should be addressed in your name, and then as follows : Poste Restante, 52 rue du Louvre, 75100 Paris RP, ☎ 233.71.60. Take your passport as identification when collecting your mail.

Telephone rates from a public telephone at any time are : Paris — London : about 7.80F for 3 minutes; Paris — New York : 48F for 3 minutes. Delays during daytime hours are usual and often lengthy — try to book your call in advance.

Health Insurance. — Even with the form E 111 you can get from a British social security office and which will save you a big percentage of doctor's or hospital bills in France, it is advisable to insure against medical expenses as, if you should require medical attention, you will have to be treated privately. Most insurance companies, travel agencies and motoring organizations have shemes at low premiums.

Nationals of non Common Market countries should make inquiries before leaving.

Currency. — There are no customs restrictions on what you take into France in the way of currency. To facilitate the export of currency in foreign bank notes, superior to the given allocation, visitors are advised to complete a currency declaration form on arrival.

Carry your money in Travellers' Cheques, obtainable from Cooks, American Express or your bank and exchangeable at banks *(hours : 9.30 am to 3.30 pm on weekdays),* exchange offices *(bureaux de change)* always found at air terminals, airports, and the larger railway stations, and in some hotels and shops — you need your passport both when buying and cashing cheques. Take a small amount of local currency for expenses on the first day.

Customs. — Going into France from the UK : your personal luggage may include, 1 bottle of spirits, 200 cigarettes or 50 cigars or 250 grammes of tobacco for those over 15; 2 cameras, 10 rolls of film per camera, a portable radio, record player (and 10 records) and a musical instrument. Returning to the UK : you may bring back duty free purchases to the value of £10, 300 cigarettes or 175 small cigars or 75 cigars or 400 grammes of tobacco, 1 bottle of spirits, 2 litres of wine. See also note above on currency.

DULY ARRIVED

To get the " feel ", the atmosphere, of Paris, besides seeing the sights described on pages 27-173 you will want to sit at a café table on the pavement, sipping a drink, go in one of the boats on the Seine, which enables you to see many of the major buildings from an unusual angle and rest at the same time, go, one week-end, to the Flea Market (p 156).

There are three types of boat : *the* **Bateaux-mouches** *(midday and evening restaurant), embarkation : Alma Bridge — Right Bank — ℐ 225.96.10 — 11 am, 2.30, 4 pm (9 pm Saturdays) except Mondays.* **Vedettes Paris-Tour Eiffel,** *embarkation : Iéna Bridge — Left Bank — ℐ 551.33.08 — 9.30 am to noon and 1.30 to 5.30 pm (9 pm Saturdays and Sundays).* **Vedettes du Pont-Neuf,** *embarkation : Vert-Galant Square — ℐ 633.98.38 — everyday 10.30, 11.15 am, noon and every 1/2 hour, 1.30 to 5 pm.* Many of the boats have glass roofs — you can sightsee spectacularly in the worst thunderstorm.

Look in the *Officiel des Spectacles* (1.20 F) published weekly on Wednesdays and available at newspaper kiosks and *Une Semaine de Paris-Pariscop* (1.80F) for what's on in the theatre, cinema, night-clubs and for sporting and athletics fixtures, exhibitions, flower shows etc. Agencies and hotels will give full details of the sumptuous reviews and music-hall entertainments at the Folies-Bergère, the Lido, the Casino de Paris, the Mayol, the Crazy Horse Saloon, the Moulin Rouge, Olympia and Bobino's.

For children especially. — There are zoos and animal enclosures in the Bois de Boulogne and Bois de Vincennes (pp 131, 135) and in the Botanical Gardens behind Notre Dame (p 139); aquaria, by the Chaillot Palace (p 49) and near the Vincennes' Zoo (p 135). Tropical fish and some animals can be found in the shops and stalls along the Quai de la Mégisserie (p 61). The Tuileries Gardens have many amusements for children from a pond where you can hire model sailing yachts to a marionette theatre. There are other theatres in several parks, a Punch and Judy show in the Luxembourg Palace gardens (p 95) and another boating pond in the Palais Royal gardens.

If it is wet go to the Grévin Waxworks Museum (p 117), the Army Museum (p 56) or the Maritime Museum (p 50).

Shops and shopping. — The big stores and larger shops are open from Monday to Saturday from 9.30 am to 6.30 pm. (A list of the department stores are to be found in the Michelin Guide 🆔 Paris Index et Plan). Smaller, individual shops may close during the lunch hour. Food shops — grocers, wine merchants and bakeries — are often closed on Mondays.

Paris still has a vast number of individually owned small shops, which makes window shopping entertaining, and masses and masses of flower shops which flame with colour.

There are also lively street markets in every quarter.

Comparative sizes, weights and measures. — Clothing : women's dresses and suits — British 34, Continental *40;* 36, *42;* 38, *44;* 40, *46,* etc; men's suits and overcoats — British 36, Continental *46;* 38, *48;* 40, *50,* etc; shirts and collars — British 14, Continental *36;* 14 1/2, *37;* 15, *38,* etc.

Weight : *1 kg* = 2 lb 3 oz; *100 grammes* = 3 1/2 oz. Length : *1 cm* = just under 1/2 inch; *1 mètre* = 39 inches; *1 km* = 5/8 mile. Volume: *1 litre* = 1 3/4 pints; *50 litres* = 11 gallons (13.21 US gal).

Temperature : *21°C* = 70°F; *15.5°C* = 60°F; *10°C* = 50°F — 98.4°F *i.e.* normal body temperature = *37°C*.

Prices and tipping (early 1979). — In shops and on menus, items are clearly marked; small extras cost approximately the following :

English newspapers (dailies)	3.50F
American newspapers (dailies)	3.00F
Petrol (per litre)	2.65F
Petrol-Super (per litre)	2.86F
English cigarettes	4.10 to 6.50F
American cigarettes	4.60 to 5.00F
French cigarettes	2.30 to 4.60F
Postage : to UK — letter 1.50; card 1.00F	
to USA - Airmail — Aerogramme 1.90F; card 1.20F	
Coffee - un café (black espresso)	1.40 to 7.00F
Coffee and milk - un café au lait	1.80 to 7.00F
Fresh lemon or orange juice - citron pressé, orange pressée	3.50 to 9.00F
A beer (bottled) - une bière bouteille	5.00 to 12F
A beer (draught) - une bière pression	3.50 to 12F

Service is often included on the bill; if in doubt ask; if it is not, add on 15 %.

Churches, Synagogues

American Church, 65 Quai d'Orsay, 7ᵉ — ℐ 551.38.90.
American Cathedral (Holy Trinity), 23 Avenue George-V, 8ᵉ — ℐ 359.17.90.
Christian Science, 36 Bd St-Jacques, 14ᵉ — ℐ 707.26.60.
Society of Friends, 114 Rue de Vaugirard, 6ᵉ — ℐ 548.74.23.
St. Michael's English Church, 5 Rue d'Aguesseau, 8ᵉ — ℐ 073.09.00.
English Methodists, 4 Rue Roquépine, 8ᵉ — ℐ 265.71.62.
Church of Scotland, 17 Rue Bayard, 8ᵉ.
St. George's (Anglican), 7 Rue Auguste-Vacquerie, 16ᵉ — ℐ 720.71.67.
St. Joseph's (English speaking, Catholic), 50 Avenue Hoche, 8ᵉ — ℐ 227.20.61.
Liberal Synagogue, 24 Rue Copernic, 16ᵉ — ℐ 727.25.76.
Great Synagogue, 44 Rue de la Victoire, 9ᵉ — ℐ 526.91.89.

TOURIST CALENDAR OF EVENTS

Palm Sunday-May	Vincennes (Reuilly Lawn)	Throne Fair
Late March/end October	Invalides	Son et Lumière (in English)
May-September	Versailles	Fountains (p 165)
June-July	Marais Quarter	Music and Drama Festival
14 July		Military march past
		Open air celebrations, fireworks
July-August-September		Summer Festival
Summer months	Sceaux Orangery	Chamber Music Festival
Early October	Montmartre	Wine harvest Festival
Second Sunday in October	Rue Lepic	Veteran cars hill race
11 November	Champs-Élysées	Military parade at the Arc de Triomphe

Special Displays of Flowers

Mid-March-Mid-April	Bagatelle	Bulbed plants
April	Bagatelle and Floral garden (Bois de Boulogne)	Azaleas
June to late September	L'Haÿ-les-Roses	Roses
June-October	Floral gardens (Vincennes and Bois de Boulogne)	Lotus, nympheas, dahlias, chrysanthenum

Commercial Exhibitions

Late April/early May	Exhibition Ground (Parc des Expositions)	Paris Fair
Late May/early June (1979-1981)	Le Bourget Airport	Paris Air Show
Early October (even years)	Exhibition Ground	Paris Motor Show

Major Sporting Events

Last Sunday in January	Vincennes racecourse	America Stakes
Palm Sunday	Auteuil racecourse	President of the Republic Stakes
First fortnight in June	Parc-des-Princes Stadium	Football Cup Final
Late May/early June	Roland-Garros Courts	French Open Tennis Championships
Whit Monday	St-Cloud racecourse	Spring Grand Prix
Second last Sunday in June	Auteuil	Paris Grand Steeple Chase
Last fortnight in June	Auteuil-Longchamp	Paris Race Meeting
Last Sunday in June	Longchamp	Paris Grand Prix
Mid-July		Finish of the Tour de France cycle race
Late June/early July	Colombes stadium	French athletics championships
September	Vincennes	Summer Grand Prix
First Sunday in October	Longchamp	Arc de Triomphe Grand Prix
1 November or Sunday closest	Auteuil	Autumn Grand Prix

USEFUL ADDRESSES

Accueil de France, 127 Avenue des Champs-Élysées, 8ᵉ — ℔ 723.72.11.
Accueil de la Ville de Paris, Hôtel de Ville, 29 Rue de Rivoli, 4ᵉ — ℔ 278.13.00.
Thos. Cook, 2 Place de la Madeleine, 8ᵉ (main office) — ℔ 260.33.20.
American Express, 11 Rue Scribe, 9ᵉ — ℔ 260.09.99.

Embassies

Australia, 4 Rue Jean-Rey, 15ᵉ — ℔ 575.62.00.
Canada, 35 Avenue Montaigne, 8ᵉ — ℔ 225.99.55.
Great Britain, 35 Rue du Faubourg St-Honoré, 8ᵉ — ℔ 266.91.42.
New Zealand, 7 ter Rue Léonard-de-Vinci, 16ᵉ — ℔ 500.24.11.
South Africa, 59 Quai d'Orsay, 7ᵉ — ℔ 555.92.37.
United States, 2 Avenue Gabriel, 8ᵉ — ℔ 296.12.02.

Hospitals

American Hospital, 63 Bd Victor-Hugo, 92 Neuilly-sur-Seine (7.5 km — 5 miles — from central Paris) — ℔ 747.53.00.
British Hospital, 48 Rue de Villiers, 92 Levallois-Perret (7.5 km — 5 miles) — ℔ 757.22.58.

English Bookshops

Brentano's, 37 Avenue de l'Opéra, 2ᵉ — ℔ 261.52.50.
Smith's, 248 Rue de Rivoli, 1ᵉʳ (English Tea Room upstairs) — ℔ 260.37.97.

Air Terminals, Airports, Airline Main offices

Aérogare de Paris, Les Invalides — ℔ 535.61.61 (Information, exchange open 24 hours, coach connections with airports, left luggage etc.).
Aérogare de Paris, Porte Maillot — ℔ 758.20.18.
Charles de Gaulle Airport, Autoroute du Nord — ℔ 862.12.12 (27 km — 17 miles — from central Paris).
Orly Airport, Autoroute du Sud — ℔ 853.12.34 (16 km — 10 miles).
Air France, 119 Champs-Élysées, 8ᵉ — ℔ 720.70.50.
Air Canada, 24 Bd des Capucines, 9ᵉ — ℔ 273.84.00.
British Airways, 38 Avenue de l'Opéra, 2ᵉ — ℔ 260.38.40.
Pan Am, 1 Rue Scribe, 9ᵉ — ℔ 266.45.45.
Qantas, 7 Rue Scribe, 9ᵉ — ℔ 266.52.00.
T.W.A., 101 Champs-Élysées, 8ᵉ — ℔ 720.62.11.

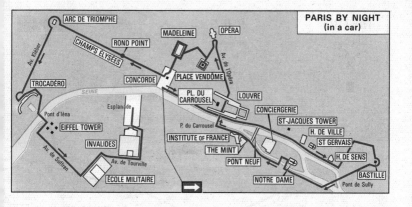

From 1 June to 15 July : Sundays to Fridays 10 pm to midnight (1 am Saturdays and days before a holiday).

The rest of the year : Sundays to Fridays sunset (5.20 to 9.45 pm) to midnight (1 am Saturdays and days before a holiday).

In summer some boat companies give tours on the Seine : (details p 9).

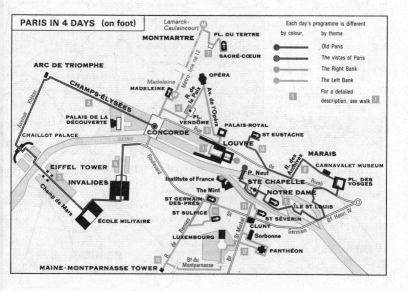

BOOKS TO READ

Artistic, architectural, historical and general background :

101 Buildings to see in Paris — A Short Architectural Guide — RENZO SALVADORI *(Canal Books)*

Paris — HORST MUNZIG *(Time Life, Collection The Great Cities)*

Bonjour Paris — FRANÇOIS BRIGNEAU *(Ed. Sun, Collection Prospects in Colour, France)*

Companion to Paris — VINCENT CRONIN *(Collins)*

The Sun King — NANCY MITFORD *(Hamish Hamilton)*

The Paris I Love *(Tudor Publishing Co.)*

The Terrible Year, the Paris Commune, 1871 — A. HORNE *(Macmillan)*

The French — How they live and work — JOSEPH T. CARROLL *(David & Charles)*

A Moveable Feast — ERNEST HEMINGWAY *(Granada Paperbacks)*

Access in Paris (Disabled Tourist's Guide) — *Obtainable from Mr. G.R. Couch, 68B Castlebar Road, Ealing, London W5*

Five English and American fiction classics :

CHARLES DICKENS — **The Tale of Two Cities**

BARONESS ORCZY — **The Scarlet Pimpernel**

ARNOLD BENNETT — **The Old Wives' Tale** (the 1870/71 siege)

HELEN WADDELL — **Peter Abelard**

ELIOT PAUL — **A Narrow Street**

There are English translations of the works of the major authors mentioned on p 21. There are also about 150 works of fiction with Paris as their setting which make amusing holiday or post-holiday reading. They range from the semi-biographical, semi-factual to light romances and fast moving detectives stories — you will find them listed in the Cumulative Fiction volumes.

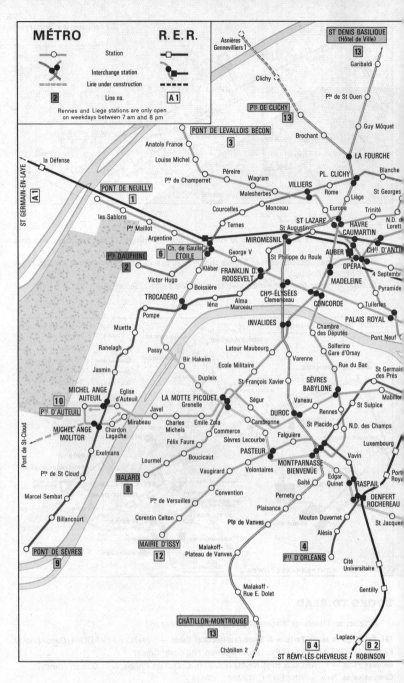

Tickets. — Tickets are obtainable in booklets of ten for 12.50F — second class (19F first class) and are valid also on buses. Booklets, *carnets*, can be purchased in *métro* booking halls (also single tickets, price : 2F second class; 3F first class), on buses, at tobacco counters and at shops with the sign R.A.T.P. outside.

All journeys, apart from those on the Sceaux spur and the R.E.R., require one ticket only no matter how long or short they are. Insert your ticket in the slot of the machine and keep it with you until you have left the *métro*. Never put a ticket in contact with metallic things; it could be demagnetized.

Tourist tickets, on production of a passport, can be bought in larger métro stations and at Services Touristiques de la R.A.T.P., 53 *bis* Quai des Grands Augustins, 6ᵉ as well as in London, SNCF (Bureau officiel); price : 38F or 63F for unlimited journeys for 4 or 7 days respectively in first class cars.

Construction. — Parisians first took the *métro* on 19 July 1900, 37 years after Londoners first took the tube (1863), 32 years after New Yorkers had begun riding on the elevated railway (1868).

Since then other capitals and major cities have followed suit : Berlin (1902), Madrid (1919), Tokyo (1927), Moscow (1935), Rome (1955), Lisbon (1959).

The first Paris line was on the Right Bank, from the Porte de Vincennes to the Porte de Maillot; the engineer responsible was Fulgence Bienvenüe and the architect for what became the standard *métro* entrance, that master of the " noodle " style, Guimard.

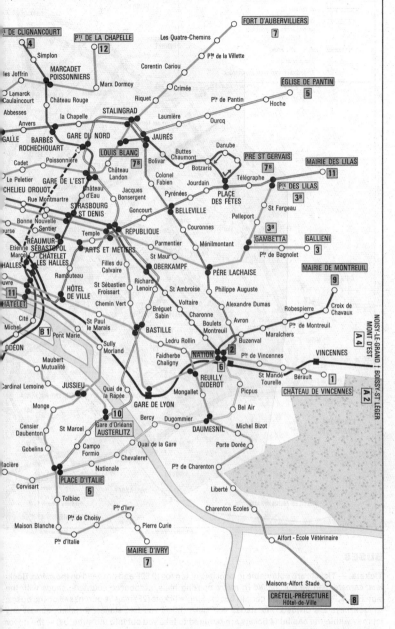

"**Going by métro**". - Lines are named after their terminals. You reach your destination - after possible changes of line - by following the direction panels. Reckon 80 seconds per station, on average. Trains start at 5.30 am. and close down at approximately 1.15 am. the next morning.

Facts and figures. — There are 183 km — 114 miles of track for the 15 lines, apart from the Sceaux spur and R.E.R. *(see below)* and 353 stations of which 135 are interchanges. No point in the capital is more than 500 m — 550 yds. from a *métro* station.

Some 4 million Parisians are transported every weekday — 1 180 million in 1976 — in 3 500 cars. In rush hours trains run every 95 seconds. 14 000 are employed in the *métro* service. (London : 254 miles of track ; 278 stations ; 4 323 cars ; 1 774 000 passengers every weekday — 546 million in 1977 ; rush hour frequency every 2 minutes ; personnel 11 702.)

Modernization. — The system is being modernized technically and aesthetically to make it more efficient and pleasanter : moving walkways are being installed, tyres fitted to reduce noise and improve suspension, platforms lengthened. The white tile walls are being replaced, stations improved and decorated with coloured glass mosaics and window displays (Opéra, Franklin-Roosevelt), good reproductions (Louvre, St-Denis-Basilique) and shops (Montparnasse, Miromesnil, St-Lazare).

The RER. — The Regional Express Network, opened in 1969 as an express system between the city centre and the far distant suburbs, already serves the Val-de-Marne in the east and St-Germain-en-Laye in the west.

It includes three lines : the St-Germain-en-Laye line, the Boissy-Saint-Léger line and the Sceaux line.

The Halles development serves as a meeting point for the RER and the north — south line.

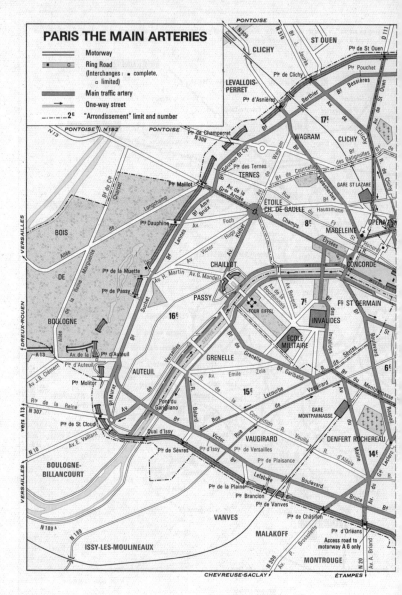

PARIS THE MAIN ARTERIES

- Motorway
- Ring Road
  (Interchanges : ■ complete,
  □ limited)
- Main traffic artery
- One-way street
- 2ᴱ "Arrondissement" limit and number

BUSES

Tickets. — Tickets are obtainable in booklets of ten for 12.50F and are valid on the *métro*. Booklets, *carnets,* can be purchased in *métro* booking halls, at tobacco counters, shops with the sign R.A.T.P. outside and on certain buses. Single tickets (2F) may be purchased on the buses.

Journeys are divided into stages — 1 ticket takes you two stages, 2 tickets almost any journey within the capital (4 tickets are required to take you out into the suburbs) — the driver will show you.

Hours. — All buses run from 6.30 am to 9 pm with some lines continuing later. Services may be reduced or suspended on Sundays and public holidays.

Bus stops are indicated by upright posts on the pavement with red and yellow panels about 2 m — 7 ft above the ground with the bus line indicated in small numerals or letters upon them.

History. — In the mid 17C there circulated in Paris, on the suggestion of the philosopher Pascal, a network of carriages known as *fiacres (p 112)* for which the fare charged was 5 *sols* or a few pence. The system worked well but eventually died, only returning under the Restoration. In 1885 carriages known as Joséphines, Gazelles, Dames Réunies, Carolines, Hirondelles or Sylphides, and seen in all parts of Paris speeding along the streets, were united to form the General Omnibus Company. Horses, in time, were replaced by trams and motor buses.

After 1918 all the road companies combined and in 1942 this joint company amalgamated with the underground. The present R.A.T.P. — Independent Paris Transport Authority — came into being in 1949.

The present problem. — In 1976, 58 routes in Paris and 138 in the suburbs covered 2 038 route km — 1 465 miles — of public thoroughfare and transported more than 686 million passengers — a large number but nevertheless a smaller total than in previous years. (London Transport : 400 bus routes; 4 018 route miles; 1 373 million passengers).

14

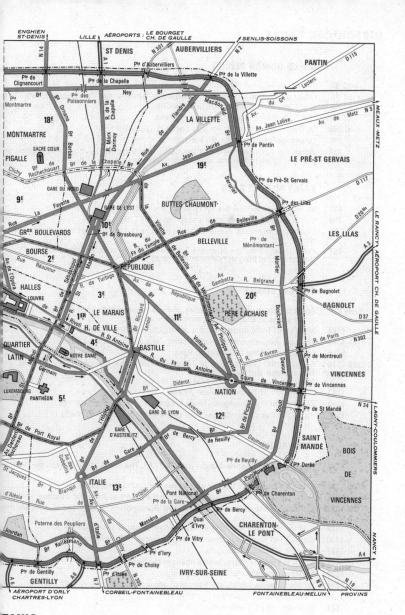

TAXIS

There are 14 300 taxis in Paris, cruising the streets day and night and parked in ranks alongside the kerb close to road junctions and other frequented points beneath signs labelled *Tête de Station*.

The hiring charge is 5F and the approximate rate 1.35F per km (1/2 mile) — depending on the time of day, area, traffic, etc... Prices are clocked up on a meter clearly visible below the centre of the dashboard. (A supplementary charge of 1F is made for taxis from station yards, air terminals, at racecourses and for baggage etc...). Add a 15 % tip.

Taxi telephone numbers and addresses
of car hiring firms are to be found
in the Michelin Guide 🛇 Paris-Index et Plan.

PRIVATE CARS

There are about 1 000 000 private cars in Paris an average of; 90 000 cars drive along the Champs-Élysées and 95 000 along the Tuileries Quays — which explains the bottlenecks, particularly as offices close in the evening. There are only 1 200 km — 750 miles — of highway and so the repercussions of just two or three major holdups...

To try and alleviate the problem, major road works have been and continue to be undertaken : 1 050 crossroads are controlled by lights; 685 km — 426 miles have been made one-way; a blue zone *(zone bleue)* has been created with controlled parking only; a grey zone *zone grise)* with parking meters; some 43 underground parking sites have been built to accommodate 41 000 cars; a ring road created *(boulevard périphérique)* — 35 km — 22 miles : also a west to east expressway (Georges Pompidou expressway) along the Right Bank (13 km — 8 miles) and a further one planned in the opposite direction along the Left Bank.

Obey the one-way and other signs, parking regulations etc. with great care : the Paris police are strict and show no particular leniency to tourists!

HISTORICAL FACTS

GALLO ROMAN PERIOD

3rdC BC	The Parisii settle on the Ile de la Cité.
52 BC	Labienus, Caesar's lieutenant, defeats the Gauls under Camulogenes, who set alight and then abandon the Ile de la Cité.
1C AD	The Gallo Romans build the city of Lutetia.
c. 250	St. Denis, first Bishop of Paris, is martyred *(pp 75, 168)*.
280	Lutetia destroyed by the Barbarians.
360	Julian the Apostate, prefect of the Gauls, is proclaimed by his soldiers Emperor of Rome when in the Cité. Lutetia becomes Paris.

EARLY MIDDLE AGES

451	St. Genevieve turns Attila away from Paris *(p 59)*.
508	Clovis makes Paris his capital and settles in the Cité.
8C	Charlemagne makes Aix-la-Chapelle (Aachen) his foremost city. Paris, abandoned, declines.
885	Paris besieged by the Normans for the fifth time is defended by Count Eudes who is elected King of France in 888 *(p 59)*.

THE CAPETIANS

Early 12C	Abelard, first studies, then teaches, in Paris. Suger, Abbot of St-Denis and minister under Louis VI and Louis VII, rebuilds the abbey.
1163	Maurice of Sully undertakes the construction of Notre-Dame.
1180-1223	Philippe Auguste erects a wall around Paris and builds the Louvre.
1215	Foundation of the University of Paris.
1223-1270	Reign of St. Louis; Pierre of Montreuil builds the Sainte-Chapelle, works on Notre-Dame and St-Denis. The king dispenses justice at Vincennes.
1253	Foundation of Sorbon College *(p 103)*.
1260	The dean of the Merchants' Guild becomes Provost of Paris *(p 115)*.
1307	Philip the Fair dissolves the Order of the Knights Templar *(p 148)*.

THE VALOIS

1358	Uprising under Étienne Marcel *(pp 66, 115)*. The monarchy moves to the Marais and the Louvre.
1364-1380	Charles V builds the Bastille and a new wall round Paris *(p 18)*.
1407	Duke Louis of Orleans is assassinated on the orders of John the Fearless.
1408-1420	Fighting between the Armagnacs and Burgundians. Paris handed over to the English.
1429	Charles VII besieges Paris in vain; Joan of Arc is wounded *(p 91)*.
1430	Henry VI of England is crowned King of France in Notre-Dame.
1437	Charles VII recaptures Paris.
1469	The first French printing works opens in the Sorbonne.
1530	François I founds the Collège de France.
1534	Ignatius Loyola founds the Society of Jesus in Montmartre *(p 76)*.
1559	Henri II is fatally wounded in a tourney *(p 79)*.
1572	Massacre of St. Bartholomew *(p 110)*.
1578-1604	Construction of the Pont Neuf *(p 70)*.
1588	The Catholic League turns against Henri III who is forced to flee Paris, after the Day of the Barricades (12 May).
1589	Paris is invested by Henri III and Henri of Navarre. The former is assassinated at St-Cloud.

THE BOURBONS

1594	Henri IV is converted to Catholicism; Paris opens her gates to him.
1605	Creation of the Place des Vosges.
14 May 1610	Henri IV is mortally wounded by Ravaillac *(p 109)*.
1615-1625	Marie dei Medici has the Luxembourg Palace built.
1622	Paris becomes an episcopal see.
1627-1664	Develpoment of the Ile St-Louis.
1635	Richelieu founds the French Academy.
1648-1653	Paris disturbed by the Fronde.
1661	Mazarin founds the College of Four Nations, the future Institut de France *(p 137)*.
1667	Colbert establishes the Observatory *(p 123)* and Gobelins Tapestry Works *(p 154)*.
17C	Construction of Versailles *(p 157)*; development of the Marais.
Late 17C	Erection of the Louvre Colonnade and the Invalides.
Early 18C	Construction of the Place Vendôme and development of the Faubourg St-Germain.
1717-1720	John Law's Bank *(p 112)*.
1722	Creation of the first Fire Brigade.
1727-1732	End of the Jansenist crisis; the St. Medard " Convulsionnaires ".
c. 1760	Louis XV has the École Militaire, the Pantheon and the Place de la Concorde constructed.
1783	Ascent of the balloonists Charles and Robert *(p 40)*.
1784-1791	Erection of the Farmers General Wall *(p 18)*.

HISTORICAL FACTS

THE REVOLUTION AND THE FIRST EMPIRE

14 July 1789	Taking of the Bastille *(p 149)*.
17 July 1789	Louis XVI at the Hôtel de Ville ; adoption of the tricolour.
14 July 1790	Festival of Federation *(p 51)*.
20 June 1792	The mob invades the Tuileries *(p 27)*.
10 Aug. 1792	Taking of the Tuileries and the fall of the monarchy *(pp 27, 40)*.
2-4 Sept. 1792	September Massacres *(pp 92, 154)*.
21 Sept. 1792	Proclamation of the Republic *(p 89)*.
21 Jan. 1793	Execution of Louis XVI *(pp 43, 142)*.
1793	Opening of the Louvre Museum.
1793-1794	The Terror *(pp 43, 142, 150)*.
8 June 1794	Festival of the Supreme Being *(pp 40, 51)*.
5 Oct. 1795	Royalist uprising suppressed by Napoleon *(p 90)*.
9-10 Nov. 1799	Fall of the Directory.
1800	Bonaparte creates the offices of Prefect of the Seine and of the Police.
2 Dec. 1804	Napoleon's coronation at Notre-Dame *(p 62)*.
1806-1814	Napoleon continues construction of the Louvre and erects the Arc de Triomphe and Vendôme Column. Stay at Malmaison.
31 March 1814	The Allies occupy Paris *(p 44)*.

THE RESTORATION

1815	Waterloo. Restoration of the Bourbons.
1821-1825	Construction of the Ourcq, St. Denis and St. Martin Canals.
1830	Fall of Charles X ; flight to Holyrood House.
1832	A cholera epidemic kills 19 000 Parisians.
1837	The first French railway line, Paris — St-Germain is opened.
1840	Return of Napoleon's body from St. Helena *(p 54)*.
1841-1845	Construction of the Thiers fortifications *(p 18)*.
February 1848	Fall of Louis-Philippe *(p 73)*. Proclamation of the Second Republic *(p 115)*.

FROM 1848 TO 1870

June 1848	The suppression of the national workshops creates disturbances in the Faubourg St-Antoine *(p 150)*.
1852-1870	Gigantic town planning undertakings by Baron Haussmann : the Halles, railway stations, Buttes-Chaumont, Bois de Boulogne and Vincennes, the Opera, the sewers, completion of the Louvre, laying of the boulevards through the old quarters of the city. Paris is divided into 20 *arrondissements*.
1855, 1867	World Exhibitions.
4 Sept. 1870	The Third Republic is proclaimed at the Hôtel de Ville *(p 115)*.

THE THIRD REPUBLIC

Winter 1870-1871	Paris is besieged by the Prussians and capitulates *(p 115)*. St-Cloud Château is burnt to the ground. Napoleon III goes into exile in England.
March-May 1871	The Paris Commune is finally suppressed by the Men of Versailles during the Bloody Week (21-28 May) ; fire, destruction (Tuileries, Old Auditor General's Office, Hôtel de Ville, Vendôme Column) and massacres *(p 153)*.
1885	State funeral of Victor Hugo.
1889	World Exhibition at the foot of the new Eiffel Tower *(p 52)*.
1900	First *métro* line opened : Maillot — Vincennes. Construction of the Grand and Petit Palais *(p 45)* ; Cubism is born at the Bateau-Lavoir *(p 76)*. The Sacré-Cœur Basilica is erected on the Butte Montmartre *(p 77)*.
1914-1918	Paris under threat of German attack is saved by the Battle of the Marne. A shell hits the Church of St-Gervais — St-Protais *(p 115)*.
1920	Interment of the Unknown Soldier *(p 47)*.
February 1934	Rioting in the vicinity of the Chamber of Deputies.
June 1940	Paris is bombed then occupied by the Germans. Hostages and resistance fighters detained at Mount Valérien *(p 171)*.
August 1944	Liberation of Paris : week of 19-26 *(pp 44, 89)*.

SINCE 1945

1950	Opening of the downstream port of Gennevilliers.
1958-1963	Construction of UNESCO, CNIT and ORTF buildings (now Radio-France House).
1964	Reorganization of departments of the Paris region : Nanterre, Créteil and Bobigny become prefectures.
1965	Paris region Town and Development Plan published.
May 1968	Strikes and demonstrations : Nanterre, Latin Quarter, the Boulevards, the Champs-Élysées.
1969	Transfer of the Halles Market to Rungis.
1970	Regional express *métro* system inaugurated. Thirteen autonomous universities created in the Paris Region.
1973	Completion of the ring road and Montparnasse Tower.
February 1974	Opening of the Paris Conference Centre.
March 1977	Election of the first mayor of Paris since 1871 (1789-1871 : 11 mayors).

PARIS YESTERDAY

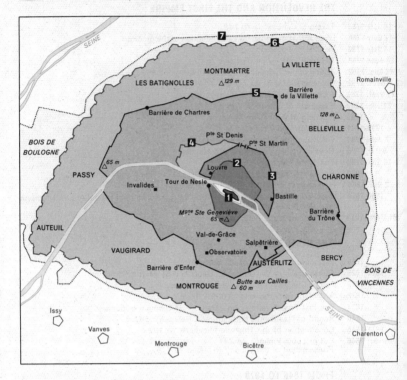

The capital's site was carved out of the limestone and Tertiary sands by the Seine at the centre of what is now the Paris Basin. At that time the river flowed at a level of 35 m — 100 ft — above its present course.

The Gallo-Roman Wall : 1. — The Parisii, taking advantage of the *Pax romana,* emerged from Lutetia, built by the Gauls and defended by the river and surrounding swamps, to settle along the Left Bank of the river *(p 100)*. The Barbarians, however, forced them to retreat, in about 276, to the Cité. On the island, they built houses, fortifications and a rampart wall *(p 65)* to defend themselves against future invasions.

The Philippe Auguste Wall : 2. — Between the 6 and 10C, the swamps were drained and cultivated, monasteries founded and a river harbour established near the Place de Grève. Between 1180 and 1210 Philippe Auguste commanded that a massive wall be built *(pp 86, 102)* reinforced upstream by a chain barrage across the river and downstream by the Louvre Fortress and Nesle Tower.

The Charles V Rampart : 3. — The Town, which was on the Right Bank (as opposed to the University on the Left Bank, and the Cité), prospered as roads were built connecting it with Montmartre, St-Denis, the Knights Templar Commandery, Vincennes Castle. By the end of the 14C, Charles V had erected new fortifications, supported in the east by the Bastille. The ramparts enclosed a Paris of just under 440 ha — 1 3/4 sq miles — and 150 000 inhabitants.

The Louis XIII Wall : 4. — In the 16C the Catholic League, Wars of Religion, the siege by Henri of Navarre kept up the pressure on the city so that Charles IX and Louis XIII extended the 14C wall westward to include the Louvre Palace.

The Farmers General Wall : 5. — The monarchy moved to Versailles. Paris now 500 000 strong, saw the erection of the Invalides, the Observatory, the Salpêtrière and the St. Denis and St. Martin Gates. The enclosed city was too small so a new wall (1784-1791) complete with 57 barriers by Ledoux was constructed *(p 138)*. " The wall, walling in Paris ", it was said, however, " makes Parisians wail ".

The Thiers Fortifications : 6. — Under the Revolution properties were broken up but little was built; under the Empire, Paris began to know problems of overcrowding and supply; gas lighting appeared during the Restoration; industry, railways and economic development brought growth to outlying villages (Austerlitz, Montrouge, Vaugirard, Passy, Montmartre, Belleville) which Thiers had enclosed in a further wall, reinforced at a cannonball's distance by 16 bastions — the capital's official limits from 1859. Twenty *arrondissements* were created in the 7 800 ha — 30 sq miles — as Haussmann began his transformation of the city (Population — 1846 : 1 050 000; 1866 : 1 800 000).

The present limits : 7. — The forts remained intact (Mount Valérien, Romainville, Ivry, Bagneux...), but the walls after serving in the city's defence in 1871, were razed by the Third Republic in 1919.

Paris' limits were defined between 1925 and 1930 as including the Bois de Boulogne and Vincennes and not extending elsewhere beyond a narrow circular belt; the area equalled 10 540 ha — 40 3/4 sq miles — and the population, in 1945, 2 700 000.

PARIS TODAY

Paris' centrifugal attraction dates from the First Empire; since then it has developed, pell mell, as the pivot of France's political, administrative, economic and cultural life. A century after Haussmann a plan was adopted in 1960 to resolve, at least, the capital's physical problems. 1965 saw the publication of a development plan.

Administrative reform. — In 1961 the **Paris Region District** was created comprising members from the mayoral and council assemblies and professional, union and cultural bodies, to examine and finance, from a regional tax, works and projects required for day to day life in the capital : the RER (p 13), Paris ring road (Boulevard Périphérique), parking space, sanitation, etc.

1964 saw the creation of seven new departments (Paris, Yvelines, Essonne, Hauts-de-Seine, Seine-St-Denis, Val-de-Marne, Val-d'Oise) which in 1966, with the unchanged Seine-et-Marne, were brought under the newly created **Préfecture de la Région Parisienne** for purposes of coordination in economic and inter-urban development and undertakings of general benefit such as the Défense scheme, the Rungis market, creation of the Paris Port Authority, hospitals, application of the Director Scheme (see below), etc.

Further coordination was instituted 1 January 1968 with the appointment of a single official to combine the deliberations of all prefectural and other bodies.

Metamorphosis. — Paris' historic, architectural and archeological treasures stand out once more thanks to the enlightened policy of André Malraux who instituted a programme of cleaning, restoration, revitalising even whole areas such as the Marais.

Engineers and planners wrestle with today's problems — highways and transport (the ring road, underground parking space, RER), supply (Rungis, Garonor), cultural centre (Georges Pompidou Centre), office expansion (Défense, Front de Seine, Maine-Montparnasse), accommodation (dormitory towns in the suburbs : Nanterre, Montreuil, Créteil, Meudon-la-Forêt...).

The departure of the Halles, the explosion of the University into thirteen autonomous universities, the decentralisation of the Higher Schools of learning, have contributed in relieving congestion at the centre. Modern hospitals, both public and private, have been erected. Green spaces have been created, aged parks and gardens refurbished...

At times, with work apparently endlessly in progress, the capital appears more like a quarry or a ship-yard... As the changes become manifest, some will tell you that vandals have taken over, others that it is becoming ever more beautiful.

Population. — The 1974 figures showed the Paris Region as being populated by more than 10 000 000 inhabitants or 18.8 % of the total population of France. This concentration lives in 2.2 % of the land area producing a density in the City of Paris of 21 900 to the km² — 56 100 to the square mile and 820 in the outer region.

While the population of Paris proper is slighty decreasing (2 300 000 in 1975), new inhabitants arrive every day to settle in the suburbs. Paris has, therefore, become the home of men and women from Brittany to Corsica, of strangers from abroad who congregate in certain areas : Jews in the Marais, White Russians in Montparnasse, Spaniards in Passy, North Africans in Clignancourt, La Villette, Aubervilliers... The true Parisian, however, remains easily identifiable among the cosmopolitan crowd : hurried, tense, protesting, frivolous, mocking, quick witted, punning — personnified in the cabaret singer, the barrow boy, the urchin.

The new Leviathan. — As France's economic metropolis, Paris consumes 20 % of the country's total output of energy in public utilities, industry and for domestic purposes.

Water, which under the Second Empire was brought to the capital by aqueducts (Vanne, Dhuys, Loing, Lunain) is now also taken from the Seine and other rivers. The Paris **sewer** system (p 145) was the giant undertaking of the engineer, Belgrand. Beneath each street is a drain of the same name. These ducts contain the pipes for drinking and industrial water, telephone and telegraph cables, and the pneumatique and compressed air tubes. Sewage is sent to the farms on the outskirts of Paris (Achères, Pierrelaye, Triel) and to the purification plant at Achères.

Reservoir dams have been constructed on the Seine (near Troyes) and the Marne (near St-Dizier) to ensure a constant supply of 650 million m³ — 660-880 million gallons of drinking water and water for industrial use daily.

Walk down any street market, past open fronted shops or through any store and you will realise that food from every region of France travels to Paris. Beef from Poitou and Nivernais, butter and cream from Normandy and Charente, cheese from everywhere, fish from Boulogne and Lorient — all come through the great modern wholesale markets at Rungis for redistribution to the people of Paris who consume annually :

560 000 tons of meat	800 million litres of wine
500 000 tons of bread	100 million bottles of mineral water
700 000 tons of potatoes	500 million eggs

The Port of Paris. — Paris, France's fourth port after Marseilles, Le Havre and Dunkerque includes some 300 port installations, 800 ha — 2 000 acres of basins and waterways and 500 km — 311 miles of riverside property (Seine, Oise, Marne, Yonne, Loing). The canals of St-Martin, St-Denis and Ourcq are administered by the city itself. Port activites are concentrated within the city of Paris at 5 main points (Bercy, Tolbiac, Javel, la Rapée, la Villette) and in the suburbs; the Port of Paris is responsible for several industrial zones as well.

In 1976 more than a fourth of the regional supplies were transferred by water (i. e. building materials : 16 million tons; petrochemicals : 5.4 million tons).

New undertakings are planned at Achères, Nanterre, la Ferté-sous-Jouarre, Vigneux, Melun and Montereau.

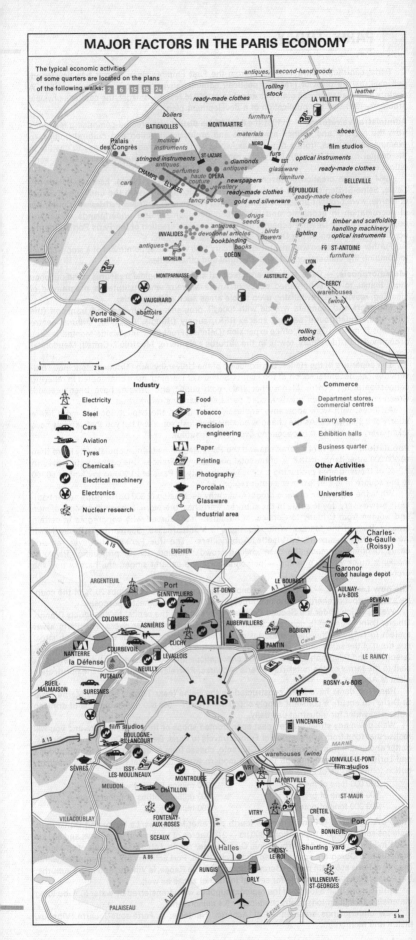

MAJOR FACTORS IN THE PARIS ECONOMY

The typical economic activities of some quarters are located on the plans of the following walks: 2 6 15 18 24

antiques, second-hand goods

rolling stock

ready-made clothes

LA VILLETTE   leather

boilers   furniture

BATIGNOLLES   MONTMARTRE   materials   shoes

Palais des Congrès   musical instruments   NORD   film studios

stringed instruments   ST-LAZARE   diamonds   EST   furs   optical instruments

CHAMPS   antiques   OPERA   perfumes   glassware   ready-made clothes

ELYSÉES   haute couture   newspapers   furniture   BELLEVILLE

cars   jewellery   ready-made clothes   RÉPUBLIQUE

fancy goods   gold and silverware   ready-made clothes

drugs   seeds   fancy goods   timber and scaffolding handling machinery optical instruments

INVALIDES   antiques   devotional articles   birds   lighting

antiques   bookbinding   flowers   FG ST-ANTOINE

MICHELIN   books   ODEON   furniture

MONTPARNASSE   AUSTERLITZ   LYON   BERCY warehouses (wine)

VAUGIRARD

Porte de Versailles   abattoirs

rolling stock

0   2 km

Industry

Electricity	Food	
Steel	Tobacco	
Cars	Precision engineering	
Aviation	Paper	
Tyres	Printing	
Chemicals	Photography	
Electrical machinery	Porcelain	
Electronics	Glassware	
Nuclear research	Industrial area	

Commerce

Department stores, commercial centres

Luxury shops

Exhibition halls

Business quarter

Other Activities

Ministries

Universities

A 15   Charles-de-Gaulle (Roissy)

ENGHIEN   LE BOURGET   Garonor road haulage depot

ARGENTEUIL   ST-DENIS   A 1   AULNAY-s/s-BOIS   SEVRAN

Port GENNEVILLIERS

COLOMBES   ASNIÈRES   AUBERVILLIERS   BOBIGNY

NANTERRE la Défense   CLICHY   PANTIN   LE RAINCY

COURBEVOIE   LEVALLOIS

PUTEAUX   NEUILLY   A 3   ROSNY-s/s-BOIS

RUEIL-MALMAISON   SURESNES   MONTREUIL

PARIS

film studios   VINCENNES   MARNE

BOULOGNE-BILLANCOURT   warehouses (wine)   JOINVILLE-LE-PONT film studios

A 13   ISSY-LES-MOULINEAUX   IVRY   ST-MAUR

SÈVRES   MONTROUGE   ALFORTVILLE

MEUDON   CHÂTILLON   CRÉTEIL   Port

VILLACOUBLAY   VITRY   BONNEUIL

FONTENAY-AUX-ROSES   SCEAUX   Shunting yard

Halles   CHOISY-LE-ROI

A 86   RUNGIS   ORLY   VILLENEUVE-ST-GEORGES

PALAISEAU   SEINE   0   5 km

20

The central area of Paris. — Paris is not only France's political capital with attendant government offices, statutory and major national undertakings and international organisation offices but also the country's industrial and commercial capital and the hub from which all means of communication radiate.

A vast labour force, available capital, a long tradition of trade and other exhibitions do much to explain the continuing attraction of the city to both French and foreign business and commercial enterprises. Industrial decentralisation, promoted since 1955, has, so far, had little obvious effect.

Paris is world famous for fashion. At the twice yearly *haute-couture* collections, lines are launched, accessories displayed, styles set. Money is made not only from the sale of made-up models but also of *toiles* or patterns to the mass-production manufacturers abroad, entire ranges of accessories from hats, shoes, belts, gloves, silk scarves to jewellery, furs, perfumes and other luxuries.

The Right Bank, now more commercial and cosmopolitan, is, generally speaking, busier and more bustling than the quieter Left Bank.

Some streets and quarters on both banks, however, have kept their association with a mediaeval craft or trade and retain something of the atmosphere if not of the Middle Ages, at least, of past centuries : the Quai de la Mégisserie of seed merchants; the Odeon area of publishing houses and bookshops; the Faubourg St-Antoine of cabinet-makers; the Rues Bonaparte and La Boëtie of antique-dealers; the Temple of second-hand dealers, particularly in clothes; St-Sulpice of makers of pious objects; the Rue de Rome of stringed instrument makers; the Rue de Paradis, of glassmakers...

There are, in addition, the streets lined by government offices (Rue de Grenelle, Chaillot), commercial organisations (Bourse, Opéra, Champs-Élysées, La Défense), the big stores and schools. And between all these is a mosaic of workshops, warehouses and small shops which, with the many massive undertakings, combine to make up Paris' infinitely various economy.

The suburbs. — The Paris region includes one quarter of French industry, one half of French commercial and financial interests; agriculture is declining. All the large manufacturing industries now have factories in the Paris periphery from the traditional to the most modern; the only exception is textiles. 1 700 000 workmen and thousands of technicians provide a buoyant economy further reinforced by the office workers in the major firms' head offices, most of which lie in the Paris business area.

Metallurgy. — While heavy industry concentrated in a bend in the Seine downstream, mechanical engineering, represented by immense factories, workshops and laboratories developed in a ring round Paris itself so that the region is the most important in France in the manufacture of cars (Renault, Citroën, Simca), machine tools, aircraft parts and the industries — electricity and electronics.

Chemistry. — The chemical works around Paris, employ a large labour force of engineers and research workers. They are concerned with a variety of other products such as rubber, paint, perfume, plastics and pharmaceuticals.

Other Industries. — In addition to the extensive new market at Rungis, the wholesale centre for all fresh food, provision industries and factories are scattered all round the Paris periphery : preserves and canning factories to the northwest; flour mills at Pantin; wine stores at Ivry and Charenton, biscuit factories at Maisons-Alfort...

Also more than 50 % of the printing and publishing houses are located in the Ile de France, which with the glass, paper and furniture industries all add to the diversity of the Paris economy besides those " service " industries essential to the maintenance and well-being of a capital city.

Index et plan MICHELIN PARIS N° 11

This MICHELIN publication contains a wealth of practical information.

■ **A street index**
Useful addresses including :

— government and municipal offices
— foreign embassies and cultural services
— churches, post offices, railway stations, department stores, etc.
— museums, sports facilities, cinemas, theatres, etc.

■ **A plan of the capital,** scale 1/10 000, showing :

— one-way streets
— public buildings, museums, theatres, post offices...
— car parks, métro stations and taxi-ranks.

■ **The leaflet Paris transports** containing :

— maps of the métro and bus routes with explanatory notes in English
— a map indicating the location of the main petrol stations and controlled parking zones.

PARIS AND THE ARTS

ARCHITECTURE

Gothic architecture. — Gothic is the true style of Paris' older buildings. **Gallo-Roman** is virtually non-existent apart from a few cradle vaulted arches still standing in the Roman baths at the Hôtel de Cluny and such heavily restored remains as the Lutetia arena; **Romanesque,** known in England as Norman, and better represented elsewhere in France, can only be seen as features in a larger whole — the small chancel columns and belfry-porch in St-Germain-des-Prés, the apse of St-Martin-des-Champs, the St-Denis Basilica crypt, and the capitals in St. Peter's, Montmartre and St-Aignan Chapel.

Gothic, however, was born in the region, arising from the combined requirements of height and increased light. An ogival style evolved, characterised inside by broken arch vaulting (St-Denis narthex and ambulatory) and outside by buttressing. These supports, it was soon discovered, could be hollowed out without diminishing their strength, and so appeared the flying buttress.

The outstanding example of Gothic development between the 12 and early 14C is to be found in Paris' greatest monument, Notre-Dame Cathedral : the vast chancel, the only slightly projecting transept, the sombre galleries at the back of the triforium are typical of **early Gothic** while firmly localizing the whole are the decorative carvings on the capitals of plants and flowers native to the Paris region. Light inside was very limited still, passing only through small narrow windows in the nave surmounted by equally small round windows or oculi, an arrangement still to be seen in the cathedral transept.

Gothic skill reached its greatest heights in the reign of St. Louis with the architect Pierre of Montreuil who, with awe-inspiring daring, replaced solid side walls by vast windows, letting the light pour in. Slender column walls only between the glass supported the roof, reinforced outside by unobtrusive buttresses or flying buttresses (the St-Martin-des-Champs refectory). The new lightness and window space inspired the glassmakers in their craft.

With the construction of its greatest masterpieces, the east end of Notre-Dame, the Sainte-Chapelle in the Cité, at Vincennes and St-Germain-en-Laye, the **radiant Gothic style** had, perhaps, reached its climax when building generally was interrupted by the outbreak of the unrest and fighting, later known as the Hundred Years War (1337-1453). The rising provoked by Étienne Marcel, the civil strife between the Burgundians and the Armagnacs explain the reason for such architecture as existed in the period being massive and sombre, almost feudal in style, epitomised by the Bastille and Men at Arms Hall in the Conciergerie.

Gothic continued into the 15C but was considerably marred by exaggerated interior decoration : purely decorative arches — liernes and tiercerons — segmented vaulting (St. Merry transept, St-Germain-l'Auxerrois), window tracery with a flame motif, pillars, unadorned by capitals, rising in a single sweep to span out directly beneath the roof (St-Séverin ambulatory) from which hung monumental keystones (St-Étienne-du-Mont). Examples of this **Flamboyant Gothic style** are the St-Jacques Tower, the Billettes Cloister and the contemporary Hôtel de Sens and Hôtel de Cluny. In these mansions, the defensive features — turrets, crenelations, wicket gates — are trimmed with richly sculptured decorations — balustrades, mullioned dormer windows — as are the early châteaux of the Loire.

Hôtel de Sens

The Renaissance. — War with Italy introduced those who went there to the Antique style and the profane in decoration. Pointed arches gave place to cradle vaulting or coffered ceilings (St-Nicolas-des-Champs), rounded bays (St-Eustache) descended on to Ionic or Corinthian capitals topping fluted columns (St-Médard). The roodscreen at St-Étienne-du-Mont is the finest example of interior decoration which elsewhere included mythological or commonplace motifs (St-Gervais stalls).

Pierre Lescot adopted the Italian style of a uniform façade broken by advanced bays crowned by rounded pediments for the Cour Carrée in the Louvre and for the Hôtel Lamoignon. Statues decorated the niches between fluted columns; cornices and a frieze surmount the doors and each floor. Inside, the ceilings are frequently coffered and decorated as above the Henri II staircase in the Clock Pavilion again in the Louvre.

Classical Architecture. — At the end of the Wars of Religion, the influence of Antiquity increased, the king once more asserted his power — events symbolised in the solidly constructed Pont Neuf.

Religious architecture turned to the Classical, a style which was to continue throughout the 17C and be characterised by a profusion of exterior columns, pediments, statues and cupolas reminiscent of the churches of Rome.

The Jesuit style of the Counter-Reformation produced the multiplicity of domes to be seen in the Sorbonne Church, the Val-de-Grâce and St-Paul-St-Louis. But this typically Baroque feature was soon modified by the architects of Louis XIV and XV — Hardouin-Mansart (The Invalides), Libéral-Bruant (Salpêtrière), Le Vau (St-Louis-en-L'Ile), Soufflot (Pantheon).

Contemporary civil constructions were characterized, in imitation of Versailles, by Classical symmetry and simplification. The Place des Vosges and Place Dauphine are true Louis XIII with the alternating use of brick and stone while the Luxembourg Palace by Salomon de Brosse has a mixture of both French and Italian elements. Immediately after came the Mansarts, Androuet Du Cerceau, Delamair and Le Muet, evolving in the Marais, a new style of architecture with their designs for the town house.

Classical architecture reached its climax between 1650 and 1750 with the majestic constructions of Perrault in the Louvre Colonnade, Le Vau, the Institute, and Gabriel, the Place de la Concorde and École Militaire.

The Antique simplicity of the Louis XVI style can be seen in the Palace of the Legion of Honour and the Farmers General Wall pavilions by Ledoux.

Luxembourg Palace

The 19C. — The Empire and Restoration had little to show, architecturally : the Madeleine, Arc de Triomphe, Carrousel Arch are classical pastiches lacking any particular originality.

The Second Empire, however, brought a fantastic new impetus to planning in the person of Baron Haussmann. A new style was rapidly imprinted on the capital — the iron and metalwork style exemplified by Baltard in St. Augustine's and the Halles, Labrouste in the Bibliothèque Nationale, Hittorff in the Gare du Nord and by Gustave Eiffel in the Eiffel Tower.

While Garnier's Opera was being built, a construction in stone which was not only one of the most successful of the period but bears comparison with larger scale edifices such as the Louvre, the Hôtel de Ville and the Hôtel-Dieu, industrial development, the discovery of new materials and techniques and the ascendancy of domestic over monumental architecture, were inaugurating close collaboration between architects and civil engineers.

The 20C. — Just as the Grand and Petit Palais, the Alexandre III Bridge and Sacré-Cœur Basilica mark a certain attachment to the past, Baudot in St. John of Montmartre and the Perret brothers in the Champs-Élysées Theatre, were discovering the possibilities of reinforced stone and concrete which the latter were to demonstrate fully in 1937 in the Chaillot Palace and the Tokyo Palace.

Since 1945, under the influence of Le Corbusier, of whose actual work the only examples in Paris are some of the University City halls, architectural design has undergone a fundamental reappraisal. The result is the wide variety of styles to be seen in the circular Radio-France House, the upraised UNESCO, the sweeping roof lines of the CNIT, the glass and aluminium façades at Orly, the new glass façades of the GAN and Manhattan Towers and Georges Pompidou Centre, whereas Charles de Gaulle airport illustrates the " concrete style ". Currently the style might be said to be vertical, so that the Paris skyline of centuries past is being redrawn as tower after tower rises high above established landmarks in the La Défense quarter, at Maine-Montparnasse, for the Science Faculty, in the Place d'Italie...

Contemporary religious architecture can best be seen at the Chantiers du Cardinal or Cardinal's Workshops.

SCULPTURE

The Gallo-Roman altar of the Paris boatmen now at the Cluny Museum *(p 100),* the capital's oldest sculpture, was followed 1 000 years later by low reliefs and statues carved by highly skilled but equally anonymous craftsmen for Notre-Dame and other churches.

From the Renaissance and for the following three centuries, the monarchy decorated the city with sumptuous religious and civil constructions which were then adorned by the sculptors to the Court : Jean Goujon (Innocents' Fountain), Germain Pilon (St-Denis), Girardon (Richelieu's tomb), Coysevox (Tuileries Gardens), Coustou (The Marly Horses), Robert Le Lorrain (Hôtel de Rohan), Bouchardon (Four Seasons Fountain) and Pigalle (St-Sulpice).

It was, however, during the mid and late 19C that Paris was gradually transformed into an open air museum with statues, particularly, multiplying in parks, gardens and streets : Carpeaux (Observatory Fountain) and Rude *(Marshal Ney)* were followed by Rodin *(Balzac, Victor Hugo),* Dalou (Place de la Nation), Bourdelle (Tokyo Palace, Champs-Élysées Theatre), Maillol (Carrousel Gardens) and Landowski *(Ste-Geneviève,* Porte St-Cloud animals).

Hector Guimard epitomized the style of 1900 in his *métro* entrances as Calder's mobile *(p 53),* Zadkine's bronzes (Père-Lachaise cemetery) and Louis Leygne and Agam's sculptures (La Défense) symbolize the work of the 20C abstractionists now appearing in parks and in conjunction with new architectural schemes.

PAINTING

Until the late 16C, early 17C, Paris remained largely unrepresented pictorially apart from the incidental scenes depicted by miniaturists, painters, engravers and illuminators such as the Limbourg brothers, who included Paris backgrounds in the *Very Rich Hours* of the Duke de Berry, and Jean Fouquet in the *Book of Hours* he pianted for Étienne Chevalier. In the 17C landscape interest in the capital began to awaken, particularly in the Pont Neuf and the Louvre and the countryside surrounding the Invalides and the Observatory. J.-B. Raguenet, Hubert Robert, Antoine de Machy and later, Bouhot and Georges Michel, and finally Méryon with his deeply toned water colours, developed a descriptive tradition which bridges the period to the late 19C when the Impressionists emerged and made Paris the world art centre.

Corot, who divided his time between painting the Paris quaysides and Ville d'Avray a few miles away, was followed by Jongkind, Lépine, Monet *(St-Germain-l'Auxerrois, Gare St-Lazare)*, Renoir *(Moulin de la Galette, Moulin Rouge)*, Sisley *(Ile St-Louis, Auteuil Viaduct)* and Pissarro *(The Pont Neuf)*, who depicted light effects in the capital at all hours and in all seasons. Paris also played an important part in the work of Seurat *(The Eiffel Tower)*, Gauguin *(The Seine by the Pont d'Iéna)*, Cézanne and Van Gogh (Montmartre scenes). Later, and more gently, Vuillard painted the peace of Paris squares and gardens.

Poulbot drawing

Toulouse-Lautrec, sketching with wit and intimacy cabaret artists before and behind the footlights, presented a totally different appreciation of the Paris scene. Equally keen of eye were André Gill, Forain, Willette and Poulbot *(p 77)* again portraying not Paris but the Parisian whether he be music-hall artist, politician *pierrot* or street urchin.

At the beginning of the 20C Paris was at its height with the **Paris School** (Derain, Vlaminck, Bonnard, Braque, Dufy, Matisse...) the inspiration of all, and the Bateau-Lavoir *(p 76)* and the Ruche *(p 119)*, the centres of good talk, night long discussion and revolution. The painters of that time who devoted most of their work to the Paris scene were Marquet and Maurice Utrillo.

The modern landscape of Paris has become familiar, particularly, through the widely reproduced paintings of the present day artists, Yves Brayer and Bernard Buffet.

MUSIC

Yesterday. — Music, in France, as elsewhere, developed most elaborately first in the church : by the end of the 12C a school of polyphony had been established in Notre-Dame, expressing in harmony the deep religious faith of the period. The Hundred Years War interrupted its development and it was only with François I that attention turned once more to the art — this time in the form of court songs and airs accompanied on the lute. In 1571, the poet, Baïf founded the Academy of Music and Poetry, to re-establish the harmony of Antiquity in poetry and music.

" That most noble and gallant art " developed naturally at the royal court, first at the Louvre, and, later, at Versailles where sovereigns, their consorts and companions disported themselves in ballets, allegorical dances, recitals, opera and comedy.

The Royal Academy of Music (1672), dominated by the personality of Lulli, encouraged sacred music to new heights in Notre-Dame (with Campra), St-Gervais and the Sainte-Chapelle (with the Couperins), St-Paul-St-Louis (Charpentier) and Notre-Dame-des-Victoires (with Lulli himself).

The Regency saw the birth of comic opera (Mouret and Monsigny) and the revitalising of opera proper by Rameau (1683-1764). Not long after, Gluck, Parisian by adoption, produced his mature operas : *Orpheus and Eurydice, Iphigenia in Aulis* and *Alcestis* (1774-1779).

Composition, since the Revolution, has centred round the National Conservatory, founded in 1795. It was there that the young Romantic school grew up with Cherubini, Auber and Berlioz who created his *Fantastic Symphony* while at the Conservatory in 1830. These were followed by César Franck, Massenet, Fauré. Paris became the international musical capital, drawing the Italians Rossini and Donizetti, the Polish Chopin *(p 74)*, the Hungarian Liszt and the Germans Wagner *(p 108)* and Offenbach, to come and stay, often for years.

1870 and the years that followed saw renewed activity with Bizet, Saint-Saëns, Charpentier and Dukas, Parisians by birth or adoption, bringing new life to symphony and opera, d'Indy founding the Schola Cantorum *(p 123)* and Debussy and Ravel co-operating with Diaghilev's Russian Ballet *(p 144)*. Finally came the Group of Six (Honegger, Tailleferre, Auric, Milhaud, Poulenc, Durey) and the rival Arcueil School of Satie and Sauguet.

Today. — Today Paris musical life is reflected in a plethora of performances by large orchestras in fine concert halls, of chamber music and organ recitals.

Quite different are the clubs, cellars and *boîtes* or night-clubs scattered throughout the Latin Quarter, along the Champs-Élysées, in Montmartre and Montparnasse.

Among the best are the Trois Mailletz *(56 Rue Galande, 5ᵉ)*, Riverbop *(65 Rue St-André-des-Arts, 6ᵉ)*, Le Caveau de la Huchette *(5 Rue de la Huchette, 5ᵉ)*, Le Slow Club *(130 Rue de Rivoli, 1ᵉʳ)*...

The construction of Notre-Dame, which began after that of St-Denis and Sens in about 1140, heralded the age of great Gothic cathedrals in France: Strasbourg (c. 1176), Bourges (c. 1185), Chartres (c. 1194), Rouen (1200), Reims (1211), Amiens (1220), Beauvais (1247).

Early English, the corresponding period in England, lasted until the end of the 13C and included in whole or in part the cathedrals of Wells (1174), Lincoln (chancel and transept : 1186), Salisbury (1220-1258), Westminster Abbey (c. 1250) and Durham (1242).

LETTERS

Paris, the inspiration of poets and novelists and the setting for so many works, has occupied a central place in French literature since the 13C when the University was founded and the Parisian dialect was adopted as the language of the court.

The people of the streets appear, at this time, in epic poems and Mystery plays *(p 62)*; individual characters and daily life in the poems of Rutebœuf and Villon (15C). Rabelais criticized Paris, but nevertheless sent Gargantua and Pantagruel to the Sorbonne and ended living in the Marais *(c. 1553 — p 86)*.

As the capital grew and attracted men of letters amongst others, it inspired a devotion in many equal to their native soil : Montaigne, Guillaume Budé, who founded the Collège de France, Ronsard and the Pléiade poets *(p 102)* and Agrippa d'Aubigné who bore witness to the religious conflicts which engulfed Paris and the rest of the country at the end of the 16C.

The 17 and 18C. — As Paris underwent alternately embellishment, under Henri XIII, and disruption, by the Fronde at the time of Louis XIV's minority, writers, intellectuals, wits and lesser mortals developed what was to be a uniquely French cultural phenomenon, the cultivated philosophic conversation of the *salons,* first at the Hôtel de Rambouillet (17C) and later at the houses of the Marquise de Lambert, Madame du Deffand, Madame Geoffrin (18C).

In contrast to the exploration and discussion of new ideas in the *salons,* the French Academy, founded by Richelieu in 1635, sought to exert a restraining influence on all branches of literature — Saint-Amand was, meanwhile, writing satire, Boileau burlesques and Madame de Sévigné her *Letters* on daily life.

In the 18C cafés — Procope, La Régence ... — developed as centres of discussion and debate; Marivaux and Beaumarchais were presenting light comedies on the capital's life style and the provincial, Rousseau, expressing his disdain of the " noisy, smoke filled, muddy " city!

It is Voltaire, outstanding in story telling, history, correspondance and memoirs, however, who, many would say, epitomises the 18C and the Paris writer at his best, with his irony and wit, light touch and perfect turn of phrase.

The Encyclopaedists typified Paris in the Age of Enlightenment as clearly as Restif de la Bretonne's *Nights of Paris* and Sébastien Mercier's *Portrait of Paris* described the daily scene in the capital.

The 19 and 20C. — The two major writers on Paris, Hugo and Balzac, were, in fact, born in the provinces. Both, in *Les Misérables* and the *Human Comedy* respectively, portrayed Paris as a character in its own right, suffering moods, influencing others... Beside these two giants, Dumas the Younger, Musset, the song-writer Béranger, Eugène Süe *(Mysteries of Paris)*, Murger *(Scenes of Bohemian Life)*, Nerval and others, pale into the background.

To the new Paris of Baron Haussmann came Baudelaire and the Parnassian and Symbolist poets and Émile Zola.

Montmartre remains transfixed in the songs of Bruant (1851-1925), the novels of Carco (1886-1958) and Marcel Aymé (1902-1967), Montparnasse in the poems of Max Jacob (1876-1944) and Léon-Paul Fargue (1876-1947). More generally descriptive are the works of Colette and Cocteau, Simenon, Montherlant, Louise de Vilmorin, Aragon, Prévert, Sacha Guitry, Éluard, Sartre, Simone de Beauvoir...

PARIS AND THE ENGLISH

Paris conjures up an image in the mind of every man and woman in Britain — the association goes back so far, the distance is so small, the atmosphere so different, the streets so wide, the buildings so massive, the landmarks so familiar from posters, pictures and films. Political exchanges have been continuous, ending in agreements to differ or often in treaties — 1763, terminating the Seven Years' War, 1814 and 1815 ending the Napoleonic era, 1856 in alliance at the end of the Crimean War, 1904 — 1910 commercial treaties which concluded in the Entente Cordiale, 1919 the Treaty of Versailles.

From the time of William the Conqueror families have intermarried; since 1420 and the recognition of Henry V as King of England and France, the English have at times penetrated to the capital.

By the 17C, aristocrats and the wealthy were completing their education with the Grand Tour of Europe with Paris as the first stop; by the mid 19C, Thomas Cook was organising group visits, since, as he stated in Cook's Excursionist and Advertiser of 15 May 1863, " We would have every class of British subjects visit Paris, that they may emulate its excellencies, and shun the vices and errors which detract from the glory of the French capital. In matters of taste and courtesy we have much to learn from Parisians... "

It was the Continental Sunday, above all, that shocked Thomas Cook, and later the Bohemianism of Montmartre and Montparnasse. But it was just this that attracted and has continued to attract many visitors from Britain ever since! A first visit to Paris for many, therefore, becomes a desire to get a kaleidoscopic view of the Eiffel Tower and the Moulin Rouge, to eat in a *bistro* and walk up the Champs-Élysées, to see the Bastille — which they can't! — and visit Versailles — which they can.

With second and third and later visits — for every Briton, once having been to Paris, surely desires to return — comes a growing interest.

Observation of what Lawrence Durrell has called " the national characteristics... the restless metaphysical curiosity, the tenderness of good living and the passionate individualism. This is the invisible constant in a place with which the ordinary tourist can get in touch just by sitting quite quietly over a glass of wine in a Paris bistro ". Comparisons with London; how much is the same and, therefore, familiar — children and adults sailing model yachts on the ponds in the Tuileries and Kensington Gardens — and yet just different enough to make you feel on holiday, how much is unique. The following pages, we hope, will help you in your discoveries.

CONVENTIONAL SIGNS

Sights

Actual walk concerned		Adjoining walk
 NOTRE DAME	★★★ **Highly recommended**	NOTRE DAME
OPÉRA *LAC INFÉRIEUR*	★★ **Recommended**	OPÉRA
ST ROCH *LAC DAUMESNIL*	★ **Interesting**	ST ROCH
HÔTEL DE VILLE Rue de la Paix *LAC DES MINIMES*	**See if possible**	HÔTEL DE VILLE Rue de la Paix
Rue de Cluny	Start of sightseeing tour	
	Sightseeing route	
	Church or monument described	
THÉÂTRE MARIGNY	Landmark mentioned	THÉÂTRE MARIGNY

Roads and railways

General maps		Detailed maps
	Motorway (access roads)	
	Dual carriageway	
	Avenue	
	Stepped road	
	Overhead railway, railway (Station)	
	Road and rail crossings : Road over rail, rail over road	

Miscellaneous

	Church or building landmark	
	Synagogue	
	Main post office	P.T.T.
	Cemetery described, landmark	
	Park described, landmark	
	(métro nearest the start or end of a walk)	M
	Basin, fountain	
	Stadium	
	Monument or statue	
	Panorama, view	
	Château described, landmark	

To choose a hotel or restaurant,
use the small, MICHELIN Red Guide :

PARIS, Hôtels et restaurants,

an extract from the current MICHELIN Guide FRANCE.

Michelin plans 🔟 or 🔟 : H 13.
Louvre métro station.

France's and, in fact, the world's largest royal palace is now famous above all as a museum.

HISTORICAL NOTES

The original fortress. — The Louvre was constructed as a fortress on the banks of the Seine by Philippe Auguste in 1200 to protect the weakest point in his new city perimeter. It stood on less than a quarter of the space now occupied by the Cour Carrée and was used as treasure-house, arsenal and archive. In the 14C the fortress ceased its military function with the erection of a new perimeter and Charles V converted it into a residence, installing his famous library in one of the towers.

A half Gothic, half Renaissance palace. — For 150 years after Charles V, France's kings preferred other palaces, until, in 1527, François I announced that he was going to take up residence in the Louvre. Rebuilding began with the razing of the keep, the knocking down of the advanced defences and the laying of a garden in their place. Only in 1546, was an architect, Pierre Lescot, commissioned to build a new royal palace. François I died the following year when the foundations were scarcely showing but building continued until the outbreak of the Wars of Religion. By this time what

(After documents in the Carnavalet Museum)

The Louvre of Charles V

came to be known as the Old Louvre consisted of the great Renaissance southwest façade of the Cour Carrée, and west and south wings with two Gothic and two Renaissance façades. All these constructions it was to retain until the reign of Louis XIV.

Construction of the Tuileries. — On the tragic death of Henri II *(p 79)*, his widow, Catherine dei Medici decided to move, with the young king, François II, to the Louvre. She did not wish to live in the palace itself, however, and in 1563 commissioned Philibert Delorme to build her a residence 500 m away in an area known as the Tuileries. Suddenly, in 1572, all work stopped when an astrologer frightened the queen into believing she would die on the site. Twenty-two years later it was resumed; Henri IV built the Flore wing; Louis XIV the Marsan; the harmony of the Delorme building was dissipated by remodelling. The Tuileries, nevertheless, remained empty of royalty until Louis XV.

The Bord de l'Eau Gallery. — Catherine also planned a covered way between the Louvre and the Tuileries following the line of the Seine. This Galerie du Bord de l'Eau, as it is called, was completed by Henri IV who added an upper storey.

The ground floor was occupied, at first, by shops and workshops; Richelieu installed the Royal Mint and printers there; Louis XIV gave rooms as studios to well known painters, sculptors, cabinet makers and architects. Living quarters were on the *entresol* and a corridor on the first floor, where five times a year the king passed to bless and touch the sick.

Construction of the Cour Carrée. — Louis XIII decided to quadruple the old Louvre since the court had become horribly cramped. Le Mercier, architect of the Sorbonne, built the Horloge Pavilion and extended it by an exact replica of Pierre Lescot's edifice. In 1659 Louis XIV commissioned Le Vau to work on the palace : the Apollo wing *(p 31)* was rebuilt and the first two floors completed (1664). Then the Sun King decided that his palace required a grandly regal exterior and he summoned the greatest architect of the time, Bernini. The Italian's ideas, however, which began with the razing of the existing palace, proved unacceptable and alternative plans, therefore, were drawn up by Le Vau, Le Brun and Claude Perrault. Perrault created the Colonnade (1667-1673), removed the Gothic wings from the Cour Carrée and replaced them with north and south façades in harmony with his colonnade. However, in 1682 the court left the Louvre for Versailles and building stopped once more.

Years of Neglect. — The palace apartments, left empty by the departed court, were let to tenants : an artists' colony including Coustou, Bouchardon, Coypel, Boucher, settled in the galleries; the colonnade was divided into dwellings; stove chimneys stuck out in rows from the wonderful façade. Taverns and jugglers' and other entertainers' shanties were built up against the walls until by 1750 the whole building had become so dilapidated it seemed in danger of being pulled down. Marigny, Minister to Louis XVI, came to its rescue.

Years of Turmoil. — On 20 June 1791 the royal family fled from the Tuileries, were arrested and returned, to be seized one year later to the day, by the Paris mob. Invading the palace the rabble pulled a red bonnet over the king's ears and made him pledge his loyalty to the nation in a toast. There followed the bloody 10 August when 600 of the Swiss Guard were massacred by the mob before the palace was sacked.

The Convention and Directory installed themselves in the opera house and apartments.

Construction and destruction. — Bonaparte expelled the last trespassers from the Louvre and began its repair. He enlarged the Carrousel Square and, on his escape from a royalist attack in the nearby street of St-Nicaise on Christmas eve 1800, erected a triumphal arch as monumental entrance to the palace forecourt. The imperial architects, Percier and Fontaine completed the Cour Carrée, reordered and decorated the royal apartments and began work on the great North Gallery along the new Rue de Rivoli. In 1810, in the Salon Carré, Napoleon married Marie-Louise.

Work on the palace stopped at the Restoration. Louis XVIII, the only king to die in the Tuileries, was succeeded by Charles X and Louis-Philippe, both of whom were expelled by the Paris mob who subsequently pillaged the royal residence.

Finally, in 1852, Napoleon III decided to complete the Louvre. While Haussmann cleared the area around the Place du Carrousel, Visconti and, later Lefuel, finished the North Gallery and constructed monumental additions to the palace's existing wings as well as providing it with north and south gates. After three centuries the Louvre, the biggest palace in the world, was finished.

During the blood soaked week of the Paris Commune of May 1871, the Tuileries was set on fire by the insurgents but the main building was saved. The Third Republic commissioned Lefuel to rebuild the Marsan and Flore pavilions.

Restoration (the base of Perrault's Colonnade has been disengaged to give the columns their full height) and cleaning have once more made the Louvre white, grand, regal.

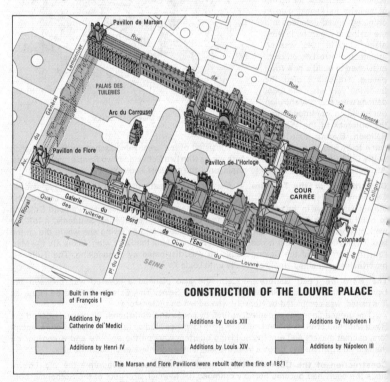

CONSTRUCTION OF THE LOUVRE PALACE

Built in the reign of François I

Additions by Catherine dei'Medici

Additions by Henri IV

Additions by Louis XIII

Additions by Louis XIV

Additions by Napoleon I

Additions by Napoleon III

The Marsan and Flore Pavilions were rebuilt after the fire of 1871

THE MUSEUM THROUGH THE CENTURIES

The dispersal of Charles V's rich library left the palace empty of treasure until François began a new collection with twelve paintings by great masters including Titian, Raphaël, Leonardo da Vinci — the *Mona Lisa* — and antique casts brought back from Italy. By Louis XIII's reign the Cabinet du Roi contained some two hundred pictures. Colbert added generously to the collection as did others, so that by the death of Louis XIV, the king's paintings numbered 2 500 scattered throughout the royal palaces. The Louvre, meanwhile, became the centre for the annual exhibition of the Academy of Painting and Sculpture.

The idea of a museum, envisaged by Louis XVI, was finally realised by the Convention which, on 10 August 1793, opened the Grande Gallery to the public.

Napoleon made the Louvre the world's richest museum by exacting a " tribute " in works of art from every country he conquered — but in 1815 the Allies took back what had been theirs.

Louis XVIII, Charles X and Louis-Philippe added to the Louvre collection which already incorporated the Museum of French Monuments created by Lenoir. The *Venus de Milo* had scarcely been rediscovered on the Island of Melos in 1820 before she was purchased by the French Government for 6 000F and brought to Paris; further Greek, Egyptian, Assyrian antiquities were collected and transported.

In 1947, the Impressionist paintings were transferred to the Jeu de Paume (p 42).

Further gifts and legacies have augmented the collections so that the catalogue now lists nearly 400 000 entries.

TOUR OF THE EXTERIOR

Start from the Place du Louvre *(description p 106).*

Colonnade**. — Perrault produced in the Louvre colonnade a work of considerable grandeur although it bears no relation to the rest of the building. Louis XIV's cypher of two coupled Ls marks the edifice; the central pediment, carved by Lemot at the time of the Empire, centred on a bust of Napoleon, replaced at the Restoration, by one of the Sun King.

Cour Carrée**. — The courtyard is the most impressive part of the Old Louvre to remain. Facing you on the left is the Pierre Lescot façade — a Renaissance delight in proportion, balance and decoration to which the sculptor, Jean Goujon, gave his all. In the centre of this west side is the Le Mercier Horloge or Clock Pavilion and further over a Classical replica of the Lescot façade. The three remaining sides, although harmonizing with the west, are not identical with it and all lack the grace of the Lescot Renaissance work. The period of each building is marked with emblazoned monograms : H interlaced with a double C and forming a D on the Lescot face are for Henri II, Catherine dei Medici and the king's favourite, Diane of Poitiers; K, H, HDB and HG on the south side, for Charles IX, Henri III, Henri IV (Henri de Bourbon) and Henri (IV) and Gabrielle d'Estrées; right of the Horloge Pavilion, LA, LB, LMT for Louis XIII and Anne of Austria, Louis of Bourbon, Louis XIV and Marie-Thérèse.

The Old Louvre. — The extent of the Old Louvre buildings can be seen in outline on the paving in the southwest corner of the courtyard. A massive keep 32 m high — 106 ft — was surrounded by ramparts, a moat and ten towers resembling those of the Conciergerie.

The main gate, 2 m wide only — 6 ft 6 in — stood between solid towers to the east.

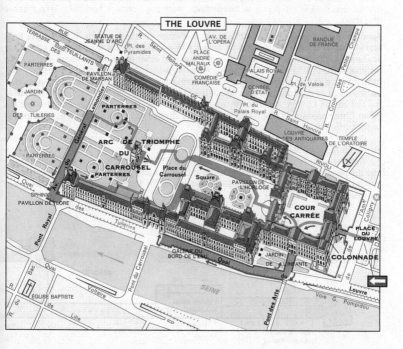

THE LOUVRE

Embankment Façade*. — Straight ahead as you walk south out of the Cour Carrée is the Pont des Arts and the Institute dome *(p 137)*; from the embankment can be seen the majestic Perrault façade and beyond, the Bord de l'Eau Gallery on which the frieze of cherubs mounted on monsters introduces a delightful, lighter note. The area after the Carrousel entrance is the part rebuilt following the 1871 fire *(p 28)*. Return and pass beneath the Horloge Pavilion.

The two arms of the Louvre. — The two arms of the palace today enclose a formal garden. It was in the 17C that the ground, crowded and vivid with military parades, tourneys and royal masques was named, after particularly brilliant celebrations in 1662, the Place du Carrousel.

The palace is impressive from the gardens but an even grander **vista***** is through the line of the Carrousel Arch, across the Place de la Concorde and, centring on the obelisk, up the Champs-Élysées, to the Arc de Triomphe.

The Carrousel Triumphal Arch**. — The Carrousel, a delightful pastiche of a Roman arch with eight rose marble columns from the Old Château at Meudon, was erected between 1806 and 1808 in celebration of the Napoleonic victories of 1805. The decoration, at one time, included the four gilded bronze horses from St. Mark's Venice, which Napoleon had brought back to France (returned 1815).

The Parterres*. — The flowerbeds, laid out in 1909 and decorated with 18 **statues*** by Maillol, mark the site of the Tuileries Palace which linked the Flore and Marsan Pavilions.

Cross to the Pont Royal to look below the great allegory on the south wall at the high relief by Carpeaux, **Flora's Triumph***, after which the corner pavilion is named.

THE LOUVRE MUSEUM★★★

Open 9.45 am to 8.00 pm. Closed Tuesdays and holidays; 5F - free on Sundays.

Some galleries or departments may be temporarily closed for rearrangement. Other areas are closed from 11.30 am to 2 pm. Moreover large-scale réorganization sometimes changes the location of certain works of art, therefore the following descriptions are subject to verification. For fuller details enquire at the information desk (main entrance, Salle du Manège) — ☎ 260.39.26 extension 3388, or at the other information desks in the museum.

Guided lecture tours (3F extra), except Sundays and Tuesdays, start at 10.30 am and 3 pm from the information desk, Salle du Manège. They are planned to include some of the most outstanding works of art. Other guided tours on a specific collection, school or period are also organized on Saturdays at 10.30 am.

Temporary exhibitions and collections shown in rotation. — Some departments are so rich that only a part of the collection can be shown at one time for lack of space — items are, therefore, shown in rotation (this applies particularly in the Drawings and Engravings Gallery in the Flore Pavilion). Pictures awaiting final hanging may be seen in the Flore Gallery.

Special exhibitions are mounted periodically around a single outstanding item or artist.

The museum's arrangement. — As in all museums of value nowadays, rearrangement in the Louvre is a continuing process. The Grande Gallery, extending from the Apollo Gallery to the Flore Pavilion is, at 442 m — 430 yds, the longest in the world. The gallery itself *(1st floor)* contains paintings; below are sculpture, above are drawings and pastels, arranged, in each case by school and period (some areas still being hung). Antiquities are arranged around the Cour Carrée *(ground and 1st floors)* with paintings from the Northern European School above *(2nd floor)*.

Familiar paintings. — You will, of course, know many of the paintings in the Louvre from reproductions. Others, you will notice, bear a striking resemblance to original paintings you are familiar with in the National Gallery in London or other galleries elsewhere — this is, in fact, not so surprising as it at first seems. An artist, preoccupied by a certain theme over perhaps a period of years, will illustrate it on several occasions with, possibly, only slight variations — such as did Leonardo da Vinci in the two versions of the *Virgin on the Rocks* now in the Louvre and London. Again the theme, by the same artist, of the Virgin, St. Anne and the Infant Christ appears as a painting in Paris (the cartoon has been lost) and as a cartoon in London (the picture has disappeared).

On the other hand the portraits of *Cardinal Richelieu* by Philippe de Champaigne are almost identical in London and in Paris.

Another occurrence is where an artist painted a series of pictures on a changing scene and the paintings have got separated as have Uccello's *Battle of San Romano,* of which one is in the Louvre, one in the National Gallery and one in the Uffizi Museum in Florence. There are many others...

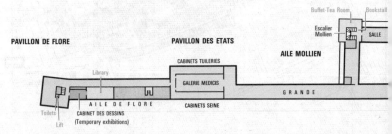

How not to succumb to exhaustion but enjoy visiting the museum!

About 3 million visitors tour the museum's 225 galleries annually. On the following pages the museum is presented by departments. Egyptian Antiquities (pp 32-33), Oriental Antiquities (p 34), Greek and Roman Antiquities (pp 34-35), Paintings (pp 36-37), Sculpture (pp 38-39), Art Objects and Furniture (p 39). The objects shown in heavy type are the Louvre's most famous treasures. If time allows only one visit, pick out a very few items from the plans and make for them only, trying not to get side-tracked by the many beautiful objects everywhere. Wear very comfortable shoes — the galleries are stone or marble paved!

There are many specialist publications in English at the main bookstall.

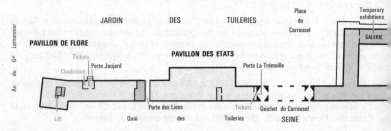

THE DEPARTEMENTS OF THE LOUVRE

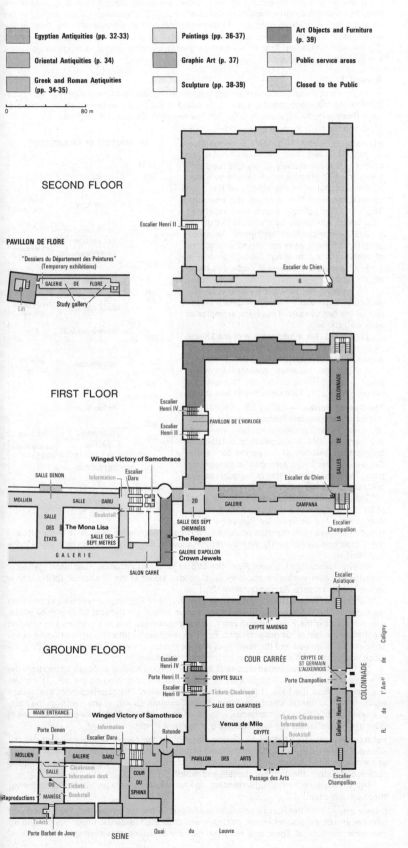

- Egyptian Antiquities (pp. 32-33)
- Oriental Antiquities (p. 34)
- Greek and Roman Antiquities (pp. 34-35)
- Paintings (pp. 36-37)
- Graphic Art (p. 37)
- Sculpture (pp. 38-39)
- Art Objects and Furniture (p. 39)
- Public service areas
- Closed to the Public

0   80 m

SECOND FLOOR

Escalier Henri II

Escalier du Chien

6

PAVILLON DE FLORE

"Dossiers du Département des Peintures" (Temporary exhibitions)

GALERIE DE FLORE

Study gallery

Lift

FIRST FLOOR

Escalier Henri IV

Escalier Henri II

PAVILLON DE L'HORLOGE

COLONNADE

LA

SALLES DE

Winged Victory of Samothrace

SALLE DENON

Information

Escalier Daru

Escalier du Chien

MOLLIEN   SALLE   DARU

Bookstall

20

GALERIE   CAMPANA

Escalier Champollion

SALLE DES ÉTATS

The Mona Lisa

SALLE DES SEPT. MÈTRES

SALLE DES SEPT CHEMINÉES

The Regent

G A L E R I E

SALON CARRÉ

GALERIE D'APOLLON
Crown Jewels

GROUND FLOOR

Escalier Asiatique

CRYPTE MARENGO

COUR CARRÉE

Escalier Henri IV

CRYPTE DE ST GERMAIN L'AUXERROIS

Porte Henri II

CRYPTE SULLY

Porte Champollion

Escalier Henri II

Tickets-Cloakroom

SALLE DES CARIATIDES

COLONNADE

Galerie Henri IV

R. de l'Am^{le} de Coligny

MAIN ENTRANCE

Winged Victory of Samothrace

Porte Denon

Information

Escalier Daru

Rotonde

Venus de Milo

Tickets-Cloakroom Information

MOLLIEN   GALERIE   DARU

PAVILLON   DES   ARTS

CRYPTE

Bookstall

SALLE DU MANÉGE

Cloakroom

Information desk

Tickets

Bookstall

COUR DU SPHINX

Reproductions

Passage des Arts

Escalier Champollion

Toilets

Porte Barbet de Jouy

SEINE   Quai   du   Louvre

EGYPTIAN ANTIQUITIES

In the 3rd and 2nd milleniums BC an Egyptian civilization flourished on the banks of the Nile. The Ancient Egyptians believed that death was only a transition on the journey to the eternal world. Everything necessary to this transformation was provided in the tomb of the deceased. It is materials from these tombs that give us an accurate picture of life during this ancient civilization. The art we have is therefore closely bound to religious traditions and the worship of the gods.

Ground Floor

In the crypt (Passage des Arts) there is in the main alcove a colossal sphinx in pink granite with the traditional head dress and the beard of the gods. The low reliefs on either side show Ramses II offering incense to the god Harmakhis in the guise of a sphinx.

Climb the stairs to reach gallery 135.

Mastaba. — *Gallery 135.* This stone funeral chapel (mastaba) was built for Akhout-Hetep, an official of the 5th dynasty of the Old Kingdom. It was common practice for officials to be buried in these mastabas in the vicinity of the great pyramid tombs of their masters, the pharaohs. This particular example shows the chapel part only, which was linked by a shaft to the underground funeral chamber containing the sarcophagus. The inner walls are carved with scenes of everyday life : hunting, fishing, scribes at work, a banquet and scenes of music and dancing.

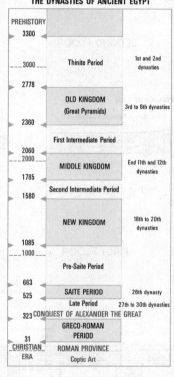

THE DYNASTIES OF ANCIENT EGYPT

PREHISTORY		
3300		
3000	Thinite Period	1st and 2nd dynasties
2778		
	OLD KINGDOM (Great Pyramids)	3rd to 6th dynasties
2360		
	First Intermediate Period	
2060 / 2000		
	MIDDLE KINGDOM	End 11th and 12th dynasties
1785		
1580	Second Intermediate Period	
	NEW KINGDOM	18th to 20th dynasties
1085 / 1000		
	Pre-Saite Period	
663		
525	SAITE PERIOD	26th dynasty
	Late Period	27th to 30th dynasties
323	CONQUEST OF ALEXANDER THE GREAT	
	GRECO-ROMAN PERIOD	
31		
CHRISTIAN ERA	ROMAN PROVINCE	
	Coptic Art	

On entering the next gallery notice the two statues of Sepa and Nesa which date from the end of the 3rd dynasty. These are examples of early civil statuary.

In gallery 133 is a masterpiece of the Thinite (Archaic) period, the **Serpent King's Stele.** Sometimes known as the stele of King Djet, the sculpture shows the religious symbols of ancient Egypt : the god Horus, symbolized by a splendid falcon, protects the King represented by a snake.

The Seated Scribe. — *Gallery 129.* Placed in the middle of the room this famous statue of a seated scribe is an incredibly realistic work dating from the Old Kingdom. It is outstanding amongst the statuary of the period for its lifelike quality. The inlaid eyes give a penetrating stare. The statue was painted in red ochre as was the tradition for male statues in Egypt.

The following passage contains the giant black diorite statue of a king of the Middle Kingdom which was usurped by Ramses II (New Kingdom). It was fairly common practice for a King to inscribe his own name in the place of the original one. On the wall is the famous lintel showing Sesostris III making an offering to the god Mentou.

Gallery 128 contains pieces from the Middle Kingdom including masks and statues of Sesostris III. Also worthy of attention is a wooden statue of the Chancellor Nakhti, who is shown in a rigid stance. *Pass on to gallery 125.*

Gallery 125 *(Galerie Henri IV)* has works from the New Kingdom, many of which came from the tombs in the Valley of the Kings. Facing you on entering is the vast black granite group, Amon protecting the King Tutankhamen, although damaged this is a masterpiece showing the King at the feet of his protector god. Egyptian religious tradition recognized Amon as the principal Egyptian god and the temples of Karnak and Luxor were dedicated to him. This tradition was interrupted only once during the reign of Akhenaton.

On the right are four seated statues of Sekhmet, the lion-headed goddess, dating from the 18th dynasty. Next is a pink granite group of four baboons, worshipping the sun. The group originally adorned the base of Ramses II's obelisk at Luxor. The counterpart of this obelisk which is still in place, stands in Place de la Concorde *(p 43).* In the centre of the room is a great granite burial sarcophagus, with its engraved sides which belonged to Ramses III (20th dynasty) who was the last great King of the New Kingdom.

Painted low relief of Sethi I. — *Galerie Henri IV.* In the centre of the wall opposite the windows. This sculpture came from the tomb of Sethi I in the Valley of the Kings near Thebes, and dates from the 19th dynasty of the New Kingdom. King Sethi is portrayed touching the necklace of Hathor, the goddess of death and rebirth.

The mummiform sarcophagii standing against the walls were an alternative to the vat shape already seen.

Coptic art. — With the Roman colonization of Egypt in the 1st century BC, the subsequent forms of artistic expression known as Coptic art, drew their inspiration from the continuing Pharaonic tradition of Egypt and from the recently introduced Mediterranean influences.

Gallery 130 shows some of the earlier works including the famous veil of Antinoüs, who was the favourite of the Emperor Hadrian. The veil shows scenes from the myth of Dionysus the god of wine. Note the mummy with wrappings which make a criss-cross pattern, and the painted portrait of the dead person mounted at the head. Gallery 132 exhibits examples of Coptic art at its zenith. In gallery 134 there is a reconstruction of part of a chapel which came from a monastery at Baouit in Middle Egypt (5-9C). The capitals and frieze running round the upper parts of the wall are intricately worked.

Retrace your steps to the Champollion Stairway via galleries 134, 132 and 130.

The objects lining the stairway came from the temple of Serapeum, the underground burial place of the deceased Apis bulls. The canopic urns held the viscera of the bulls. On the second intermediate landing is a statue of the bull Apis, the sacred animal of the god Ptah.

First Floor

Bust of Amenophis IV. — *Upper landing of the Champollion Stairway.* This highly impressive fragment of the statue of Amenophis IV (Akhenaton) came from the temple of Aten at Karnak. This was the pharaoh who abandoned the religion of his predecessors (Amon) in favour of the solar disc or globe of Aten. The period was known as the Amarnan revolution, and it was Amenophis's successor Tutankhamen who reinstated Amon.

Gebel-el-Arak knife. — *Gallery 236-A.* This knife, in a glass case in front of the wall mirror, is a masterpiece from the early Thinite Period. The blade is of flint and the delicately carved ivory handle portrays hunting and battle scenes.

Other works of the Old Kingdom, the same period as the Seated Scribe, to be noted in gallery 238-B are the head of King Didoufri in red sandstone, who reigned when the great pyramids were being built; the man's head known as Salt Head of painted limestone. To the right is a rare wooden statue of the same period portraying a couple, a favourite Egyptian theme.

Pectoral ornament and rings of Ramses II. — *Gallery 240-C.* These colourful royal jewels exemplify the refinement of these crafts at the time of the New Kingdom. They are of gold with precious stones inlaid. Note the Egyptian royal beasts, the sacred cobra and vulture appear once again. The gallery also contains domestic objects from the Middle Kingdom.

Gallery 242-D has furniture and funerary objects which accompanied the dead person on his journey to the eternal world. Note the striking colour of the varnished statues. Note in gallery 244-E the portrait bust of King Amenophis IV, the Pharaoh who abandoned the religion of his fathers. In a case is a small but delicate statue of the king with his wife, Nefertiti.

The Statue of Queen Karomama. — *Gallery 246-F.* This celebrated bronze statue showing the Queen holding her arms forward, has been beautifully moulded exhibiting a knowledge of techniques in this Late Dynastic Period. Amongst the exhibits in this and gallery 248-G, dating from the Saite Period are the blue enamelled statuettes and the array of small bronzes depicting a large number of the Ancient Egyptian deities. The figure in the passage is known as the Healing Statue and represents a man holding a stele.

Gallery 250-H has works showing the influence of both the Mediterranean (Greek and Roman) and the Ancient Egyptian civilizations : funerary jewels, gold and silver objects, and in the centre of the room the great bronze statue of the falcon headed god, Horus. This work testifies to the skill of the Egyptian bronze craftsmen.

FIRST FLOOR

Escalier Henri IV
Escalier Henri II
SALLES DE LA COLONNADE
Bust of Amenophis IV
Gebel-el-Arak Knife
Karomama
Ramses II's Jewels
250 248 246 244 242 240 238 236
GALERIE
CAMPANA
Escalier Champollion

GROUND FLOOR

Escalier Henri IV
Porte Henri II
Escalier Henri II
COUR CARRÉE
GALERIE HENRI IV
GALERIE D'ALGER
126
Sethi I and the goddess Hathor
125
127
CRYPTE
134 132 130
128
Mastaba
135 133 131 129
Seated Scribe
Passage des Arts
To first floor
Escalier Champollion

0   50 m

1 THE LOUVRE ★★★

ORIENTAL ANTIQUITIES

The Far Eastern part of the collection is displayed in the Guimet Museum (p 145).

The Mesopotamian civilization which grew up on the banks of the Tigris and Euphrates lacked the uniformity which was common in later civilizations, being an amalgam of peoples, cultures and languages. A series of rival and successive empires vied with one another for political domination : Sumer, Babylonia and Persia.

On the whole they were a military and warlike people and destruction was rife, however many buildings, cities, palaces and temple like towers called *ziggurats* have survived. An added aid to reconstituting their way of life was the fact that they made use of a written script — using cuneiform symbols — inscribed on clay tablets *(see galleries II and XVIII).*

Stele of the Vultures. — *Gallery I.* This work commemorates a victory of Eannatum, the ruler of the city state of Lagash. Wars were frequent due to the great rivalry between the various independent city states which existed during the Summerian Kingdom.

Stele of Naram-Sin. — *Gallery I.* This stele in rose coloured sandstone shows the King, Naram-Sin of Akkad, climbing a mountain, surrounded by his soldiers. Naram-Sin was one of the first five rulers of the Akkadians, a southern Mesopotamian population, neighbours to the Sumerians. The king wears the horned crown usually reserved for the gods.

ARCHAEOLOGICAL SITES OF MIDDLE EAST

Statues of Prince Gudea and Ur-Ningirsu. — *Gallery II.* These masterpieces of Mesopotamian art, massive in their proportions, are carved out of hard diorite. Prince Gudea was ruler of the city of Lagash in Sumer. This type of statue usually carried an inscription and was probably intended for the temples of Lagash.

The Intendant, Ebih-il. — *Gallery III.* The seated figure (3rd millenium BC) with his staring eyes inlaid with blue and the typical skirt of *kaunakes,* a hairy material, was found in the temple of Ishtar (the goddess of war and love) in the town of Mari on the middle Euphrates. Also from Mari are the mural paintings of the Royal Palace and the fiercesome lion which used to guard the entrance to the Temple of Dagan.

Code of Hammurabi. — *Gallery IV.* Hammurabi conquered a greater part of Mesopotamia and in so doing destroyed Mari and founded the Old Babylonian Empire centred on the city of the same name. This black basalt stele is inscribed with 282 laws in the Akkaid language and cuneiform script. The King is shown receiving the laws from the god of Justice.

The Old Babylonian Empire was followed by the Assyrian and Persian Empires.

Archers of the Persian Kings. — *Gallery VIII.* After the fall of the Assyrians the province of Elam, on the borders of Mesopotamia, was incorporated in the Persian Empire.

The ruling Achemenide Dynasty, of which Darius was the most famous, had its centres at Susa and Persepolis. The great capital (gallery VII) and the enamelled brick panels showing the archers, came from Darius' palace at Susa.

With the arrival of the Greeks under Alexander the Great a new period of break up began. Romans and Parthians divided up the Empire on Darius' death.

Note in gallery VII the gigantic capital taken from Artaxerxes Palace at Susa.

Assyrian Low Reliefs. — *Galleries XXII-XXIV.* The powerful Assyrian kingdom to the north of the lands of Babylonia had a fine art style. The great Assyrian monarchs decorated their palaces with low reliefs e.g. King Assurbanipal's at Nineveh and Sargon's at Khorsabad. Examples to be seen here are the winged bulls which guarded the palace entrance and the sculpture of the giant and hero Gilgamesh who is shown strangling a lion. King Sargon and his ministers are also visible.

GREEK AND ROMAN ANTIQUITIES

This department is at present being reorganized and certain exhibits are liable to have changed places. The reference letters used in the text refer to the plan on p 35 and do not necessarily correspond with the official designation of the galleries.

Ground Floor

Lady of Auxerre (M). — The exact origin of this statue which came from the museum of Auxerre (a town to the southeast of Paris) is unknown. It is one of the oldest known Greek statues and the rigid stance is typical of the austere Dorian style. This departs from the rigid frontality of Egyptian statues, with the folding of the right arm over the body.

Hera of Samos (N). — This column-like statue of the goodess Hera (wife of Zeus and patroness of marriage and birth) shows a rigidity typical of the Archaic period. One can discern a search for form, under the meticulous folds of her garments.

The Horseman Rampin (N). — The head is original while the rest is a cast of the statue in Athens. Again from the Archaic Period (mid- 6th century BC) with a certain angularity of line, the pose is less rigid with the head turned slightly to the left. Note the famous Antique smile and the care for detail in the portrayal of the curls, hair and beard.

Sculpture from the Athenian Parthenon (P). — The Parthenon in Athens was rebuilt between 442 and 433, after the Persians had destroyed the original. In this the Classical Period Greek art was at its height. The Parthenon was decorated by the great sculptor Phidias. Shown here is a fragment of the frieze which went right round the temple. Young Athenian maids bring an embroidered veil to Athena the patron goddess of Athens.

Venus de Milo. — This is one of the most accomplished statues of antiquity dating from the 2nd century BC (Hellenistic period) when there was a greater search for realism. Poised and supple the marble has acquired an undeniable plastic beauty. Note the contrast between the simple lines of the nude torso and the complex folds of the drapery.

Winged Victory of Samothrace (Q). — *On the landing of the Daru Stairway.* This is another masterpiece of the Hellenistic style of the 3rd century BC.

The statue was found in pieces on the island of Samothrace. The Greeks commonly represented Victory by a winged woman. Here the sculptures soaring movement seems to defy space. Note nearby the palm and ring finger which were found in 1950 at the same spot as the sculpture.

The Caryatid Gallery (101). — The hall built for Henri II by Pierre Lescot, got its name from the monumental statues, carved by Jean Goujon, which uphold the balcony. It was here in 1558 that Mary Stuart married the future François II. The works shown here are from the end of the 5th to the 4th century BC when a new style was created by Praxiteles.

First Floor

Apollo of Piombino. — This bronze statue was found in the sea near Piombino, Italy, and is a masterpiece of pre-Classical work (5th century BC). The lips and eyebrows are inlaid with copper.

Athlete's Head. — This bronze, one of the most beautiful heads in Antiquity was found at Benevento in Italy. Note the perfect features of this youth and the victor's crown.

Ephebe of Agde. — This magnificent bronze statue was found in the former Greek port of Agde in 1964.

The Cervetri Sarcophagus. — The Etruscans created a powerful centre of civilization in Italy transmitting fruits of their Hellenised civilization to the Romans. Their art was essentially funerary. In the middle of the room is a large terra cotta sarcophagus portraying a married couple sharing a banquet. The figures are lifelike and the greatest attention has been paid to minute details.

Tanagra Figurines (IX). — These terra cotta statuettes are full of life, marvels of grace and delicacy. They were probably offerings having a religious meaning and are examples of 4th century Attic pottery.

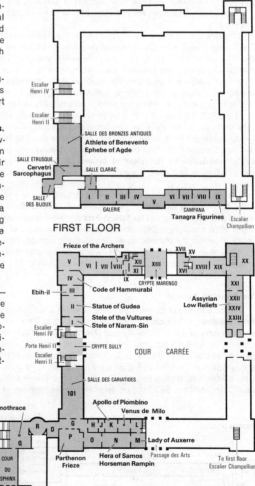

FIRST FLOOR

GROUND FLOOR

PAINTINGS

How to find the different Schools of Painting (Second Floor, p 31)

French	Primitives	Salle Duchâtel
	16C	Salon Carré
	17-18C	Grande Galerie — Second Floor West
	19C	Aile Mollien — Salles Mollien, Denon, Daru — Second Floor South
	Beistegui Coll.	Aile de Flore (First Floor)
Italian	Primitives	Grande Galerie
	16C	Salle des États
	17C	Salle des Sept Cheminées (plan p 31)
	17-18C	Aile de Flore (First Floor)
Flemish and Dutch	Primitives	Cabinets Seine
	16-17C	Cabinet Tuileries
	17C	Salle Van Dyck — Galerie Médicis — Salle des Sept Mètres
Spanish	14-18C	Pavillon de Flore (First Floor)
German	15-16C	Cabinets Seine
English	17-19C	Second Floor West

The French School

French primitive paintings (14-16C) can be seen in the Salle Duchâtel and the Salon Carré. In a period when religious subjects were the rule the painting of Jean le Bon against the traditional gold background is unique in that it was the first real example of portrait painting. Note the Altar-cloth of Narbonne, an ink on silk painting showing Scenes of the Passion.

The **Avignon pietà** (1) a masterpiece of early French painting shows great feeling. Compare the two portraits by Fouquet (*Charles VII, Guillaume Jouvenel*) the greatest painter of the 15C. The portraits of Jean Clouet show a truthfulness and care for detail (**François I**-2).

17C. — The Grande Galerie opens with early works of the Great Classical period. The cold landscapes and sombre mythological subjects of Nicolas Poussin (4th and 5th bays on the left : *Orpheus and Eurydice* and the *Four Seasons*, a series of 4 landscape paintings) one of the " Roman " French painters are in contrast to the golden hazes of Claude Lorrain's architectural scenes.

The canvases of Simon Vouet (2nd bay on the right) show a decidedly Baroque influence. The scenes of everyday life evoking a peace and nobility, by Le Nain (the *Meal of the Peasants, The Blacksmith's Shop; A Family of Peasants*) and of society by Philippe de Champaigne (*Portrait of a Man*) hang opposite the compositions of La Tour preoccupied with the effects of light (*St. Joseph the Carpenter*, **The Adoration of the Shepherds** and *Magdalen with the Candle*). The portraits of *Louis XIV* by Rigaud, **Richelieu** by Champaigne, *Séguier* by Le Brun, the first painter to Louis XIV, evoke the formality and solemnity of court life.

In the 18C reaction set in and styles changed : attitudes became less formal and portraits were smiling (the portraits by Largillière and Fragonard's, *Inspiration*, **Music**); lighthearted scenes in bucolic landscapes (Lancret : *Innocence* and *The Music Lesson* and works by Boucher and Chardin). The age of enlightenment is aptly evoked in the dreamy quality of Watteau's **Embarkation for the Island of Cythera** (3) and his mysterious canvas **Gilles** (4). The works of Greuze had a more serious moral tone (The two paintings illustrating the *Paternal Curse*).

The Neo-Classical style of the Empire is best seen in the vast historic canvas by David of the **Coronation of Napoleon** (5), his portrait of *Madame Récamier* and the less formal paintings of Girodet and Ingres (**The Turkish Bath** (6), the *Grande Odalisque*). Romanticism triumphs in the violent scenes of Delacroix (**Scenes of the Massacres of Scio** (7), *Death of Sardanapalus, Liberty Guiding the People*) and Géricault's poignant shipwreck scene **Raft of Medusa** (8) Note the realism in Courbet's works as he portrayed everyday scenes (*Burial at Ornans*). Then follows the picturesque Romanticism of Corot (*Views of the Roman Countryside*).

The Spanish School

The golden age of Spanish painting provides a variety of contrasts. El Greco's canvas of **Christ Crucified** (9) is typical of his mannerist style. The realism of Ribera with his taste for the bizarre or even brutal subject (**The Club Foot** — 10) and of Murillo in **The Young Beggar** (11) with its striking lighting effects, contrast with the mystical works of Zurbaran and Baroque exaltation of Carreno de Miranda (*The Foundation of the Trinitarian Order*). Velazquez as court painter revelled in the rich colours and varied textures of fine garments as seen in his portraits of royalty (*Infanta Marguerita, The Queen Marie-Anne of Austria*). The Beistegui Collection (Aile de Flore) contains Goya's masterpiece of portraiture, *The Solana*.

The Italian School

The works of the Italian primitives of the 14 and 15C, the precursors of the Renaissance, are displayed in the Grande Galerie with the Venetian, Paduan and Bolognese pictures on the left and the Florentine and Siennese ones on the right. Cimabue's **Virgin and Angels** (12) faces Giotto's **St. Francis of Assisi** (13) which is one of the first paintings to include an authentic landscape background and a living person as subject. Note the predominance of blue in Fra Angelico's **Coronation of the Virgin** (14) and the rose pink of Sassetta's *Triptych of St. John*. The Virgin and Child remained a favourite subject (Fra Filippo Lippi, Botticelli and Perugino) but portraits become more expressive : **Saint Sebastian** (15) by Mantegna; *Christ in Benediction* by Bellini and the *Visitation* and *Portrait of an Old Man and his Grandson* by Ghirlandajo.

The Italian Renaissance is epitomized in the **Mona Lisa** (16), the portrait painted, by Leonardo da Vinci, of the wife of a rich Florentine. This famous work of art is small, the colours are sombre — but the clear features, enigmatic expression, and the beautiful hands, are strangely compelling and memorable. Alongside is the **Virgin and Infant Jesus with Saint Anne** (17) also by Leonardo. Amongst several religious scenes by Raphael note the portrait known as *Balthazar Castiglione*. The Venitians added a profusion of colour and life to their works : Giorgione (*Open Air Concert*), Tintoretto (**Suzanna Bathing** — 18), Titian (*François I, Woman at her Toilet*), and the vast Veronese painting, **Wedding at Cana** (19) in which Christ appears beside the Emperor Charles V, 16C Venetian high society and the artist as a cello player.

The artists of the Baroque style show a search for lighting effects : Guido Reni's naked figures against sombre backgrounds (*Ecce Homo, St. Sebastian*); Guercino's streaming light in his *Adoration of the Shepherds;* the intense luminosity of Piazzetta's *Assumption* and the striking contrasts of Caravaggio (**The Death of the Virgin** — 20, *The Fortune Teller*). The 18C is represented by Tiepolo (*Carnival Scene, The Charlatan*) and Guardi with 8 Venetian scenes.

The Dutch and Flemish Schools

The works of the Flemish primitives are characterized by the oval face, the carefully draped garments and the taste for familiar details : Van der Weyden (*Greeting of the Angel*) and Jan van Eyck's **Madonna with the Chancellor Rolin** (21). A certain realism appears in the works of Hieronymus Bosch (*The Ship of Fools*) and Bruegel the Elder (*The Beggars*).

The peaceful landscapes and still lifes of Jan Bruegel, son of the above and known as Velvet Bruegel, precede the small *genre* canvases of the life of the bourgeois of the period by Teniers, Ter Borch and Vermeer (*The Lace-maker*). The sombre colours of the Frans Hals portraits are often lightened by a white collar : the **Bohemian Girl** (22) is exceptional for its naturalness and life.

Rubens' richness of colour, his love of luxurious materials and clothes, the life-like sensual painting of the human form, even in his religious works, make his paintings stand out — *Portrait of Helen Fourment (2nd floor)*, his second wife, *Adoration of the Magi (2nd floor)* and *The Fair*.

The **Medici Gallery** (23) contains the of 21 paintings by Rubens — an official commission for Marie dei Medici which turned out a masterpiece *(p 94)*. Among Rubens' disciples were the more reserved and extremely elegant Van Dyck (**Portrait of Charles I of England** — 24) and the altogether different Jordaens, bursting with realism and colour (*The Four Evangelists*).

Rembrandt is represented by 4 **self-portraits** (25), landscapes and the **Pilgrims of Emmaus** (26).

The German School

The German Renaissance school is represented by a fine *Self-portrait* of Dürer as a young man, a *Venus* by Lucas Cranach and the portrait of the humanist *Erasmus* by Holbein the Younger.

The English School

Apart from Hans Holbein and Van Dyck, who were official painters to the English court the English School is represented by works in the great tradition of English portrait painting : Lawrence, Reynolds (*Master Hare*), Raeburn (*Captain Robert Hay of Spot*) and Gainsborough (*Conversation in a Park, Lady Alston*). In addition there are several Constable landscapes.

GRAPHIC ART (Pavillon de Flore)

The 90 000 drawings, engravings, charcoal sketches and water colours of the Drawings and Engravings department are shown in rotation *(Second Floor, galleries 1-4, see plan p 31)*.

FIRST FLOOR

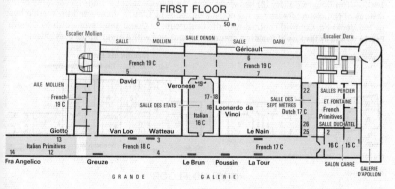

SCULPTURE

Pavillon des États *(enter by the Porte La Trémoille)*

French Romanesque. — *Gallery 1.* With the upsurge of faith and consequent church building in the early Middle Ages, various local schools of sculpture developed. The Romanesque gallery contains pieces from religious buildings. To the left of the stairway is a carved capital from the Church of Ste-Geneviève in Paris, showing Daniel between two lions. To the right is the Head of Christ from Lavaudieu, in painted and gilded wood. Against the wall is a moving Burgundian Descent from the Cross. Against the end wall is a low relief showing St. Michael and the Dragon — a lively composition.

French Gothic. — *Galleries 2, 3 and 4.* This period saw the building of the great Gothic cathedrals in France and their adornment with religious statuary. The rigid spirituality is evident in the head of St. Peter (2), with the stylised curls and beard and the two statue-columns from Notre-Dame de Corbeil representing King Solomon and the Queen of Sheba.

In the next gallery a variety of regional styles is evident : compare the Virgin and the Child from Burgundy (mid-15C) with the Mary Magdalene (second half 15C, Meuse), the latter shows more naturalness and approaches the Renaissance in style. Striking in this gallery is the tomb of Philippe Pot, the seneschal of Burgundy, which is surrounded by 8 hooded figures with heads bowed by grief who bear the armoured figure of the man.

In the upper gallery is a masterpiece of Gothic sculpture the **Virgin of Isenheim,** from Alsace. The spirituality of the Middle Ages is evident in this work. The other upper galleries display northern European Gothic sculpture.

French Renaissance. — On the back wall of gallery 6 is a marble high relief by Michel Colombe, portraying St. George fighting the dragon. There is a distinctly Renaissance influence in the framing.

Gallery 7 *(Salle Jean Goujon)* contains some of the best examples of French Renaissance work. In the middle is the harmonious composition of **Diana the Huntress** by the 16C sculptor, Jean Goujon, which personifies elegance and grace. Also by the same sculptor the three low reliefs on the far wall represent **Nymphs** and Tritons. These graceful pieces came from the Fountain of the Innocents in Paris (p 109). Worthy of note also are the low reliefs in the middle window recess (the four Evangelists and a Descent from the Cross). In the first window alcove is the **Three Graces,** a funerary monument for the heart of Henri II by Germain Pilon.

Italian sculpture. — Note Donatello's low relief of the **Virgin and Child** *(3rd alcove from the left)* und the details of 2 angels by Verrocchio. There are various enamelled terra cottas by della Robbia. This gallery gives access to gallery 9, *(on the ground floor)* where **The Slaves** of Michelangelo are displayed. These masterpieces of controlled strength and profound emotion were carved between 1513 and 1520 and were intended for the tomb of Pope Julius II.

Pavillon de Flore *(enter by the Porte Jaujard)*

On entering turn left and make for gallery I at the far end.

18C. — The first gallery contains examples of statuary taken from royal and princely palaces such as Versailles, Marly and Petit-Bourg. The works date from the early decades of the 18C, when the style moved from a classicism to a freer style known as Rococo. Louis XV is presented as Jupiter and Marie Leczinska as Juno. Gallery 2 has works taken from the Grande Cascade and park at Marly, done by Antoine Coysevox and Nicolas Coustou. The small pieces of the next gallery, contrast with the pompous statues of the previous rooms. Included amongst the busts is a portrait of *Nicolas Coustou* by his younger brother Guillaume. The rotunda displays Cupid cutting his bow from the club of Hercules, by Edme Bouchardon. Note how the supple lines of the arc moves with the movement of the body. Sketches for this study hang on the walls.

The monumental works in gallery 5 show a return to a more Classical style and realism in portraiture. Note the statue of *Voltaire* in the Classical manner.

Jean-Antoine Houdon was the master of French sculpture in the closing decades of the 18C. He was especially renowned for his portraits. Displayed around the statue of Diana the *Huntress* are a series of **Houdon Busts :** Rousseau, Voltaire, Franklin, Washington, Madame Adélaïde, one of the daughters of Louis XV and two charming busts of the Brongniart children.

The works in gallery 7 show a return to the purity of the antique art after the liberties of the Rococo style. Note the care taken for the living model as in Julien's *Dying Gladiator.*

19C. — The Empire Gallery (8) has works from the Neo-Classical period. The severity of the statues of Napoleon (dressed in his coronation robes by Claude Ramey and the marble bust by the Venetian, Canova) contrast with the two groups of Cupid and Psyche also by Canova. **Psyche revived by the Kiss of Cupid** is a graceful composition with a great tenderness of feeling.

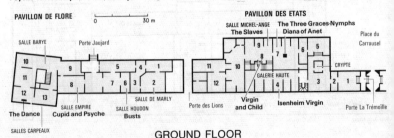

GROUND FLOOR

In gallery **9** the medallions of David of Angers are full of vigour (Bonaparte, George Sand and Alfred de Musset). The force and energy of Rude's head of *La Marseillaise,* a study for the Arc de Triomphe *(p 47),* contrasts with the charm of his *Young Neapolitan Fisherman.*

The works of Antoine-Louis Barye in gallery **10** keenly evoke the animal kingdom, a much neglected subject, and show great realism and vitality. Admire the magnificent *Lion and Snake* a combat of force and cunning, the *Tiger and Crocodile* and the *Pawing Bull.*

Jean-Baptiste Carpeaux was the official sculptor of the Second Empire. His works shown in gallery **11** are dominated by the masterpiece **La Danse.** This statue was commissioned for the façade of the Paris Opera *(p 73).* The exuberance and joy which emanates from this whirl of figures contrasts with the gloom of the group, Ugolin and his children.

ART OBJECTS AND FURNITURE

Apollo Gallery★★★. — *First floor (plan p 31).* This was a stateroom when the Louvre was a royal palace and Le Brun's masterpiece provides a Grand Siècle setting for all that remains of the royal treasures of France. The **Crown Jewels** include the **Regent** diamond, 137 carats, purchased by the Duke of Orléans in 1717 from England, St Louis' and Napoleon's crowns, insignia, chalices and reliquaries in gold and precious stones.
Go through the Egyptian galleries to the Champollion Stairway.

Colonnade Galleries★★. — The first three Colonnade Galleries have splendid panelling and coffered ceilings going back to the 16 and 17C. They are taken in part from the Château Neuf de Vincennes (**1**), the King's Bedchamber (**2**) and the King's State Chambers (**3**) of the Louvre. The galleries which follow contain art objects from the Middle Ages and the Renaissance.

Harbaville Triptych. — *Gallery 4.* This 10C Byzantine ivory triptych shows Christ, the Virgin and Saint John the Baptist surrounded by other saints. This masterpiece is accompanied by other early Christian and Romanesque ivories, enamels and bronzes.

Ivory Virgin. — *Gallery 5.* Amidst a display of valuable French Gothic treasures is the Ivory Virgin, a masterpiece from the treasure of the Ste-Chapelle *(p 68).* This is one of the most beautiful Parisian ivories, dating from the 13 and 14C. Note also the painted ivory Coronation of the Virgin. The highly coloured Limousin enamels attract the attention in particular the ciborium by the master enameller Alpais.

The Renaissance works of art begin in gallery **6** where you should pause before the slender Tuscan statue of St. John the Baptist and the works of Riccio.

The Maximilian Tapestries. — *Gallery 7.* On the walls of this the great Renaissance gallery hang a magnificent set of 12 tapestries *(one hangs in the preceding gallery)* entitled " The Hunts of Maximilian ". These were woven in Brussels in 1535 for the Emperor Charles V and are characteristic of the Renaissance style of Brussels tapestry. The gallery has a rich collection of French painted enamel work including a self-portrait of Jean Bouquet and pieces by famous Limoges masters such as the Limosins and Pénicauds. There are fine pieces of Italian faience from the workshops of Urbino and Gubbio and examples of Bernard Palissy's (1510-1589) work, who was the first Frenchman to produce elaborately decorated pottery.

The galleries in the north wing of the Cour Carrée are devoted in part to French furniture from the 16-19C. Explanatory panels on the walls enable the visitor to date the pieces.

The Boulle Cupboards. — From 1660 onward the majesty and greatness of the Louis XIV period was reflected in all the decorative arts (see galleries **11-16**). Furniture of the period was rather heavy and opulent and was veneered with tortoiseshell, inlaid with brass and ivory or gilded. André-Charles **Boulle**, the royal cabinetmaker was particularly associated with this style. In the gallery called after him (**13**) are two Boulle **cupboards** in ebony inlaid with mother of pearl, copper and pewter and ornamented with gilded bronze mounts.

The Cressent Commode. — In the 18C, the Regence style followed Rococo, with its characteristic curvilinear forms. Charles **Cressent**, cabinetmaker to the Duke of Orléans, was a leading exponent of this style — see his famous **Monkey Commode** (**16**).

Gobelins Tapestry. — In the Condé Gallery (**29**) are the wonderful Gobelins tapestries on a rose background, known as the **Loves of the Gods,** after Boucher. In gallery **30** a writing desk by Riesener stands near a splendid flat desk by Benneman, which was used by Napoleon in the Tuileries. Galleries **33** and **34** contain furniture by Riesener for Marie-Antoinette. There are several fine Empire pieces including the Throne of Napoleon I and the cradle of his son (**36**).

FIRST FLOOR

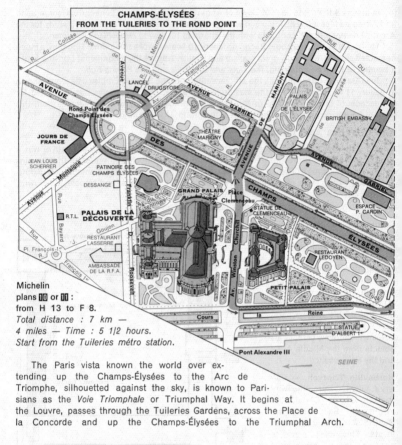

CHAMPS-ÉLYSÉES
FROM THE TUILERIES TO THE ROND POINT

Michelin
plans 10 or 11 :
from H 13 to F 8.
Total distance : 7 km —
4 miles — Time : 5 1/2 hours.
Start from the Tuileries métro station.

The Paris vista known the world over extending up the Champs-Élysées to the Arc de Triomphe, silhouetted against the sky, is known to Parisians as the *Voie Triomphale* or Triumphal Way. It begins at the Louvre, passes through the Tuileries Gardens, across the Place de la Concorde and up the Champs-Élysées to the Triumphal Arch.

THE TUILERIES GARDENS★★   10 or 11 : from H 12 to G 11

The gardens, the Jardin des Tuileries, beautifully situated beside the Seine, epitomise the formal French style of design.

The first garden. — In the 15C the area was used as a rubbish tip by butchers and tawers of the Châtelet district, the clay soil for making tiles — *tuiles* — hence the name : Tuileries.

When, in 1563, the Queen Mother, Catherine dei Medici, decided to build a château next to the Louvre (p 27), she bought land from the Tuileries for an Italian style park. This included fountains, a maze, a grotto, decorated with terra cotta figures by Bernard Palissy, and a menagerie and silkworm farm.

The park became the fashionable airing place and as such broke new ground, for hitherto fashion and elegance had always been displayed indoors.

Le Nôtre's French Garden. — By 1664 the gardens required attention : Colbert entrusted the embellishment to Le Nôtre, born near the Marsan Pavilion and a gardener at the Tuileries, like his father and grandfather before him. He raised two terraces lengthways and of unequal height to level the sloping ground ; created the magnificent central alley vista ; hollowed out the pools ; designed the formal flowerbeds, quincunxes and slopes.

Colbert was so delighted that he wanted the gardens kept for the royal family but was persuaded by the writer, Charles Perrault, to allow the public to enjoy them also.

In the 18C the gardens' appeal was increased by such attractions as chairs being available for hire and toilets being built.

In 1783 the physicist, Charles, and the engineer, Robert, made an early balloon flight from the gardens.

The Revolution. — On 10 August 1792, Louis XVI and his family fled the Tuileries Palace, crossed the gardens and sought refuge with the Legislative Assembly. The Swiss Guards also tried to escape but two thirds of them were slaughtered in the gardens by the mob.

The Festival of the Supreme Being, organised by the painter David on 8 June 1794, opened in the gardens before proceeding to the Champ-de-Mars (p 51).

The Tuileries today. — The part of the Tuileries designed by Le Nôtre remains unaltered although the effect of his positioning of occasional statues has been jeopardized by less satisfactory additions, apart from those by Maillol which are outstanding.

If you have a special interest turn to p 178 where the Museums are classified by subject.

TOUR

The modern area of the Tuileries, between the wings of the Louvre and the Carrousel Arch are described on p 29. Start from the Flore Pavilion, where the Avenue du Général-Lemonnier meets the quay and two sphinxes, brought back after the capture of Sebastopol in 1855, stand guard.

The Bord de l'Eau Terrace. — Walk up the steps to the waterside terrace from which there is a **view★★** overlooking the gardens, the Seine and, in the background, the Louvre. This was the playground of royal princes and the sons of Napoleon I and III.

An underground passage beneath the terrace, communicating with the Place de la Concorde, enabled Louis-Philippe to escape from the palace in 1848.

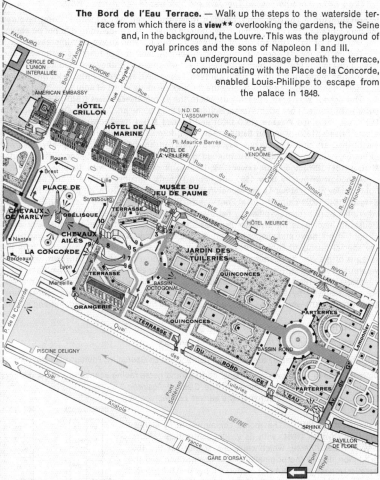

Walk towards the formal gardens.

The Parterres. — The small grille, marked by a ditch, formerly divided the royal garden from the public area.

The **statues★★** between the Général-Lemonnier Avenue and the round basin are by Coysevox, Nicolas Coustou and Le Pautre; the figures and decorative vases lining the paths circling the basin are copies from Antiquity.

Quincunxes. — The central alley affords a magnificent **vista★★★**. On either side are areas of greenery, the first ornamented with **statues★** illustrating the speed of the chase : *Apollo and Daphne* by Nicolas Coustou on the right: *Hippomenes* (Guillaume Coustou) and *Atalanta* (Le Pautre) on the left.

The Octagonal Basin and Terraces. — The huge octagonal basin and the adjoining statues, terraces, slopes, stairways were designed as a single architectural composition.

1) The Seasons (N. Coustou and Van Clève)
2) Arches from the Tuileries Palace *(p 27)*
3) Bust of Le Nôtre (Coysevox). The original is in St-Roch *(p 90)*
4) The Tiber in the Antique manner
5) The Rhône and the Saône (G. Coustou)
6) The Nile in the Antique Manner
7) The Rhine and the Moselle (Van Clève)
8) Commemorative tablet of the balloon ascent of Robert and Charles in 1783
9) Fame on a winged horse★★ (Coysevox)
10) Mercury on a winged horse★★ (Coysevox)

Until 1716 there was no exit from this end of the Tuileries, the moat at the foot of the Louis XIII wall cutting it off from the Esplanade or future Place de la Concorde. A swing bridge was constructed over the moat and ornamented in 1719 by Coysevox's winged horses which were brought for the purpose from Marly. The bridge disappeared when Louis-Philippe had the Place de la Concorde redesigned.

Steps and ramps afford access at several points to the terraces *(the Feuillants on the north side, the Bord de l'Eau on the south)* which run the length of the gardens and culminate in the Jeu de Paume and Orangery Museums.

The pavilions were built at the time of the Second Empire and serve as painting gallery annexes to the Louvre; the national collection of Impressionist Paintings was transferred to the **Jeu de Paume** in 1947 and the **Orangery** *(closed)* kept for temporary exhibitions.

■ JEU DE PAUME MUSEUM★★★ ▯▯ or ▯▯ : G 11

Open 9.45 am to 5 pm; closed Tuesdays and holidays; 5F — Sundays : 2.50F.

Impressionism. — The Barbizon school (Th. Rousseau, Millet), which followed Corot, favoured the dark tones of trees and the night. By contrast other artists endeavoured to put on canvas the vibration of light, the colours of impression. They became known as " impressionists ".

The Impressionists were not interested in painting historical or religious pictures or portraying day to day life : for them light was all — they analysed it, they watched its play. Their observation made them turn to sunlit gardens, snow, mist, and flesh tints. Paint was applied in small brightly coloured dabs to give the fleeting, unstable effect of light.

The school was born at Honfleur where the young **Claude Monet** (1840-1926) and **Sisley** (1839-1899) studied light effects under Boudin and the Dutchman, Jongkind. On their return to Paris, they rejoined **Pissarro** (1830-1903) and **Edouard Manet** (1832-1883) and with their fellow artists **Cézanne** (1839-1906) and **Bazille** (1841-1870), formed an active group in opposition to the established art circles of the day. **Degas** (1834-1917), meanwhile, although originally a follower of Ingres, held himself apart and continued to do so until the end of the Second Empire. **Berthe Morisot** (1841-1895) and **Fantin-Latour** (1836-1904) exhibited regularly with the others.

Although dispersed after 1880, the Impressionists remained faithful to the painting of light : Sisley at Moret-sur-Loing, Monet in the Seine Valley and Cézanne at Aix-en-Provence. **Gauguin** (1848-1903) painted first at Pont-Aven in Brittany before setting out for the South Seas where his work became typified by flat planes of colour surrounded by dark outlines; Henri Rousseau, known as the **Douanier Rousseau** (1844-1910), brought a very personal expression of light in his naïve and allegorical pictures; the Dutchman, **Van Gogh** (1853-1890), discovered the special quality of light in Provence, although it was not enough to save him from the ravages of his own temperament and suicide at Auvers-sur-Oise. His canvases, with their vigorous strokes of pure colour, can now be seen as the early forerunners of Fauvism.

Seurat (1859-1891) by a highly detailed stippling technique broke down all colour masses. He was followed by **Signac** (1863-1935) and briefly, by Pissarro. Finally there was **Toulouse-Lautrec** (1864-1901) who was primarily interested in the theatre and its bizarre lighting effects.

TOUR

Following the order of the galleries note in particular :

Entrance Hall. — On display are two large paintings of *La Goulue* by Toulouse-Lautrec.

Galleries I and II. — Shown are Degas' portraits and horse racing scenes; his ballet dancers reveal his concern for movement. In The *Glass of Absinthe* the juxtaposition of the figures on the canvas communicates pathos.

Galleries VI and VII. — The rooms contain works by Manet : the cool *Olympia* (1864) with its vividly contrasting colours; *Déjeuner sur l'herbe*, which caused a scandal at the 1863 exhibition due to the originality of the composition and the permissiveness of the subject matter — it became the group's public manifesto; the *Portrait of Emile Zola;* and the *Fifer* where the lone young figure, uncluttered by details communicates a feeling of immediacy.

Gallery VIII. — Featured by Monet are two canvases : the *Wild Poppies* and *Peace Beneath the Lilac Trees.* Sisley's *Barges at Bougival Lock* reveals his sensitivity to nature; while Jongkind paints picturesque views of old Paris.

Gallery X. — *1st floor.* Five canvases of the *Rouen Cathedral* by Monet, reveal, by their unique colour sequence, the school's originality. The artist rented a room facing the west door and painted more than twenty versions of the same scene, clearly exemplifying the group's theory on ever changing light effects — at different times of day and seasons of the year — even on a subject so apparently inert as cathedral stone.

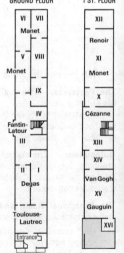

Gallery XI. — In this room the *Houses of Parliament* by Monet is shown. Renoir with his shimmering palette evokes a joy of living personified by the feeling of well being exuded by his figures : *Le Moulin de la Galette, Young Girl at the Piano*, the *Nymphéas* series.

Gallery XIII. — Cézanne sought to reduce nature to its basic geometric form : cone, square, sphere as shown in : *The Suicide's House, Woman with Coffeepot, Still Life with Apples and Oranges* and the *Cardplayers.*

Galleries XIV and XV. — Van Gogh through his contact with the Impressionists lightened his palette as shown in the *Church of Auvers.* Gauguin's firm outlined and 2-dimensional paintings of Tahiti illustrate a world so different from his fellow artists : *Women of Tahiti, Arearea, Le Repas* and the *White Horse.*

THE PLACE DE LA CONCORDE★★★   ⓾ or ⓫ : G 11

Everything — the site, the size, the general elegance of the square — combines to impress.

HISTORICAL NOTES

In honour of the " Well Beloved ". — Paris aldermen, wanting to find favour with Louis XV, commissioned Bouchardon to sculpt an equestrian statue of the Well Beloved, as he was known, and organised a competition to find an architect for the square. Servandoni, Soufflot, Gabriel and others all submitted plans. The winner was Gabriel who designed an octagon with an area of nearly 84 000 m² — 21 acres — bordered by a dry moat and balustrade. Eight massive pedestals, in pairs and intended later to support statues, were to mark the oblique corners. Twin edifices with fine colonnades were to be constructed to flank the opening of the Rue Royale. Work began in 1755 and continued until 1775.

In 1770, at a firework display to celebrate the marriage of the Dauphin and Marie-Antoinette, the crowd panicked and 133 people were crushed to death in the moat. In 1792 the royal statue was toppled and Louis XV Square became the Square of the Revolution.

The guillotine at work. — On Sunday 21 January 1793 a guillotine was erected near where the Brest statue now stands, to perform the execution of Louis XVI. The King arrived from the Rue Royale, he climbed the steps of the scaffold, calm and serene, and above the roll of the drums tried to make his last words heard : " My people, I die innocent of the crimes of which I am accused; may my blood consolidate the happiness of France ". Beginning on 13 May, the " nation's razor ", by now installed near the grille to the Tuileries, cut the necks of a further 1 343 victims including Marie-Antoinette, Mme du Barry, Charlotte Corday, the Girondins, Danton and his friends, Mme Roland (p 66), Robespierre and his confederates. Only after two years, in 1795, did the sound of the fall of the blade of the guillotine cease to be heard in the square. The Directory, in hope of a better future, renamed the blood soaked area, Concorde.

Completion. — The Concorde Bridge was opened in 1790 and the square's decoration completed in the reign of Louis-Philippe by the architect Hittorff. The king decided against a central statue which all too easily might become an object of contention with any change in regime and selected, instead, an entirely non-political monument, an obelisk. Two fountains were added similar to those in St. Peter's Square in Rome. The north fountain represents river navigation and the south fountain maritime navigation. Eight statues of towns of France were commissioned for the pedestals provided by Gabriel. Cortot sculpted Brest and Rouen, Pradier Lille and Strasbourg. It was at the foot of this last figure, executed after a famous actress of that time, Juliette Drouet, that the poet-politician, Déroulède, rallied patriots after 1870 when the town of Strasbourg was under German rule.

THE SQUARE

Obelisk★. — The obelisk comes from the ruins of the temple at Luxor. It was offered by Mohammed Ali, Viceroy of Egypt, to Charles X in 1829 when seeking French support, but only reached Paris four years later, in the reign of Louis-Philippe. The monument, 3 300 years old, is covered in hieroglyphics; it is 23 m tall — 75 ft — and weighs more than 220 tons. The base depicts the apparatus and stratagems used in its transport and erection on the square (Maritime Museum p 50) — Cleopatra's Needle in London, offered by the same ruler to Queen Victoria, comes from Heliopolis and is 2 m shorter 6 ft-6 in.

G. Coustou : The Marly Horses (detail)

Views★★★. — The best point from which to get a view of the Champs-Élysées — Triumphal Way is the obelisk. The view is framed by the Marly Horses as you look up the avenue towards the Arc de Triomphe, and by the Winged Horses of the Tuileries towards the Louvre. There are good vistas also, north to the Madeleine and, south, to the Palais-Bourbon.

The two mansions★★. — Gabriel's colossal mansions on either side of the opening to the Rue Royale are impressive without being overbearing; the colonnades inspired by that at the Louvre are even more elegant than the original and the mansions themselves, one of the finest examples of the Louis XV style.

The right pavilion, the **Hôtel de la Marine,** was originally the royal furniture store, until, in 1792, it became the Admiralty Office. Today it houses the Navy Headquarters and the Ministry of Environment. The pavilion, across the street, was at first occupied by four noblemen. It is now divided between the French Automobile Club and the Hôtel Crillon, a world famous luxury hotel. It was in this building on 6 February 1778 that the Treaty of Friendship and Trade between the King, Louis XVI and the 13 independent States of America was signed. Benjamin Franklin was among the signatories for the States. On the Rue Royale side, a plaque in English and French commemorates this treaty by which France officially recognized the independence of the U.S.A.

The two mansions on their far sides from the Rue Royale (p 72) are bordered respectively by the American Embassy (on the left) and the former Vrillière mansion, designed in the 18C by Chalgrin and where Talleyrand died in 1838.

THE CHAMPS-ÉLYSÉES*** ⑩ or ⑪ : from G 11 to F 8

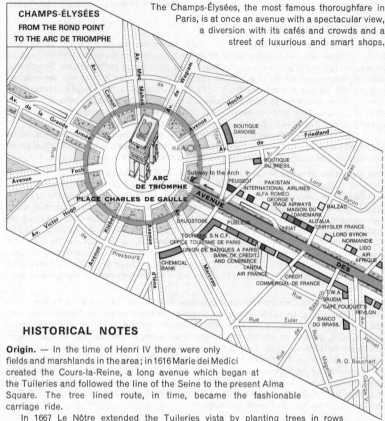

CHAMPS-ÉLYSÉES
FROM THE ROND POINT
TO THE ARC DE TRIOMPHE

The Champs-Élysées, the most famous thoroughfare in Paris, is at once an avenue with a spectacular view, a diversion with its cafés and crowds and a street of luxurious and smart shops.

HISTORICAL NOTES

Origin. — In the time of Henri IV there were only fields and marshlands in the area; in 1616 Marie dei Medici created the Cours-la-Reine, a long avenue which began at the Tuileries and followed the line of the Seine to the present Alma Square. The tree lined route, in time, became the fashionable carriage ride.

In 1667 Le Nôtre extended the Tuileries vista by planting trees in rows on the plain known as the Grand Cours. The calm shades were renamed the Elysian Fields — Champs-Élysées — in 1709. In 1724 the Duke of Antin, Director of the Royal Gardens, extended the avenue to the Chaillot Mound — the present Étoile; his successor, the Marquis of Marigny, prolonged it in 1772 to the Neuilly Bridge. Two years later Soufflot, reduced the road gradient by lopping the mound by more than 5 m — 16 ft — the surplus rubble being dumped and producing the still apparent rise in the Rue Balzac.

The fashion. — At the end of the 18C the Champs-Élysées were still wild, deserted, unknown and only six private mansions had been built within their precincts. Of these, one, the Hôtel Massa, was later transported stone by stone and re-erected near the Observatory (p 123). The Allies, who occupied Paris in 1814, alloted the green area in the centre of the capital, the English and the Prussians camping in the Tuileries and Place de la Concorde, the Russians beneath the trees in the Champs-Élysées. The ensuing delapidation took two years to clean up.

The avenue, by 1828 in the City's care, was embellished by fountains, footpaths, gas lighting. During the time of the Second Empire it became a favourite meeting place and the curious, seated on either side of the thoroughfare, might see cavaliers and their escorts riding side-saddle, tilburies and broughams, eight abreast in a cloud of dust. Café orchestras (the Alcazar rebuilt by Hittorff in 1840), restaurants, panoramas, circuses attracted the elegant who swelled in number when there were race meetings at Longchamp or the great world exhibitions (1844, 1855, 1867, 1900...).

In the gallant Widows' Alley, now the Avenue Montaigne, crowds gathered to dance beneath the three thousand blinding gas flares as Olivier Metra conducted polkas and mazurkas with gay abandon or in the nearby Winter Garden, to listen to Sax, the musician playing his new instrument, the saxophone.

The heart of the nation. — Today there is little that is aristocratic about the avenue, but it still sparkles, it still appeals to all.

On 14 July, military processions with bands playing used to draw immense numbers. In 1974 the processions took place from the Place de la Bastille to the Place de la République and in 1975 on the Cours de Vincennes. At times of great national emotion, the triumphal avenue is the spontaneous rallying point for the people of Paris : the procession of the Liberation (26 August 1944), the manifestation of 30 May 1968, the silent march in honour of General de Gaulle on 12 November 1970.

Every day of the week, year in year out, Parisians and tourists alike may be seen congregated upon this famous avenue, seated at its cafés or idly walking its shaded alleys until far into the night.

WALK

The Marly Horses**. — These two magnificent marble groups *(Africans Mastering the Numidian Horses)* were originally commissioned from Guillaume Coustou for Marly, Louis XIV's superb château near Versailles, which was destroyed during the Revolution. A special trailer drawn by sixteen horses brought the marbles to their present site in 1795.

Bear right in the square and left along the Avenue Gabriel.

Avenue Gabriel and Avenue Marigny*. — The Avenue Gabriel runs along the back of the well shaded gardens of the mansions on the Faubourg St-Honoré *(p 143)* : the American Embassy (once the house of the gastronome Grimod de La Reynière, whose culinary judgment was absolute), the Interallied Union Circle, the British Embassy, the Élysée Palace (fine Cock iron grille wrought in 1905 — *p 143*). To the left are a landscaped garden and the Espace Pierre Cardin.

Turn left in the Avenue de Marigny. Beside the Marigny Theatre, you will find the Stamp Market in full operation on Thursdays and Sundays.

There is a good **view**** looking towards the Invalides *(ill. p 55)*. Straight ahead the statue of Clemenceau, the Father of Victory, by François Cogné (1932) marks the opening of the Avenue Winston Churchill.

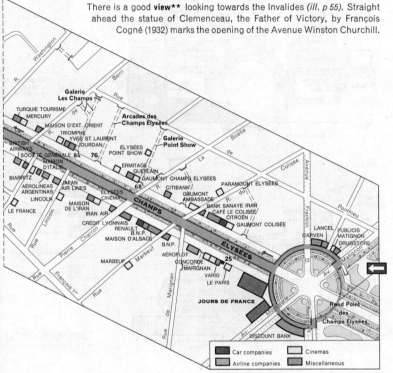

The Petit Palais and the Grand Palais. — The halls were built for the 1900 World Exhibition. The palaces' stone, steel and skylight architecture and very varied exterior decoration has always had critics as well as admirers but the constructions, nevertheless, have gradually come to be admitted as part of the Paris urban scene.

The Petit Palais houses the **Museum of Fine Arts of the City of Paris*** *(open 10 am to 6 pm; closed Mondays and holidays; 8F, 5F on Saturdays; special charges for temporary exhibitions)*.

The museum is divided into the Dutuit (antiques, mediaeval and Renaissance art objects, paintings, drawings, books, enamels, porcelain), Tuck (18C furniture and art objects) and City of Paris 19C collections (Géricault, Ingres, Delacroix, Carpeaux, Corot, Courbet, Barbizon school, Impressionists, 1900 Art, O. Redon, Vuillard and Bonnard). It is widely known also for outstanding temporary exhibitions — Tutankhamen, Ingres, Florentine and Pompeii frescoes, Rembrandt...

An Ionic colonnade before a mosaic frieze forms the façade of the **Grand Palais** along its entire length. Enormous quadrigae crown the corners; elsewhere the decoration is 1900 " modern style ". Inside, the single hall space is covered, above ground by a flat glass dome.

The Grand Palais, long the home of annual exhibitions and shows (art, cars, domestic equipment, children, etc.), has been entirely remodelled. It now comprises conference rooms with attendant facilities, a library, a closed-circuit television an exhibition area of just under nearly 5000 m² — 6000 sq yds — known as the National Galleries of the Grand Palais *(entrance: Avenue du Général Eisenhower)* and is intended as a cultural centre (Picasso, Chagall, Matisse, Fernand Léger, Miro exhibitions).

A further area on the west side has been given to the Palais de la Découverte *(p 46)*.

To the south, the **Alexandre III Bridge,** also built for the 1900 World Exhibition, is another example of the popular steel architecture of the 19C.

Palais de la Découverte**. — *Avenue Franklin-Roosevelt. Open 10 am to 6 pm : planetarium lectures 3 and 4 pm. Closed Mondays, 1 January, 1 May, 14 July, 15 August, 25 December. 3F (7F including the planetarium).*

This museum of scientific discoveries, founded in 1937, is a centre both for higher scientific study and for popular enlightenment. Diagrams, lectures and demonstrations, experiments, documentary films and temporary exhibitions illustrate progressive stages and the most recent discoveries in the sciences. The **planetarium*,** beneath its dome, presents a clear and fascinating introduction to the heavens.

Walk along the Cours-la-Reine to the statue of King Albert I of Belgium.

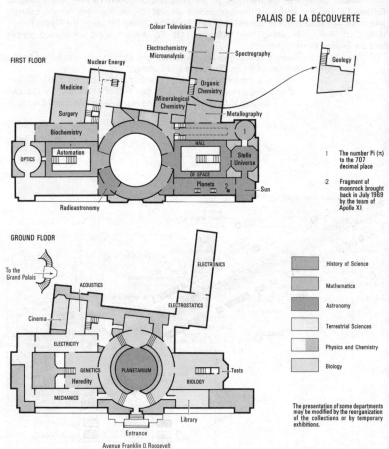

PALAIS DE LA DÉCOUVERTE

FIRST FLOOR

Colour Television
Electrochemistry Microanalysis
Spectrography
Geology
Nuclear Energy
Medicine
Organic Chemistry
Mineralogical Chemistry
Surgery
Metallography
Biochemistry
OPTICS
Automation
HALL
Stella Universe
OF SPACE
Planets
Sun
Radioastronomy

1 — The number Pi (π) to the 707 decimal place

2 — Fragment of moonrock brought back in July 1969 by the team of Apollo XI

GROUND FLOOR

To the Grand Palais
ELECTRONICS
ACOUSTICS
ELECTROSTATICS
Cinema
ELECTRICITY
GENETICS
Heredity
PLANETARIUM
Tests
BIOLOGY
MECHANICS
Library
Entrance
Avenue Franklin D. Roosevelt

History of Science
Mathematics
Astronomy
Terrestrial Sciences
Physics and Chemistry
Biology

The presentation of some departments may be modified by the reorganization of the collections or by temporary exhibitions.

From the Concorde to the Rond-Point. — The Champs-Élysées, in this area, is planted with trees, landscaped, bordered with grand old chestnut alleys, scattered with occasional pavilions and even a small children's funfair. In Louis XVI's time the Ledoyen Restaurant was a modest country inn where passers-by paused to drink fresh milk from the cows grazing outside.

The Rond-Point itself, a circular crossroads 140 m — 153 yds — in diameter, by Le Nôtre, juxtaposes Second Empire buildings (the **Jours de France** magazine on the left) with such ultra-modern shops as the Matignon Drugstore or Lancel and, at the start of the Avenue Montaigne *(see map p 144)*, luxury shops and broadcasting centres (Europe No. 1, Radio-Télé-Luxembourg and FR 3).

From the Rond-Point to the Arc de Triomphe. — The section of the avenue from the Rond-Point is the second widest thoroughfare in Paris, it measures 71 m overall — 22 m pavements lining either side of the 27 m roadway (233 ft, 72 and 89 ft — Avenue Foch : 120 m — 394 ft).

The Second Empire private houses and amusement halls which once lined it have vanished so the capital's principal avenue appears here as a street without historical memories. The only exception is No. 25, a mansion built by La Païva, a Polish adventuress, who became first a Portuguese marchioness and later a Prussian countess and whose house was famous for the dinners she gave which were attended by the philosophers Renan and Taine and the Goncourt brothers, and for its probably unique onyx staircase. The Coliseum, an amphitheatre built in 1770 to hold 40 000 spectators, has left its name to a street, a café and a cinema.

The Champs-Élysées today is a commercial thoroughfare, a place of spectacle and a tourist venue. Airline offices, motocar showrooms, banks alternate with cinemas and big cafés. The dress and fashion houses of the Arcades Gallery at No. 76 — the former entrance to the well-known Lido (now moved to the Normandie) — provide attractive and elegant window displays. Point Show at No. 68 and Les Champs at No. 84 are examples of a new style of multi-purpose centres where pubs, restaurants, cinemas and shops are to be found under one roof.

THE ARC DE TRIOMPHE★★★   ⬜⬜ or ⬜⬜ : F 8

The arch and the **Place Charles-de-Gaulle★★★** which surrounds it, together form one of Paris' most famous landmarks. Twelve avenues radiate from the arch which, in that it commemorates Napoleon's victories, evokes at the same time, imperial glory and the fate of the Unknown Soldier whose tomb lies beneath.

Historical Notes. — By the end of the 18C the square was already star shaped although only five roads so far led off it. At the centre was a semicircular lawn.

1806 : Napoleon commissioned the construction of a giant arch in honour of the French fighting services. Chalgrin was appointed architect.

1810 : With the new Empress Marie-Louise due to make her triumphal entry along the Champs-Élysées and the arch only a few feet above ground, owing to two years of difficulty in laying the foundations, Chalgrin was compelled to erect a dummy arch of painted canvas mounted on scaffolding, to preserve appearances.

1832-1836 : Construction, abandoned during the Restoration, was completed under Louis-Philippe.

1840 : The chariot bearing the Emperor's body passed beneath the arch in a moving ceremony.

1854 : Haussmann redesigned the square, creating a further seven radiating avenues, while Hittorff planned the uniform façades which surround it.

1885 : Victor Hugo's body lay in state for a night beneath the arch, draped in crape for the occasion, before being transported in a pauper's hearse to the Pantheon.

1919 : On 14 July the victorious Allied armies, led by the marshals, marched in procession through the arch.

1920 : 11 November, the Unknown Soldier began his vigil.

1923 : 11 November, the flame of remembrance was kindled for the first time over the tomb of the Unknown Soldier.

1944 : 26 August, Paris, liberated from German occupation, acclaimed General de Gaulle.

Circling the Arch. — It is suggested that first you walk round the square to see from a distance the arch's proportions and the relative scale of the sculpture.

Chalgrin's undertaking, inspired by Antiquity, is truly colossal, measuring 50 m high by 45 m wide — 164 × 148 ft — with massive high reliefs as its chief adornment. Unfortunately Etex and Cortot intrigued with Thiers against their fellow artist Rude and succeeded in cornering three of the four groups of sculpture — Rude's is the only group with a hint of inspiration. Pradier filled the cornerstones of the principal faces with four figures sounding trumpets.

A frieze of hundreds of figures, each 2 m tall — 6 ft — encircles the arch in a remarkable crowded composition; above, a line of shields rings the coping.

Facing the Champs-Élysées : **1)** The Departure of the Volunteers in 1792, commonly called The Marseillaise, Rude's sublime masterpiece. — **2)** General Marceau's funeral. — **3)** The Triumph of 1810 (by Cortot) in celebration of the Treaty of Vienna. — **4)** The Battle of Aboukir.

Facing the Avenue Wagram : **5)** The Battle of Austerlitz.

Facing the Avenue de la Grande-Armée : **6)** Resistance (by Etex). — **7)** The Passage of the Bridge of Arcola. — **8)** Peace (by Etex). — **9)** The capture of Alexandria.

Facing the Avenue Kléber : **10)** The Battle of Jemmapes.

On reaching the Champs-Élysées once more, take the underground passage which starts from the right pavement to the arch.

The names of the greatest victories won during the Revolution and the Empire appear upon the shields at the summit. Beneath the monument, the Unknown Soldier rests under a plain slab; the flame of remembrance is rekindled each evening at 6.30 pm.

Lesser victories are engraved on the arch's inner walls together with the names of 558 generals — the names of those who died in the field are underlined.

The Arch Platform. — *Access : 10 am to 5.45 pm from April to September : 4.15 pm the rest of the year. Closed Tuesdays, 1 January, 1 May, 1 and 11 November, 25 December; 5F — Sundays and holidays 2.50F.*

There is an excellent **view★★★** of the capital generally from the platform and, in the foreground, of the twelve avenues radiating from the square. Standing on the arch you find yourself halfway between the Concorde and the La Défense Quarter *(p 167)*, at the climax of the Champs-Élysées — Triumphal Way.

Assembled in a small museum in the arch are mementoes of its construction and the celebratory and funerary ceremonies with which it has been associated.

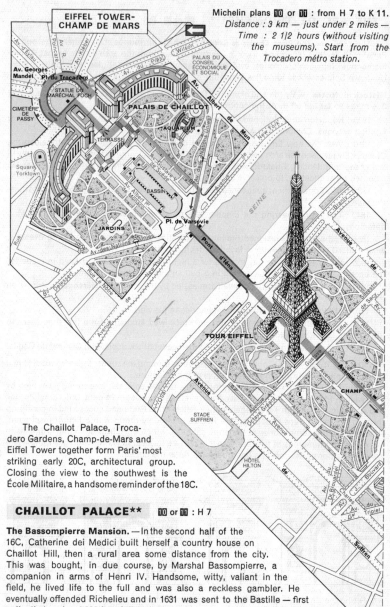

EIFFEL TOWER-
CHAMP DE MARS

Michelin plans 🔟 or 🔟 : from H 7 to K 11.
Distance : 3 km — just under 2 miles —
Time : 2 1/2 hours (without visiting
the museums). Start from the
Trocadero métro station.

The Chaillot Palace, Troca-
dero Gardens, Champ-de-Mars and
Eiffel Tower together form Paris' most
striking early 20C, architectural group.
Closing the view to the southwest is the
École Militaire, a handsome reminder of the 18C.

CHAILLOT PALACE★★ 🔟 or 🔟 : H 7

The Bassompierre Mansion. — In the second half of the
16C, Catherine dei Medici built herself a country house on
Chaillot Hill, then a rural area some distance from the city.
This was bought, in due course, by Marshal Bassompierre, a
companion in arms of Henri IV. Handsome, witty, valiant in the
field, he lived life to the full and was also a reckless gambler. He
eventually offended Richelieu and in 1631 was sent to the Bastille — first
gallantly burning 6 000 love letters it was said.

The Convent of the Visitation. — Henrietta of England, wife of Philip of Orleans,
took over the mansion on Bassompierre's death, as a Convent of the Visitation of
Holy Mary — Parisians happily referred to the nuns as the Sisters of Bassompierre!
The convent became known for great preachers : Bossuet, Bourdaloue and Mas-
sillon, and as a place of retreat for great ladies of the court : Marie Mancini, Mazarin's niece,
Mlle de la Vallière — for both of whom it seemed politic to withdraw from the attentions of
Louis XIV.

Grandiloquent projects. — Napoleon chose Chaillot as the site for a palace for his son, the
King of Rome. Stupendous plans were drawn up by Percier and Fontaine; the convent was
razed; the top of the hill levelled; the slope lessened; the Iéna Bridge built — then the Empire
fell. Blücher demanded that the bridge be destroyed since it commemorated a Prussian
defeat but Louis XVIII interposed, saying that he would sit in the centre in his sedan and be
blown up with it.

The Trocadero. — The name Trocadero was given to the area in 1827 after a military tourna-
ment on the site had re-enacted the French capture four years previously of Fort Trocadero,
near Cadiz. The square, the Place du Trocadéro, was laid out in 1858; twenty years later, at the
time of the 1878 Exhibition an edifice, said to be Moorish inspired, was erected upon it. In 1937
this was replaced by the present Chaillot Palace.

*If you want to know the meaning of an **abbreviation** or **conventional sign** used in*
this guide, consult the table on p 26.

THE SQUARE, THE PALACE EXTERIOR AND THE GARDENS

The Place du Trocadéro. — The semicircular square, dominated by an equestrian statue of Marshal Foch, is a centre point from which major roads radiate to the Alma Bridge, the Étoile, the Bois de Boulogne and the Passy quarter — the wall at the corner of Avenue Georges-Mandel marks the boundary of Passy cemetery *(p 152)*.

Chaillot Palace. — The spectacular, low-lying palace of white stone, consisting of twin pavilions linked by a portico and extended by wings curving to frame the wide terrace, was the design of architects Carlu, Boileau and Azéma. The palace's horizontal lines along the brow of the hill make a splendid foil to the vertical sweep of the Eiffel Tower when seen from the Champ-de-Mars or from almost any of the capital's viewpoints. The pavilion copings, back and front, bear inscriptions in letters of gold by the poet Paul Valéry. Low reliefs and sculptures by forty artists adorn the wings and steps to the gardens, bronze gilt statues the terrace.

Looking across to the Champ-de-Mars, you get a wonderful **view★★★**, in the foreground, of the Seine and the Left Bank, and beyond dominating all, the Eiffel Tower. Beyond again, in the far distance is the École Militaire.

The scene changes completely so that even the Eiffel Tower loses its predominance, when the fountains at the head of the pool pore out.

Beneath the palace terrace is one of the capital's largest theatres *(access through the hall in the left pavilion)*. Under skilled directors and talented actors, it became from 1951 to 1972 the home of the Peoples National Theatre — Théâtre National Populaire, the T.N.P. Known now as the Chaillot National Theatre this modernized theatre serves as a multi-purpose cultural centre, seating 1 800. On the left below the steps to the gardens is the small Gémier Theatre erected in 1966 as an experimental playhouse.

The Gardens★. — Beyond the walls on either side of the long rectangular pool in direct line with the Iéna Bridge, the final slopes of Chaillot Hill lead down, beneath flowering trees, to the banks of the Seine.

The pool, bordered by stone and bronze gilt statues, is at its most **spectacular★★** at night when the powerful fountains are floodlit.

The **Trocadero Aquarium** contains freshwater fish *(open : 10 am to 5.30 pm — 6.30 pm 15 May to 30 September; 2.50F)*.

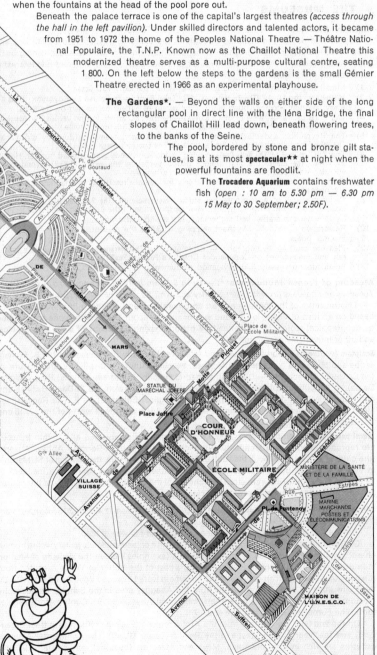

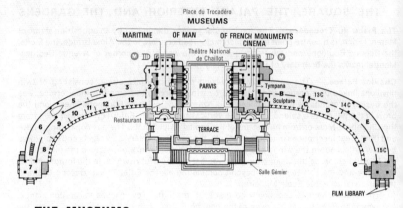

■ THE MUSEUMS

Maritime Museum**. — *Open 10 am to 6 pm; closed Tuesdays and holidays; 6F.*

French sea power and shipping throughout the centuries is displayed by life size and scale models of naval and mercantile ships, oceanographic research vessels, fishing boats and pleasure craft. Prows, pictures, dioramas, and mementoes of naval heroes add interest to the displays; films shown.

1) Model ships : Christopher Columbus' **Santa Maria** ; the early 19C **Océan**.
2-3) Vessels of the 16, 17 **(The Royale)** and 18C **(Soleil Royal** ; with figures by Coysevox ; **Louis XV**, a toy belonging to the young king). Fine group of galleys dominated by **The Réale**.
4) The Ports of France, a series of 13 canvases by the 18C artist, Joseph Vernet. The **Astrolabe**, the sloop of the 19C navigator and Antarctic explorer, Dumont d'Urville.
5) The Revolution and the 1st Empire. Model of an early steamship (Jouffroy d'Abbans). **The Valmy**, modelled in ebony, ivory and silver. The **Emperor's Barge** (1811).
6) The 19C model of **The Belle Poule** in which Napoleon's body was returned from St. Helena in 1840. **The Gloire**, the first armour plated vessel in the world (1859). World War I vessels. Main staircase leads to temporary exhibits.
7) From 1919 to the present. Naval vessels including aircraft carriers, landing crafts and submarines.
8) Reconstruction of a hydrographic studio. Bathyscaphe. **The Redoutable**, a nuclear submarine. Docks and naval shipyards. The transportation of the Luxor obelisk (1831).
9) Underwater exploration and archeology, life saving and diving.
10) Restoration of models. Merchant shipping, 1837 to the present.
11) Fishing boats.
12) Pleasure craft — hydrography — exploration — **The Hérétique**, Alain Bombard's sailing raft and mementoes of Commander Charcot's **Pourquoi Pas?**
13) Small foreing vessels ; old navigation instruments.

Museum of French Monuments**. — *Open 9.45 am to 12.30 pm and 2 to 5.30 pm; closed Tuesdays and holidays (except Easter Sunday and Whit Sunday); 5F — Sundays : 2.50F.*

This museum of the monumental art and mural painting of France in reproduction was based on an idea of Viollet-le-Duc and was opened in about 1880. The exhibits are grouped by geographical region, by school and by period, making evolutions of style, geographical and other influences, easy to follow.

Sculpture *(double gallery on the ground and 1st floors)* : **A**. Early Romanesque art — **B**. Romanesque sculpture and tympana from Moissac, Vézelay, Autun — **C**. Military architecture of the Crusades Campaigns. — **D**. Gothic cathedral statuary (Chartres, Amiens, Reims, Notre-Dame). — **E**. Sculpture of the 13 and 14C (recumbent figures from the St-Denis Basilica and other churches) and 15C (palace ornaments, fountains, Calvaries). — **F**. The Renaissance (Jean Goujon, Ligier Richier, Germain Pilon). — **G**. Busts and small works of the 17, 18 and 19C (Pigalle, Houdon, Rude).

Mural painting *(pavilion upper floors)* : the most important Romanesque and Gothic frescoes are reproduced on lifesize architectural replicas : the crypt of St-Germain Abbey, Auxerre (the oldest frescoes in France), the vault of St-Savin-sur-Gartempe, the chancel of St. Martin's at Vic, the apse of Berzé-la-Ville, the dome of Cahors Cathedral, the dance macabre of La Chaise-Dieu Abbey Church, etc. The richness of the colours and the vitality of the figures are amazing when seen so unexpectedly close to.

Museum of Man** (Musée de l'Homme). — *Open 10 am to 6 pm, 1 April to 30 September (5 pm the rest of the year); closed Tuesdays and holidays; 5F.*

The subject of the museum is the races of man and his way of life.

On the first floor are an anthropological gallery and a palaeontological gallery where human characteristics are compared by means of fossils (examples include the skeleton of Menton man discovered on the French Riviera in 1872, a cast of the Hottentot Venus executed from the body of a South African native and the mammoth ivory Lespugue Venus) and from Africa, five collections on prehistory (frescoes from the Ahaggar area in the Sahara), ethnography (costumes, tools, arms, jewellery) and art (mediaeval Abyssinian art, Central African sculpture). The European Gallery is at the end.

On the 2nd floor are displays from the Arctic regions (Eskimo crafts, masks from Greenland) and the Near and Far East and the Pacific (Easter Island). The Continental America galleries are rich in pre-Columbian, Maya and Atzec art (beautiful rock crystal skull and statues of the god Quetzalcoatl).

Cinema Museum*. — *Visit by appointment :* ☏ 704.24.24; 5F.

The history of motion pictures, from the very beginning of photography, is evoked in a series of sixty galleries. Reynaud's *théâtre optique* (1888), Marey's photographic rifle, Edison's kinetoscope, the Lumière brothers' kinematograph and photorama, posters, models (some of them were executed by the Russian director Eisenstein), settings (the robot of Fritz Lang's *Metropolis),* costumes and dresses worn by film stars (Rudolph Valentino, Greta Garbo) illustrate the film world. Over 3 000 objects show the evolution of the technical aspects of filming : shooting, staging, projection. Excerpts from various films complete this picture of the cinema world.

Film Library (Cinémathèque). — *Trocadero Gardens, Albert-de-Mun side.* This film library, one of the richest in the world, has a total of 50 000 films. As many as 4 to 5 films are shown daily. It is a meeting place for the professionals and amateurs of the film world. *Programmes at the box office and in the press. 5F.*

THE CHAMP-DE-MARS*   Ⅱ or Ⅲ : J 8

The Champ-de-Mars is now a vast formal garden closed at one end by the École Militaire and at the other by Chaillot Hill. Bestriding it is the Eiffel Tower.

The parade ground. — When Gabriel had completed the École Militaire, he replaced the surrounding market gardens which ran down to the Seine by a parade ground or Champ-de-Mars — Martian Field (1765-1767). The public was first admitted in 1780.

In 1783 the physicist, Charles, launched the first hydrogen filled balloon from the ground which came down 20 miles away near Le Bourget. Blanchard, a year later, launched a balloon complete with basket and ailerons... in which he landed on the far side of Paris at Billancourt.

The Festival of Federation. — It was decided to commemorate the 14 July 1790, the first anniversary of the taking of the Bastille, by a Festival of Federation on the Champ-de-Mars. Stands were erected; mass was celebrated by Talleyrand, Bishop of Autun, assisted by 300 priests at the national altar in the centre of the ground. La Fayette, at the altar, swore an oath of loyalty to the nation and the constitution which was repeated by the listening crowd of 300 000 and finally by Louis XVI, in the midst of the general enthusiasm.

Festival of the Supreme Being. — In 1794, Robespierre had the Convention decree a state religion recognising the existence of a Supreme Being and the immortality of the soul. These hypotheses were solemnly affirmed on 8 June at a mammoth festival presided over by Robespierre, the Incorruptible, as he was known. The procession began in the Tuileries and ended on the Champ-de-Mars.

Less than two months later Robespierre's own head fell to the guillotine.

The capital's fairground. — From time to time the ground has been given over to exhibitions; on 22 September 1798 the Directory commemorated the anniversary of the Republic with an Industrial Exhibition destined to replace the old Saint-Germain and Saint-Laurent Fairs — an innovation was the payment of exhibitors.

World exhibitions were held in 1867, 1878, 1889, 1900 and 1937 — the Eiffel Tower remains as a souvenir of the Exhibition of 1889. In the same year, the army exchanged the ground with the City of Paris for a terrain at Issy-les-Moulineaux.

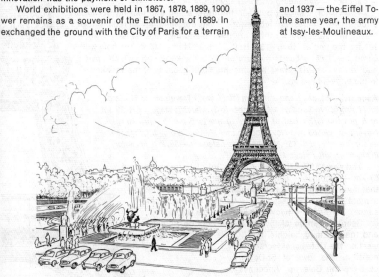

The Champ de Mars from the Trocadero Gardens

The gardens. — The present gardens, laid out by C. J. Formigé, were begun in 1908 and completed in 1928. Part is landscaped with grottoes, arbors, cascades and a small pool at the foot of the tower and part is formal. Wide strips on either side along the Suffren and La Bourdonnais Avenues were sold for building and are now lined by large private houses and blocks of luxury flats.

THE EIFFEL TOWER★★★   ▣ or ▣ : J 7, J 8

The tower is the capital's look out and Paris' best known monument. When it was erected it was the tallest construction the world had ever known but since then its 300 m — 984 ft — have been topped by sky-scrapers and telecommunication towers elsewhere. The additions made for television transmission have increased its height by another 20.75 m — 67 ft to 320.75 m — 1 051 ft.

Historical notes. — The idea of a tower came to Eiffel as a natural conse-quence of his study of the use of high metal piles for viaducts. The first project dates from 1884; between 1887 and 1889 three hundred skyjacks put the tower together with the aid of two and a half million rivets.

Eiffel, in his enthusiasm, cried " France will be the only country in the world with a 300 m flagpole ".

Artists and writers, however were appalled; among the 300 who signed a protest were Charles Garnier of the Opera, the composer, Gounod, and the poets and writers François Coppée, Leconte de Lisle, Dumas the Younger, Maupassant... Equally the tower's very boldness and incredible novelty brought it great acclaim and by the beginning of the century it had become a subject of celebration by other poets and dramatists, Apollinaire, Cocteau... and painters such as Pissarro, Dufy, Utrillo, Seurat, Marquet... Since then its form, appearing as millions of souvenirs, has become familiar everywhere.

In 1909, when the concession expired, the tower was nearly pulled down — it was saved through the importance of its huge antennae to French radio telegraphy; from 1910 it also became part of the International Time Service.

In 1916 it was made the terminal for the first radio telephone service across the Atlantic. French radio has used it as a transmitter since 1918 and television since 1957. The top platform serves as the base for a revolving light beacon (replaced recently by a fixed red light) and an aircraft meteo-rological and navigation station.

Nobody now questions the tower's aesthetic appeal or its utility — it has taken its place on the capital's skyline and beckons a welcome to all who come to Paris.

The tensile masterpiece. — The tower's weight is 7 000 tons; the dead-weight of 4 kg per cm² — 57 lbs per sq inch — is about that of a man sitting in a chair. A scale model made of pig iron 30 cm high — 11.8 inches — would weigh 7 grams or 1/4 oz; 35 to 40 tons of paint are used every seven years when it is repainted.

The sway at the top in the highest winds has never been more than 12 cm — 4 1/2 inches — but the height can vary by as much as 15 cm — 6 inches — depending on the temperature.

The visitor, standing between the tower's feet and looking upwards through the interesting latticework of pig iron, gets an incredible feel-ing of the stupendous : there are three platforms : the 1st is at 57 m — 187 ft ; the 2nd at 115 m — 377 ft; the 3rd at 274 m — 899 ft. The bold will climb the 1 652 steps to the top; others will take the lifts which have had to have special brake attachments fitted because of the variation in the angle of ascent.

Ascent. — *Stages 1 and 2 : 10 am (10.30 am, 1 November to 31 March) to 11 pm (6 pm Sundays 1 November to 31 March); stage 3 : 10.30 am to 5 pm the latter half of March; 10 am to 6 pm, 1 April to mid-November, closed mid-November to mid-March. Fare by lift : stage 1 — 4F, 2 — 10F, 3 — 15F; by the steps : stage 1 — 3F, 2 — 5F. After 6.30 pm, by lift : stage 1 — 8F, 2 — 11F.*

The **view**★★★ for the visitor to the 3rd platform may extend 67 km — 42 miles — if the atmosphere is really clear — but that is rare. Paris and its surrounding suburbs appear as on a giant map — the best light is usually one hour before sunset. Through a window Eiffel's rooms can be seen.

Bearings can be taken west on the Bois de Boulogne and the St-Cloud heights, north-west on the Défense skyscrapers, north on the town of St-Denis, east on the Bois de Vincennes and the zoo rock point and, south, on Orly Airport.

Beneath the tower is a bust by Bourdelle of the engineer, Eiffel, who presented the country with one of the most frequented French monuments : more than 3 000 000 visitors in 1976.

THE ÉCOLE MILITAIRE★★   ⬛ or ⬛ : K 9

The École Militaire, the French Military Academy, and one of the finest examples of French 8C architecture, was perfectly sited by its architect at the end of what is the Champ-de-Mars.

HISTORICAL NOTES

Construction. — Thanks to Mme de Pompadour, Louis XV's favourite, the financier and supplier to the army, Pâris-Duverney, obtained, in 1751, permission to found and personally to supervise the building of a Royal Military Academy where young gentlemen without means would be trained to become accomplished officers. The parade ground was given the name Champ-de-Mars.

Jacques-Ange Gabriel, architect of the Petit Trianon at Versailles and of the Place de la Concorde, produced sumptuous plans which the financier duly modified. The final construction nevertheless remains incredibly magnificent when one remembers that it was designed as a barracks. The king took no interest in the future school and, in fact, money to pay for the building was raised from a tax imposed on playing cards.

The academy numbered 500 students; the course lasted three years. In 1769 Louis XV agreed to lay the foundation stone for the chapel; by 1772 the buildings were complete.

Bonaparte the Military Cadet. — In 1777 the Royal Academy became the Higher Officers' School. In 1784 Bonaparte, who had been to the lesser military academy at Brienne and was then 15, was admitted on the recommendation that he would " make an excellent sailor ". He passed out as a lieutenant in the artillery with the mention that he would " go far in favourable circumstances ".

The Military Tradition. — The institution was suppressed by the Revolution, but the buildings, which had been enlarged in the 19C, have retained their military tradition both as quarters and instruction centre. The Swiss Guards of the Ancien Régime, the National Guard of 1848, have been replaced by French and Allied officers attending the School of Advanced War Studies, the Staff College, the Higher Schools of National Defence and Army Ordnance.

THE EXTERIOR

The impressive **central pavilion** which you see as you approach up the Champ-de-Mars, is ornamented with eight superb Corinthian columns each two storeys high; completing the decoration are a carved pediment, trophies, allegorical figures and a crowning quadrangular dome. Low lying wings frame the main building. The barracks on either side are 19C.

Facing the central pavilion, is the equestrian statue of Marshal Joffre by Real del Sarte (1939).

Leave the **Village Suisse** (antique and second-hand dealers' shops — *open Thursday to Monday, 10.30 am to 12.30 pm and 2 to 7 pm* — on your right, to circle the academy by way of Suffren and Lowendal Avenues until you come to the Place Fontenoy. (Lowendal commanded part of the French army which defeated the British and Dutch at Fontenoy in 1745).

From the semicircular square, you look across the sportsground to the **main courtyard★★**, lined on either side by beautiful porticoes with paired columns. At the back is the central pavilion, flanked by colonnaded buildings ending in advanced wings.

Inside, the chapel, the main staircase, the Marshals' Saloon and the Guardroom on the first floor are remarkably decorated (*guided tours on written application to the Général Commandant Militaire, École Militaire, 1 Place Joffre. The Chapel is open to the public on Sundays, 9 am to noon*).

Fontenoy Square has entirely lost its 18C character. The huge blocks on its east side include the Ministries of Health, Merchant Navy and Post Office, on its south side lies UNESCO.

UNESCO HOUSE★   ⬛ or ⬛ : K 9

Displays, debates, film shows for groups on application : ☏ 566.57.57.

The home of UNESCO (United Nations Educational, Scientific and Cultural Organization) was opened in 1958 and is the most truly international undertaking in Paris, the membership by 142 states and construction jointly of the buildings by Breuer, Nervi and Zehrfuss, American, Italian and French architects respectively, demonstrating unique cooperation.

The buildings. — The main building, in the form of a Y supported on piles, houses the secretariat (sales counters in the entrance hall with souvenirs, newspapers, periodicals and stamps). A second building with fluted concrete walls and an accordion pleat designed roof contains the conference halls and committee rooms. The small cubic construction four storeys high beside the Japanese garden, is a secretariat annexe. Additional accommodation was provided in 1965, by means of two floors being constructed underground and lit naturally by six low level patios, and in 1970, at No. 1 Rue Miollis.

Decoration. — The decoration is also the result of international artistic cooperation. There are frescoes by the Spaniard, Picasso, and the Mexican, Tamayo, a monumental statue by the Englishman, Henry Moore (*Figure in Repose*), a black steel mobile by the American, Calder, *Sun and Moon*, walls by the Spanish ceramic artists, Miro and Artigas, mosaics by the French, Bazaine and Herzell, a relief by Jean Arp, tapestries by Lurçat, and the French-Swiss, Le Corbusier, and a Japanese garden by Noguchi. In and around the later annexes are works by the Italian, Giacometti, the Spanish, Chillida, the Venezuelan, Soto and the American, Kelly.

The overall impression is a remarkable synthesis of mid 20C art.

Michelin plans ⅒ or ⑪ : from H 10 to K 10.
Time : 4 to 5 hours (including visits to the museums). Start from the Invalides métro station.

In 1974 the Invalides celebrated their tercentennial. This is the most outstanding single monumental group in Paris. The adjacent Army Museum, is rich and spectacular.

HISTORICAL NOTES

Barracks for 4 000 men. — Before Louis XIV's reign, old soldiers, invalided out of the service, were, in theory, looked after in convent hospitals. In fact most were reduced to beggary.

In 1670 the Sun King founded the Invalides on the edge of what was then the Grenelle Plain. Funds were raised by a levy on acting soldiers' pay and on the sales of the local district markets over a period of five years. Construction of the vast edifice capable of providing quarters for 4 000 began in 1671 to plans by Libéral Bruand and was completed only five years later. A dome, added to the original undertaking by Jules Hardouin-Mansart, lifted the project out of the utilitarian into the monumentally inspired.

Pillage. — On the morning of 14 July 1789 rebels advanced on the Invalides in search of arms. They crossed the moat, disarmed the sentries and entered the underground rifle stores. As further crowds blocked the stairs fierce fighting broke out in the half darkness. The mob finally made off with 28 000 rifles towards the Bastille.

Napoleon's return. — The major event in the history of the Invalides was the return of Napoleon's body in 1840. After seven years of negotiation with the British Government, the French King, Louis-Philippe, was able to dispatch his son, the Prince of Joinville, to St. Helena in the frigate, *The Belle Poule (model in the Maritime Museum; p 50)* to collect the Emperor's remains. On the prince's arrival on 8 October, the coffin was exhumed and opened for two minutes during which it was seen that the body of the Emperor who had been dead nineteen years, had remained in a state of perfect preservation; those present, including the generals Gourgaud and Bertrand, the 19C historian Las Cases and Napoleon's valet, Marchand, viewed the Emperor once more in his guardsman's uniform.

The coffin, after its long sea voyage, was disembarked at Le Havre and brought up the Seine to Paris where it was landed at Courbevoie. The funeral was held on 15 December 1840. A snowstorm enveloped the city as the hearse passed beneath the Arc de Triomphe, down the Champs-Élysées and across the Concorde Square to the Esplanade.

The coffin lay under the cupola and in St. Jerome's Chapel until the tomb, designed by Visconti, was completed. The transferring took place on 3 April 1861.

The institution's decline. — During the 19C the number of inmates steadily decreased; now they number less than 100. The buildings today are occupied by the Invalides National Institute, the Army Museum and Army Medical Department.

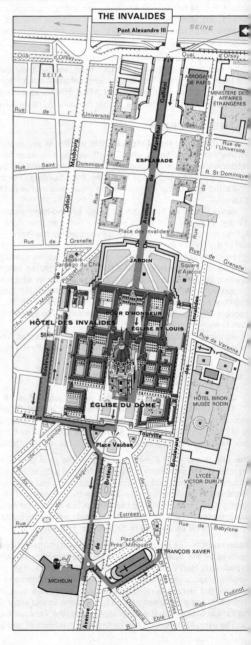

THE INVALIDES

THE INVALIDES★★★   (Hôtel des Invalides)   ▢▢ or ▢▢ : J 10

Arrive, if possible, from the north, for from the Alexandre III Bridge, there is a superb **overall view★★★** of Libéral Bruand's Classical style buildings and Mansart's crowning gold dome.

Esplanade. — *Presently under construction.*

The Esplanade, designed and constructed between 1704 and 1720 by Robert de Cotte, Mansart's brother-in-law, affords a spectacular vista 500 m long and more than 250 m wide, ending of course in the Classically balanced Invalides buildings.

The Paris Air Terminal, Les Invalides, stands on the left, fitting into the surroundings. On the right, there can usually be seen at midday, Frenchmen playing lively contests of *boules* — a game of skill but with little in common, despite the name, with English bowls.

The Alexandre III Bridge and the Invalides

Garden. — Preceding the Invalides are a garden, bordered by a wide dry moat, ramparts lined by 17 and 18C bronze cannon and an 18 piece triumphal battery used to fire salutes on such occasions as the 1918 Armistice and 14 July 1919 Victory March.

The battery, removed by the Germans in 1940 and returned in 1946, now stands disposed on either side of the entrance.

Façade★★. — The façade is majestic, in style and line, in proportion and size — it is 196 m long — 645 ft. At the centre is a magnificent doorway, flanked at either end by pavilions. Decoration appears in the form of trophies surrounding the dormer windows and in the equestrian statue of Louis XIV supported by Prudence and Justice in the rounded arch above the entrance.

The first statue by Guillaume Coustou (1735), damaged during the Revolution, was replaced by the present figure by Cartelier in 1815.

Restoration work on the **lateral walls★** has uncovered noble buildings on the right side and on the left, alongside the Boulevard de Latour-Maubourg, the fine proportions of Jules-Robert de Cotte's Order of Liberation Chancellery and the original trench.

Main courtyard★. — Go through the entrance to the main courtyard, lined on all sides by two superimposed arcades.

Four central pavilions with carved pediments break the even architectural lines as do the sculptured horses, trampling the attributes of war, at the corner angles of the roof. The dormer windows are decorated, like those on the façade, with trophies. The fifth window to the right of the east central pavilion *(left on entering)* has a peculiar history : Louvois, who had been in charge of the construction of the Invalides, had had his arms emblazoned on the buildings in several places; Louis XIV ordered them to be removed. A mason thereupon thought up the idea of encircling a window with the paws of a wolf, making a play on the intendant's name and surveillance; *loup voit* — the wolf sees all.

The end pavilion, which is the most ornate, serves as the façade to St. Louis' Church. At the centre is the Seurre statue of Napoleon, known as the Little Corporal, which stood for some years at the top of the column in the Place Vendôme.

In the Classical courtyard with its perfect proportions, its steeply pitched slate roofs and cobbled paving, there is an impressive series of cannon lined up along the walls : note the " Griffon " (1528) which weighs 15 589 kg — 34 295 lbs — and was taken by the French before Coblenz (Germany) in 1799, the " Catherina " (1487) bearing the name of Sigismund of Austria, the " Württemberg culverin " (16C) with its chiselled breech and its barrel entwined by a snake.

Church of St-Louis-des-Invalides★. — The church, also known as the Soldiers' Church, was designed by Libéral Bruand before Mansart added the dome to the group and is cold and functional. The only decoration derives from the captured enemy banners overhanging the upper galleries. A window behind the high altar enables one to see through to the baldachin in the Dome Church.

The organ, enclosed in a loft designed by Hardouin-Mansart, is a magnificent 17C instrument on which Berlioz's *Requiem* was played for the first time in 1837.

The banners were more numerous at the end of the Empire but when the Allies entered Paris in March 1814, the Invalides governor burnt 1417 of them in the courtyard; the history of each is commemorated on the church pillars.

In the crypt *(not open)* lie former governors of the Invalides and 19 and 20C marshals and generals of the field, including Joffre, Leclerc, Giraud and Juin.

Conserved in an urn is the heart of Mademoiselle de Sombreuil, daughter of the Governor of 1789. During the massacres of September 1792, her filial love moved the murderers to spare her father.

■ THE ARMY MUSEUM*** (Musée de l'Armée) 🔟 or 🔟 : J 10

Open 10 am to 6 pm, 1 April to 30 September (5 pm the rest of the year). Closed 1 January, 1 May, 1 November and 25 December. Ground floor, east : films shown on the two World Wars; 5F (ticket also valid, two consecutive days, for the Dome Church, the Museum of Relief Maps and Plans and films shown).

The galleries of one of the world's richest army museums lie on either side of the main courtyard. *Some galleries may be closed for reorganization.*

The number and diversity of arms and armour and their often lifelike display, enables one to follow, in every detail, the evolution of military defence and attack. The splendid royal chased harnesses, the Renaissance swords, daggers, rapiers and the firearms signed by the most famous gunsmiths, make every visitor pause.

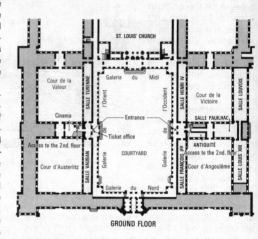

Among the countless souvenirs of French military history, are some with a story of glory or gallantry — the wooden leg of General Daumesnil *(p 133)* — some are tragic — the bullet which killed Turenne — and some are moving — the Emperor's flag of farewell flown at Fontainebleau as he signed his abdication in 1814, and the 1918 Armistice bugle on which the cease-fire was sounded. Napoleonic mementoes are also exhibited. There are also lead soldiers and cardboard figures and documents from the two World Wars (maps, films, models).

Military History	Gallery	Access
Prehistory - Early Middle Ages	Antiquité	Ground floor, west
Middle Ages and Ancien Régime		
— Arms, armour (7-16C)	François Ier	
— Arms, armour (16 and 17C)	Henri IV, Louis XIII	Ground floor, west
— History of swords, rapiers and fire arms	Pauilhac	
— Regimental arms	Louvois	
— Mementoes from Louis XIII to Louis XVI Period	Ancienne Monarchie	2nd floor, east
The Revolution		
— Mementoes from the Revolutionary, Directoire and Consultate Periods	La Fayette 1re République	2nd floor, east
The First Empire		
— Mementoes from Napoleonic Period : his family, his marshals, his campaigns	Napoléon	2nd floor, east
— The Emperor's hat, sword and medals	Turenne	Ground floor, east
The Restoration	Restauration	2nd floor, east
The National Guard	Entrance Hall	2nd floor, east
The July Monarchy - 2nd Republic	Bugeaud	2nd floor, east
The Empire - The Second World War		
— Equestrian armour	Vauban	Ground floor, east
— Flags and banners (1800-1918)	Turenne	Ground floor, east
— Regimental arms	Louvois	Ground floor, west
	Alliés	3rd floor, west
— Mementoes from the First World War	1914-18	2nd floor, west
	Alliés	3rd floor, west
— Mementoes from the Second World War	1939-45	2nd floor, west

■ MUSEUM OF RELIEF MAPS AND PLANS 🔟 or 🔟 : J 10

Open 10 am to 12.15 pm and 2 to 6 pm, 1 April to 30 September (4.45 pm the rest of the year); closed Sunday mornings, Tuesdays, 1 November, 11 November, 25 December. Same ticket as for the Army Museum. Access through the Army Museum (last floor, east).

A collection of 43 models of French strongholds executed from 1668 to 1870 illustrates military fortification since the time of the great military architect Vauban.

■ MUSEUM OF THE ORDER OF LIBERATION** 🔟 or 🔟 : J 10

Pavillon Robert-de-Cotte, 51 bis Boulevard de Latour-Maubourg. Open 2 to 5 pm; closed Sundays, in August, Easter, Whitsun, 1 November, and 25 December.

The Order of Liberation, created by General de Gaulle at Brazzaville in 1940, honoured as " companions ", those who made an outstanding contribution to the final victory. The list, which was closed in 1946 consists of service personnel and civilians, a few overseas leaders including King George VI, Winston Churchill and General Eisenhower, and several French towns (Paris, Nantes, Grenoble, Vassieux-en-Vercors and Ile de Sein). The memory is also perpetuated of French heroes and major operations of the Resistance.

THE DOME CHURCH★★★ 🔲 or 🔲 : J 10

Stand in the centre of the Place Vauban; from here you have a **general view★★** of the Dome Church on the far side of Mansart's original trench, now restored and spanned by an unobtrusive drawbridge.

It is one of the major masterpieces of the age of Louis XIV. In this building Hardouin-Mansart perfected the French Classical style which had first appeared in the Carmelite Church (p 154) and been developed in St-Paul-St-Louis (p 79), the Sorbonne (p 103) and the Val-de-Grâce (p 122). To complete the Baroque effect, the original plan envisaged the creation before the south face, of a colonnaded esplanade in the manner of Bernini before St. Peter's. Instead, to afford a good vista, a wide avenue was cut through the then open countryside, the Avenue de Breteuil.

The Dome arose when Louis XIV commissioned Hardouin-Mansart to build a church to complement the Invalides buildings of Libéral Bruand and to epitomise the splendour of his reign. In 1677 therefore, work began on the Dome Church, oriented towards the north and joined to the Soldiers' Church by a common sanctuary. It was completed by Robert de Cotte in 1735.

The Dome Church stands, finally, as the greatest example of the French 17C or *Grand Siècle* religious architecture, just as Versailles does of the civil architecture of the same period.

In 1793 the Revolution transformed the two churches, which were still united, into a Temple to Mars. It was also decided to transfer to them the captured enemy standards previously hung in Notre-Dame. With Napoleon's interment of Turenne in the church in 1800, it became a military mausoleum, receiving also countless trophies from the imperial campaigns.

It was guarded by the old soldiers, known as the *grognards* or grumblers, billeted in the Invalides barracks.

In 1842, two years after the return of Napoleon's body (p 54), Visconti enlarged the central altar, replaced the original baldachin and had the crypt dug to receive the coffin. The big window was constructed only in 1873. These alterations disturbed the inner balance, but the grandeur remains.

Façade. — The façade consists, in the usual Jesuit style, of a projecting central section flanked by outer wings. All are the same height, thus avoiding heavy connecting areas.

Between the Doric columns at ground level are statues of St. Louis by Nicolas Coustou and Charlemagne by Coysevox; above a projecting entablature are Corinthian columns, statues of the four Virtues and a pediment carved by Coysevox.

Twelve additional statues which originally also adorned the façade were destroyed during the Revolution.

The dome. — Hardouin-Mansart's masterpiece captures the imagination both by its sweeping lines and its dignity; it has a beauty all its own whether standing out against a clear summer sky or rising, almost invisibly, a deeper shadow, against the darkness of the night.

The design was based on a prodigious knowledge of balance and proportion which enabled it to rise in a single thrust without buttressing. Forty columns separate the windows round the drum; the cupola base, pierced by round arched windows, is ornamented with consoles while above, divided into twelve sections, rises the massive gilded dome, decorated with trophies, garlands and other ornament. Windows in the form of helmets provide air and light inside. Crowning all are an elegant lantern and a spire which rises 107 m — 351 ft — into the sky.

The dome's covering of lead sheeting, attached by copper nails to the wood frame was gilded for the first time in 1715 and has been restored several times since — in 1813, 1853, 1867 and 1937. On this last occasion 260 tons of lead were laid on the frame before craftsmen applied 350 000 sheets of gold leaf, weighing only 6 kg — 13 1/4 lbs.

The Dome Church

If you can, spare the time to look at the un-tourist sights of Paris : the Bourse (p 118), Radio-France House (p 155), the Rungis Market (p 107) near Orly Airport, the sewers (p 145), the Flea Market (p 156), the cemetery for dogs at Asnières.

Interior. — *Same times as for the Army Museum (p 56) but closed at 7 pm in July and August.*

The decoration is sumptuous : painted cupolas, walls orned with columns and pilasters and low reliefs by the greatest contemporary artists and inlaid marble pavements.

1) Tomb of Joseph Bonaparte, elder brother of Napoleon, King of Spain.
2) Monument to Vauban by Etex. The Emperor himself commanded that the military architect's heart be brought to the Invalides.
3) Foch's tomb by Landowski.
4) Ornate high altar surrounded by twisted columns and covered by a baldachin by Visconti. Vaulting decoration by Coypel.
5) General Duroc's tomb.
6) General Bertrand's tomb.
7) At the back — the heart of La Tour d'Auvergne, first grenadier of the Republic; in the centre, the tomb of Marshal Lyautey.
8) Turenne's tomb by Tuby.
9) St. Jerome's Chapel (carvings by Nicolas Coustou). The tomb at the foot of the wall is Jerome Bonaparte's, younger brother of Napoleon, King of Westphalia.
10) The Emperor's tomb.

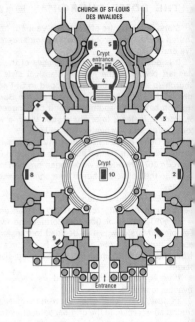

CHURCH OF ST-LOUIS DES INVALIDES

The Cupola. — The cupola itself is impressive. Painted on the pendentives are the four Evangelists by Charles de la Fosse and then, in ascending order, the Kings of France (in medallions) and the Twelve Apostles by Jouvenet. On the cupola itself a vast composition by La Fosse of St. Louis presenting Christ with the sword with which he conquered the infidels.

Napoleon's tomb★★★. — The majesty of the setting perfectly befits the Emperor's image. Visconti designed a circular crypt in which to stand the red porphyry sarcophagus upon a base of green granite from the Vosges. It was completed in 1861.

The Emperor's body is placed in six coffins, each contained inside the other : the innermost is of tin sheeted iron; the second of mahogany; the third and fourth of lead; the fifth of ebony; the last of oak.

The crypt. — At the base of the stairs, behind the baldachin, two massive bronze statues stand guard at the crypt entrance, one bearing an orb, the other the imperial sceptre and crown. Low reliefs around the gallery depict institutions founded by the Emperor.

The sarcophagus stands at the centre of the inlaid marble pavement, designed as a star while, against the pillars circling the crypt, are twelve colossal statues by Pradier symbolizing Napoleon's campaigns from the Italian victories of 1797 to Waterloo in 1815.

In the *cella,* before a statue of the Emperor in his coronation robes, lies the King of Rome. He died in Vienna in 1832 and remained in the crypt of the Habsburgs before being transferred to Paris on 15 December 1940 exactly one century after his father, and finally entombed in 1969.

From the Invalides to St. Francis Xavier

Walk from the Place Vauban along the Avenue de Breteuil to No. 46.

The Michelin Tourist Services. — In France in 1900 there were 3 000 vehicles on the road — phenomena which threw country folk into a panic. Car owners bought petrol at the local grocer and it was for these car owners and drivers that André Michelin, brother of Édouard who manufactured tyres, compiled a little red book : the Guide FRANCE. This, with its selection of hotels and restaurants and pages of practical information, has grown in size and fame until it is now known to seasoned travellers the world over complete with its star award system for restaurants.

The young André Michelin next created in Paris, in 1908, a Car Travellers' Information Bureau which provided enquirers with itineraries and road information. He went on to supply the local authorities with name plates for towns and villages, to undertake, in 1910, the mapping of France to a scale of 1 : 200 000 — 1 inch : 3 miles — the numbering of all roads (1913) and the production, from locally quarried pumicestone near Clermont-Ferrand, of large square milestones covered in distinctive vitreous enamel. After the 1914-1918 War, guides were published to the Battlefields and in 1926, the Regional Guide Brittany, the first tourist guide in the series now known as the Michelin Green Tourist Guides.

Michelin, formerly located at No. 97 Boulevard Pereire with nearly three quarters of a century of experience, and still at work producing and improving maps and guides for the motorist and the tourist, is to be found at No. 46 Avenue de Breteuil. *Reception, Information and Sales Offices : open 9 am to noon and 1 to 4.30 pm; closed Saturdays and Sundays; ☎ 539.25.00*

The façade of the building is adorned with a series of ceramic panels which evoke the part played by Michelin in the first great cycle and motor races. The large tiled panel to the right, *le coup de la semelle,* demonstrates their concern for the quality and performance of the tyres.

Look left up the Avenue de Breteuil for a good view of the Invalides Dome before skirting St. Francis Xavier Church, a late 19C Romanesque pastiche, and returning to the métro.

Michelin plans ▯▯ or ▯▯ : from J 14 to K 16.
Total distance : 11 km — 7 miles.

The Cité is the heart of Paris and is an eternal magnet through its beauty, its architecture and its history.

We suggest that you divide your visit into four half-day walks :
1. A walk circling the two islands by means of the quays *(start : St-Michel métro) pp 60-61.*
2. Notre-Dame and its quarter *(access : Cité métro station) pp 62-65.*
3. The Law Courts, Ste-Chapelle and the Conciergerie *(access : Cité métro station) pp 66-70.*
4. The Ile St-Louis *(access : Cité or Pont-Marie métro stations) p 71.*

The Cité from the Samaritaine store terrace

HISTORICAL NOTES

Lutetia. — Between 250 and 200 BC Gaulish fishermen and boatmen of the Parisii tribe discovered and set up their huts on the largest island in the Seine — Lutetia was born. The township, whose Celtic name meant " habitation surrounded by water ", was conquered by Labienus' Roman legions in 52 BC. The Gallo-Roman town prospered on river transport, so that the vessel which was later incorporated in the capital's coat of arms *(p 115)* is a reminder both of the shape of the island and of the way of life of its earliest inhabitants. The boatmen's existence has been confirmed by the discovery of one of their pagan altars beneath Notre-Dame *(p 101).*

In the 4C the name Lutetia was changed to that of its inhabitants and thus became Paris.

St. Genevieve. — In 451 Attila crossed the Rhine at the head of 700 000 men; the Parisians began to flee at his approach until Genevieve, a young girl from Nanterre who had consecrated her life to God, calmed them assuring them that the town would be saved by heavenly intervention. The Huns arrived, hesitated, and turned, to advance on Orleans. Parisians adopted the girl as their protector and patron.

Ten years later the island was besieged by the Franks and suffered famine; Genevieve escaped the enemy watch, loaded boats with victuals in Champagne and returned, again miraculously avoiding detection. She died in 512 and was buried at King Clovis' side *(p 105).*

The Count of Paris becomes King. — In 885, for the fifth time in forty years, the Normans sailed up the Seine. The Cité — the island took the name in 506 when Clovis made it his capital — was confronted by 700 ships and 30 000 warriors bent on advancing into Burgundy. Assault and siege proving unsuccessful, the Normans took their boats out of the water, mounted them on logs and rolled them on land round Paris. Eudes, Count of Paris and the leader of the resistance, was thereupon elected king.

Cathedral and Parliament. — During the Middle Ages the population spread from the island along both banks of the river. But while the episcopal see remained under Sens (Paris did not have its own archbishop until 1622), schools were established within the cathedral's shadow which were to become famous throughout Europe. Among the teachers were Alexander of Paris, inventor of the poetic alexandrine line and, at the beginning of the 12C, the philosopher Abelard, whose moving romance with Heloise began in the cloister of Notre-Dame. Chapels and convents multiplied on the island : St-Denis-du-Pas (where St. Denis' martyrdom is said to have begun), St-Pierre-aux-Bœufs (the porch is now the St-Séverin porch), St-Aignan *(p 65),* St-Jean-le-Rond (where unwanted children were abandoned), were but a few of the belfried edifices which by the end of the 13C numbered at least twenty-three.

The Cité, the seat of parliament, the highest judiciary in the kingdom was, inevitably, involved in revolutions and uprisings such as that attempted by Étienne Marcel in the 14C and the Fronde in the 17C. During the Terror of 1793-94 the Conciergerie prisons were crowded, while next door, the Revolutionary Tribunal continued to sit in the Law Courts, endlessly pronouncing merciless sentences.

Transformation. — Under Louis-Philippe and to an even greater extent, under Napoleon III, the entire centre of the island was demolished : 25 000 people were evacuated. Enormous administrative buildings were erected : the Hôtel-Dieu, a barracks (now the police prefecture), the commercial courts. The Law Courts were doubled in size; the Place du Parvis before the cathedral was quadrupled; the Boulevard du Palais was built ten times wider than before.

In August 1944 the Paris police barricaded themselves in the prefecture and hoisted the tricolour. For three days they held the Germans at bay until relieved by the arrival of the French Army Division under General Leclerc.

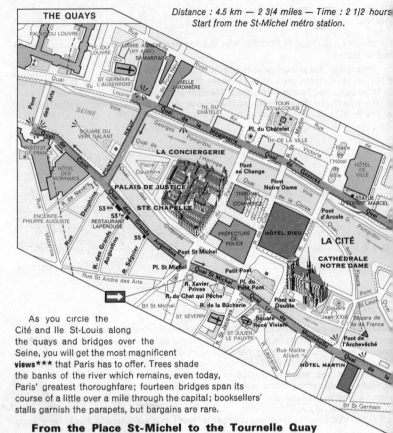

THE QUAYS

Distance : 4.5 km — 2 3/4 miles — Time : 2 1/2 hours
Start from the St-Michel métro station.

As you circle the
Cité and Ile St-Louis along
the quays and bridges over the
Seine, you will get the most magnificent
views★★★ that Paris has to offer. Trees shade
the banks of the river which remains, even today,
Paris' greatest thoroughfare; fourteen bridges span its
course of a little over a mile through the capital; booksellers'
stalls garnish the parapets, but bargains are rare.

From the Place St-Michel to the Tournelle Quay

Quai St-Michel. — Bookshops line the quay, broken only by two old and narrow streets.

The **Petit Pont** (1853) stands on the site of the oldest river crossing in Paris — the Romans built a wooden bridge there as a terminal to their Orleans Road (now the Rue St-Jacques). It was first constructed in stone in 1185 by Bishop Maurice of Sully, architect of Notre-Dame, and defended by the Petit Châtelet or Lesser Barbican. It was the only bridge which minstrels were allowed to cross toll free in the Middle Ages.

Quai de Montebello. — From the quay, and particularly the small René-Viviani Square (p 99) the **view**★★★ of Notre-Dame is quite superb (*illustration p 62*).

In the 17C the two hospital buildings, the Hôtel-Dieu, on the river bank and the Cité respectively, were linked by a bridge, the **Pont au Double,** so named because the toll levied by the hospital was a *double tournois* or a doubloon struck in Tours (coin minted in Tours — until the 13C — had only 75 % of the value of Parisian coin). The present bridge was built in 1885.

Quai de la Tournelle. — Among the old houses lining the Tournelle Quay which lies just before the Archevêché Bridge (1828) is No. 47, the **Hôtel Martin** (1630) and variously a private house, a community of young girls, a bayonet forge — during the Revolution — a hospital pharmacy — during the Empire — and now a Public Health Museum. Some collections have been transferred to No. 13 Rue Scipion (5ᵉ) while awaiting the completion of restoration work.

From the Pont de la Tournelle to the Châtelet

No. 15, opposite the Tournelle Bridge, is the very old Tour d'Argent restaurant where Henri IV is said to have discovered the use of a fork (*museum open to restaurant patrons*).

The Tournelle Bridge was first built in wood in 1370 and has been reconstructed several times since. A statue of St. Geneviève by Landowski marks it out from its neighbours.

It was at this point in the Middle Ages that a chain curtain, to stop attacks from the river was suspended from a tower in the now vanished 14C **Tournelle Castle**, across the Seine to the Barbeau Tower (*p 86*) on the Right Bank. Splendid **view**★★★ of Notre-Dame from the bridge.

Sully Bridge. — This bridge, which dates from 1876, rests on the tip of the Ile St-Louis. From the first section there is a good **view**★ of Notre-Dame, the Cité and the Ile St-Louis. On the right the Quai St-Bernard is bordered by the Pierre and Marie Curie University buildings (*p 139*), so that students once more walk the same area as did their mediaeval predecessors attending St. Victor s Abbey. In the 17C, before the quay was built, noblemen and even Henri IV, accompanied often by the Dauphin, used to come to the river foreshore to bathe.

At the centre of the bridge, on the Ile St-Louis, is a formal garden, noisy with small children, and all that remains of the Bretonvilliers Mansion terraced gardens (*p 71*).

The **view**★★ from the bridge's second section is delightfully unspectacular — the Anjou Quay and Lambert Mansion, the Célestins' Quay, Marie Bridge and St-Gervais belfry.

Henri-Galli Square. — The small green Henri-Galli Square at the end of Sully Bridge contains a few stones from the Bastille. In the Middle Ages the area between the Hôtel Fieubet (p 79) and the Arsenal Library was occupied by the Celestine Monastery; while on your right, that between the Boulevard Morland and the river bank was **Louviers Island.** It was joined to the mainland in 1843.

The Quais des Célestins and Hôtel de Ville. — Walk left, along the Celestine Quay (p 86) from where there is an attractive **view*** of part of the Ile St-Louis and the Marie Bridge.

The **Marie Bridge***, named after one of those who sold off land on the Ile St-Louis, marks the start of the Hôtel-de-Ville Quay where the International City of the Arts stands (p 86).

In line with the Louis-Philippe Bridge on your left, are the Pantheon and St-Étienne-du-Mont (pp 104, 105).

A little further on, behind the equestrian statue of Étienne Marcel, is the Hôtel de Ville (p 114).

Quai de Gesvres. — As you walk along this quay which begins at the Arcole Bridge (rebuilt 1888), you find yourself alternately looking at the caged birds and garden plants displayed by the shops, and gazing across the river at Haussmann's monumental creations — the Hôtel-Dieu, police headquarters, commercial courts and the Law Courts. On the right the tall St-Jacques Tower (p 111) marks the narrow Rue St-Martin.

The **Notre-Dame Bridge** (1913) was the Greater Bridge in Roman times, as opposed to the Lesser Bridge on the far side of the island. Burnt down by the Normans and rebuilt on piles in 1413, it was the first to be given an official name, and the houses built upon it were the first to be numbered in Paris. It fell down in Louis XII's reign, but was rebuilt and lined by identical houses with richly decorated façades, since it was on the royal route of solemn entries into Paris. One of the houses can still be seen, for Watteau painted it in the 18C for his friend Gersaint, the picture dealer (West Berlin, Charlottenburg).

From the Place du Châtelet to the Place St-Michel

The Quai de la Mégisserie. — The **Pont au Change** or Money Changers' Bridge in front of the Châtelet Square (p 111), established in the 9C by Charles the Bald, was closely occupied all through the Middle Ages by jewellers and money-changers. It was to this bridge that all foreigners and visitors to Paris had to come to change their money.

Walk along the Mégisserie Quay, so called because until the Revolution, the quayside was the public slaughterhouse (mégisserie : tawing). Now there are pet shops and seed merchants. An attractive **view**** extends over the Law Courts, Conciergerie, and the old houses along the Horloge Quay and Pont-Neuf. At the end of the Pont-Neuf stand the Belle Jardinière and Samaritaine department stores — from the terrace of Samaritaine shop no. 2 (lift) there is an excellent **view***** over the whole of Paris. Continue by the Pont-Neuf and the Conti Quay to the Pont des Arts (closed for reconstruction).

The Pont des Arts. — The '' academic '' bridge faces the Institut de France (p 137). In 1803 the bridge was novel on two counts : it was the first to be built of iron and it was for pedestrians only — there were chairs to sit on and glasshouses with rare plants to shelter in, in case of rain. It was a toll bridge and on the day it was opened 65 000 Parisians paid to walk upon it.

The **view***** is outstanding encompassing the Pont-Neuf and the Vert Galant Square (p 70). Behind the Square are the Law Courts, the Sainte-Chapelle spire and the towers and spire of Notre-Dame; visible beyond a row of plane trees are the two theatres of the Place du Châtelet (p 111), the top of the St-Jacques Tower, the Hôtel de Ville and the St-Gervais belfry; downstream the Louvre, the Grand Palais and the Carrousel Bridge.

The Quais de Conti and Grands-Augustins. — The Conti Quay runs beside the Institut de France, the Mint (p 136), before arriving at the Pont-Neuf, where, in 1906, the scientist, Pierre Curie, was run over by a horse-drawn carriage and killed. At the corner of Rue Dauphine beneath an arcade, is the curious Rue de Nevers (p 136).

Continue from the Pont-Neuf to the Place St-Michel by way of the Grands-Augustins Quay. The quay, the oldest in Paris, was built in 1313 by Philip the Fair and in 1670 was named after the then celebrated Great Augustine Monastery (p 136) which stood in its own grounds between the Rue Dauphine and the Rue des Grands-Augustins.

In the 17C house at No. 51 is the famous restaurant of Lapérouse.

The Place St-Michel, which dates from the time of Napoleon III, was the scene, in August 1944, of student fighting against the Germans.

NOTRE-DAME CATHEDRAL★★★   🔟 or 🔟 : K 15

The cathedral of Paris, can be seen in all its radiant glory from the parvis or Viviani Square. Notre-Dame has a perfection all its own, with balanced proportions and a façade in which solid and void, horizontal and vertical, combine in total harmony. It is a beautiful religious edifice and one of the supreme masterpieces of French art.

Notre-Dame from Viviani Square

Construction. - For 2 000 years prayers have been offered from this spot : a Gallo-Roman temple, a Christian basilica, a Romanesque church preceded the present sanctuary founded by Bishop Maurice of Sully. A man of humble origin, he had become a canon at the cathedral and supervisor of the diocese by 1159 and, shortly afterwards, undertook to provide the capital with a worthy cathedral.

Construction began in 1163, during the reign of Louis VII. To the resources of the church and royal gifts, were added the toil and skill of the common people : stone masons, carpenters, iron workers, sculptors, glassworkers, moved with religious fervour, worked with ardour under Jean of Chelles and Pierre of Montreuil, architect of the Sainte-Chapelle. By about 1345 the building was complete — the original plans had not been modified in any way.

Ceremonial Occasions. — Long before it was completed, Notre-Dame had become the setting for major religious and political occasions : St. Louis placed the Crown of Thorns in the cathedral in 1239 until the Sainte-Chapelle was ready to receive it; in 1302 Philip the Fair went to the cathedral solemnly to open the first States General; ceremonies, acts of grace, state funerals, the Te Deum, processions, have followed down the centuries; the young Henry VI of England was crowned there in 1430; Mary Stuart was crowned there on becoming Queen of France by her marriage to François II; and Marguerite of Valois stood alone in the chancel while the Huguenot, Henri of Navarre, waited at the door as their marriage ceremony was performed in 1572 — although he came later to agree that " Paris is well worth a mass " and attended subsequent ceremonies inside the cathedral !

With the Revolution, the Church of Our Lady was dedicated to the cult of Reason and then of the Supreme Being. All but the great bell were melted down and the church interior was used to store forage and food. On 2 December 1804 the church was decked with hangings and ornaments to receive Pope Pius VII for the coronation of the Emperor (see the picture by David in the Louvre : *p 36*). After the anointing, however, Napoleon seized the crown from the pontiff and crowned first himself and then Josephine.

Restoration. — Gradually the building began to fall into disrepair, until in 1841, in accordance with popular feeling roused by the Romantic Movement and Victor Hugo's novel *The Hunchback of Notre-Dame,* the July Monarchy ordered that the cathedral be restored. A team of men under Viollet-le-Duc worked for twenty-three years on the statuary and glass, on removing additions, repairing the roof and upper parts, re-ordering the doors and chancel and erecting the spire and the sacristy. Notre-Dame emerged virtually unscathed from the Commune of 1871 and the Liberation of 1944 and remains the focal point for great occasions in Paris' history : the magnificent Te Deum of 26 August 1944 and the Requiem Masses for General de Gaulle on 12 November 1970 and President Pompidou on 6 April 1974.

■ PLACE DU PARVIS

The square, the zero point from which all road distances are measured, is dominated by the grandiose façade of Notre-Dame, somewhat diminished by the parvis having been quadrupled in size and the surroundings opened out by Haussmann in the 19C.

In the Middle Ages, when mysteries were played before churches and cathedrals, the porch represented paradise from which the word parvis evolved.

The Hôtel-Dieu. — The Hôtel-Dieu hospice, founded in the 7C had, by the 17C, been enlarged to two buildings linked by the Pont au Double *(p 60)*. In about 1880 these buildings were replaced on the island by the present Hôtel-Dieu and a square laid on the old site with, at the centre, a statue of Charlemagne.

Excavations. — Archaeologists in search of Lutetia have taken the opportunity of excavating beneath the parvis. Fragments of a 3C rampart and part of the porch of the Merovingian Cathedral of St. Stephen, which preceded Notre-Dame, have been uncovered, as well as capitals, Gallo-Roman coins and pottery which are displayed in the crypt adjoining the car park.

THE NOTRE-DAME FAÇADE★★★

The façade's overall design is majestic and perfectly balanced. The central portal is taller
nd wider than the others; that on the left is surmounted by a gable *(see below)* — it was a
mediaeval practice to avoid monotony by dissymmetry.

The Kings' Gallery. — The twenty-eight statues are of the Kings of Judea and Israel. A similar
allery can be seen in the cathedrals of Amiens, Reims and Chartres. In 1793 the Commune took
them for the Kings of France and shattered them on the parvis; Viollet-le-Duc restored them.

The Rose Window Level. — The design of the great rose window, nearly 10 m — 30 ft —
cross, is so perfect that it has never shifted in over 700 years. It forms a halo to the statue
f the Virgin and Child supported by two angels, before it. In the lateral bays, surmounted by
elief arches, are statues of Adam and Eve. The ensemble portrays the Redemption after
he Banishment from the Garden of Eden.

The Grand Gallery. — The gallery is a superb line of ornately carved arches linking the towers.
At the balustrade's buttress corners Viollet-le-Duc placed fantastic birds, monsters and
emons which, although large, are
carcely visible from below.

The Towers. — The twin towers, majes-
c, graceful, and 69 m high — 226 ft —
re pierced by slender lancets more
han 16 m in height (50 ft).

Emmanuel, the great bell in the
outh tower, tolled only on solemn oc-
asions, weighs 13 tons and its clap-
er nearly 500 kg — 9 3/4 cwts. It is said
hat when it was recast in the 17C,
women threw gold and silver jewellery
nto the heated bronze, which is why
he tone is so pure.

scent. — *Open 1 April to 30 September
0 am to 5.45 pm (4.15 pm the rest of
he year); closed Tuesdays and 1 Janu-
ry, 1 May, 14 July, 1 November, and
5 December. Access at the foot of the
orth tower Rue du Cloître Notre Dame;
F — Sundays and holidays 2F.*

The north tower upper chapel con-
ains original portal statues and paint-
ngs. Steps lead to the south tower
latform from which you get a splendid
iew★★★ of the spire and flying but-
resses, the Cité and Paris generally.

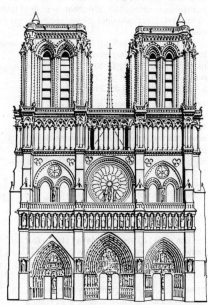

THE WEST FACE PORTALS★★★

In the Middle Ages the portals looked completely different : the multicoloured statues
tood out against a gilt background affording a bible in stone from which those who could
ot read could learn the scriptures and the legends of the saints. Today without colour, they
evertheless remain worthy of examination in detail.

From left to right are :

The Portal to the Virgin. — The tympanum, a model to sculptors throughout the Middle
Ages, shows below, the Ark of the Covenant, prophets and kings, above, a Dormition in the
resence of Christ and, at the apex, the Coronation of the Virgin.

The arching is delicately beaded, leaves, flowers and fruit framing angels, patriarchs,
ings and prophets of the celestial court. The Virgin and Child at the pier are modern. The
mall low reliefs on the side walls and arch shafts show the labours of the months and the
igns of the zodiac. The statues in the embrasures were added by Viollet-le-Duc.

Portal of the Last Judgment. — The tympanum, on its two remaining lintels, illustrates the
Resurrection and, above, the Weighing of Souls, the good being led to heaven by angels, the
amned to hell by demons. Christ sits in Majesty at the apex with the Virgin and St. John.

The six archivolts show the celestial court; below Abraham receives souls. The statue of
Christ at the pier and the Apostles in the embrasures are 19C; the Wise and Foolish Virgins
eneath open and shut doors to Paradise on the archway shafts are modern.

Portal of St. Anne. — The cathedral's oldest statues, carved in about 1170 some sixty years
efore the portal was erected, and intended for a narrower door, fill the tympanum's two
pper levels. At the apex are a Virgin and Child with Maurice of Sully (standing) and Louis VII
kneeling), consecrating the cathedral. The 12C central lintel shows the Life of the Virgin,
he lower, that of St. Anne and St. Joachim (13C).

The archivolts illustrate a celestial court; the pier supports a long and slender statue of
t. Marcel, Bishop of Paris in the 5C when he is said to have delivered the capital from a
ragon — he is sticking his crozier down the monster's throat. *(The original statue is in the
orth tower chapel.)* The embrasure and buttress statues are modern.

THE CATHEDRAL INTERIOR★★★

Notre-Dame impresses immediately by its size, its lighting, the noble uplift of its lines. A congregation of 9 000 can be accommodated within its 130 m length, 48 m width and 35 m height — 427 × 158 × 115 ft. *(A 10 min. film retracing the history of Notre Dame can be seen in the south tower).*

General Plan. — The plan is the prototype of all large Gothic cathedrals. In the 13C the upper windows and galleries were enlarged and lowered respectively to increase the light reaching the chapels off the outer aisles. Flying buttresses were then added to support the roofing. Part of the 12C architecture can still be seen at the transept crossing in the small rose and tall windows. The redoubtable pillars (1) supporting the towers measure 5 m across — 16 ft.

The stained glass of the Middle Ages was succeeded by clear glass with *fleur-de-lys* design in the 18C and monotone glass in the 19C; the modern glass by Le Chevalier, installed in 1965, returned to mediaeval manufacturing processes and colours. The 1730 organ, now with 109 stops and 6,100 pipes, is the biggest in France *(concerts : Sundays at 5.45 pm).*

Chapels. — Notre-Dame is entirely surrounded by chapels. They were built between the buttresses in response to the great number of foundations made by guilds and the rich in the 13 and 14C. This called for a lengthening of the transepts, which would have otherwise lost their profile.

In accordance with a tradition renewed in 1949, the goldsmiths of Paris offer a work of art to the cathedral every year in May — the most beautiful are by Le Brun (2, 3) and Le Sueur (4). On the left are the tombstones of a 15C canon (5), and of Cardinal Amette (6).

Transept. — The diameter — 13 m — 42 1/2 ft — and lightness of the transept rose **windows★★** is brilliant evidence of the rapid advances made in architecture in the Gothic period. The north rose (7) which has remained practically intact since the 13C, shows Old Testament figures around the Virgin; in the restored south rose (8) Christ sits surrounded by saints and angels.

The statue of St. Denis (9) by Nicolas Coustou makes a pair, against the transept pillars at the entrance to the chancel, with the beautiful 14C **Virgin and Child★** (10) — Our Lady of Paris, previously in St-Aignan *(p 65).* A pavement inscription recalls the conversion of the 20C poet Paul Claudel (11).

Chancel. — Louis XIII, childless after twenty-three years of marriage, consecrated France in 1638 to the Virgin — a vow materialised in the redecoration of the chancel by Robert de Cotte. Of this there remain the stalls, and a *pietà* by Nicolas Coustou (12), flanked by statues of Louis XIII (13) by Guillaume Coustou and Louis XIV (14) by Coysevox.

It was at this time that the stone chancel screen was cut back leaving, of the remarkable 14C **low reliefs★**, only scenes from the Life of Christ (15) and His Apparitions (16).

Mausoleums of bishops of Paris, buried in the crypt, line the ambulatory (17-24).

Treasury. — *Open 10 am to 5 pm; closed Sundays and holidays; 3F.*

The Crown of Thorns, the Holy Nail and a fragment of the True Cross are displayed on Sundays in Lent and Good Friday in the main area of the cathedral.

EXTERIOR★★★

Notre-Dame's lovely exterior presents an excellent summary of 13C architecture.

North Face. — A canons' cloister, now destroyed, gave its name to the street and north transept face.

The magnificent **Cloister Portal★★★** erected in about 1250 by Jean of Chelles, on the experience acquired at the Sainte-Chapelle, served as a model throughout the Gothic period.

The great and finely worked transept rose rests on a clerestory with which it forms an unprecedented and delicate opening 18 m — 58 ft — high. Below the rose is the many gabled carved doorway, richly decorated by comparison with the thirty years older doors of the main west face. On the lower level of the tympanum are events from the Life of the Virgin and above scenes from a mystery play.

The portal's jewel is the figure at the pier, a superb **Virgin★★★** (the Child was lost during the Revolution) with a gentle smile and the infinite nobility of a 13C masterpiece.

Opposite, at No. 10, is the **Cathedral Museum** (*open Saturdays and Sundays, 1 November to 30 June, 2.30 to 6 pm; 2F*) which evokes the cathedral's major historical moments since the 17C.

The **Red Door★**, a little further along, has, on the tympanum, the Virgin being coronated by her Son between St. Louis and Margaret of Provence. This door was reserved to the canons of the chapterhouse.

Seven 14C **low reliefs★** inlaid into the chancel chapels' foundations depict the Death and Assumption of the Virgin.

John XXIII Square. — From this square, opened as a formal garden with a Neo-Gothic fountain in 1844 and always crowded with mothers and children, there is an outstanding view of the **east end★★★** of the cathedral with its intricate decoration of balustrades, gables, pinnacles, gargoyles and the 14C flying buttresses rising 15 m — 50 ft — into the air to form the boldest mediaeval crown of all.

If you take a few steps back you can see the 13C roof. Viollet-le-Duc reconstructed the **spire★★** above the transept to the original plans, using at least 500 tons of oak and 250 tons of lead, so that it could rise once more to 90 m — 295 ft. He included himself among the decorative copper figures of Evangelists and Apostles!

Beyond the 19C sacristy is the magnificent **St. Stephen's portal★★★**, a pair with the cloister door but even richer in sculpture. A railing prevents a close approach. It was begun in 1258 and has a tympanum illustrating the life and stoning of St. Stephen to whom the church preceding the cathedral had been dedicated.

Cross the parvis to the Place Louis-Lépine.

THE NOTRE-DAME QUARTER★

Place Louis-Lépine. — A colourful and almost rural **flower market** lights up the cold administrative blocks of the Hôtel-Dieu, the police headquarters and the commercial courts which have surrounded the square on three sides since the Second Empire. On Sundays birds replace the flowers for sale in the square named after the popular prefect who, in addition to many reforms, gave the Paris police their white truncheons and whistles.

The Ancien Cloître Quarter★. — By way of the Corse Quay, lined with flowershops and the Fleurs Quay, where there are none, make for the Ancien Cloître Quarter.

ÎLE DE LA CITÉ

Although considerably restored, the quarter is the only reminder of what the Cité looked like in the 11 and 12C when students such as Abelard (*p 59*) attended the cathedral school which was later to merge with the Sorbonne.

Go down to the Rue des Ursins which is level with the old banks of the Seine, the site, until the 12C, of Paris' first quay, the Port St-Landry, before it was transferred to the Hôtel de Ville foreshore.

At the end of the narrow street stand the remains of the Cité's last mediaeval **church**, St-Aignan (at No. 19), where a few Romanesque capitals can still be seen. Priests celebrated mass secretly in the chapel during the Revolution.

Turn left into the Rue de la Colombe where there is a curious tavern at the top of some steps and traces of the Lutetian Gallo-Roman wall can be seen in the pavement.

Nos. 22 and 24 in the Rue Chanoinesse, on the left, are the last of the mediaeval canons' houses; note the 16C doorways and stone posts in the courtyard.

By way of the Rue du Cloître-Notre-Dame, walk left round John XXIII Square.

Ile-de-France Square. — This ancient upstream point of the island now bears, at its tip, the **Deportation Memorial** (sculpture by Desserprit), funeral urns and the tomb of the Unknown Deportee.

The **view★★★** of the cathedral from the square includes the whole east end.

THE LAW COURTS★★★ (Palais de Justice) ▢▢ or ▢▢ : J 14

On the Ile de la Cité stands not only the Gothic splendour of Notre-Dame but the seat of the civil and judicial system — the Law Courts. It forms with the Sainte-Chapelle and the Conciergerie an architectural ensemble of great historical interest.

The King's Palace. — The Roman governors, the Merovingian kings, the early Capetian kings, lived in turn on the Cité, establishing administrative quarters, building a dwelling of the finest stone for royal use, inaugurating a mint and, lastly, constructing a chapel and keep.

In the 13C St. Louis lived in the Upper Chamber (today the First Civil Court), dispensed justice in the courtyard and built the Sainte-Chapelle; Philip the Fair constructed the Conciergerie, a sumptuous palace " more beautiful than anyone in France had ever seen "

On 22 February 1358, the mob under Étienne Marcel *(p 115)* entered the apartments of the Dauphin, the future Charles V, whose father John the Good had been taken prisoner by the Black Prince at Poitiers and held in England, and slew his counsellors before his eyes. On regaining control, Charles V left the palace, preferring to live at the Louvre or outside Paris — an example followed by Charles VII, Henri IV and Louis XIV who all subdued Paris; Louis XVI, Charles X and Louis-Philippe, who refused to abandon the palace, all lost their thrones.

Parliament's Palace. — Parliament, installed in the former royal residence, was the kingdom's supreme court of justice. Originally its members were nominated by the king, but in 1522 François I sold the rights which thus became hereditary. Conflicts between the officers of state and the king were settled by courts presided over by the monarch.

Judges, barristers, clerks and others thronged the lesser courts in the palace. Fires were frequent : the Great Hall was badly damaged in 1618, the Sainte-Chapelle spire in 1630, the Debtors' Court in 1737, the Marchande Gallery in 1776. In 1788 Parliament demanded the convocation of the States General — not a good idea — the General Assembly announced its suppression and the Convention sent the members to the guillotine.

Palace of Justice. — The Revolution overturned the judicial system. New courts were installed in the old building which took the name of Palace of Justice. Restoration began in 1840 and continued until 1914, interrupted only by the Commune fire, after which the building was given the façade which now overlooks the Place Dauphine and the wing on the Orfèvres Quay.

(After a Bibliothèque Nationale photo, Paris)

The Palace in the 17C

Conciergerie. — *Tour : p 69.* The name Conciergerie was given in the old palace to the part controlled by a person of high degree : the *concierge* or keeper of the king's mansion — a remunerative office involving the licensing of the many shops within the palace walls.

Among pre-Revolutionary prisoners were several who had made successful or unsuccessful attempts on successive kings' lives : Montgomery on Henri II; Ravaillac on Henri IV...

At the Revolution as many as 1 200 men and women were held at one time in the Conciergerie; during the Terror the building became the antechamber to the Tribunal, which in nine cases out of ten meant the guillotine. Among those locked in the cells were : Queen Marie-Antoinette; Mme Elisabeth, sister to Louis XVI; Charlotte Corday who stabbed Marat; Mme du Barry, the favourite of Louis XV; the poet André Chénier; Philippe-Égalité; the chemist, Lavoisier; the twenty-two Girondins condemned by Danton who, with fifteen of his companions, was in turn condemned by Robespierre, who was himself condemned with twenty of his followers by the Thermidor Convention, and finally the public prosecutor Fouquier-Tinville, and the president, judges and juries of the Revolutionary Tribunal. In all nearly 2 600 prisoners left the Conciergerie between January 1793 and July 1794 for the capital's guillotine placed successively on the Place du Carrousel, Place de la Concorde, Place de la Bastille, Place de la Nation (where in 40 days 1 306 heads fell) and finally returning to Place de la Concorde.

TOUR OF THE LAW COURTS

The palace is open from 9 am to 6 pm except on Saturdays and Sundays and all the courts, galleries and halls may be entered with the exception of the Bustes Gallery, and the Juvenile Court (Galerie des Bustes, Tribunal pour Enfants).

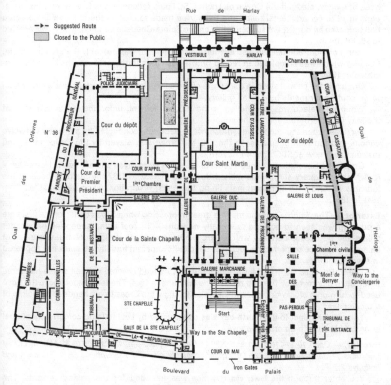

The May Courtyard. — The courtyard, which overlooks the Boulevard du Palais is separated from it by a fine Louis XVI wrought iron gateway. The name of this forecourt was due to a very old custom by which the clerks of the court — an important corporation — planted a tree on the 1 May in this courtyard. The tree used in these celebrations, which were similar to the traditional English festivities, came from one of the Royal Forests.

The imposing buildings round the courtyard were erected after the fire of 1776. A small yard to the right abuts on the old Conciergerie wicket gate *(plan p. 69)* through which the victims of the Terror passed on their way to the tumbrils beneath the watchful eyes of the curious and the *tricoteuses* — the women knitting — perched upon the steps.

From the Marchande Gallery to the Harlay Vestibule. — Turn left in the Marchande Gallery formerly the most animated part of the building, bustling with plaintiffs, lawyers, clerks, court officials and hangers-on, to walk down the Sainte-Chapelle Gallery. Turn right, up the Procureur de la République's Corridor and right again up a passageway which skirts the lively petty court area (Chambres Correctionnelles). Turn right at the end into the Duc Gallery, getting an open **view*** of the Sainte-Chapelle from the corner.

Turn left beyond the ornate Chamber of the Civil Court of Appeal, into the Première Présidence Gallery and leave on the left the **C.I.D.** (Police Judiciaire) known to all admirers of Inspector Maigret. From the vast and empty Harly Vestibule steps lead to the Assize Court *(open only when in session)* on the right. At the end is the Chamber of the Court of Cassation *(frescoes and tapestries — but not often open).*

From the Harlay Vestibule to the May Courtyard. — Walk down to the right the Lamoignon Gallery (glance at the St. Louis Gallery in passing, on your left) and the following Prisoners' Gallery.

Enter the **Lobby** (Salle des Pas-Perdus), formerly the Gothic Great Hall of Philip the Fair, twice destroyed and reconstructed most recently after the Commune of 1871. The two Classical aisles, crowded with plaintiffs, barristers in their gowns but without the English distinctive wig, clerks and officials, are now the busiest place in the building — Balzac called it " the cathedral of chicanery ".

Notice the tortoise — a malicious dig at the delays in the law — in the monument, on the right, of the 19C barrister, Berryer. At the end on the left is the former apartment of St. Louis, later the Parliamentary Grand Chamber, when Louis XII had it decorated with a fine ceiling, then the Revolutionary Tribunal under Fouquier-Tinville (1793 - 94 — *p 66*) and now the **First Civil Court.**

Walk down the grand Louis XVI staircase built by the architect Antoine, noting the old shop names.

■ THE SAINTE-CHAPELLE*** 🔲🔲 or 🔲🔲 : J 14

The chapel is a Gothic marvel — the deep glow of its windows one of the great joys of a visit to Paris.

Historical Notes. — Baudouin, a French nobleman and Emperor of Constantinople, when in need of money, pledged the Crown of Thorns. St. Louis redeemed the Crown from the Venetians in 1239. For additional relics and the shrine made to contain them, he paid two and a half times the amount spent subsequently on the Sainte-Chapelle building, which was erected to shelter them.

Pierre of Montreuil (known also as Pierre of Montereau) was probably the architect of the building which was completed in record time — less than thirty-three months — and consecrated in 1248.

Originally the chapel stood in the centre of the court, linked at the upper level of the porch to St. Louis' apartments by a small gallery.

When the palace was remodelled in the 18C, parliament, unfortunately, built a wing of the May Courtyard abutting on the chapel.

Services, when the chapel was in use, were elaborate, conducted by a chapter of twelve canons and fourteen chaplains; in the 17C the organ was played by the Couperins — the instrument is now at St-Germain-l'Auxerrois.

During the Revolution, although some of the relics were saved and are now in Notre-Dame (p 64), the reliquary shrine was melted down. From 1802 to 1837 the building became the judiciary archive with filing cabinets lining the walls; restoration, when it came, took from 1841 to 1867.

Exterior. — The Sainte-Chapelle made a great impression when it was built : for the first time a building was seen to possess practically no walls — its roof being supported on slender pillars and buttresses between which were windows nearly 15 m high — 50 ft. It was a feat of balance — balance so perfect, in fact, that despite its apparent fragility, no crack has appeared in seven centuries.

The spire rises 75 m — 246 ft — into the sky. Its lead covered wooden frame has three times been destroyed by fire and rebuilt, the last time in 1854. The lead angel above the apse used to turn on a clockwork mechanism so as to show the Cross in his hands to all points of the compass.

The small adjunct to the fourth bay was constructed by Louis XI and comprises a chapel at ground level with an oratory above.

Interior. — *Open 10 to 11.45 am and 1.30 to 5.45 pm (4.45 pm, 1 October to 31 March) closed Tuesdays, 1 January, 1 May, 25 December (possibly closed 1 November); 5F — Sundays and holidays 2.50F.*

You enter through the **lower chapel** which was intended for the palace servants. The chamber is 17 m wide and only 7 m high — 56 × 23 ft. Columns, garishly decorated in the 19C, uphold the central vault, and are supported, in their turn, by elegantly pierced flying buttresses. The pavement is made up of the tombstones of canons buried beneath it.

Two spiral staircases lead to the **upper chapel**, a wondrous jewel, which attracts even the faintest ray of sunlight. The **stained glass windows***** are the oldest in Paris and amongst the finest to be produced in the 13C in their vividness of colour and the vitality of the thousands of small characters they portray; the 1 134 scenes on glass spread over an area of 618 m² — 6 672 sq ft — form a veritable illustrated bible. The mid-19C restorations are hard to detect.

The windows should each be read from bottom to top and left to right, except for Nos. **6, 7, 9** and **11** which must be read lancet by lancet.

UPPER CHAPEL

1) Genesis - Adam and Eve - Noah - Jacob.
2) Exodus - Moses on Mount Sinai.
3) Exodus - The Law of Moses.
4) Deuteronomy - Joshua - Ruth and Boaz.
5) Judges - Gideon - Samson.
6) Isaiah - The Tree of Jesse.
7) St. John the Evangelist - Life of the Virgin - The Childhood of Christ.
8) Christ's Passion.
9) John the Baptist - Daniel. — 10) Ezekiel.
11) Jeremiah - Tobias. — 12) Judith - Job. — 13) Esther.
14) Kings : Samuel, David, Solomon.
15) St. Helena and the True Cross - St. Louis and the relics of the Passion.
16) 15C Flamboyant rose window : the Apocalypse.

The vessel is encircled by blind arcades with capitals delicately carved with leaf motifs; against each pillar stands a statue of an apostle holding one of the Church's twelve crosses of consecration — six of the figures are old (brown on the plan).

The statues, in spite of their modern colouring, are extraordinarily lifelike (others are in the Cluny Museum : p 99).

Two small niches in the third bay were reserved for the king and the royal family. In the next bay, on the right, is the door to the oratory built by Louis XI : a grille enabled him to follow the service without being seen.

The reliquary shrine stood at the centre of the apse in a gallery covered by a wooden baldachin and reached by twin circular staircases enclosed in openwork turrets. The staircase on the left, which dates back to when the chapel was built, was often mounted by St. Louis who then, himself, opened the door to the shrine, inlaid with sparkling jewels.

The porch onto the terrace is a reconstruction with a 19C tympanum and pier.

■ THE CONCIERGERIE★★ 🔟 or 🔟 : J 14

The Conciergerie includes three superb Gothic halls built by Philip the Fair in the 14C.

The Exterior. — The best **view★★** is from the Mégisserie Quay on the Right Bank from where you can also see the four towers reflected in the Seine. The crenelated Bonbec Tower, on the right, which is the oldest, got its name babbler, because it was used as a torture chamber. The twin towers in the centre of the 19C Neo-Gothic façade commanded the palace entrance and the bridge of Charles the Bald. The Argent Tower on the right contained the treasure. The square 14C Horloge Tower has since 1370 housed the first public clock to be installed in Paris. The carvings on the face are by Germain Pilon (16C — restored). The silver bell, having chimed the hours for the monarchy, was melted down in 1793.

The Interior. — *Enter through No. 1 Quai de l'Horloge and go through to the Guardroom. Guided tours : 10 to 11.25 am, and 1.30 to 5.25 pm, (4.25 pm 1 October to 31 March). Closed Tuesdays in winter and 1 January, 1 May, 1 November, 25 December. 5F — Sundays and holidays 2.50F.*
Guardroom★ (Salles des Gardes). — Stout pillars with interestingly carved capitals support the Gothic vaulting in this room which now lies some 7 m — 23 ft — below the level of the 16C quay.
The Hall of the Men-at-Arms★★ (Salle des Gens d'Armes). — This magnificent four aisled Gothic hall has an area of 1 800 m² — 19 375 sq ft. Exactly above was the palace's Great Hall and the royal apartments.

Kitchens (Cuisines). — The four huge chimneys and fires in the kitchens were each intented for a separate purpose — spit roasting, boiling cauldrons, etc. — and between them, could serve the royal family and 2 000 to 3 000 others.

The " Rue de Paris ". — The Rue de Paris, was the name given to the last bay, closed by a grille from the Hall of the Men-at-Arms, as it led to the quarters of the executioner, known tradition-ally as Monsieur de Paris. During the Terror, penniless prisoners slept in it on the ground.

Prisoners' Gallery. — The gallery, off the Rue de Paris, was the busiest part of the building, with prisoners arriving and departing, lawyers, police and gaolers.

From the 1st floor, the police escorted the prisoner down the spiral staircase, situated in one of the turrets of the Bonbec Tower, and into the gallery (through a door on the right which has since been walled up). This room gave onto the council room which on one side served as the men's prison yard and on the other side it opened onto a staircase (**3**), which led to the Tribunal. The prisoners were most likely herded into the room, which is now used as the kitchens for the Conciergerie restaurant and from there, one by one, they were taken to a neighbouring room where they were sat on a stool and their last toilet was performed.

Their hands were roped behind their backs, collars ripped wide and hair cut from the napes of their necks before walking through the wicket gate to the clerk of the court (register office) — abutting on the May Courtyard — and out to the tumbrils.

Marie Antoinette's Prison. — The cell (**1**) where the queen lived from 2 August 1793 to 16 October 1793 in-cluded the area now a chapel. A screen separated the queen from the day and night watch. The cell now communicates with the next one (**2**) in which first Danton and then Robespierre are said to have been held.

The Girondins' Chapel. — The chapel was trans-formed into a collective prison when twenty-two Girondins were held there together in 1793.

The museum contains Marie-Antoinette's cruci-fix and other mementoes, contemporary documents, a cell door, a guillotine blade, etc.

The Women's Courtyard (Cour des Femmes). — In the centre, as always, is a pathetic patch of grass and a tree. In the corner is the Place of the Twelve (**4**) where men and women prisoners could talk and where the twelve selected daily for the guillotine said their farewells.

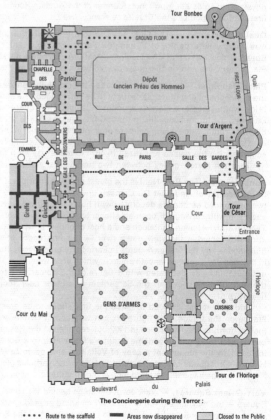

The Conciergerie during the Terror :

•••• Route to the scaffold   ■■■ Areas now disappeared   ▢ Closed to the Public

■ LAW COURTS QUARTER* (Palais de Justice)

For a long time the Cité ended in the west in a sort of river level archipelago, separated from the main island by the arms of the Seine. It was on one of the islets that Philip the Fair had the stake erected in 1314 for the Grand Master of the Order of Templars, Jacques de Molay, watching him burn from his palace window. The King's Garden (Jardin du Roi), which

Marie dei Medici converted into Paris' first Botanical Garden, extended from the islands to the Conciergerie.

It was only at the end of the 16C that Henri III decided to re-order the Cité point : the mud-filled ditches were drained, the islets joined (the Vert-Galant Square is at the old ground level), the central earth terrace of the future Pont Neuf built up and the south bank raised by some 6 m — 20 ft. By about 1580 the new terrain was ready for the builders.

TOUR *(plan p 65)*

Start from the Horloge Tower. Facing you are the Commercial Law Courts built in 1865 on the site of the former St. Bartholomew's, the royal parish church from the 9C to the Revolution. Cross the vestibule to look at the dome which rises majestically to a height of 42 m — 141 ft. Opposite the May Court,

DOWNSTREAM END OF THE ILE DE LA CITÉ IN 15 C

the construction of the Boulevard du Palais by Haussmann did away with the gallows area.

A little further on, a tablet marks the site of St. Michael's, the palatine chapel until the time of St. Louis (13C). Leave on your left the Marché-Neuf Quay where **Théophraste Renaudot**, physician to Louis XIII, Huguenot, founder of the Auction Rooms, Public Assistance and the first printed periodical, the *Gazette de France,* lived.

Quai des Orfèvres. — The Quai des Orfèvres — literally the gold and silversmiths' quay — was the jewellers' centre of 17 and 18C Paris : Strass, inventor of the synthetic diamond, Boehmer and Bassenge who fashioned Marie-Antoinette's necklace, had their shops on the Place Dauphine and on the quay, today known at No. 36 as the headquarters of the C.I.D.

Place Dauphine. — In 1607 Henri IV ceded the land between the palace and the Pont-Neuf for the development of a triangular square to be surrounded by a series of houses constructed of brick, white stone and slate to a uniform design. The square was named in honour of the Dauphin, the future Louis XIII. In the 18C the square was the scene, each spring, of the Exhibition of Youth, when young painters presented their works in the open air.

Only a few façades, such as No. 14, look as they did originally. Further on, the side of the square facing the palace was razed in 1874 to make way for a monumental staircase.

Take the narrow gulley between two heavily restored houses of 1608 to the Pont-Neuf.

Pont-Neuf*. — The Pont-Neuf is the oldest of the Paris bridges. The two halves begun in 1578 to the designs of Androuet Du Cerceau and completed in 1607 are not strictly in line. The twelve rounded arches are decorated with humourous grotesques, the half circles resting on each pile with carvings of open-air shops, tooth drawers at work, comic characters such as Tabarin and the Italian Pantaloon and a host of gapers and pickpockets. The Pont-Neuf's other attributes included the view down river — the first unencumbered by houses and other buildings — and the first pavements in Paris to be properly separated from the hurtling traffic in the roadway. A pump beneath an arch, which drew water from the river to supply the Louvre until 1813 and was decorated with a figure of the woman of Samaria giving Jesus water at the well, became known as the Samaritain — a name later adopted by a department store nearby *(p 61).*

Suddenly it was decided to place the first statue to be erected on a public highway in France on the bridge. The figure chosen was an equestrian bronze of Henri IV. This was melted down by the Revolution in 1792 but replaced at the Restoration by the present figure, cast in bronze from the Vendôme Column's first statue by a Bonapartist who is said to have included in the monument a copy of Voltaire's epic poem *La Henriade* (on the League and Henri IV), a statuette of Napoleon and various written articles glorifying the Emperor !

The bridge has been restored many times but the basic construction remains unchanged.

Vert-Galant Square*. — Walk down the steps behind the Henri IV statue. The Vert-Galant Square — the nickname given to Henri IV, meaning gay old spark — at the extreme tip of the island, is a peaceful spot from which to enjoy a **view**★★ of the Pont-Neuf and the river.

THE ILE ST-LOUIS**   🔟 or 🔟 : K 15, K 16

Calm quays and unpretentious classical architecture make the Island of St. Louis one of the most attractive places in Paris.

Originally there were two islands, the Ile aux Vaches and the Ile Notre-Dame, where in the Middle Ages judicial duels were held known as the Judgments of God. The contractor, Marie, early in the reign of Louis XIII, together with two financiers, Poulletier and Le Regrattier, obtained permission from the king and chapter of Notre-Dame to join the islets and to construct two stone bridges linking the new island to the mainland. In return they were to be allowed to sell the land for building. The work began in 1627 and was completed by 1664. The Ile St-Louis, therefore, like the nearby Marais (p 79), is Classical in style. But

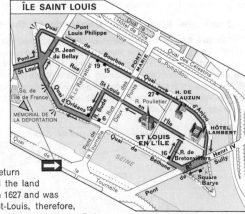

what makes the island unique is its atmosphere of old world charm and provincial calm. Writers, artists and those who love Old Paris have taken up their abode in its peaceful setting.

TOUR

On the island you see a 17C house at almost every step : nobly proportioned façades, most bearing historical or anecdotal tablets, wrought iron balconies and tall brick chimneys. Behind massive panelled doors, studded with bosses and great nails, are inner courts where the stone sets and mounting blocks have not changed since the days of horse-drawn carriages.

Quais de Bourbon and Anjou. — At the end of the new St-Louis Bridge turn left and follow the Bourbon Quay round the picturesque tip of the island where chain linked stone posts, canted 18C medallions, anglers and the view of St-Gervais Church combine to make an altogether delightful **scene***. A little further on are two magnificent mansions (Nos. 19 and 15) which once belonged to parliamentarians — steep mansard roofs, mascaroons, spacious stairwells encircled by wrought iron balusters, indicate their former splendour.

The Anjou Quay, beyond the **Marie Bridge***, is lined by some of the island's finest mansions. The Marquise de Lambert, hostess of a famous literary *salon*, lived at No. 27 (p. 79).

Hôtel de Lauzun*. — *Enter through No. 17. Apply at : Chef du Cabinet de l'Adjoint au Maire chargé de la Questure, Hôtel de Ville, ☎ 277.15.40, ext. 57-07.* The mansion, erected in 1657 by Le Vau for the caterer to the army, Gruyn, who was imprisoned shortly afterwards for corruption, belonged for only three years to the Duke of Lauzun, Saint-Simon's brother-in-law, who nevertheless left it his name. The poet, Théophile Gautier, lived there in the 1840's, also Baudelaire, Rilke, Sickert and Wagner. The house now belongs to the City of Paris and is used for official guests.

Inspite of the plain façade and modest size of many of the rooms, the **interior decoration**** which is splendid with gilded panelling, painted ceilings, tapestries, Italian style false perspective, and woodwork, makes it one of the richest private mansions of the 17C.

Hôtel Lambert or **Le Vau*.** — *No. 2 Rue St-Louis-en-l'Ile; not open.* The mansion of President Lambert de Thorigny, known as Lambert the Rich, was built in 1640 by Le Vau and decorated by Le Sueur (whose designs may be seen at the Louvre) and Le Brun.

From the Hôtel Lambert to St-Louis-en-l'Ile. — The Square Barye has been laid out at the tip of the island — last trace of the former terraced gardens of the financier, Bretonvilliers.

No. 16 Quai de Béthune, previously known as the Balcony Quay from the number of overhanging balconies, was the house of the Duke of Richelieu (great nephew of the cardinal). Turn right into the Rue de Bretonvilliers which ends beneath an arcade, part of the former mansion of the same name, then left into the Rue St-Louis-en-l'Ile, the island's main street.

St-Louis-en-l'Ile Church**. — The church is marked outside (No. 21) by an unusual iron clock and an original pierced spire. Building began in 1664 to plans by Le Vau, who lived on the island, but was only completed in 1726. The interior, in the Jesuit style, is ornately decorated, with woodwork gilding and marble of the *Grand Siècle* (17C), statuettes and enamels. A plaque presented in 1926 in the north aisle bears the inscription : " In grateful memory of St. Louis in whose honor the City of Saint Louis, Missouri, USA is named ".

From the Church to the Louis-Philippe Bridge. — Continue along the Rue St-Louis-en-l'Ile to No. 51 which, in the middle of the 19C, was the archbishopric and where there is a very fine doorway surmounted by a bearded human mask supported by dragons, also a majestic balcony. The Rue Budé, on the left, comes out onto the Orléans Quay which you follow to the right, leaving on your left the Polish Library and the small Adam-Mickiewicz Museum (No. 6).

From the quay there is a splendid **view***** of the east end of Notre-Dame and the Left Bank. Leave the island by the modern Rue Jean-du-Bellay and the Louis-Philippe Bridge.

Michelin plans ⓮ or ⓯ : from F 12 to G 11.
Distance : 3 km — 2 miles — Time : 2 hours. Start from the Concorde métro station.

The Place de la Concorde, the Madeleine, the Opera and the Place Vendôme form a quadrilateral, linked by some of the most elegant streets in Paris. In the evening the pavements are thronged with lively crowds attracted by the cinemas and theatres.

From the Place de la Concorde to the Madeleine

The **Rue Royale**, running between the two great mansions designed by Gabriel in the 18C *(p 43)*, has a double vista : ahead to the Madeleine, its immense pediment raised high on its line of columns, and, backwards, to the white mass of the Palais-Bourbon beyond the slender Concorde obelisk. Luxury shops (Villeroy & Boch, Christofle, Jansen), great restaurants, superb provision and catering establishments (Maxim's, Fauchon's), to be found in the Rue Royale itself or close to the Madeleine, add a quiet opulence. At the end of the 18C the writer, Mme de Staël, lived in No. 6, and Gabriel, the architect, in No. 8.

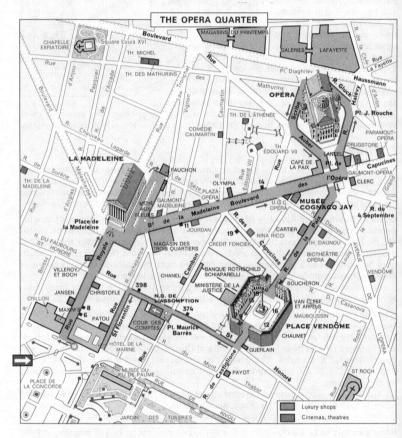

THE OPERA QUARTER

THE MADELEINE★★   ⓮ or ⓯ : F 11, G 11

The Madeleine is the name by which the Church of St. Magdalen is known to everyone in Paris, and everyone knows it, thanks to its surprising Greek temple appearance and its dominant position at the juncture of the Boulevards and the street from the Concorde.

Construction. — Few churches can have had such a stormy history. It was begun by one architect, in 1764; a second razed what had already been erected to begin on a building modelled on the Pantheon; all work ceased between 1790 and 1806 when Napoleon announced that on this spot there should be erected a temple to the glory of the Grand Army. Once more the existing building was razed, this time so that a Greek temple might be constructed. The architect was Vignon; work proceeded slowly once more.

In 1814 Louis XVIII confirmed that the Madeleine should indeed be a church, but in 1837 the building was almost selected for use as Paris' first railway terminal. The church's vicissitudes ended with its consecration in 1842 although its priest was shot by the Commune in 1871.

Tour. — From the square look up the monumental flight of steps (28) to the majestic colonnade of Corinthian columns — 52 in all, each 20 m tall — 66 ft. These support the surrounding sculptured frieze, the gigantic pediment, the Lemaire sculpture of the Last Judgement. The reliefs on the massive bronze door were inspired by the Ten Commandments. Inside, three domes on pendentives light the single aisle and semicircular chancel. At the high altar is a picture of the Magdalen. From the steps there is a splendid view down the Rue Royale, beyond the obelisk to the Palais-Bourbon and the Invalides dome.

From the Madeleine to the Opera

Boulevard de la Madeleine. — Immediately on your left, as you start to walk towards the Opera, is a flower market, while on your right the Trois-Quartiers store marks the meeting point of the Madeleine, Chaussée d'Antin and Place Vendôme quarters. No. 11, the former sweet shop, A la Marquise de Sévigné, is where Alphonsine Plessis died, the original *Lady of the Camelias* of Alexandre Dumas the Younger and Marguerite in Verdi's *Traviata*.

Boulevard des Capucines. — The boulevard and street, which contains fine houses — No. 19 built in 1726, and, opposite, the old Foreign Ministry where Stendhal died in 1842 — were named after a Capuchin monastery which stood formerly to the south. The boulevard was the scene of the call to arms, barricades and street fighting throughout the night of 23 February 1848 which was followed by the abdication of Louis-Philippe.

Beyond the Olympia music-hall, (No. 28) on the left, are the Rue Édouard-VII, named after Edward VII's visit to Paris in 1910, and, at No.14 a tablet commemorating the first public showing of 16 m — 52 ft — films by the Brothers Lumière on 28 December 1895.

Cognacq-Jay Museum★★. — *25 Boulevard des Capucines. Open 10 am to 5.40 pm. Closed Mondays and holidays; 3F, free on Sundays.*

The Louis XV and Louis XVI panelled rooms contain outstanding oils and pastels by Boucher, Fragonard, La Tour, Greuze, Canaletto, Gainsborough, furniture signed by the greatest 18C cabinet-makers, busts and precious ornaments. The harmony and taste of the collection give a wonderful impression of gallant and sophisticated life in the Age of Enlightenment.

Place de l'Opéra. — Haussmann did not see the Opera Square simply as a setting for the National Musical Academy but as a circus from which a number of roads should radiate and constructed his boulevards accordingly. Public opinion, at the time, was divided as to whether the square was not altogether too vast; today it barely copes with the milling traffic.

Luxury shops quarter the small central area; the Café de la Paix terraces provide an international meeting place for those with time to spare; elegant displays at the other corners invite window shoppers to gaze at leather, scarves and gifts at Lancel and jewellery at Clerc.

THE OPERA★★   ⅡⅡ or ⅡⅡ : F 12

The celebrity of France's first home of opera, the prestige of its opera and ballet companies, the architectural magnificence of the great staircase and foyer, the sumptuous decoration of the auditorium, invite the tourist to treat himself to an enjoyable evening.

Construction. — The site of Garnier's Opera House was determined by Haussmann's town planning project. In 1820 the idea developed of building a new opera house, forty years later a competition was held to find an architect. Charles Garnier, a 35-year-old architect, winner of the Rome prize in 1848 but otherwise unknown, was unanimously chosen from the 171 contestants. The foundation stone was laid in 1862; the opera was opened, at last, in 1875.

Garnier dreamed of creating a Napoleon III style of architecture, but the opera house created no new school, having insufficient originality; it is, nevertheless, remarkable and, in its way, is the most successful monument of the Second Empire.

It is also the biggest theatre in the world with a total area of 11 000 m² — 118 404 sq ft — and a stage so large that it can accommodate 450 players. But this area and the annexes are so extensive that the auditorium seats only 2 200.

Modern music and dance now figure frequently in the programme of the Opera. The company sometimes performs on other Parisian stages (Palais des Sports, Palais des Congrès). The permanent company numbers 1 100.

Exterior. — The main façade overlooks the Place de l'Opéra. At the top of a flight of steps and preceding the arcades to the theatre are statues including a Paul Belmondo copy of Carpeaux' **Dance★★** (the original is in the Louvre).

A majestic balcony fronts the foyer. Above are the dome over the auditorium and a triangular pediment marking the stagefront. As you bear right, round the building, you get some idea of its size. The projecting wing was originally for subscribers who could drive to this private entrance in their carriages.

The so-called Emperor's Pavilion, on the Rue Scribe, had a double ramp to enable the sovereign to ride straight to the royal box in his carriage. The pavilion is now occupied by the extensive Opera **Library** and **Museum** *(open 10 am to 5 pm; closed Sundays and holidays and the fortnight following Easter; 1F).*

Interior. — The only way of seeing inside the opera house is to go to a performance. However the **great staircase★★** is visible from the main entrance hall *(open from 11 am onwards).* The **main foyer★**, the **auditorium★** are remarkable and at their best on state occasions. Original features are the incorporation in the design by Garnier of marbles of every hue — white, blue, rose, red and green — from all the quarries of France, the magnificent six ton chandelier and a false ceiling inspired by opera and ballet, painted by Chagall in 1964.

From the Opera to the Place Vendôme

The **Rue de la Paix**, laid in 1806 over the site of a Capuchin chapel, was originally known as the Rue Napoléon. Napoleon, on his column, can be seen with his back towards it. The beautiful jewellers, shops, Cartier among others, which line the street have made its name a synonym for elegance and luxury throughout the world.

THE PLACE VENDÔME★★   🔟 or 🔢 : G 12

The Place Vendôme is a superb display of the majesty of French 17C architecture. In about 1680, Louvois, Superintendent of Buildings, conceived the idea of building upon the land to the north of the Rue St-Honoré, a square which would serve as a setting for a monumental statue of Louis XIV and be surrounded by suitable buildings housing academies, the National Library, the Mint. In 1685, the Duke of Vendôme's mansion and the neighbouring Capuchin convent were purchased and Hardouin-Mansart was commissioned to design the square, (originally known as the Place des Conquêtes but soon renamed Place de Vendôme or Louis-le-Grand). In 1686 the equestrian statue of the king by Girardon was unveiled.

But the square was just a beautiful façade for only gradually were the lots at the back taken up; the first building was completed in 1702, the last in 1720. The royal statue was destroyed by the Revolution and the square temporarily renamed Place des Piques. In 1810 Napoleon placed the Austerlitz column at its centre.

The Square. — Uniform arcades at ground level, above, pilasters rising two floors and finally, steeply pitched roofs with a continuous series of dormer windows, surround the square. The effect is not of monotony but of perfection of proportion and style, to which variety is added by the graceful, and again uniform, pedimented façades of the principal buildings standing obliquely at each of the square's four corners.

As you walk round the square (224 × 213 m — 245 × 233 yds) by the right, every house evokes a memory or a name : No. 19 is the former Hôtel d'Évreux (1710); No. 15 is now the Ritz Hotel; Nos. 13 and 11, now the Ministry of Justice, were formerly the Royal Chancellery — the official measure for the metre was inlaid in the façade in 1848; No. 9, at the end of the 19C, was the house of the military governor of Paris. Chopin died at No. 12 in 1849; No. 16 was the home of the German, Dr. Mesmer, founder of the theory of mesmerism...

The square, like the Rue de la Paix, is the place for great names among jewellers, perfumers, bankers : Van Cleef & Arpels, Boucheron, Elizabeth Arden, Schiaparelli, Rothschild.

The Column. — The column's stone core is entwined in a spiral made from the bronze from 1 200 cannon captured at the Battle of Austerlitz (1805).

The first statue to be placed at the top of the column was of Napoleon as Caesar; in 1814 he was replaced by Henri IV, who was removed for the 100 Days. Louis XVIII hoisted a colossal *fleur-de-lys*; Louis-Philippe re-established Napoleon, this time in military uniform. The Commune tore down the column in 1871; the Third Republic re-erected it and placed upon it a replica of the original statue.

(By permission of U.A.P.)

The Place Vendôme

From the Place Vendôme to the Place de la Concorde

The windows of the Rue St-Honoré between the Rue de Castiglione and the Rue Royale are a window-shoppers paradise. The street's repute goes back many years, even centuries : before the Revolution, the court, the nobility, the treasury, all came to shop, whether for dress or finance. At No. 374 Mme Geoffrin established a *salon* which was frequented by all the great names of Louis XV's reign. A few steps away, in the Rue Cambon, is the house from which Coco Chanel reigned over the fashion world for half a century.

The **Church of N.-D. de l'Assomption,** now the Polish Church, was formerly the chapel of the Convent of the Sisters of the Assumption on the Place Maurice-Barrès. This round 17C building is capped by a disproportionately large dome. Inside are a 17C fresco on the dome of the Assumption by Charles de la Fosse, and respectively at the altar and to its right, an Annunciation by Vien (18C) and an Adoration of the Magi by Van Loo. Abutting on the church is the Cour des Comptes (Auditor General's Office, 1912).

No. 398 is the site of the house in which Robespierre lived until the eve of his execution on 9 Thermidor.

Jean Patou, the couturier's, is on your right as you walk down the Rue St-Florentin to the Place de la Concorde.

To cross Paris and find your way in the Suburbs, use the map
Outskirts of Paris, No. 🔟🔟

Michelin plans ⅒ or ⑪ : from C 14 to D 12.

Distance : 5 km — 3 miles — Time : 4 hours. Start from the Place Clichy métro station.

" There is more of Montmartre in Paris, than of Paris in Montmartre " goes the saying.

The " Butte ", as it is known locally, is the part of Paris most full of contrasts — anonymous boulevards run close to delightful village streets and courts, steep stone steps lead to open terraces, Sacré-Cœur pilgrims tread the streets beside nightclub revellers.

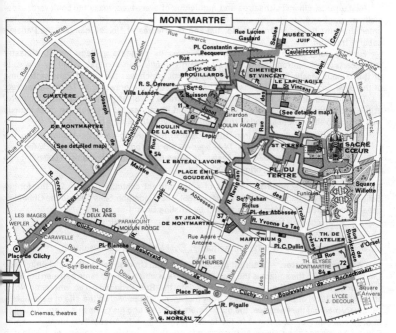

HISTORICAL NOTES

Martyrs' Mound. — Although it is known that the name Montmartre derives from the Mound of Mercury, a local legend dating from the 8C prefers ascription to the local martyrs, St. Denis or Dionysius, first Bishop of Paris, the priest, Rusticus, and the deacon, Eleutherius. These are said, in about 250 AD, to have been first tortured on the grill in the Cité and then decapitated, whereupon Denis picked up his blood covered head and walked north to the place now known as St-Denis *(p 168).*

A powerful abbey. — The Rue des Abbesses perpetuates the memory of the forty-three mother superiors of the Benedictine convent established on the hill in the 12C and used by the King of Navarre, the future Henri IV as his headquarters four centuries later when he laid siege to Paris in 1589. He failed to take the city before his next campaign, his only conquest it is said, being that of the 17 year old abbess, Claude de Beauvilliers.

In the reign of Louis XIV the " upper " convent and its chapel, St. Peter's, at the top of the hill, were abandoned in favour of the " lower " convent on the hillside below. 1794 saw the name of the hill changed, provisionally, to Mont-Marat, the last abbess guillotined and the convent buildings razed.

Shortly afterwards the gypsum quarries, whose miles of underground galleries threatened to undermine the hill, were abandoned and the thirty old flint and grain mills were also closed.

The early days of the Commune. — In 1871, after the fall of Paris, the people of Montmartre collected 171 cannon on the hill to prevent their capture by the Prussians. Forces sent by the government seized the cannon on 18 March but were unable to remove them, the generals being taken prisoner and shot by the crowd — a bloody episode which was to mark the beginning of the Commune. Montmartre remained under Federal control until 23 May.

Bohemian Life. — Throughout the 19C artists and men of letters were drawn to the free and easy, picturesque way of life as lived on the Butte. Berlioz, the writers and poets, Nerval, Murger and Heine, were the precursors of the great generation of 1871-1914; young painters sought inspiration on the Place Pigalle, artists' models and seamstresses led a free, Bohemian existence. The early poets' circles transformed themselves into café groups from which flowed songs (Aristide Bruant), poems, humour, drawings (Caran d'Ache, André Gill, Toulouse-Lautrec). Everyone went to the newly opened Moulin-Rouge (1889) to applaud the singers, clowns and dancers — Yvette Guilbert, Valentin le Désossé, Jane Avril, La Goulue.

The Butte, thanks to the Lapin Agile café and Bateau-Lavoir studios, remained, until 1914, the capital's literary and artistic centre, then inspiration moved to Montparnasse *(p 119)* and Montmartre abandoned itself to night life.

From the Place de Clichy to the Place du Tertre

Boulevard de Clichy. — The bustling Place de Clichy stands on the site of one of the city barriers built by Ledoux and valiantly defended against the Allied attack of 1814.

Walk along the Boulevard de Clichy, laid along the line of the Farmers General wall and now lined with cinemas and large popular restaurants with seafood as their speciality. On the Rue Caulaincourt corner stood the Gaumont-Palace, the largest auditorium in Paris, on the site of the former Hippodrome built at the time of the World Exhibition of 1900 to seat 8 000.

Restaurants, cinemas, theatres and nightclubs of every type, make the boulevard, especially at night and on Sunday afternoons, the centre of *la vie parisienne* and cosmopolitan entertainment; the Deux-Anes at No. 100 and Dix-Heures at No. 36 maintain the Parisian cabaret tradition.

Further along is the **Place Blanche,** which owes its name to spillage from the plaster laden carts crossing from the quarries beneath the hill. It is dominated still by the sails of the famous **Moulin-Rouge,** the French music-hall, which was the cult of Paris at the time of the *Belle Époque* and which has been immortalized in the drawings of Toulouse-Lautrec.

The next square, the **Place Pigalle** and the streets of pleasure leading from it, were, at the end of the 19C, lined by artists' studios and literary cafés, of which the most famous was the Nouvelle Athènes. Today the quarter is brilliantly lit and populous.

> The Rue Pigalle leads from the square to the Rue de La Rochefoucauld and the **Gustave Moreau Museum** *(No. 14 — open 10 am to 1 pm and 2 to 3 pm; closed Mondays, Tuesdays, August, 1 January, Easter, 25 December; 5F)* which contains 11 000 paintings and drawings by this original 19C artist.

Boulevard de Rochechouart. — Places of entertainment continue : at No. 118 the former Belle-en-Cuisses cabaret. It was at No. 84, in 1881, that Rodolphe Salis opened the Chat-Noir cabaret night-club made famous in a song by Aristide Bruant :

Je cherche fortune	Au clair de la lune
Autour du Chat Noir	A Montmartre le soir.

Belle Époque façade (No. 72) on the former Élysée-Montmartre music-hall.

The Abbesses' Quarter. — Walk left up Steinkerque and Orsel streets to the quiet little Place Charles-Dullin. On the square is the small **Atelier Theatre** which grew to fame between the wars.

Bear left from the Rue des Trois-Frères into the Rue Yvonne-Le-Tac where, at No. 9, stands the Chapel of the Auxiliatrices Order *(not open to the public)* on the site of a mediaeval sanctuary marking the **Martyrium,** the place where St. Denis and his companions are presumed to have been decapitated. It was in the former crypt that on 15 August 1534 Ignatius Loyola, Francis Xavier and their six companions made apostolic vows in the service of the Church from which was born the Society of Jesus. Six years later the order was recognized by Pope Paul III.

Continue to the Place des Abbesses. On the right is Jehan-Rictus Square, on the site of the former town hall of Montmartre where Verlaine was married in 1870. Opposite is the **Church of St. John of Montmartre,** designed by Baudot and the first to be built of reinforced concrete. The building is still interesting in the bold use made of its structural material, the slenderness of its pillars and beams, particularly as it was completed as long ago as 1904. The church's rose facing has earned it the local nickname of the Brick St. John.

Take a look at the colourful market of open fronted shops and costermongers' barrows in the Rue des Abbesses.

On the right the Rue Ravignan scales the " Butte ".

The Bateau-Lavoir. — This world renown artistic and literary Mecca, which disappeared in a fire in 1970 — just as it was to be preserved, preceded, in the evolution of art, the no less outstanding Ruche of Montparnasse *(p 119).* Located at No. 13 in the delightful **Place Émile-Goudeau★** this small wooden building saw the birth in 1900 of modern painting and modern French poetry. It was here that Picasso, Van Dongen, Braque, and Juan Gris, freed colour and created cubism — with Picasso's famous *Demoiselles d'Avignon* — and Max Jacob, Apollinaire and Mac Orlan broke away from traditional poetic form and expression.

A few old streets★. — The Rue Ravignan ends at the Place J.-B.-Clément (at the end of the street, on the left is a former water tower) which you cross to take the Rue Norvins on the right. The **crossroads★** formed by the meeting of the Rue Norvins, the Rue des Saules and the Rue St-Rustique will be known to many visitors from Utrillo's paintings. Even today it is typical of the old Montmartre.

Nearby, in the Rue Poulbot on the right, is the **Historial,** or waxworks museum where fourteen dioramas pinpoint the greatest events in Montmartre's history *(guided tours, 10 to 11.30 am and 2 to 5.30 pm; closed 1 January and 25 December; 7F).*

The minute Place du Calvaire commands an exceptional view of Paris.

Other Michelin Green Guides available in English

- Brittany
- Châteaux of the Loire
- Dordogne
- French Riviera
- Normandy

- Austria
- Germany
- Italy
- London

- New York City
- Portugal
- Spain
- Switzerland

Place du Tertre**. — This longstanding meeting place has an almost village atmosphere at times, particularly in the morning. At night, however, it is transformed into the tourist centre of Montmartre as crowds wander under the flaring lights, pause before the café-cabarets (La Mère Catherine, Le Clairon des Chasseurs), glance at the paintings of unknown artists.

No. 21 is the house of the Free Commune founded in 1920 by Jules Dépaquit to keep alive the imaginative and humorous traditions of

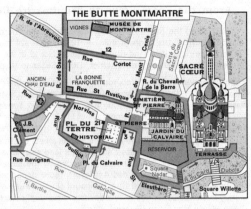

the Butte. No. 3, once the local town hall, is now Poulbot House where children from surrounding streets, popularized in the artist's delightful line drawings (1879-1946 — *illustration p 24*), foregather on Sunday mornings.

■ ST. PETER'S CHURCH★   ⑩ or ⑪ : C 14, D 14

The church, the Église St-Pierre, only remaining building of the great Abbey of Montmartre and, after St-Germain-des-Prés and St-Martin-des-Champs, one of the oldest churches in the capital, was begun on the site of an earlier basilica to St. Denis in 1134 and completed before the end of the century. The nave vaulting was reconstructed in the 15C; the banal west façade in the 18C.

Interior. — Four marble columns with capitals said to have come from a Roman temple which crowned the mound, have been placed in pairs, against the inside of the façade in line with the columns of the nave, and in the chancel, where the oldest ogive arches in Paris (1147), their torri very roughly hewn, meet above the single bay. In the north aisle is the tombstone of Queen Adélaïde of Savoy, wife of Louis VI the Big, who spent her last days in the abbey which she had founded in 1133.

The Romanesque style capitals are worn originals or replacements. The apse and aisles are lit by modern stained glass designed by Max Ingrand (1953).

The Calvary Garden. — *Restoration and excavations in progress. Not open to the public.*

The garden is on the site of the old Benedictine abbey and cloister; the Calvary dates only from 1802. In 1794 the Convention used the church apse as a suitable site for the new invention by the engineer, Chappe, of a telegraph station linking Paris and Lille. The simple grace of St. Peter's belfry contrasts sharply with the rounded mass of the Sacré-Cœur.

St. Peter's Cemetery. — North of the church lies the very old and minute church cemetery *(open only 1 November)* in which are buried the explorer, Bougainville, the sculptor, Pigalle, the brothers Debray, original owners of the Moulin de la Galette and Montmartre's first Mayor, Félix Desportes.

Bear left round the vast Montmartre reservoir towards the Sacré-Cœur terrace. This overlooks the Square Willette laid out in 1929 and approached by steps and slopes and also a funicular. The square commands, from its height of some 100 m — 350 ft — above the Seine, a magnificent **view**** of Paris *(viewing table)*.

■ THE SACRÉ-CŒUR BASILICA★★   ⑩ or ⑪ : C 14, D 14

Construction. — After the disastrous Franco-Prussian War of 1870, some Catholics vowed to raise money by public subscription to erect a church to the Sacred Heart on Montmartre hill. The proposal was declared a state undertaking by the National Assembly in 1873.

Abadie, who had become known for his restoration of St. Frontius' Church in Périgueux, recalled the old church's design as he drew Romano-Byzantine plans for the new basilica. It was begun in 1876 (Abadie died in 1884 when only the foundations had been laid and was thus succeeded by various architects), completed only in 1910 and not consecrated until 1919; it cost 40 million francs. For half a century worship has continued, without interruption, within its walls.

The Edifice. — The tall white outline is as much a part of the Paris skyline as the Eiffel Tower. The basilica's many cupolas are dominated by the dome and 80 m high campanile — 262 ft. The total effect is impressive even if the aesthetic appeal is arguable.

The interior, well adapted to the basilica's role as a pilgrim church, is decorated with mosaics. On the chancel vaulting Luc Olivier-Merson has evoked France's devotion to the Sacred Heart. The stained glass windows, shattered during 1944, have now been replaced.

Ascent of the dome *(access through the north aisle, 9 am to 6.30 pm from Palm Sunday to 30 September; 9.30 am to 5.30 pm the rest of the year; 3F)* affords a bird's-eye view of the church interior and, from the gallery outside on a clear day, a circular **panorama***** extending over 50 km — 30 miles. The crypt *(same access and times; 5F)*, with the same ground plan as the church, contains the treasure and an audio-visuel history of the basilica.

In the belfry hangs the Savoyarde, cast in 1895 at Annecy, given by the Savoy dioceses and, at 19 tons, one of the world's heaviest bells.

From the Sacré-Cœur to Montmartre Cemetery

Walk along the Rue du Chevalier-de-la-Barre. The narrow and often deserted, Rue St-Rustique marks Paris' highest point — 129.37 m — 424 ft.

Continue right, down the Rue des Saules. No. 12 in the Rue Cortot had as tenants, over the years Renoir, Othon Friesz, Utter, Dufy, Suzanne Valadon and her son, Utrillo.

Round the vineyard. — Walk round the famous Montmartre vineyard where at the beginning of October, the grape harvest is always a great and festive event. Beyond, the **Montmartre Museum** (17 Rue St-Vincent — open 2.30 (11.30 am on Sundays) to 5.30 pm; closed Tuesdays and holidays : 5F) is rich in mementoes of life in the quarter in its heyday and of Clemenceau, one time local mayor. The house itself was the country residence of the actor Rosimond.

The **crossroads*** where the Rue des Saules meets the Rue St-Vincent is one of the most delightful corners of the Butte : small steps lead away mysteriously, the road rises steeply beside the cemetery, a country air enhanced by the famous **Lapin Agile,** half hidden by an acacia. This former Cabaret des Assassins, rechristened when André Gill painted it a new sign, was, between 1908 and 1914, the haunt of writers and artists, who began the tradition of literary evenings continued to this day (every evening, except Mondays, at 9 pm) were Francis Carco, Pierre Mac Orlan, Picasso, Vlaminck...

Continue down the Rue St-Vincent on the left, where on the far side of the Place Constantin-Pecqueur you will find the Rue Lucien-Gaulard and, on the far right, the modest **St. Vincent cemetery** where the artist Steinlen, the musician Honegger, the painter Utrillo, the writer Marcel Aymé and many others lie buried.

Beyond the Rue Caulaincourt is a small **Museum of Jewish Art** (42 Rue des Saules; 3rd floor — open Tuesdays, Thursdays, Sundays, 3 to 6 pm; closed Jewish holidays; ☎ 257.84.15; 4F) including devotional objects, models of synagogues and works by Chagall and Pissarro.

The Château des Brouillards. — Walk up the steps from the Place Constantin-Pecqueur. On the left is the Rue de l'Abreuvoir, named after the water trough once used by the cattle which grazed the mound and still a peaceful thoroughfare. Turn right into the shaded alley skirting the **Château des Brouillards,** an 18C folly, later a dance hall. Its grounds, at the end of the Rue Simon-Dereure, have become the Square Suzanne-Buisson. The statue of St. Denis stands where he is said to have washed his decapitated head.

The Moulin de la Galette Quarter. — Work underway; to be finished June 1979.

Opened in 1910, **Avenue Junot** gave onto the Montmartre maquis where mills still turned their sails to the wind; amidst the artist's studios and private houses are at No. 11 the Hameau des Artistes, and at No. 25 the Villa Léandre. Walk back to No. 1 where the new entrance to the Tertre Theatre will be.

To the right of the crossroads with the Rue Giradon stood the former dance hall, the Moulin de la Galette which was the rage at the turn of the century and inspired many painters including Renoir, Van Gogh, Willette... The windmill which has topped the hall for more than six centuries, is the old Blute-fin (restauration in progress; closed) defended against the Cossacks in 1814 by the heroic Debray whose corpse was finally crucified upon the sails. On the terrace stands the 1736 Paris north bearing (p 123) : will be open after work is completed.

The Radet Mill (p 89) will return to its place, at the corner of Rue Lepic.

Walk down the steeply winding **Rue Lepic,** the old quarry road, and the scene each autumn of a veteran car rally (p 10). Van Gogh lived with his brother at No. 54.

Turn right into the Rue Joseph de Maistre; left into the Rue Caulaincourt; across the steel bridge (which spans the Montmartre Cemetery — 1795) down to the other side of the Rue Caulaincourt and the cemetery.

Montmartre Cemetery*. —
Access by the stairs on the left.

1) Lucien and Sacha Guitry (playwrights and actors).
2) Emile Zola (novelist).
3) Hector Berlioz (composer).
4) Greuze (painter).
5) Heinrich Heine (poet and writer).
6) Fragonard (painter).
7) Th. Gautier (poet and critic).
8) Alexandre Dumas the Younger (novelist).
9) Ernest Renan and Ary Scheffer (philosopher; painter).
10) Edgar Degas (p 42) (Impressionist painter).
11) Léo Delibes (composer).
12) J. Offenbach (composer).
13) Edmond and Jules de Goncourt (novelists).
14) Stendhal (H. Beyle) (novelist).
15) Alfred de Vigny (poet and dramatist).
16) Louis Jouvet (p 144) (actor).
17) Alphonsine Plessis, the Lady of the Camelias (p 73).

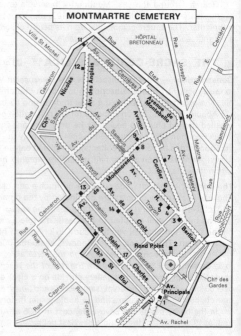

MONTMARTRE CEMETERY

Michelin plans 🔟 or 🔟 : H 16, H 17 — J 16, J 17.
Distance : 9 km — 6 miles — Time : one day — 4 separate walks or visit only the buildings drawn in perspective on the map (pp 80-81). Start from the St-Paul-le-Marais métro station.

The quarter, after general restoration, has an atmosphere all its own. The 16, 17 and 18C private town houses, in many cases of considerable size and beauty are often associated with the great families of France and notable events in her history. They are known as *Hôtels* — Hôtel Carnavalet, etc. — as are larger town houses throughout France.

A swamp. — It was in the 13C that the swamp lying on either side of the raised Rue St-Antoine, a highway since Roman times, was cleared. Philippe Auguste's wall and the Charles V wall ending in the powerful Bastille fortress in the east, brought the Marais within the city bounds — an event confirmed by the flight of several monarchs from the royal palace to the more powerful strongholds of the Hôtels St-Paul and des Tournelles.

A fashionable quarter. — By the beginning of the 17C the then Place Royale, now Place des Vosges, had become the focal point of the Marais. The Jesuits had settled along the Rue St-Antoine, the nobility and courtiers had built splendid houses off the main streets. It was at this time that the *Hôtel,* a discreet Classical building, standing between entrance court and garden, developed as a distinctive feature in French architecture and women of the world attracted free-thinkers and philosophers through their *salons* — the brilliant conversational groups who frequented their houses.

Then gradually the nobility began to move west, the quarter ceased to be fashionable and, after the taking of the Bastille, was virtually abandoned.

An architectural treasurehouse. — Inspite of the restoration of certain houses — the Hôtels Carnavalet, Sully — the disrepair of this area seemed almost impossible; it is only recently, under the 1962 Malraux Law that the 126 ha — 300 acre quarter has been restored and a living community created *(Festival in June).*

1 ST-PAUL QUARTER 🔟 or 🔟 : J 16

From the 14C the Rue St-Antoine, which was unusually wide, became the local meeting place and the setting for all popular celebrations including jousting — it was here that Henri II received the fatal blow to his eye in a tourney with his Scots captain of the guard, Montgomery. The king died in the Hôtel des Tournelles; Montgomery was executed (1574).

■ CHURCH OF ST-PAUL-ST-LOUIS★ 🔟 or 🔟 : J 16

In 1627 the Jesuits, on land donated by Louis XIII, added to their fifty year old monastery a church (completed in 1641) which they dedicated to St. Louis.

The tall classically ordered **façade** with superimposed columns hides the dome, the great novelty of the Jesuit style.

The **interior** has a single aisle and inter-communicating chapels, cradle vaulting and a cupola with a lantern above the transept crossing. Tall Corinthian pilasters line the walls. The twin stoups at the entrance were given by Victor Hugo. In the chapel to the left of the high altar there is a Mater Dolorosa in marble by the 16C, Germain Pilon.

From St-Paul-St-Louis to the Place des Vosges

Bear right into the Rue St-Paul.

Former Hôtel St-Paul. — The residence of Charles V in 1360 and, briefly of Charles VI, who made it a house of revelry.

Hôtel d'Aubray or **de la Brinvilliers.** — No. 12, Rue Charles-V has a fine wrought iron banister in the left wing. In the 17C it belonged to a notorious poisoner, the Marquise de Brinvilliers.

Hôtel Fieubet. — The house on the Square Henri-Galli *(p 61)* was built by Jules Hardouin-Mansart in 1680 for Marie-Thérèse's chancellor, Gaspard Fieubet.

Follow the route marked to return to the Rue St-Antoine, Glance, in passing, at the **Hôtel des Parlementaires de la Fronde,** which has been restored and converted into flats.

Hôtel de Béthune-Sully★. — *62 Rue St-Antoine.* The house was built in 1624 by Jean Androuet Du Cerceau and bought ten years later by Sully, former minister of Henri IV.

The main gate, between massive pavilions, has been restored and opens once more onto the inner **courtyard★★**, an outstanding Louis XIII architectural group with an ordered decoration of carved pediments and dormer windows and a series of figures representing the Elements and the Seasons. Inside *(guided tours Wednesdays, Saturdays and Sundays at 3 pm; 7F)* are fine 17C painted ceiling and panelling.

No. 21, Rue St-Antoine, the **Hôtel de Mayenne** or **Ormesson** (restored) is the same period.

St. Mary Temple. — *No. 17.* The chapel, now a Protestant church, was built in 1632 by François Mansart for the Convent of the Visitation. The dome above the rotunda nave is a compromise between the ultimate in Italian Baroque and French Classicism.

Walk past the statue of the 18C playwright Beaumarchais to the boulevard of the same name, where behind No. 21, stands the **Hôtel Mansart de Sagonne,** a beautiful colonnaded house at the far end of a garden. The house was built by Jules Hardouin-Mansart for himself and decorated by Mignard, Le Brun and Coypel. Turn left for the Place des Vosges.

■ THE PLACE DES VOSGES★★ 10 or 11 : J 17

This is Paris' oldest square.

The Hôtel des Tournelles. — The house, acquired by the crown in 1407 on the assassination of the Duke of Orleans, was where Louis XII ended his days and Henri II died, fatally wounded in a joust *(details p 79)*. His widow, Catherine dei Medici, who had come to hate it, had it pulled down.

The Place Royale. — In 1605 Henri IV determined to transform the Marais into a splendid quarter with a vast square (140 m — 459 ft — on its north-south side and 127 m — 348 ft — on its east-west side) at its centre in which all the houses would be " built to a like symmetry. " On its completion in 1612, the Royal Square became the centre of elegance, courtly parades and festivities and also, a duelling ground, despite Richelieu's interdict.

At the Revolution the square lost its central statue of Louis XIII (melted down but replaced in 1818) and named in 1793 after a political aim, Indivisibility and from 1800-1814 after the department which paid its taxes the most promptly, the Vosges; it was then renamed the Place Royale from 1815-1870 and since the Third Republic it has kept its present name — Place des Vosges.

The square today. — The 36 houses retain their original symmetrical appearance with arcades, two storeys with alternate stone and brick facings and steeply pitched slate roofs pierced by dormer windows. The **King's Pavilion** on the south side and the largest house in the square, is balanced by the Queen's Pavilion to the north and linked to the Rue St-Antoine by the Rue de Birague.

No. 9, the **Hôtel de Chaulnes** is the Academy of Architecture; No. 1 *bis* where Madame de Sévigné was born (1626); No. 17 where the preacher Bossuet lived; No. 21 where Richelieu lived (1615-1627) before moving to the Petit Luxembourg *(p 95)*.

No. 6, the former Hôtel de Rohan-Guéménée, now **Victor Hugo House★**, was the home of the poet from 1833 to 1848 : mementoes, MSS, furniture executed by the poet himself. *(Open 10 am to 5.40 pm; closed Mondays and holidays; 3F, free Sundays)*.

Return to the St-Louis Church by the Rue de Turenne (No. 23, the former **Hôtel Colbert de Villacerf**, *being restored*) and the Rue de Sévigné (No. 7, the **Hôtel Bouthillier de Chavigny**).

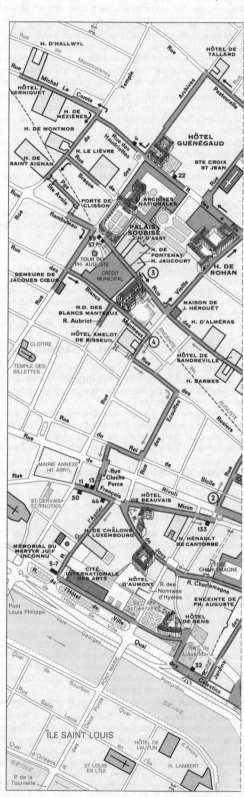

2 THE CARNAVALET QUARTER 📖 or 📖 : J 16, J 17

Turn right out of the Rue de Rivoli into the Rue Pavée (No. 10 with the curious interlaced façade is a synagogue). Near the juncture with the Rue Malher there stood, until 1848, a double prison : the Greater Force for men political prisoners, the Lesser Force for women. In September 1792, 171 prisoners were massacred inside its walls by the mob.

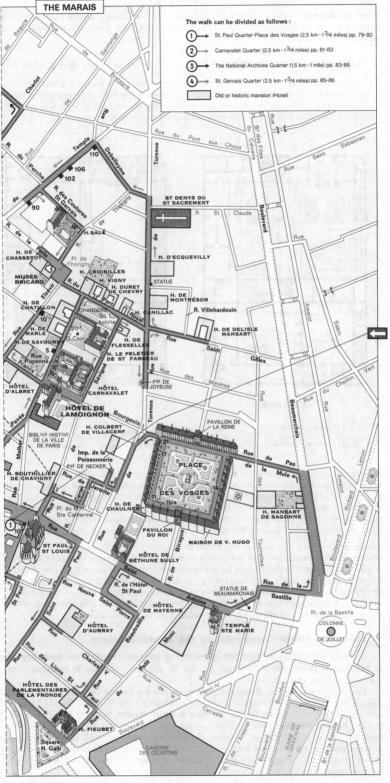

Hôtel de Lamoignon**. — *24 Rue Pavée*. The Hôtel d'Angoulême, built in about 1585 for Diane, the legitimized daughter of Henri II, was bought in 1658, by Lamoignon, president of the first parliament to sit in Paris. There he entertained Racine, Mme de Sévigné, the Jesuit preacher, Bourdaloue, and the poet and critic, Boileau. On the far side of the courtyard the majestic building is divided by six Corinthian pilasters which rise unbroken to the cornice — the first example in Paris of the Colossal Order. Two rudimentary wings are crowned with curved pediments adorned with attributes of the chase and crescent moons (allusions to the goddess Diana). An unusual square turret overlooks the street.

Historical Library of the City of Paris. — *Open 9.30 am to 6 pm; closed Sundays, holidays and 1st fortnight in August.* Founded in 1763 the library is rich in French Revolution documents. The **reading room*** is beautiful with its painted ceiling and 17C tapestry.

■ THE HOTEL CARNAVALET* *Entrance : 23 Rue de Sévigné* 🔟 or 🔟 : J 16, J 17

The mansion (1544), was given its Renaissance appearance by Mansart in 1655.

Marie de Rabutin, the Marquis de Sévigné, who wrote the famous *Letters* which, with a light touch and quick wit give a lucid picture of day to day events, lived in the house from 1677 to her death in 1696. The buildings surrounding the three garden courts are 19C.

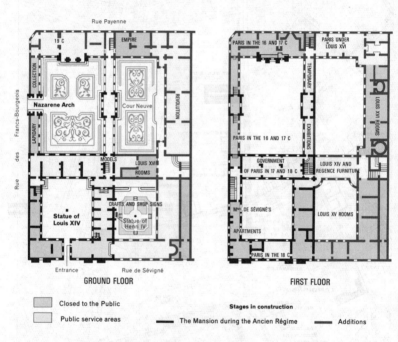

GROUND FLOOR	FIRST FLOOR

Closed to the Public
Public service areas

Stages in construction
━━━ The Mansion during the Ancien Régime   ━━━ Additions

Exterior. — Jean Goujon carved the lions at the main entrance which is 16C, and the keystone cornucopia in which the supporting globe was later recarved into a carnival mask in allusion to the mansion's name. The contemporary **statue*** of Louis XIV in the courtyard is by Coysevox ; the building at the end is Gothic; only the four statues of the Seasons are Renaissance. The large figures on the wings are 17C; the cherubs with torches decorating the end of the left wing are again by Jean Goujon. The Nazarene Arch *(Rue des Francs-Bourgeois)* is 16C.

Museum**. — *Open 10 am to 5.40 pm; closed Mondays; 5F, free on Sundays and holidays.* The museum is an extraordinary, well ordered conglomeration within a single house of mementos of the Marquise de Sévigné, George Sand and other writers, the history of Paris from Henri IV to the *Belle Époque* (early 20C), fascinating inn and shop signs and vivid souvenirs of the Revolution. On the first floor several rooms have been reconstituted with painted panelling and ceilings transferred from other houses in the Marais and Louis XIV and Régence Louis XV and XVI furniture and furnishings to look much as they did in their prime.

From the Hôtel Carnavalet to the Soubise Palace

On leaving the museum, walk left up the Rue de Sévigné — No. 29 is the **Hôtel Le Peletier de Saint-Fargeau,** now part of the museum. No. 52, opposite, the **Hôtel de Flesselles,** bears the name of Paris' last provost.

Turn right *(Rue du Parc-Royal)* and right again into the Rue de Turenne to see the 17C Joyeuse fountain by No. 41. Retrace your steps and continue north up the Rue de Turenne, past the Rue Saint-Gilles, by No. 22, the **Hôtel de Delisle-Mansart,** to No. 54 Rue de Turenne, the 17C **Hôtel de Montrésor** (now a school) — look up at the beautiful Virgin on the Rue Ville-hardouin corner. No. 60 Rue de Turenne, the **Hôtel d'Ecquevilly** generally known as the **Hôtel du Grand Veneur** or Master of the Royal Hunt House, has a fine façade decorated with emblems of the chase and a magnificent **grand staircase*** adorned with huntsman's weapons and trophies *(to visit apply to the caretaker).*

Church of St-Denys-du-St-Sacrement. — The church, built in the form of a Roman basilica at the time of the Restoration, contains a remarkable Delacroix **Deposition*** (1844) — at the back of the chapel to the right of the entrance *(electric hand-switch)*.

On the Rue Vieille-du-Temple are early 17C houses (Nos. 110, 106, 102). No. 90 was the Marais Theatre, where in 1636 *The Cid* by Corneille was presented. Turn back into the Rue des Coutures-St-Gervais before passing the rear façade of the Hôtel Salé.

Hôtel Salé (or **Hôtel Aubert-de-Fontenay** or **Hôtel de Juigné**). — *5 Rue de Thorigny*. The house was built in 1656 for a salt tax collector, hence the malicious name given it by Parisians, Hôtel Salé or Salted. It is now closed and a Picasso Museum will be installed after restauration of the house.

Hôtel Libéral-Bruand. — *1 Rue de la Perle*. Built in 1685 by the architect of the Invalides for himself *(to see the courtyard, ask the caretaker)* and later bought by the Bricards, this elegant mansion now houses a **Lock and Metalwork Museum** known also as the **Bricard Museum*** *(open 10 am to noon and 2 to 5 pm; closed Mondays, Tuesdays, holidays and August. 5F)*. In five well lit rooms the art of the lock is followed from the Roman era to the Empire; 20C ironwork is also on display. The Bricard workshops, which still produce art metalwork, can also be seen.

Nos. 3 and 5 is the **Hôtel de Chassepot** *(being restored)*.

Rue du Parc-Royal. — The street, consisting of 17C houses overlooking the Léopold-Achille Square, retains definite character in spite of considerable disfiguring. No. 12 is the **Hôtel Croisilles,** No. 10 **Vigny,** No. 8 **Duret-de-Chevry,** No. 4, **Canillac.**

Rue Payenne. — Turn right, down the Rue Payenne, where on your left is the Square Georges-Cain, a stone garden lined on two sides by the elegant orangery and façade of the Hôtel Saint-Fargeau. Opposite, the **Hôtel de Chatillon** (No. 13), has a paved courtyard and an interesting staircase, and the **Hôtel de Marle** or **de Polastron-Polignac** next door (No. 11), a fine mask above the entrance and a wagon roof attributed to Philibert Delorme. The house is a Swedish cultural centre.

It was at No. 5 that Mansart and Clotilde de Vaux, inspiration of the 19C positivist philosopher, Auguste Comte, died. Followers of Comte's doctrine " Love is a first principle, Order is the basis of method and Progress life's objective " met in their unusual Chapel of Humanity.

Turn right into the **Rue des Francs-Bourgeois.** This old street was originally known as Pulley Street after the pulleys on the looms in the local weavers' shops. It took its present name in 1334 when almshouses were built in it for the poor who were known as " the men who pay no tax " or *francs bourgeois*.

Hôtel d'Albret. — *No. 31*. The house, built in the 16C for the Duke of Montmorency, Constable of France, was remodelled in the 17C. It was in this house that the widow of the playwright Scarron, the future Marquise de Maintenon, became acquainted with Mme de Montespan. Appointed in 1669 governess to the latter's children by Louis XIV, she subsequently herself became the king's mistress. The façade was interestingly reordered in the 18C.

Turn right into the Rue Elzévir. The **Hôtel de Savourny** is at No. 4. Glance at the noble rear façade of the Hôtel de Marle as you reach No. 10.

Return again to the Rue des Francs-Bourgeois. No. 35, the **Hôtel Barbes** and No. 26, the **Hôtel de Sandreville,** were both built around 1630 while the **Hôtel d'Alméras** at No. 30 dates from 1598. It has a curious rams' head gateway.

On the corner of the Rue Vieille-du-Temple, at No. 54, stands the **House of Jean Hérouet*,** treasurer to Louis XII. Built in about 1510, it still has early mullioned windows and an elegant corbelled turret. Nearby, stood in the 15C the **Hôtel Barbette,** the discreet residence of Queen Isabela of Bavaria who began the fashion for masked balls, at the time the King, Charles VI, was living at Hôtel St-Paul. She described the plight of her husband, who was subject to fits of madness, and her own situation with cynicism : " The King embarrasses me when he is mad and infinitely more when he is not ". Continue along the Rue des Francs-Bourgeois.

Walk past the Crédit Municipal bank, a former pawnbroker's, and you will see on the left, at No. 57 *bis* one of the towers of Philippe Auguste's 800 years old perimeter wall. At No. 59, against the wall is a fragment of the façade of a 1638 *Hôtel*.

3   THE NATIONAL ARCHIVES   ▯▯ or ▯▯ : H 16

The extensive National Archives of France are kept in the Soubise Palace and the Hôtel de Rohan. The beauty of the buildings, their pure Louis XV style decoration and the documents themselves make a visit worthwhile on several counts.

The Clisson Manorhouse. — In about 1375 the Constable of France, Olivier de Clisson, companion in arms of Du Guesclin, began to build a manorhouse on the site of the present buildings. Only the **entrance*** remains, flanked by a pair of corbelled turrets *(58 Rue des Archives)*.

In 1553 the manor passed to the Guise family who made it their headquarters, during the Wars of Religion. The massacre of St. Bartholomew (1572) was planned here.

Soubise Palace. — In 1700 Madame de Soubise, the wife of François de Rohan, Prince of Soubise, acquired the house thanks to generous gifts from Louis XIV. Most unusually for the time, plans were entrusted to an unknown architect, Delamair, who incorporated the Clisson gateway into the new house. Simultaneously the architect was occupied with building a second house for another member of the Rohan family, the Cardinal Bishop of Strasbourg. The outstanding decoration inside the Soubise Palace is due to Boffrand, a pupil of Mansart.

The Archives. — The National Archives established under the National Assembly in 1789 have been housed in the Soubise Palace since 1808 where the 6 000 million government and legal papers and personal archives occupy nearly 280 km — 175 miles of shelving. The Hôte de Rohan, converted into the imperial printing house under Napoleon, was taken over as an annexe in 1927. Other annexes are to be found Rue des Francs-Bourgeois, No. 58 is the **Hôtel d'Assy**, No. 56 **de Fontenay** and No. 54 **Jaucourt.**

■ SOUBISE PALACE★★ *(60 Rue des Francs-Bourgeois)* ▯▯ or ▯▯ : H 16

The main building, the former Guise mansion, stands behind the façade built by Delamair in 1705. It overlooks an elegantly majestic **courtyard★★** created on the site of a former riding school, hence its plan. The statues of the Seasons on the façade (copies), the reclining figures of Glory and Magnificence on the pediment, and the groups of children, are all by Robert Le Lorrain.

The apartments★★. — The most gifted painters (Boucher, Natoire, Van Loo) and sculptors of the period (1735-1740) worked with exquisite fantasy in decorating in the Rococo style the woodwork, panelling and high reliefs of the magnificent apartments on the ground floor of the Prince of Soubise *(same times and ticket as for the Hôtel de Rohan)* and on the first floor of the Princess.

Historical Museum of France★★. — *Open 2 to 5 pm except Tuesdays and holidays; 2F. Temporary exhibitions are frequent.* Among the great historical documents on display are the Edict of Nantes (1598) and its Revocation (1685), the Concordat of 1802 between Napoleon and the Holy See and, among the domestic documents, the acts of foundation of the Sainte-Chapelle and the Sorbonne, a model of the Bastille and Napoleon's testament.

■ HÔTEL DE ROHAN★★ *(87 Rue Vieille-du-Temple)* ▯▯ or ▯▯ : H 16

Guided tours : Mondays, Wednesdays, Thursdays and Fridays at 3.30 pm; 2F (ticket also for Soubise Palace apartments).

The house's official name, Hôtel de Strasbourg, can still be seen above the entrance.

The main façade overlooks the garden, which the mansion has in common with the palace. The courtyard, less in size than that of the palace, has stables on its right hand side crowned by the wonderful **Horses of the Sun★★** by Robert Le Lorrain.

A staircase leads to the **cardinals' apartments★★** *(temporary exhibitions).* Among the first salons, decorated with Aubusson tapestries (after cartoons attributed to Boucher), are the sumptuous Gold Salon and the amusing small Monkey Room with animal decorations by Christophe Huet.

The smaller rooms, such as the Fable Room, are delightfully furnished.

The National Archives Quarter

Walk left along the Rue Vieille-du-Temple on leaving the Hôtel de Rohan. Bear left again into the Rue des Quatre-Fils and then right into the Rue Charlot.

Ste-Croix-St-Jean Church. — *Open 9 am to noon, in the afternoon apply at 6 ter Rue Charlot or 13 Rue du Perche.* This much restored church was erected in 1624 as a Capuchin monastery chapel and was attended by Mme de Sévigné when she lived in the Rue de Thorigny. The chancel is rich with 18C gilded panelling from the former Billettes Church; to the left stands a remarkable **statue★** of St. Francis of Assisi by Germain Pilon (16C), and to the right St. Denis by the Marty brothers (17C). The ecclesiastical ornaments worn by Abbot Edgeworth de Firmont when celebrating mass before Louis XVI in the Temple on the morning of his execution *(p 148)* are displayed in the sacristy.

Turn left beyond the church into the Rue Pastourelle. At the corner of the Rue des Archives, at No. 78, the **Hôtel de Tallard** will recover after restoration the Classical aspect given it by Bullet and its medallions. Continue left down the Rue des Archives.

Hôtel Guénégaud★★. — *No. 60.* The house, built between 1648 and 1651 by Mansart was minimally remodelled in the 18C. Note the plain harmonious lines, the courtyard ornamented with six bronze stags' heads, the noble staircase and the small formal garden.

The **Museum of the Chase★★** *(open 10 am to 6 pm, 1 April to 30 September — 5 pm from the rest of the year; closed Tuesdays and holidays; 6F)* displays arms froms prehistory to the 19C *(1st floor)* and trophies and souvenirs from M. Sommer's (who restored the *Hôtel*) own big game expeditions *(2nd floor).* On the stairs and in the red, blue and green salons are pictures by the animal painters, Desportes, Oudry and Carle Vernet. Walk left in the Rue des Quatre-Fils to see the garden and rear façade. No. 22 was where in the 18C Mme du Deffand for many years held a famous *salon.* Retrace your steps and continue along the Rue des Haudriettes (look at the monumental fountain, dating from 1705, at the corner) and the Rue Michel-le-Comte to No. 19, all that remains of the **Hôtel de Mézières,** No. 21, the **Hôtel Verniquet** — named after the geometrician who at the end of the 18C completed one of the first detailed maps of Paris *(p 97)* and No. 28, the **Hôtel d'Hallwyl,** *(being restored),* built by Ledoux, architect to Louis XVI, where Mme de Staël was born in 1766.

Return to the Rue du Temple and turn right.

Hôtel de Montmor. — *No. 79.* The house, erected in the reign of Louis XIII for his treasurer Montmor, known as Montmor the Rich, was remodelled in the 18C. Montmor's son invited the great physicians and doctors of the day to join the Abbot Gassendi; these meetings anticipated the founding of the Academy of Science (1666).

The façade, pierced by tall windows overlooking the first court, is adorned with a balcony surmounted by a carved pediment. A vaulted passage to one side led to the garden at the back. The stair ramp is a remarkable piece of wrought ironwork. In the Rue de Braque examine the **Hôtel Le Lièvre** (Nos. 4 and 6) built in 1663 and possessing twin doorways and balconies and, at No. 4, a formal grand staircase.

Return to the Rue du Temple.

Hôtel de Saint-Aignan. — *No. 71.* The house, built in 1650 by Le Muet, was acquired in 1680 by the Duke of Saint-Aignan, Colbert's son-in-law and joint tutor with Fénelon, of Louis XIV's three grandsons. A monumental gateway decorated with fantastic masks precedes the courtyard which is overlooked by the main, colossally ordered façade. The left side of the courtyard, in fact, is a facing applied by Le Muet to the Philippe Auguste wall to achieve a uniform effect. The stables have attractive pointed vaulting.

Walk down the 19C Passage Ste-Avoie turn left into the Rue Rambuteau. Bear right at the crossroads, down the Rue des Archives. No. 4 was **Jacques Cœur's house,** Chancellor of the Exchequer to Charles VII. Walk back to the Rue des Blancs-Manteaux on the right, and into the Rue Aubriot *(p 133).*

Church of Notre-Dame-des-Blancs-Manteaux. — The Crédit Municipal bank stands on the site of a monastery founded by St. Louis in 1258 for the mendicant order of the Serfs of the Virgin whose members wore white cloaks *(blancs manteaux).* In 1695 the Benedictines of St. William, the Guillemites, who had replaced the earlier order at the end of the 13C, rebuilt the old monastery chapel. At the time of the Second Empire, Baltard, architect of the Halles, took the 18C façade of the Church of St-Eloi, when this was removed from the Cité and applied it to Notre-Dame-des-Blancs-Manteaux.

The interior has a remarkable collection of woodwork — an inner door, organ loft, communion table — and a magnificent Flemish **pulpit★** in which marquetry panels are inlaid with ivory and pewter and framed in gilded and fretted woodwork in the Rococo style of 1749.

Continue left to the Rue Vieille-du-Temple.

4   THE ST-GERVAIS QUARTER   🔟 or 🔟 : J 15, J 16

Hôtel Amelot de Bisseuil★ (or **Hôtel des Ambassadeurs de Hollande).** — *47 Rue Vieille-du-Temple.* The present mansion replaced an earlier building in 1655, the mediaeval residence of the Marshals of Rieux, companions in arms of Du Guesclin and Joan of Arc.

The 17C house, which has been remodelled at various periods, was at one time let to the Dutch ambassador's chaplain, hence its name. By 1776 the house, by now the home of the playwright, Beaumarchais, who had completed *The Barber of Seville* and was at work on *The Marriage of Figaro,* had become a gathering point for arms awaiting dispatch to the American rebels.

The **gateway★,** decorated with masks and allegories, is one of the Marais' most outstanding. *(Ring to see the courtyard — the house is not open to the public.)* The house and wings on either side are ornamented with sculptured motifs and four monochrome sundials. Low reliefs and paintings, dating form the 17C, have been recovered inside.

Hôtel des Ambassadeurs de Hollande
Detail of the gate

Jewish Quarter. — Turn left in the Rue des Rosiers and right in the Rue des Écouffes. The two streets are typical of the Jewish quarter which has grown up in Paris' 4th *arrondissement;* ritual objects, kosher meat and oriental specialities can be seen in shops with Hebrew painted fascias.

Bear right into the Rue du Roi-de-Sicile, which cuts through what was once the domain of Charles of Anjou, brother of St. Louis, King of Naples and Sicily (1266-1285).

Turn left into what is now the Rue Cloche-Perce and in the 13C and later centuries was known as the Rue de la Grosse-Margot.

It was in this same street now cut by the Rue de Rivoli and two series of steps that the poet François Villon, and his companions in the 15C led a debauched life.

Rue François-Miron. — This road, once a highway across the marshes, still bears the name of a local magistrate of the time of Henri IV. In the Middle Ages it began on the low St-Gervais hill *(p 114)* and was bordered by the town houses of several abbots of the Ile-de-France : the half-timbered and much restored Nos. 11 and 13 date back to the reign of Louis XI in the 15C; the beautiful Marie Touchet, mistress of Charles IX, is said to have lived at No. 30 where a minute Renaissance courtyard can still be seen beyond the entrance passageway.

The modern history of the Hôtel de Vigny *(p 83)* symbolizes, to a great degree, that of the Marais today. In 1961, when scheduled for demolition, the house was found to contain a good 17C painted ceiling, saved and restored by a group of young Parisians who had already drawn attention to the possibility of there being other undiscovered treasures in the quarter. The first festival and the Malraux Law of 1962 set in motion the greatest urban restoration programme ever undertaken in France. The group meanwhile, working below Nos. 44-46 Rue François-Miron have uncovered outstanding Gothic *cellars★ (under restoration)* which once belonged to the Paris house of Ourscamp Abbey on the Oise. *To visit apply to the Association pour la Sauvegarde et la mise en valeur du Paris historique, Hôtel de Beauvais (68 Rue François-Miron; ☎ 887-79-31; 2 to 6 pm; closed Sundays and Mondays).*

Turn down the Rue Geoffroy-l'Asnier towards the Seine. No. 26, the **Hôtel de Châlons-Luxembourg**, built in 1610 has a carved main gate and an interesting brick and stone façade. Opposite, at No. 17, is the **Memorial to the Unknown Jew** with an undying flame to the Jewish victims of National Socialism in the crypt and above a museum of the Jewish struggle against Hitlerism *(open 10 am to noon and 2 to 5 pm except Saturdays; 2F)*.

Turn left, before reaching the river, into the Rue de l'Hôtel-de-Ville, where on your left is the long modern façade of the **International City of the Arts** (1965), which provides studios and lodging for a year to French and foreign painters, composers and sculptors.

The fine rear façade of the Hôtel d'Aumont *(see details below)* is on your left.

Cross the Rue des Nonnains-d'Hyères, and walk past a small garden towards the massive walls and mullion windows of the Hôtel de Sens.

■ HOTEL DE SENS★ ▥ or ▦ : J 16

The Hôtel de Sens, the Hôtel de cluny and Jacques Cœur's house are the only great mediaeval private residences to remain in Paris.

The first was constructed between 1475 and 1507 as a residence for the archbishops of Sens of which Paris was a dependence until 1622. During the period of the Catholic League in the 16C it became a centre of intrigue with frequent visits by Louis I of Guise, Cardinal of Lorraine. In 1594 Monsignor de Pellevé died of apoplexy within its walls while a *Te Deum* was being sung in Notre-Dame to celebrate Henri IV's entry into Paris. In 1605 Queen Margot, Henri IV's first wife, came to live in the mansion after long exile in the Auvergne.

In 1760 the house was occupied by the office of the Lyons stage coach which made a journey reputed to be so unsafe that passengers used to make their wills before setting out. In 1911 the City of Paris bought the residence and undertook the considerable restoration required.

The mansion. — *Illustration p 22.* The old houses which originally surrounded the mansion have been cleared away so that it now stands apart. Its façade is ornamented with corner turrets and a tall dormer window with a stone finial. A large and a small door each with basket handle vaulting are surmounted by pointed arches. Walk through the Flamboyant porch into the courtyard, where you will see a square tower, cut by a machicolated balcony and enclosing a spiral staircase. Turrets and beautiful dormer windows again adorn the façades.

The **Forney Library** *(open Tuesdays through Fridays 1.30 to 8.30 pm; Saturdays 10 am to 8.30 pm; closed Sundays, Mondays and holidays)* includes decorative and fine arts and industrial techniques.

From the Hôtel de Sens to the Rue St-Antoine

Quai des Célestins. — Walk down to the embankment from which there are excellent **views★** of the Ile St-Louis and the Pont Marie. No. 32 stands on the site of the **Barbeau Tower** which marked the beginning of the Philippe Auguste perimeter wall on the Right Bank. The tower was first replaced by an indoor tennis court which, in 1645, was taken over briefly by Molière and the Illustrious Theatre *(p 137)* before he left for the provinces.

The Philippe Auguste Wall. — Turn left up the Rue des Jardins-St-Paul, which once skirted the city wall of which a long section, complete with crenelated ramparts and intersected by two towers, can still be seen. The length which formed part of the perimeter between the Barbeau Tower and the St-Paul Postern is the largest fragment still in existence.

Rabelais died, in this street, in 1553. At the end can be seen the Jesuit style east end and dome of St-Paul-St-Louis Church.

Walk left long the Rue Charlemagne and the Rue de Jouy.

Hôtel d'Aumont. — *7 Rue de Jouy.* At the beginning of the 17C Le Vau built a house on this site for Michel-Antoine Scarron, uncle of the burlesque poet and father-in-law of the Marshal Duke of Aumont, Governor of Paris at Louis XIV's succession. The house was remodelled and enlarged by François Mansart and decorated by Le Brun and Simon Vouet; the formal garden was probably designed by Le Nôtre. The façades and inner court are almost severe in line.

During the 19C the mansion suffered considerable damage but it has now been restored by the City of Paris to serve as the Paris administrative court.

Turn right at the end of the street into the Rue François-Miron.

Hôtel de Beauvais★. — *No. 68.* In the 13C the Abbot of Châalis had his town house on this site. Below were mediaeval **cellars★** *(to visit apply to the Association pour la Sauvegarde et la mise en valeur du Paris historique — details p 85)* with pointed vaulting which have been excavated.

In 1654 Catherine Bellier, known as One-Eyed Kate, first woman of the bedchamber to Anne of Austria and forty years old, displayed such personal gallantry to the sixteen years old Louis XIV that she won a fortune in favours. In addition, for her services, her husband, Pierre Beauvais, and she were enobled and granted the site of the former town house of the abbots of Châalis. They commissioned the architect, Lepautre to build them a sumptuous mansion which he did even purloining stone from the Louvre to do so. When Mozart came to Paris at the age of seven in 1763, accompanied by his father and sister, he stayed in this house. The façade has lost its exterior decoration. The covered entrance, where stone guards still protect the walls, extends to a vestibule where Doric columns support a cupola. Beyond is a courtyard of uneven triangular shape with a rams' head decoration — Kate's canting arms! The stairway on the left has a carved stone banister, a rare ornament in the Marais.

No. 82, the **Hôtel Hénault-de-Cantorbe** has attractive balconies and a pleasant inner courtyard. The house, where Voltaire's sister Mme de Dompierre lived, stands at No. 133 Rue St-Antoine. Note the balcony supported by two winged dragons.

THE PALAIS-ROYAL - AVENUE DE L'ÔPÉRA ★★

Michelin plans 10 or 11 : G 12, G 13 - H 13.
Distance : 3 km — 2 miles — Time : 3 hours. Start from the Palais-Royal métro station.

In this part of Paris the Palais-Royal, the Bibliothèque Nationale and St-Roch Church remind one vividly of the city's past in contrast to the Avenue de l'Opéra and the Rue de Rivoli which seem to epitomize the present. To the right of the métro station is the **Louvre des Antiquaires** *(open Tuesdays to Saturdays 11 am to 7 pm)* a building containing 240 antique shops.

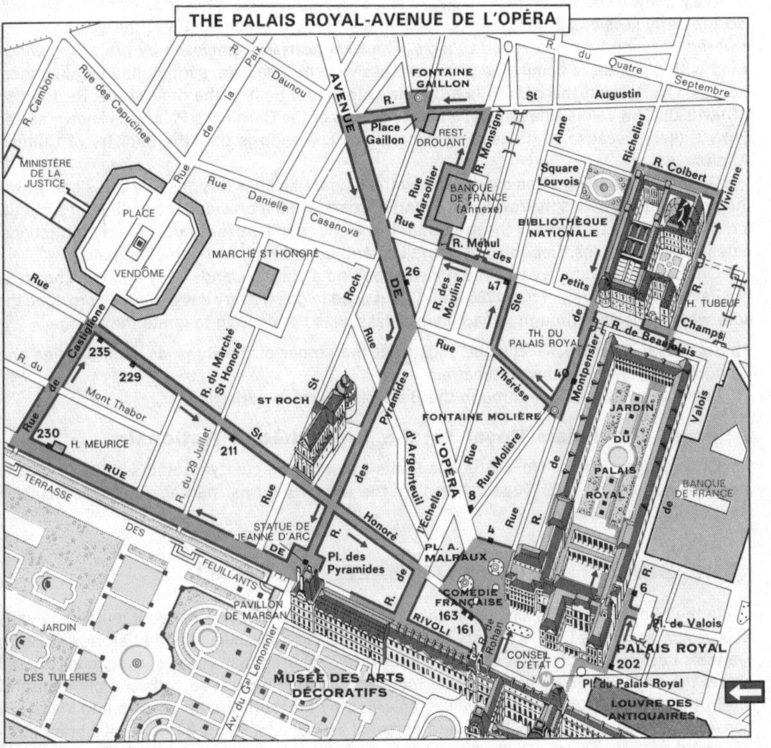

THE PALAIS-ROYAL★★ 10 or 11 : H 13

The façades of Richelieu's palace, now the office of the Council of State can be seen though not entered. The quiet garden has retained its 18C atmosphere.

The Cardinal's Palace. — In 1624, Richelieu, who had just become prime minister, acquired a mansion near the Louvre with grounds extending to the Charles V perimeter wall. In 1632 he commissioned Le Mercier to build the huge edifice which became known as the Cardinal's Palace.

The Royal Palace. — The Cardinal on his deathbed in 1642 left his mansion to Louis XIII who soon followed him to the grave. His widow, Anne of Austria, with her son, the young Louis XIV, then quit the vast discomforts of the Louvre for the smaller and more beautiful mansion which henceforth became known as the Royal Palace. The Fronde in 1648 forced their hasty departure. When Louis XIV returned to Paris he went to live in the Louvre and lodged Queen Henrietta Maria, widow of Charles I of England, and then her daughter, Henrietta in the palace.

The Orleans. — After a lightning illness had carried off Henrietta, the palace was given in apanage to her husband Philippe of Orleans, brother of Louis XIV and subsequently to his son, appointed Regent during the minority of Louis XV. Philippe II of Orleans was highly gifted and also highly dissolute — palace suppers at that period were notorious.

In 1780 the palace passed to Louis-Philippe of Orleans, who being short of money, undertook the construction round three sides of the garden, of apartment houses with ground level shopping arcades and uniform façades. The three new streets skirting the frontages were called after the younger Orleans brothers : Valois, Montpensier and Beaujolais. The palace precinct became the favourite idling place for Parisians. Between 1786 and 1790 the same architect, Louis, was commissioned by Philippe-Égalité to build the Théâtre-Français, now the Comédie-Française *(p 91)*, and the Théâtre du Palais-Royal.

Decline. — During the Revolution, the garden became virtually an open air club and the palace a bawdy house and gambling centre until, in 1801, Napoleon converted it to commercial use. Louis XVIII returned the mansion to the Orleans and it was from there that Louis-Philippe set out for the Hôtel de Ville, in 1830, to be proclaimed king. The July Monarchy closed the gaming houses (1838) and the popularity of the arcade shops began to decline.

The Commune set it on fire in 1871 and although it has been restored (1872-1876), the garden and surrounding antique and book shops are now, for the most part, very quiet.

THE PALACE AND THE GARDEN

The palace façade overlooking the square consists of a central building and two receding wings decorated with 18C carvings of military trophies and allegorical figures.

The east wing now stands on the site of the theatre Richelieu had built and in which Molière created his major plays between 1661 and 1673 (when he collapsed on stage while acting out *Le Malade Imaginaire : p 90*). It later became an opera house, where Lulli's works continued to be performed until it was burnt down in 1763.

Walk a few steps up the Rue Valois. At No. 6 (beautiful balcony) in 1638 Richelieu conducted the early sessions of his new foundation, the French Academy. Enter the palace by the covered passage from the Rue de Valois. The **main courtyard***, enclosed by projecting wings lined with galleries, is dominated by an impressive central façade, surmounted by allegorical statues. Overlooking the garden is a double colonnade, built at the time of the Restoration (1814-1830). The Valois side gallery, all that remains of the Cardinal's Palace, is known as the Prow Gallery because of its nautical decoration. The wing is now the Ministry of Cultural Affairs.

Go through to the garden overlooked by the elegant façades designed by Louis and where the present quiet belies the rowdyism of earlier years when it provided the setting for a circus, a riding school, a ballroom, a theatre—until this went up in flames—shops, funfair attractions, cafés where Jacobins, Republicans, Royalists and others met, and gambling halls.

On the grass, on an ivy covered pedestal behind a statue, stands a toy cannon, known as the Palais-Royal cannon. From 1786 until 1914 it used to go off every day at midday provided the sun, when reflected through a magnifying glass, was hot enough to ignite the charge.

Palais-Royal Theatre. — The 18C theatre at the corner of the Rues de Montpensier and Beaujolais is now a vaudeville theatre.

Leave the Royal Palace through the Beaujolais terrace peristyle.

From the Palais-Royal to the Bibliothèque Nationale

On your way pass at No. 8 Rue des Petits-Champs, the courtyard and sombre brick and stone façade of the 1633 Tubeuf Mansion, the library's formal garden, Colbert's mansion (1665) and **Louvois Square.**

THE BIBLIOTHÈQUE NATIONALE★ ⏢ or ⏢ : G 13

In the Middle Ages the kings of France collected manuscripts; Charles V mustered nearly 1 000 volumes in the Louvre Library *(p 28);* Charles VIII and Louis XII had libraries at Blois; François I at Fontainebleau. A copyright act in 1537 ensured that a copy of every book printed enters the royal, now national, library — today extended to include records and photographs.

In the 17C the Tubeuf Mansion was enlarged by Mansart and on coming into Mazarin's possession housed his 500 pictures and personal art objects. By 1666 the Royal Library numbered 200 000 volumes and Colbert decided to move it to his own mansion in the Rue Vivienne; fifty-four years later, it was moved again when it was added to the original Mazarin collection.

The Library Today. — The Bibliothèque Nationale, or '' Nationale '' is divided into departments, covering 16 500 m² — 177 600 sq ft : Printed Books (7 million volumes dating from the 15C and including two Gutenberg Bibles, first editions of Villon, Rabelais, Pascal...); Periodicals and Newspapers; Manuscripts (including Charlemagne's Gospel, the Bible of Charles the Bald and the St. Louis Psalter; MSS of Hugo, Proust and Pasteur...); Prints, Engravings and Photographs; Maps and Plans (13 — 20C); **Medals, Coins and Antiques*** (*closed for re-arrangement;* 700 000 art objects — coins, medals, cameos...); Music; record library.

Tour. — The west side of the main courtyard is by the 18C architect, Robert de Cotte. The staircase on the right leads to displays of books acquired under the copyright law (the 19C, Second Empire reading room — *members only* — can be seen through a window). At the end is the Mansart Gallery *(free access during exhibitions)* and, opposite, the State Room fine 18C panelling containing the original plaster bust of *Voltaire* by Houdon (*p 91*). The philosopher's heart was placed in the statue's pedestal. The great staircase leads to the Medal Room and the magnificent **Mazarin Gallery*** by Mansart (*often used for temporary exhibitions*).

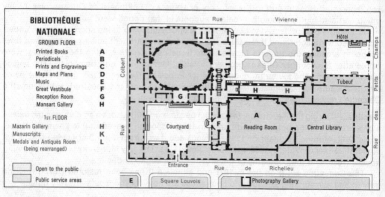

BIBLIOTHÈQUE NATIONALE

GROUND FLOOR

Printed Books	A
Periodicals	B
Prints and Engravings	C
Maps and Plans	D
Music	E
Great Vestibule	F
Reception Room	G
Mansart Gallery	H

1st. FLOOR

Mazarin Gallery	H
Manuscripts	K
Medals and Antiques Room (being rearranged)	L

Open to the public

Public service areas

From the Bibliothèque Nationale to St-Roch Church

On leaving the library, walk left down the Rue de Richelieu to the Rue Molière.

Molière Fountain. — The 19C fountain by Visconti stands not far from what is now No. 40 Rue de Richelieu, the site of Molière's house. It was there that he was taken when he collapsed on stage at the first Palais-Royal Theatre, on 17 February 1673. The playwright was 51.

Make for the Rue des Petits-Champs by way of the Rues Thérèse and Ste-Anne — No. 47 is the house Lulli had built in 1671, borrowing 11 000 *livres* from Molière to do so. Musical motifs can be seen upon the façade.

The Rue des Moulins gets its name from the windmills which stood upon a hillock built of public waste like the neighbouring Butte St-Roch. The mound was razed in 1668, but one of the mills, the Radet, was saved and transported to Montmartre where it is being restored (*p 78*).

The brief Rue Méhul leads to the old Ventadour Theatre where Victor Hugo's melodrama, *Ruy Blas,* was first played in 1838. The building is now an annexe of the Bank of France.

Walk to the Rue Monsigny and the Rue St-Augustin on the left. Facing the **Gaillon fountain** erected in 1707 on the square of the same name (remodelled by Visconti in 1827), is the Restaurant Drouant, known in the world of letters as the place from which the names of the Goncourt prizewinners are announced annually in autumn.

On reaching the Avenue de l'Opéra turn left.

Avenue de l'Opéra**. — This luxurious thoroughfare was begun simultaneously at either end by Haussmann in 1854 and completed in 1878.

The most serious obstacle in the road's path was the Butte St-Roch, which covered the area between what are now the Rue Thérèse and the Rue des Pyramides and rose to sufficient height for Joan of Arc to position her large supporting cannon upon it when her troops were preparing to attack the St. Honoré Gate (*p 91*).

The mound had been partly levelled off in 1615 but remained a poor area until the end of the 17C when the slums were demolished and the vast heaps of rubble were utilised to build up the lowlying areas around the Champ-de-Mars.

The Avenue de l'Opéra, still not quite a hundred years old, has become one of Paris' prestige streets where big business and commerce reign. For the tourist the avenue is the place for making purchases : perfume, scarves, gifts and *articles de Paris* (fancy goods). It is also a business district with many large banks, building societies and international bookshops (*see Useful Addresses p 10*). More obvi-

Avenue de l'Opéra

ously the avenue and the streets off it have become a communication centre with the French Government Tourist Board at No. 8, the Havas Travel Agency at No. 26, and foreign tourist and air and shipping lines occupying offices all around.

Turn right into the Rue des Pyramides and, after crossing the Rue d'Argenteuil where Corneille died in 1684, continue to the square, **Place des Pyramides,** at the end of which there stands an equestrian statue of Joan of Arc by the 19C sculptor, Frémiet, to which many make an annual pilgrimage.

Rue de Rivoli*. — The Rue de Rivoli, between the Place des Pyramides and the Rue de Castiglione on the right, crosses the site of the former Tuileries **Riding School.** In 1789 the school was hastily converted into a meeting place for the Constituent Assembly. Sessions were subsequently held there by the Legislative Assembly and the Convention, until on 21 September 1792, the day following the French victory over the Prussians at Valmy (commemorative tablet on a pillar in the Tuileries railings opposite No. 230), it became the setting for the proclamation of the Republic and the trial of Louis XVI.

It was Napoleon who, in 1811, had this part of the avenue constructed, although it was not to be completed until nearly the middle of the century.

The houses facing the Tuileries are of uniform design above arcades lined, in strange contrast, with both luxury and souvenir shops.

In 1944 the Rue de Rivoli was the scene of a momentous decision in the capital's own history when the German General von Choltitz, Commandant of Paris, who had his headquarters at the Meurice Hotel at No. 228, refused to obey Hitler's orders to blow up the capital's bridges and principal buildings when the tanks of General Leclerc's division and the Resistance were known to be approaching. Instead he allowed himself to be taken prisoner on 25 August and Paris to be liberated intact.

Turn right up the Rue de Castiglione, known formerly as the Passage des Feuillants after the Benedictine monastery which it skirted, and right again, into the Rue St-Honoré.

The Rue St-Honoré at the time of the Revolution. — The **Feuillants Monastery,** which had grounds extending to the Tuileries riding school, augmented its income by building an apartment house which can still be seen between Nos. 229 and 235 in the Rue St-Honoré. It was here that the short-lived Feuillants Club of moderates who, in line with La Fayette, Bailly, Sieyès and Talleyrand, disassociated themselves from the extremist Jacobin group, met in 1791.

No. 211 is the former Noailles Mansion where General La Fayette married one of the daughters of the house in 1774. It is now the St. James and Albany Hotel. On the left there used to be a **Jacobin Monastery** (a Dominican order of St. James). In 1789 a club installed itself in the monastery and took its name, becoming famous during the Revolution under the leadership of Robespierre.

The Rue du Marché St-Honoré now cuts across the site of the monastery church and a market dating back to 1810 occupies the ground on which the monastery once stood.

St-Roch Church, on the left, was the site on 13 Vendémiaire — 5 October 1795 — of bloody fighting. A column of royalists leading an attack on the Convention, then in the Tuileries, aimed to march through the Rue St-Roch. Bonaparte, however, who was in charge of the defence, mowed down with machine-gun fire the men massed on the church steps and perched on its façade. The bullet holes can still be seen.

Some idea of the scale of Haussmann's earth moving undertakings can be gained from the fact that to enter the church nowadays you have to walk up twelve steps, whereas before the construction of the Opera Avenue, you had to go down seven.

■ CHURCH OF ST-ROCH★ 🔟 or 🔟 : G 13

The Church of St-Roch is particularly interesting for its works of art of the 17 and 18C.

Construction. — The foundation stone of the church dedicated to the early 14C saint who tended those suffering from the plague in Italy, was laid by Louis XIV in 1653. The Moulins hillock site compelled the architect, Le Mercier, to reorientate the church so that it faces south to north.

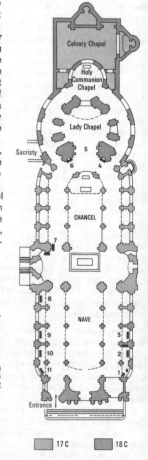

Calvary Chapel

Holy Communion Chapel

Lady Chapel

Sacristy

5

6   4

CHANCEL

7

CHANCEL

8

NAVE

9   3

10   2

11

Entrance

17 C   18 C

Funds soon ran out but work was able to continue after a lottery had been organized in 1705. Instead of completing the nave, a series of chapels one behind the other were constructed beyond the apse, lengthening the church from the planned 80 to 125 m — 262 to 410 ft (5 m — 16 ft shorter than Notre-Dame) and obliterating all unity of design. In consequence, in line behind the altar are a Lady Chapel by Jules Hardouin-Mansart, with a tall richly decorated dome, a Communion Chapel with a flat dome and finally a Calvary Chapel *(closed for restoration).*

In 1719 a gift of 100 000 *livres* from John Law *(p 112),* recently converted to Catholicism, enabled the nave to be completed. Robert de Cotte designed the façade in the Jesuit style in 1736.

Among those buried in St-Roch in the Lady Chapel and side chapels are the playwright Corneille, the garden designer Le Nôtre, the Abbot de l'Épée *(p 123),* the philosophers Diderot and d'Holbach and Mme Geoffrin, hostess of a famous 18C *salon.* The 17C mariner, Duguay-Trouin, has been transferred to Saint-Malo.

Works of Art :

1) Tomb of Henri of Lorraine, Count d'Harcourt by Renard (17C) and bust of the 17C Marshal de Créqui by Coysevox (17C).
2) Funeral monument of the astronomer, Maupertuis by d'Huez and statue of Cardinal Dubois by Guillaume Coustou.
3) Tomb of Duke Charles de Créqui.
4) Godefroy de Bouillon Victorious by Claude Vignon (17C). Funerary plaque to Duguay-Trouin.
5) The Triumph of the Virgin, painting by J. B. Pierre on the dome *(illumination : apply to the sacristan).* The **Nativity★** at the altar by the Anguier brothers, was brought from the Val-de-Grâce.
6) Resurrection of the Son of the Widow of Naïm by Le Sueur (17C).
7) Le Nôtre bust by Coysevox and funerary inscription.
8) Monument to the Abbot de l'Épée (19C).
9) Bust of the painter Mignard and statue of his daughter by Lemoyne (18C).
10) Baptism of Christ by Lemoyne. Medallion by Falconet.
11) Baptismal Chapel : frescoes by Chassériau (19C).

Continue left down the Rue St-Honoré to the Rue de l'Échelle, so called after the ladder or flight of steps leading to a scaffold which stood on the site during the Ancien Régime. The ecclesiastical courts then sent polygamists, perjurers and blasphemers to the steps where they were exposed in shame before the public.

On the right is the Marsan Pavilion, which, with the Flore Pavilion (reconstructed), are all that remain of the Tuileries Palace, burnt down in 1871 *(p 27).*

MUSEUM OF DECORATIVE ARTS★★ ⬛⬛ or ⬛⬛ : H 13

107 Rue de Rivoli. Open 10 am to noon and 2 to 5 pm, Sundays 10 am to 5 pm; closed, Tuesdays ; 5F.

50 000 selected exhibits in a space more compact than the Louvre provide a vivid panorama of the evolution in form and taste in sculpture, painting, furniture, tapestry, banqueting settings and all forms of decoration in France.

The temporary exhibitions organized by the Centre for Industrial Innovation on the ground floor are often extremely interesting *(noon to 6 pm; closed Tuesdays; admission charge variable)*.

On the second floor, displays illustrate the development of items of everyday life from Gothic times to the 18C (sculpture, tapestries, furniture, arms and musical instruments...). A collection of Dubuffet's works can be found on the same floor; paintings, drawings, gouaches and sculpture were donated by the artist himself.

The third floor is a good example of a living museum with rooms faithfully reconstructed with contemporary paintings and furnishings to illustrate life in France from the reign of Louis XVI to that of Napoleon III.

The fourth floor is entirely devoted to art from the principal countries of Europe, Islam and the Orient.

Art courses (drawing, modelling, metal engraving) are offered. *Information can be obtained at the Secrétariat des Ateliers : ☎ 260.32.14. ext 933, Mondays and Fridays 2 to 6 pm.*

On leaving the museum, you pass on your right the latest Louvre façade (remodelled during the Third Republic). The statues in the niches are of the generals of the First Empire.

Turn left into the Rue de Rohan, which leads to the Place André-Malraux. The street runs over the original site of the Quinze-Vingts Hospice which in the reign of Louis XVI was transferred by Cardinal de Rohan, the institution's administrator, to barracks in the Rue de Charenton where it remains to this day *(p 150)*.

■ PLACE ANDRÉ-MALRAUX ⬛⬛ or ⬛⬛ : H 13

From this altogether Parisian crossroads — formerly known as the place du Théâtre Français — created in the time of Napoleon III and decorated with attractive modern fountains there is a splendid view up the Avenue de l'Opéra.

Comédie-Française. — In 1680 Louis XIV combined the former Molière company with that at the Hôtel de Bourgogne *(p 109)* at the same time granting it the sole right of performance in the capital. The new company took the name Comédie-Française.

The company, however, found itself the butt of hostility simultaneously from the Sorbonne and the orthodox and was compelled to move home frequently — from the Guénégaud *(p 137)* to the Rue de l'Ancienne-Comédie *(p 137)*, the Palais des Tuileries *(p 27)* and the Odéon *(p 94)*.

At the Revolution a dispute broke out in the company between players who supported the Republicans and those favouring the Royalists. In 1792 the former, led by Talma, took over this theatre.

Napoleon showed a great interest in the Comédie-Française, in Talma — and also in the leading lady, Mlle Mars. In 1812 he presented the company with a foundation making it an association of currently acting and apprentice players and players on pension. Today the theatre is still under a director nominated by the state.

On 21 February 1830 the company, playing *Hernani*, was involved in the famous battle — a battle of taste — which marked Victor Hugo's triumphal *début* as a playwright.

The repertoire of the Comédie-Française has, by tradition, been classical, with set rules in style of acting and in interpretation — Molière, Corneille, Racine, Marivaux, Musset, Beaumarchais. Recently, however, works by foreign and 20C French authors have been admitted — Pirandello, Claudel, Giraudoux, Anouilh...

In the foyer are Houdon's famous bust of **Voltaire★★** *(p 88)* and the chair in which Molière was sitting when taken fatally ill on stage *(p 88)*.

At No. 161 Rue St-Honoré was the Café de la Régence founded in 1681 in the Place du Palais-Royal and forced to move in 1854 when the square was enlarged. It is now the home of the Moroccan Tourist Office.

Memories of Joan of Arc. — Joan came to the gate in the Charles V perimeter wall which stood where No. 163 Rue St-Honoré is now, when leading her attack on the capital in 1429. She had already freed Orleans *(see Michelin Green Guide Chateaux of the Loire)* and accompanied the King to Rheims for his coronation, but her task, as she saw it, was far from complete. Paris was still in the hands of the English under the Regent Bedford who wished not only to retain the city but to make it safe enough to bring over the young Henry VI and crown him in Notre-Dame, King of England and France.

The girl soldier paused to pray at the small St-Denis-de-la-Chapelle (the church, now remodelled, is at No. 16, Rue de la Chapelle, 18ᵉ), before undertaking her attack on the gate fort defended by a moat. Realising this would have to be filled in, she moved to measure the water's depth with her lance when she was wounded in the thigh by an arrow. She was given first aid in what is now No. 4 in the square while her men beat a hasty retreat. Henry VI was crowned in Notre-Dame (1431).

Although this is the only episode linking Joan of Arc with the capital there are, in addition to the medallion by Réal del Sarte on the Café de la Régence façade, four statues of her in the city — in the Place des Pyramides *(p 89)*, Rue de la Chapelle, Place St-Augustin *(p 142)* and at 41 Boulevard St-Marcel *(p 141)*.

ST-GERMAIN-DES-PRÉS - LUXEMBOURG ★★

Michelin plans ▥▥ or ▥▥ : from J 13 to L 13.
Distance : 2.5 km — 1 1/2 miles — Time : 2 1/2 hours. Start from St-Germain-des-Prés métro.

This old quarter on the Left Bank is known for beautiful churches and the Luxembourg gardens, for its narrow streets, antique shops, restaurants, cafés and cellars.

ST-GERMAIN-DES-PRÉS CHURCH★★   ▥▥ or ▥▥ : J 13

The church, the oldest in Paris, and the palace of the once powerful abbots are all that remain of the famous Benedictine abbey.

The Merovingian necropolis. — In 542 King Childebert, son of Clovis, on his return from Spain with a piece of the True Cross and St. Vincent's tunic, had a monastery built in the open fields *(prés)* to shelter the relics. He was buried in the church as were subsequent members of his line until King Dagobert (639 — *p 168*). He lies beside St. Germanus, Bishop of Paris, after whom the church had taken its name of St-Germain-des-Prés or St. Germanus in the Fields.

A powerful abbey. — St-Germain-des-Prés was from the 8C, a link in the prodigious chain across Europe of 17 000 Benedictine abbeys and priories and in its own right, sovereign ruler of a domain of some 17 000 ha — 42 000 acres. Spiritually it acknowledged only the pope.

The monastery was sacked four times in forty years by the Normans and the present church is, therefore, a rebuilding dating in its earliest parts from 990 to 1021.

There followed enlargement of the chancel in 1163 — an addition consecrated in person by Pope Alexander III at a service from which the bishop of Paris was excluded, as a mark of the order's independence — the building of Gothic cloisters, a refectory and a Lady Chapel in the 13C by Pierre of Montreuil, making the monastery a most beautiful mediaeval group.

In the 14C while Paris was being given its third defence perimeter by Charles V *(p 18)*, the abbey surrounded itself with a crenelated wall intersected by towers and preceded by a moat connected with the Seine. These fortifications remained until the end of the 17C when they were replaced by houses, so creating the district of St-Germain *(p 124)*.

A centre of learning. —The Cluniac rule was followed in the abbey from the 11 to the 16C when it became debased; it was reformed in 1515 and in 1631 and then attached itself to the austere Congregation of St. Maur which earned the community a reputation for holiness and learning.

Decadence. — The abbey was suppressed at the Revolution: the rich library was confiscated, the church, from which the royal tombs disappeared, turned into a saltpetre works and the greater number of its buildings sold, knocked down or burnt. In spite of everything, however, the nave was saved although the twin transept towers disappeared. The vessel received a decoration of somewhat stiff frescoes between 1841 and 1863 by the painter, Flandrin.

TOUR

Exterior. — With all that has happened to it, inevitably the 11C Romanesque church has altered considerably in appearance. Of the three original towers there remains only the massive one above the façade, one of the oldest in France. The top arcaded storey, rebuilt in the 12C was restored in the 19C and, in the same century, crowned with the present steeple. The original porch is hidden by an outer door added in 1607; on the right, the presbytery is an 18C addition. The twin square towers at the end of the chancel were truncated instead of being repaired in 1822. The chancel itself, rebuilt in the middle of the 12C when its buttresses were strengthened by a series of flying buttresses, is contemporary with Notre-Dame.

The small square to the south is on the site of the monks' cemetery and in September 1792 was the setting for the massacre of the 318 priests and monks who had been locked up in the adjoining Abbey Prison. The former abbatical palace *(p 93)* can be seen behind the apse.

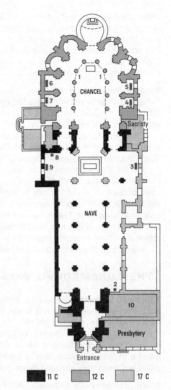

Interior. — St-Germain, built as a monastery chapel, is not large — it measures 65 × 21 × 19 m high — 213 × 69 × 62 ft. Proportions and carving are diminished by the irritating 19C multicolour restoration.

To the right of the cradle vaulted porch is the St. Symphorian Chapel where St. Germanus was buried. Excavations in the chapel in 1971 uncovered several additional sarcophagi and carvings. The Gothic vaulting above the nave and transept, similar to that in the chancel, replaced an earlier wooden roof in 1646; the capitals are copies of the 11C originals now in the Cluny Museum (p 99). The frescoes above the arches are by Flandrin, a student of Ingres.

The chancel and ambulatory remain 12C. Originally the arches, some of which are still semi-circular, supported galleries but in 1646 these were converted into a purely ornamental triforium; the 6C marble shafts in the slender columns are from the original Childebert church and along with the remains found in St. Symphorian Chapel and Notre-Dame are the only traces of Merovingian buildings in Paris.

The chancel capitals are typically Romanesque.

1) Modern wrought iron grille by Raymond Subes.
2) Our Lady of Consolation (1340).
3) Tomb by Girardon (17C).
4) Mausoleum of James Douglas, a 17C Scottish nobleman attached to the court of Louis XIII.
5) Descartes' and the learned Benedictines, Mabillon and Montfaucon's, tombstones.
6) Boileau, the poet and critic's, tombstone.
7) Tomb of William Douglas, a Scottish nobleman attached to the court of Henri IV.
8) Statue of St. Francis Xavier by N. Coustou.
9) Tomb of John Casimir, King of Poland, who died in 1672, Abbot of St-Germain-des-Prés.
10) St. Symphorian Chapel (closed).

11 C   12 C   17 C

From St-Germain-des-Prés to the Luxembourg

A Picasso sculpture, *Homage to Apollinaire,* has been placed in a small square on the corner of the Place St-Germain-des-Prés and the Rue de l'Abbaye amidst fragments of the Lady Chapel built by Pierre of Montreuil and removed from the church in 1802 (the portal is in the Cluny Museum garden, p 99). Walk along the quiet Rue de l'Abbaye where at No. 16 can be seen the rebuilt but nevertheless remarkable west façade of the refectory designed in 1239 by Pierre of Montreuil and burnt down in 1794, (the original refectory itself stood at Nos. 14-12, the chapter-house at No. 11).

Abbatical Palace. — The former abbatical palace (Nos. 5 to 1) is an impressive brick and stone edifice which was constructed in 1586 by the Cardinal-Abbot Charles of Bourbon, proclaimed King of France in 1589 during the League. His reign, as Charles X, however, was shortlived since he died the following year, a prisoner of his nephew Henri IV. The palace was sold in 1797. The angle pavilion and part of the Renaissance façade have been restored to their original aspect.

The Old Streets*. — Turn left into the **Rue de Fürstemberg,** an old fashioned street with a charming square shaded by paulownia and white-globed lamp-posts. The street was built in 1699 by the cardinal of the same name, through the acquisition of the monastery stable-yard. The Nos. 6 and 8 are the remains of the outbuildings.

Delacroix, leader of the Romantic painters set up his studio in No. 6 which is now the **Eugène Delacroix Museum** (open 9.45 am to 5.15 pm; closed Tuesdays; 2F).

Bear right into the curious winding **Rue Cardinale,** again opened (1700) by Fürstemberg, this time overlooking the monastery tennis court and still partially lined by old houses (Nos. 3 to 9). The Rue Cardinale ends picturesquely as you continue past the Petite Boucherie passage to the Rue de l'Abbaye on the right and subsequently the Rue de l'Échaudé (1388).

The construction of the Boulevard St-Germain brought about the disappearance, in about 1870, of the meeting point of several small roads which had served as the abbey's place of public chastisement. Justice was meted out on thieves, counterfeiters, pimps, who were punished by gibet and pillory — a penalty suppressed by Louis XIII in 1636. Two Huguenots, surprised in secret meeting in 1557, had their tongues torn out before being burned alive at this spot by the abbey authorities.

The old St-Germain Fair. — Cross the boulevard into the Rue de Montfaucon which at one time led to the St-Germain fairground.

The fair, founded in 1482 by Louis XI for the benefit of the abbey, lasted until the Revolution (1790), its annual celebration an important event in the Paris economy. In 1818 the site was made over to the local market which flourishes still although a part was taken in 1900 to build university examination halls.

Make for the Carrefour de l'Odéon by way of the Rues Mabillon, Lobineau and Quatre-Vents and then bear right into the Rue de Condé. It was in this street, lined still by old houses, that Beaumarchais wrote the *Barber of Seville* in 1773 (No. 26). Continue to the Place de l'Odéon.

Place de l'Odéon. — This semicircular square was created in 1779 in the former Condé house grounds and has always been a place of repute. The houses surrounding it have plain façades; the roads leading to it were named after famous writers : Corneille, Racine, Voltaire (now renamed Casimir-Delavigne), Molière (Rotrou), Crébillon, Regnard. No. 1, the Café Voltaire, was frequented by the Encyclopaedists and, at the turn of the 20C, by Barrès, Bourget, Mallarmé and Verlaine; it is now the Benjamin-Franklin American Library.

Théâtre National de l'Odéon. — In 1782 a theatre was built in the gardens of the former Condé mansion to accommodate the French Comedians who for the past twelve years had been installed in the Tuileries Palace Theatre. The new theatre, built in the antique style of the day, was given the name Théâtre Français.

Came the Revolution; the company divided and in 1792 those for the Republic left under Talma for the theatre in the Rue Richelieu, the present Comédie-Française (p 91). The Royalists who remained were soon removed to prison.

In 1797 a new company took over the theatre, renamed it the Odeon and failed. In 1807 the building was burned down but was reconstructed and the company started up again. In spite of the success of the play by Alphonse Daudet, the *Arlésienne* (1872) to music by Bizet, the theatre never became popular until 1946 when it began to specialize in 20C plays. It changed its name to Théâtre de France and for several years, with a company headed until 1968 by Jean-Louis Barrault and Madeleine Renaud, became the best filled theatre in Paris. Inside is a modern ceiling designed in 1965 by André Masson.

Walk down the Rue Rotrou and turn right for the Luxembourg Palace.

THE LUXEMBOURG PALACE AND GARDENS★★ 🔟 or 🔟 : K 13, L 13

The devil Vauvert. — The site, after the abandonment of the encampment and villas of Gallo-Roman times, became a desert and later the haunt of a ghostly highwayman named Vauvert, after his lair in an old ruin. Terror spread far and wide until in 1257 the Carthusians, installed by St. Louis at Gentilly, suggested to the king that they rid the neighbourhood of the outlaw. They succeeded and when they had established themselves in the area received so many gifts that they were able to construct a vast monastery. The monks' tree nursery (*pépinière*) and vegetable garden (*potager*) became known as the most beautiful in the capital.

Marie dei Medici's Palace. — After the death of Henri IV, his Queen, Marie dei Medici, who no longer enjoyed living at the Louvre, decided to build herself a palace which would recall the house of her youth in Tuscany. In 1612 she bought the mansion of Duke François of Luxembourg and a considerable adjoining area; in 1615 her architect, Salomon de Brosse, began to construct the queen a palace inspired by the Pitti Palace of Florence.

The building was much admired and in 1621 Rubens was commissioned to paint a series of 24 large pictures retracing allegorically the queen's life — the pictures now hang in the Medici Gallery in the Louvre (pp 30, 37).

The day of deceit. — In 1625 the queen installed herself in the palace but her joy was short-lived for she had entered into opposition with Richelieu. She extracted a promise from her son, Louis XIII, on 10 November 1630 to dismiss the Cardinal but it was revoked twenty-four hours later and she was banished to Cologne where she died in 1642. The palace reverted to its original Luxembourg title and, although abandoned, remained crown property until the Revolution.

The palace as parliament. — In 1790 when the monastery was suppressed, the gardens were enlarged and the palace vista extended the full length of the Avenue de l'Observatoire. Under the Terror the palace became a prison, receiving before they were sent to the guillotine the Noailles family, Danton and his followers, the poet Fabre d'Églantine and the lawyer and writer Camille Desmoulins and many others. The building next became a parliamentary assembly for the Directory, the Consulate, the Senate and its successor the Peers' Chamber. Chalgrin, architect of the Arc de Triomphe and the Odéon, completely transformed the interior, while from 1836 to 1841 Alphonse de Gisors enlarged it on the garden side by the addition of a new front to the main building and two projecting wing pavilions in the style of the original building. At various dates Marshal Ney, the conspirator Louis-Napoleon Bonaparte (the future Napoleon III) and members of the Commune who turned against it, were all tried in the palace. In the Second World War the building was occupied by the Germans. On 25 August 1944 it was freed by Leclerc's Division and the French Resistance.

It is now the seat of the **Senate,** the French Upper House. The Senate is composed of 283 members chosen by an electoral college consisting of deputies, departmental and municipal councillors. Should the Presidency of the Republic fall vacant, the Senate President will exercise the functions of Head of State in the interim.

THE PALACE

*Individual tours : Sundays 9.30 to 11 am and 2 to 4 pm; 0.50F. Group tours on written appli-
cation to the Secrétariat Général de la Questure du Sénat, 15 Rue de Vaugirard, 75006 Paris.*

To give a Florentine air to his design for the palace, Salomon de Brosse employed bosses,
ringed columns and Tuscan capitals but he kept the French style ground plan of a courtyard
surrounded by a central building, two wings at right angles and closed by twin arcaded galleries meeting in a central gateway surmounted by a cupola *(illustration p 23)*. The fine balus-
traded terrace has been recently reconstituted according to Brosse's original plan.

Inside, the library is decorated with **paintings★** by Delacroix *(Dante and Virgil walking in
Limbo, Alexander placing Homer's poems in Darius' gold casket)*. The ceiling of the library
annexe is decorated with a painting of the *Signs of the Zodiac* by Jordaens. In the Golden
Book Room are the 17C panelling and paintings which once adorned Marie dei Medici's
apartments. The Senate council chamber, the state gallery and most of the saloons were
furnished during the reign of Louis-Philippe. The main staircase by Chalgrin leads to the
gallery in which the Rubens paintings were hung at one time.

Two inner courts, below the level of the Allée de l'Odéon, are decorated in the French
gardens style.

The Petit Luxembourg, now the residence of the president of the Senate, comprises the
original Hôtel de Luxembourg presented to Richelieu by Marie dei Medici and also the cloister
and chapel of a convent founded by the queen.

The Luxembourg Museum, originally placed in the Orangery, has been transferred to the
National Museum of Modern Art *(p 144)*.

The Senate has extended its premises to a series of buildings across Rue de Vaugirard.
The architecture of this group harmonizes well with the surrounding edifices. In the ground
floor galleries, can be seen exhibitions of Coins and Medals and Sèvres Porcelain. Incorporated in the new buildings are, at No. 36, the doorway of a mansion built by Boffrand in 1716 and
round the corner at No. 15 Rue Garancière, the façade of another mansion adorned with
mascaroons representing the Seasons.

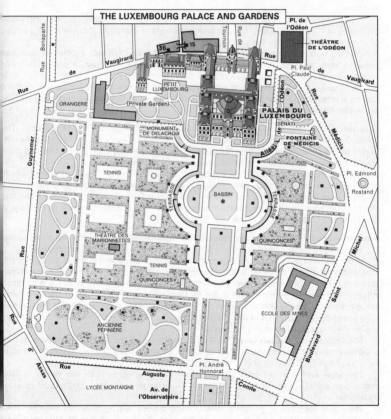

THE GARDENS

The gardens, which in themselves are most attractive, provide the most extensive green
open space on the Left Bank and are often crowded with mothers and small children, students
and young people.

Basically the design is formal, the only free, more English style garden being along the
Rue Guynemer and the Rue Auguste-Comte.

The tradition of husbandry of the Carthusians continues in the courses in arboriculture
and apiculture given in what was once a corner of the Carthusian tree nursery (near the Rue
d'Assas).

Statues began to invade the lawns under Louis-Philippe and today have reached such numbers that they seem to confront one at every step. The best, among this not artistically impressive crowd of figures, is the Delacroix group by Dalou. Queens and illustrious women of France line the terrace.

The **Medici Fountain★** (1624) which stands in a green setting at the very end of a long pool shaded by plane trees, shows obvious Italian influence in its embossed decoration and overall design. In a niche the jealous cyclops, Polyphemus, waits to crush Acis and Galatea (by Ottin 1863) while on the Rue de Médicis side is a low relief of Leda and the Swan (1807).

From the Luxembourg Palace to St-Germain-des-Prés

Walk to the Place St-Sulpice by way of the Rue de Tournon and, on the left, the Rue St Sulpice, a street like many in the quarter lined with shops selling devotional objects.

Place St-Sulpice. — Started in 1754, it was originally intended that the square should be semicircular with uniform façades modelled on that at No. 6 (at the corner of the Rue des Canettes), designed by Servandoni, the 18C Italian architect and painter who worked principally in France *(see below)*. The project for the uniform square fell through.

At the centre of the square stands a fountain erected by Visconti in 1844. It is so fashioned that it includes at the cardinal points of the compass, the portrait busts of four great men of the church : Bossuet, Fénelon, Massillon and Fléchier. None were ever made cardinals and in a play upon words — *point* in French means : both point and never — the fountain is known as *The Fontaine des Quatre Points Cardinaux* — the Fountain of the Cardinal Points or the Four Cardinals who never were.

CHURCH OF ST-SULPICE★★   ▢▢ or ▢▢ : K 13

Construction. — The church, dedicated to the 6C Archbishop of Bourges, St. Sulpicius, was founded by the Abbey of St-Germain-des-Prés as a parish church for the peasants living in its domain.

It has been rebuilt several times and was enlarged in the 16 and 17C, reconstruction beginning in 1646 with the chancel. Six architects were in charge successively over a period of one hundred and thirty-four years.

By 1732 work was due to begin on the façade but it was felt that a different style was required from the Graeco-Roman which had been adopted up till then. A competition was organized which was won by the Florentine, Servandoni, who proposed a fine Antique style façade in contrast to the rest of the edifice. Servandoni's project was adopted but modified first by Maclaurin and then by Chalgrin. Delacroix' genius dominated the twenty artists who worked on the interior mural decorations.

Exterior. — The final façade differs considerably from Servandoni's original concept. The colossal pediment has been abandoned; the belfries are crowned not by Renaissance pinnacles but by balustrades; the towers are dissimilar, the one on the left being taller and more ornate than the one on the right which was never completed.

Walk back along the south side of the church, down the Rue Palatine. The transept façade is in the Jesuit style with two superimposed orders and heavy connecting ornaments.

Seen from the corner of the Rue Palatine and the Rue Garancière, St-Sulpice is a building of some size, shouldered by massive buttresses designed as inverted consoles and ending in the dome and corbelled apse of the Lady Chapel.

Interior. — Enter through the south transept door (Rue Palatine). The interior, which measures 113 m long by 58 m wide by 34 m high — 371 × 190 × 112 ft — is extremely impressive.

In the transept, a copper band oriented from north to south and inlaid in the pavement, crosses from a plaque in the south arm to an obelisk in the north arm. During the winter solstice a ray of sunshine, passing through a small hole in the upper window in the south transept, strikes marked points on the obelisk in the far transept at midday exactly. At the spring and autumn equinox the ray falls on the copper plaque. This 1744 meridian *(p 123)* thus serves daily as a midday timepiece. The Christ against the Pillar, the Mater Dolorosa and the Apostles beside the chancel columns are by Bouchardon.

The decoration of the **Lady Chapel★** at the centre of the east end of the church, was supervised personally by Servandoni. In the altar niche is a Virgin and Child by Pigalle; on the walls hang paintings by Van Loo and on the dome is a fresco by Lemoyne.

The **organ loft★** was designed by Chalgrin in 1776. The organ itself was rebuilt in 1862 and is considered one of the finest in France. The church has a long and august musical tradition.

Mural paintings★ full of Romantic ardour were carried out by Delacroix between 1849 and 1861 on the walls of the first chapel on the right. On the vaulting is St. Michael killing the dragon; on the right wall Heliodorus is being driven from the Temple (the story is that Heliodorus, a minister of the King of Syria, coveted the treasures of the Temple and was struck down by three avenging angels, one of whom can be seen on horseback); on the left wall Jacob struggles with the Angel.

Two stoups against the second pillars of the nave have been made from giant shells given to François I by the Venetian Republic and then by Louis XV to St-Sulpice Church in 1745. Their rock supports were carved by Pigalle.

Return to St-Germain-des-Prés by the Rue des Canettes, Duckling Street, which takes its name from the low relief at No. 18 — and the Rue des Ciseaux with its many old houses.

Michelin plans ⑩ or ⑪ : K 14.

Distance : 2 km — 1 mile — Time : 2 1/2 hours. Start from the St-Michel métro station.

This is one of Paris' mediaeval quarters with narrow, winding streets, old and modern schools, university buildings, churches and the treasure filled Hôtel de Cluny.

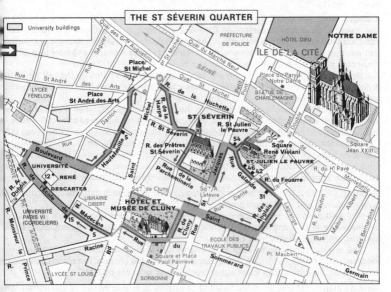

THE ST SÉVERIN QUARTER

From the Place St-Michel to St-Séverin and St-Julien-le-Pauvre. — Leave by the Rue de la Huchette and almost immediately bear right into the Rue de la Harpe, an old Roman road. At the end turn left into the Rue St-Séverin for the church *(p 98)*.

Walk left round the church by way of the Rue des Prêtres-St-Séverin and the Rue de la Parcheminerie or Parchment Street, so called after public letter writers and copyists who lived there. Once past the east end of the church in the Rue St-Jacques, bear right into the Rue Galande for St-Julien-le-Pauvre *(p 99)*.

From St-Julien-le-Pauvre to the Hôtel de Cluny. — On leaving the church turn left into the **Rue Galande,** the Lyons — Paris Roman road where cellars and pointed mediaeval arches have been unearthed at Nos. 46 and 54 and at No. 42 a carved stone above the door shows St. Julian the Hospitaller in his boat. The Rue du Fouarre, on the left, was one of the places where university lectures were given in the open air in the Middle Ages and got its name from the bundles of straw *(fouarre)* on which the students sat. Dante is said to have attended lectures in this street in 1304.

Continue down the Rue Galande (15C gable at No. 31) to turn right at the bottom into the Rue des Anglais, named after the English students who lived there in the Middle Ages. At the end, turn right in the Boulevard St-Germain, left into the Rue de Cluny and right again (Rue Du Sommerard) for the Hôtel de Cluny *(pp 99-100)*.

From the Hôtel de Cluny to the Place St-Michel. — Continue along the Rue Du Sommerard and across the Boulevard St-Michel to the Rue de l'École-de-Médecine, another old Gallo-Roman road.

At No. 5 the long gowned Brotherhood of Surgeons, founded by St. Louis in the 13C, performed anatomical operations of every kind until the 17C Barbers or short gowned surgeons were only allowed to undertake bleeding and confinements. The 1695 lecture theatre has been incorporated in the Paris III University. Glance along the Rue Hautefeuille, on the right, where there is a 16C corner turret. At No. 15 stood a Franciscan monastery of high repute in the Middle Ages for its teaching. In Louis XVI's reign, the geometrician **Verniquet** worked there on the first trigonometrical plan of Paris. Shortly afterwards, in 1791, the revolutionary group formed by Danton, Marat, Camille Desmoulins and Hébert took over both the monastery and its name, the Cordeliers. Marat lived opposite and it was there that he was stabbed in his bath by Charlotte Corday on 13 July 1793. The present buildings, now a university centre (Paris VI), were built between 1897 and 1900 to house the School of Practical Medicine. Of the vast conventual buildings, only the monks' Flamboyant Gothic refectory-dormitory remains in the courtyard *(not open)*.

The central part of the former **Medical School** (No. 12), now known as the René Descartes University (Paris V), dates back to 1775. An Ionic colonnade precedes a large courtyard at the centre of which stands a statue of the 18C French anatomist, *Bichat*, by David d'Angers. In pre-Revolutionary times students of medicine and surgery were taught separately; they were united in 1808. All students now complete their practical studies in the eleven university medical centres of the Paris region.

Continue round the school and along the Boulevard St-Germain to the Rue Hautefeuille, on the left. The old street, in which No. 5, with an attractive 16C turret, was once a residence of the abbots of Fécamp, ends in the Place St-André-des-Arts, a square with picturesque houses on the site of a church of the same name. Beyond is the Place St-Michel.

CHURCH OF ST-SÉVERIN★★   ▣ or ▣▣ : K 14

The ambulatory of this Gothic church is one of the great successes of Flamboyant art. The church has an attractive garden and old charnel house and is the setting for concerts every Tuesday.

Construction. — In the 6C there lived in this area, which was then open country, a hermit by the name of Séverin who persuaded Clodoald, grandson of King Clovis and future saint (St. Cloud in France), to take holy orders. An oratory, in due course, was raised to his memory but was burned down by the Normans. It was replaced first by a chapel and later by a church dedicated not to the original Séverin but to a Swiss namesake, St. Severinus.

By the end of the 11C, St-Séverin was serving as the parish church for the Left Bank; the following century Foulques de Neuilly was preaching from its pulpit the 4th Crusade, which was to found the Latin Empire of Constantinople (1204).

Building of the present church began in the first half of the 13C when a master builder, maintaining the Romanesque façade, began to reconstruct the first three bays of the nave in the Gothic style. This substitution of Romanesque by Flamboyant Gothic continued until 1530.

In 1681 the capricious Grande Mademoiselle, cousin to Louis XIV, who had broken with her own parish church of St-Sulpice, adopted St-Séverin and, pouring moneys from her vast fortune, had the chancel modernized by the architect, Le Brun. Under his supervision pillars were faced with marble and wood; pointed Gothic arches were transformed into rounded arcades.

Exterior. — Chapel and aisle bays are covered by ridge roofs, each gable being ornamented with mouldings and monster gargoyles.

The west door, which is 13C, comes from the Church of St-Pierre-aux-Bœufs which stood on the Ile de la Cité and was demolished in 1839. Above, windows, balustrades, the rose window, are all 15C Flamboyant Gothic.

The original porch can be seen on the north side of the tower (the tympanum has been recarved). Still on the north side, in the corner formed by the chapels, is a niche containing a statue of St. Severinus. The tower superstructure and spire are both 15C.

Ground plan. — The width of the building compared to its length, strikes you immediately on entry. This extra breadth occured in the 14 and 15C when the church's enlargement was being mooted but land was only available on either side. The original building with single side aisles was, therefore, flanked by outer aisles and a series of chapels. There is no transept. The Communion Chapel, on the north side, is a 17C addition.

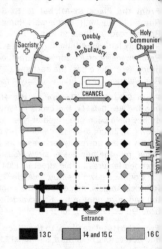

The actual dimensions are : length 50 m width 34 m and height 17 m — 164 × 112 × 56 ft *(cf. the proportions of Notre-Dame, p 64).*

Nave. — The first three bays of the nave are far superior to the rest. Their short columns are ornamented with capitals while above the broken arch arcades rises the triforium, a narrow gallery replacing an earlier wide tribune similar to those of Notre-Dame. The bays of the triforium are filled, like those of the windows above, with a regular tracery of trefoils and roses.

In the following Flamboyant style bays, the columns lack capitals; the tracery in the arcades is angular and complicated.

The sides towards the nave of the capitals along the aisles are carved with the figures of angels, prophets and urchins. The organ is as outstanding as the Louis XV organ loft. The two apostle paintings in the north aisle are 17C.

Chancel. — The chancel's five absidal arches stand higher than those lining the chancel; the Flamboyant vaulting follows a single, much compartimented, design.

The church's wonder is the double **ambulatory★★**, circling the chancel. As you walk, the fall of the rib tracery onto the column stems recalls strolling through a grove of palm trees. On the central pillar the ribs continue in further ornament as spirals down the shaft.

In the chapel adjoining the sacristy, a late 15C mural painting represents the Last Judgment.

Windows★. — The beautiful stained glass in the upper windows is late 15C; the bay in the west end illustrating a Tree of Jesse behind the organ is 16C; the modern glass in the east end chapels is by Bazaine.

Leave the church by the south door (4th bay).

Charnel House. — A small garden exists, where there was formerly a burial ground surrounded by a charnel house. Part of the galleries although restored, look much as they did in mediaeval times. They are the only ones still extant in Paris today. (The practice was to remove the bones of the dead from their graves and put them in cavities in the charnel house walls as the burial ground became overcrowded).

It was in this burial ground that in 1474 the first operation was made for gall stones. An archer, condemned to death, was a sufferer and was offered his freedom by Louis XI should he survive an experimental operation that a surgeon of the time wished to try out. The operation was successful; the archer was cured and freed.

ST-JULIEN-LE-PAUVRE CHURCH★   ⅠⅠ or Ⅲ : K 14

This corner of Paris has an appeal all its own with its small local church in a picturesque setting and an unforgettable view of Notre-Dame.

Construction. — Several of the chapels which have stood successively on this site since the 6C have been named St. Julian — after the 3C Martyr, Bishop of Brioude; after the Confessor, the mediaeval Bishop of Le Mans, known as the Poor because he gave so much away that his purse was always empty; and finally after the ferryman and Hospitaller. In the end it was the name of the mediaeval bishop which prevailed : St. Julian the Poor.

The present building was constructed by the monks of Longpont, a monastery a few miles outside Paris, between 1165 and 1220 (when Notre-Dame was being built).

From the 13 to the 16C the University held its assemblies, including the election of chancellor; in the church, but in 1524 the students made such a rumpus and damaged the interior so gravely that university proceedings were barred henceforth. In 1655 the priory was suppressed and the church attached as a chapel to the Hôtel-Dieu Hospital. Since 1889 it has been a Malachite Chapel.

The square. — The square, on the site of a couple of the church's bays, is more a close than a square. It is bordered to its right by a night-club in the cellars of an old house. The **view★★** across the opening of the Rue Galande to St-Séverin is one of the best known of old Paris and is still being faithfully reproduced by painters. An iron wellhead, originally over a well inside the church, now stands against the doorway near two paving stones from the old Orleans — Lutetia Roman road (Lutetia was the Roman name for Paris). No. 14 in the Rue St-Julien-le-Pauvre dates from the 17C and was at one time the house of the governor of the Petit Châtelet or Lesser Barbican.

The Church. — The portal onto the square was constructed only in 1651 when two bays of the nave and the south aisle were removed. The north face and chancel, flanked by twin absidal chapels, overlook the Square René-Viviani.

Inside, although the nave, which lacks a transept, was recovered with cradle vaulting in 1651, the Gothic vaulting over the aisles was left. The chancel, the most beautiful part of the building, is closed by a wooden iconostasis on which hang icons or holy pictures. The two chancel pillars have **capitals★** remarkably carved with acanthus leaves and harpies. There is also an unusual 15C tombstone in the south aisle.

René-Viviani Square. — The small church close was enlarged in 1928 to its present size, care being taken to preserve the Robinia or false acacia planted in 1680, the second oldest tree in Paris, and now supported with a prop. (The species was introduced from the United States by the botanist, Robin, and called after him.)

The **view★★★** is remarkable : St-Julien itself stands out clear and white behind a curtain of trees; the street St-Julien-le-Pauvre bustles with life beneath the picturesque jumble of roofs; the Ile de la Cité; and finally, and above all, Notre-Dame seen from a three quarters angle in all its mass, its delicacy and its grandeur (*illustration p 62*).

THE HÔTEL DE CLUNY AND ITS MUSEUM★★   ⅠⅠ or Ⅲ : K 14

The old residence of the Abbots of Cluny, the ruins of the Roman baths and the wonderful museum, make a supremely interesting group.

HISTORICAL NOTES

The Roman baths. — The present ruins cover about one third of the site which must have been occupied at the beginning of the 3C by a vast Gallo-Roman public bath house, constructed by the powerful guild of Paris boatmen. By the end of the 3C it had been sacked and burnt to the ground by the Barbarians.

The residence of the Abbots of Cluny. — About 1330, Pierre de Châlus, Abbot of Cluny-en-Bourgogne bought the ruins and the surrounding land on behalf of the influential Burgundian Abbey to build a residence for abbots visiting the college founded by the abbey near the Sorbonne. Jacques of Amboise, Bishop of Clermont and Abbot of Jumièges in Normandy rebuilt the residence to its present design between 1485 and 1500.

The house received many guests including Mary Tudor, eldest daughter of Henry VII who at 16 had been married to Louis XII of France, a man in his fifties who only survived three months. The queen passed her period of mourning in the residence strictly watched by Louis' cousin and successor, François I, lest she should bear a child which might cost him his throne. In fact when Mary was discovered one night in the company of the young Duke of Suffolk the king compelled her to marry the Englishman there and then in the chapel and then despatched her straight away to England. In the 17C the house served as residence for the papal nuncios, the most illustrious being Mazarin.

Abandonment. — At the Revolution the residence was sold for the benefit of the state. It had a variety of owners — a surgeon who used the chapel as a dissecting room, a cooper, a printer, a laundrywoman. The navy installed an observatory in the tower and discovered 21 planets. The baths were covered with six feet of soil and vegetables and an orchard planted.

The founding of the museum. — In 1833 a collector by the name of Alexandre Du Sommerard came to live in the house. On his death in 1842 the mansion and its contents were purchased by the state and opened as a museum in 1844. The garden is now also open to the public.

■ THE HOUSE★★

The Hôtel de Cluny with that of Sens and Jacques Cœur's house, is one of the three large private houses dating back to the 15C to remain in Paris. The mediaeval tradition can be seen in several features such as the crenelations and turrets although these have only a decorative function. Comfort and delicate ornament are important elements in the mansion's design.

Enter the main courtyard where there is a beautiful 15C well curb. The left wing is decorated with arches; the central building has mullioned windows while above, a frieze and Flamboyant balustrade, from which gargoyles spurt, line the base of the roof which in its turn is ornamented with picturesque dormer windows swagged with coats of arms. A pentagonal tower juts out from the central building to contain a wide spiral staircase; corner turrets encase other, narrower, stairs.

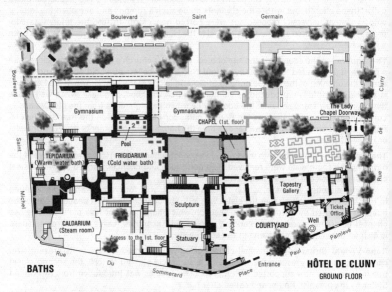

■ THE MUSEUM★★

Open 9.45 am to 12.45 pm and 2 to 5.15 pm; closed Tuesdays and some holidays; 5F.

The museum's twenty-four galleries are entirely devoted to the Middle Ages; the collection as a whole, gives an outstanding picture of the period.

The Baths★ (Thermes). — Excavations have determined the plan of these public baths dating from 200 AD. The best preserved area, the frigidarium (room X) which measures 21 × 11 m — 69 × 36 ft, was 14.5 m — 47 1/2 ft high and had walls 2 m — 6 1/2 ft thick was built of small quarry stones divided by red brick courses. The ribbed vaulting rests on consoles carved as ships' prows — an unusual motif which has inspired the idea that the building was constructed by the Paris boatmen. This same guild, in the reign of Tiberius, (14—37 AD), dedicated a pillar to Jupiter which was discovered beneath the chancel of Notre-Dame and is now on view in the court; it is known as the **Boatmen's Pillar (1)** is Paris' most ancient piece of sculpture.

Room X contains fragments of sculpture from Notre-Dame before 1793. Among the exposed pieces are **21 heads★★ (2)** from the King's Gallery. Discovered in April 1977 during the excavation of Hôtel Moreau in the 9th *arrondissement,* these works date from 1210-1230. Inspite of their condition, the heads evoke an unexpected freshness and a surprising intensity.

The tapestries. — Several rich series of tapestries, woven in the south of the Netherlands and the Loire Valley in the 15 and early 16C, are of the " thousand flower " type, which is typified by harmony and freshness of colour, love of nature, and the grace of the people and animals portrayed. The most perfect example is **The Lady and the Unicorn★★★** series (room XI rotunda, 1st floor). In the six hangings the lion (chivalric nobility) and the unicorn (bourgeois nobility), standing on either side of a richly clad lady, probably symbolize the armorial bearings of different members of the Le Viste family from Lyons. Five of the hangings are believed to depict allegories of the senses but the sixth remains unexplained. Note the blue-green grass and uniform red backgrounds, the lack of decoration, the richness of the animal and plant life. Earlier are small 16C panels embroidered with the Norman English leopards.

The decorative arts in the Middle Ages. — In addition to the tools and utensils of everyday life, the museum possesses pieces of sculpture (original statues from Notre-Dame and the Sainte-Chapelle, rooms IX, X), jewellery gold and silverwork, furniture, illuminated manuscripts, arms and armour, ironwork, liturgical vestments, stained glass, etc.

The chapel★ (room XX). — The chapel, on the first floor, was formerly the abbots' oratory. It has elegant Flamboyant vaulting which falls upon a central pillar and twelve niches, each with its console and carved canopy and formerly containing the statue of a member of the Amboise family. Below there now hang fine tapestries from Auxerre Cathedral illustrating the life of St. Stephen. A stone staircase with an open well leads down to the garden.

Michelin plans 🔟 or 🔟 : K 13 - L 14, L 15.
Distance : 2.5 km — 1 1/2 miles — Time : 4 hours. Start from the Maubert-Mutualité métro.

This is an unusual walk among university faculty buildings and famous schools with the Sorbonne, the Pantheon and St-Étienne-du-Mont Church as the principal landmarks.

HISTORICAL NOTES

Gallo-Roman Lutetia. — In the 3C Lutetia was a small town of some six thousand inhabitants : Gauls occupied the Ile de la Cité, Romans the summit and some slopes of what was later known as Mount St. Genevieve. All the usual public monuments associated with any city colonized by the Romans are to be found : an aqueduct, in this case 15 km — 9 miles — long from the Rungis plain, to bring water to the public baths, a network of paved roads to serve the first Latin quarter, a temple to Mercury crowning Montmartre Hill. Lutetia itself was crossed by the great Soissons — Orleans road, so congested with traffic that it was made oneway.

The preaching of St. Denis on the Ile de la Cité would lead one to presuppose the existence of a Christian church of some kind from the year 250 AD, although no trace of such a building has been discovered. Shortly afterwards the Barbarian invasions ravaged the entire Left Bank with fire (276-280).

The mediaeval Alma Mater. — In the 12C teachers, clerks and students threw off the tutelage of the bishops of the Ile de la Cité *(p 65)* and moved to the area around the St. Genevieve and St. Victor Monasteries on the Left Bank. In 1215 Pope Innocent III authorised the group's incorporation so founding the University of Paris, the first in France.

Students came from provincial France and abroad, registering under disciplines — theology, medicine, the liberal arts, canon law — or by " nationality ", in the colleges founded upon the hill : Sorbon College, 1253; Harcourt College, 1280 on the ruins of the Lutetia Theatre and now St-Louis Lycée; Coqueret College *(p 102)*; Scottish College *(p 151)*; Clermont College, founded by the Jesuits in 1550 and now Louis-le-Grand Lycée; St. Barbara's, Navarre and many others.

The youthful student crowd, turbulent and a terror to the local populace, did not even hold the king in respect. The University had its own jurisdiction of which it was extremely jealous, in 1407 even compelling the royal marshal, who had hanged several students, to come personally and cut down the corpses from the gibet before seeking the Sorbonne's pardon.

The Franciscans (St. Bonaventura), Dominicans (St. Albert the Great, St. Thomas Aquinas) and later the Oratorians (Malebranche, Massillon) and the Jesuits also drew thousands of students and although the University tried, on several occasions, to prevent their following courses, it failed.

From tutelage to autonomy. — In 1793, the Convention disbanded all universities; Latin ceased to be the official language of scholarship.

In 1806 Napoleon founded the Imperial University of France, with a series of academies as the actual bodies of instruction. But university tradition and the enormous influx of students made the system unwelcome and finally unworkable...

New buildings were erected in the Rue des Saints-Pères, Halle aux Vins, Censier and elsewhere and lately in the suburbs, Orsay, Nanterre, Châtenay-Malabry... but still did not prevent the student uprising of May 1968.

October 1970 saw the disappearance of the University of Paris as such and the creation, in its place, for the student population of some 200 000, of thirteen autonomous universities in the Paris region, each with a full range of disciplines, its own curricula and examinations.

The Latin Quarter. — The quarter remains the home of students and younger people of all nationalities, of Bohemianism and fantasy. The Boulevard St-Michel, or Boul' Mich, as it is known, is the heart of the area with its café terraces, publishing houses and bookshops, particularly around the Librairie Gibert, selling new and secondhand books, textbooks, French and foreign language editions, luxury volumes and paperbacks.

In the surrounding streets " cellars ", night-clubs, exotic restaurants, experimental cinemas provide night long entertainment.

GALLO ROMAN PARIS

The courses of roads, the aqueduct and ramparts are based on excavation findings

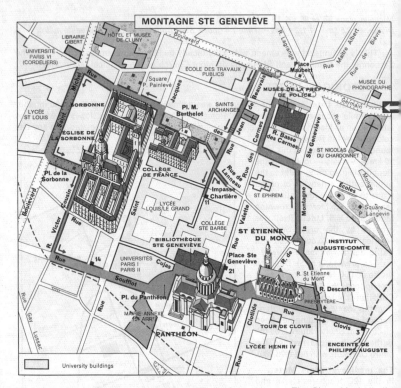

MONTAGNE STE GENEVIÈVE

University buildings

From the Place Maubert to the Place de la Sorbonne. — The Place Maubert, the "Maube" as it is called by students, wanderers and idlers, is the traditional meeting place, the forum of the Latin Quarter, the Court of Miracles of the Left Bank. Barricades have gone up in times of popular uprising.

Leave the Place Maubert by the Rue Jean-de-Beauvais where, in the 14C, the **Beauvais College Chapel** was erected. Since 1882 the much restored chapel has been the seat of the Romanian Orthodox Church in Paris (*No. 9 bis; open Sundays and holidays during offices; other days by permission of the Archpriest*).

The street crosses the Rue des Écoles which, when it was laid in 1651, caused the 150 year old print shop of the erudite publishing house of Estienne to be pulled down.

Coqueret College, where in the 16C under the Hellenist master, Dorat, the students included the poets Ronsard, Antoine de Baïf and, later, Rémy Belleau, Jodelle, Pontus de Tyard and du Bellay, who together formed the Pléïade literary group, stood at No. 11 in the Impasse Chartière, left of the Collège de France. Coqueret itself has been incorporated in St. Barbara's.

The **Rue de Lanneau,** by the entrance to the Chartière blind alley, is picturesque with 16C houses. Turn left for the Collège de France.

Continue by way of the Rue des Écoles, past the main façade of the Sorbonne to the Boulevard St-Michel where you turn left for the Place de la Sorbonne (*description p 103*).

From the Place de la Sorbonne to the Place du Panthéon. — On leaving the church take the Rue Victor-Cousin on the left and then the Rue Soufflot. The **Jacobin Monastery** Church, founded by the first brothers of St. Dominique, who arrived in Paris in 1217, on the site of a former Chapel to St. James, stood at No. 14. Jacques Clément who assassinated Henri III in 1589 was a brother in the monastery, also Humbert II, last of the line of Dauphiné princes who, by taking holy orders, brought his province under the French crown.

From the Place du Panthéon to the Place Maubert. — Walk down the Rue Clovis, past St-Étienne-du-Mont, to the Rue Descartes. On the corner is a presbytery erected by the Duke of Orleans when he retired to the St. Genevieve Abbey where he died in 1752.

A large section of the **Philippe Auguste perimeter wall** (*p 18*) can be seen from a little farther along. It originally stood 10 m high — 33 ft and here lacks only its crenelations.

Return to the Rue Descartes and turn right to skirt the former École Polytechnique (recently moved to the outskirts of Paris) which replaced the earlier Navarre College, founded in 1304 by Jeanne of Navarre, wife of Philip the Fair; and is now the Institut Auguste Comte. The institution, originally intended for seventy poor scholars later numbered among its students Henri III, Henri IV, Richelieu and Bossuet. The École Polytechnique, founded by the Convention in 1794, moved to its present site in 1805. Two years of military discipline and scholarship "for country, science and glory" ensure a high standard of technical knowledge among the few selected. The "X", as they are known, have included such diverse personages as Foch, the positivist philosopher Auguste Comte, Borotra, André Citroën and the French Presidents, Albert Lebrun and Valéry Giscard d'Estaing. Women were admitted for the first time in 1972.

Continue down the Rue de la Montagne-Ste-Geneviève, turn left into the Rue des Écoles to reach the Police Museum (*p 105*) in the Rue des Carmes.

■ THE COLLÈGE DE FRANCE ▥ or ▥ : K 14

The Collège de France has a great past and an equal present. The building stands on the site of large Gallo-Roman baths discovered in 1846 *(map p 101)* of which nothing remains.

Three Language College. — The mediaeval university spoke only Low Latin; the Classical authors were proscribed; Virgil was unknown. In 1530, at the suggestion of the humanist, Guillaume Budé, François I created a new centre of learning with twelve " king's readers " freed from Sorbonne intolerance, scholasticism and disdain of pagan literature. The teachers received payment from the king and so could give instruction free.

In the " three language college " students learned to read the greatest Latin, Greek and Hebrew authors. Henri II installed the staff and students in two colleges, Cambrai and Tréguier which were replaced on the same site in the 17C by Louis XIII with the Royal College of France. New subjects of study were added : mathematics, medicine, surgery, philosophy, Arabic, Syriac, botany, astronomy, canon law and, in the reign of Louis XV, French literature.

The College today. — In 1778 the building was reconstructed by Chalgrin and, at the Revolution, took its modern name of Collège de France. 19C reconstructions have been replaced in the 20C by vast additions. The poor labs, on the Rue des Écoles and Rue St-Jacques in which Claude Bernard worked on the function of the pancreas from 1847 to 1878 have disappeared in favour of new halls and laboratories and equipment such as the cyclotron on which Frédéric Joliot-Curie produced fission in a uranium particle. Other outstanding members of the College have been Cuvier (zoologist), Ampère (physicist), Michelet (historian), Champollion (Egyptologist), Renan and Bergson (philosophers), Marcelin Berthelot (chemist), Paul Valéry (poet) and more recently François Jacob (physician). The college retains total scholastic independence although dependent financially, since 1852, on the state.

■ THE SORBONNE ▥ or ▥ : K 14

Foundation. — In 1253 a college for sixteen poor students who wished to study theology was founded by a Paris canon, Robert of Sorbon — named, in accordance with mediaeval custom, after his native village of Sorbon in the Ardennes — and the King, Saint Louis, to whom the priest was confessor. From such a simple beginning was to develop the Sorbonne, the centre of theological study in pre-Revolutionary France and the seat of the University of Paris.

It was in the same buildings that three printers summoned from Mainz by Louis XI established the first printing house in France in 1469.

Political and religious struggles. — The theological faculty at Philip the Fair's request condemned the Templars which resulted in their dissolution; in the Hundred Years War, the Sorbonne sided with the Burgundians and the English, recognising Henry V of England as King of France and seconding one of their greatest advocates, Bishop Pierre Cauchon as prosecutor in the trial of Joan of Arc. The Sorbonne steadfastly opposed all Protestants and, in the 18C, the philosophers.

From Richelieu to the present day. — Richelieu, on his election as Chancellor of the Sorbonne, put in hand reconstruction of the buildings and church (1624-1642). In 1792 the Sorbonne and University were suppressed; in 1806 they were re-established by Napoleon. Between 1885 and 1901 large scale rebuilding and expansion prepared the way for the Sorbonne to become the principal centre of higher learning in France. Then came 1968 when the Sorbonne and Nanterre became the focal points of student unrest, sparking off the popular uprisings of May 1968 and instigating a reform of the university system throughout France.

The Sorbonne houses the offices of Paris III and Paris IV Universities.

THE PRESENT BUILDING

The building is a remarkable feat of design when one realises that it includes twenty-two lecture halls, two museums, sixteen examination halls, twenty-two lecture rooms, thirty-seven rooms for the teaching staff, two hundred and forty laboratories, a library, a physics tower, an astronomy tower, offices, the chancellor's lodge, etc.

The most interesting areas — the entrance, the main staircase and great lecture hall with Puvis de Chavannes' famous painting the **Sacred Wood★** — overlook the Rue des Écoles *(apply to the caretaker).*

The main courtyard, lined on the left by the library wing and dominated by the chapel's Classical pediment and cupola, is the students' central meeting place, the place where debate starts, where talk never ceases. To some degree it is also, traditionally, the university sanctuary. Decorative panels by Weerts beneath the arches illustrate the traditional Lendit Fair held at St-Denis and formerly a great university occasion (11 June).

The Sorbonne Church★. — *Open only when there are temporary exhibitions.*

The church was erected by Le Mercier between 1635 and 1642 in the Jesuit style. The façade, unlike St-Paul-St-Louis *(p 79)*, is not so proportioned as to overwhelm the rest of the building and its design of two (instead of three) superimposed orders became the style model.

The **face★** overlooking the main courtyard of the Sorbonne is completely different : above the ten Corinthian columns marking the doorway, rise, first the transept, then the cupola. The effect is outstanding and worth walking into the courtyard to see.

Inside, in the chancel is the **tomb★** of Cardinal Richelieu, the white marble magnificently carved by Girardon in 1694 to drawings by Le Brun. The tomb was violated in 1794 when the church became the Temple of Reason.

The cupola pendentives were painted by Philippe de Champaigne.

MONTAGNE STE-GENEVIÈVE ★★

■ **PLACE DU PANTHÉON** 🔟 or 🔟 : L 14

The Rue Soufflot and the semicircular square are lined by the symmetrical buildings of the former Law Faculty (by Soufflot, 1772) now the offices of Paris I and Paris II Universities and buildings by Hittorff, 1844.

St. Genevieve Library. — Until it was replaced in the middle of the 19C by the St. Genevieve Library, Montaigu College stood on the left, on the corner of the Rue Valette. The college was known for its teaching, its austere discipline and its squalor — its scholars were said to sleep on the ground amidst lice, fleas and bugs. Manuscripts and incunabula from St. Genevieve Abbey were transferred by Labrouste to the new building in 1850 to form the nucleus of the new library. *Reader's ticket holders only.* Behind the library is St. Barbara's College, founded in 1460 and the last of the Latin Quarter Colleges to survive.

A hexagonal tower dating from 1560 and known as Calvin's Tower, stands in the courtyard at No. 21 Rue Valette. It is all that remains of Fortet College where, in 1585, the Duke of Guise founded the Catholic League which was to expel Henri III from Paris.

Henri-IV Lycée. — It was on this site that Clovis, following his victory over the Visigoths at Vouillé near Poitiers, had a rich basilica erected in 510 in which he and his wife Clotilda were both buried and also St. Genevieve. The widespread devotion to the saint soon called for the foundation of an abbey which came under the rule of Augustine canons and rivalled the Abbey of St-Germain-des-Prés in spiritual, juridical and territorial power. Mediaeval piety was expressed on all occasions by vast processions walking behind the saint's shrine through the decorated streets of Paris to the sound of ringing church bells.

The Revolution suppressed such festivities and even the abbey so that there remain only the refectory (along the Rue Clotilde), Gothic cellars and the church belfry, known as **Clovis' Tower.** Since 1796 the buildings have been occupied by the Henri-IV Lycée.

THE PANTHEON★★ 🔟 or 🔟 : L 14

The Pantheon's renown makes it one of the capital's most popular sights.

A royal vow. — Louis XV, when he fell ill at Metz in 1744, vowed that if he recovered he would replace St. Genevieve Abbey's half ruined church by a magnificent edifice. He entrusted the fulfilment of his vow to the Marquis of Marigny, brother to the Marquise de Pompadour.

Soufflot, Marigny's *protégé,* was charged with the plans. In his effort to combine the nobility and purity of Antiquity and the sweeping lines of the Middle Ages, he designed a vast church 110 m long by 84 m wide by 83 m high — 361 × 276 × 272 ft — in the form of a Greek cross. At the centre he placed a huge dome beneath which would lie the saint's shrine. The foundations were laid in 1758 but financial difficulties intervened — Marigny ran three lotteries to find sufficient money — and it was only completed by Soufflot's pupil, Rondelet, in 1789.

The Temple of Fame. — In 1791 the Constituent Assembly decided that the now closed church should henceforth " receive the bodies of great men who died in the period of French liberty " — the church thus became the national Pantheon. Mirabeau, Voltaire, Rousseau were buried there, and for a short time, Marat also.

Successively the Pantheon has been a church under the Empire, a necropolis in the reign of Louis-Philippe, a church again under Napoleon III, headquarters of the Commune and finally a lay temple (Victor Hugo was buried within it in 1885).

TOUR

Exterior. — The Constituent Assembly ordered the blocking of Soufflot's forty-two windows which has deadened the design in spite of the frieze and garland which encircle the building. Two storeys were also removed from the towers flanking the apse.

The **dome**★★, which has an iron framework, can only be appreciated from some distance.

The peristyle is composed of fluted columns supporting a triangular pediment, the first of its kind in Paris. In 1831 David d'Angers carved a representation upon it of the Nation distributing palms presented by Liberty to great men including Bonaparte, La Fayette, Voltaire and Rousseau.

Interior. — *Open April to September 10 am to 5.40 pm (4.10 pm October to March). Closed Tuesdays, 1 January, 1 May, 1 November, 25 December; 5F; Sundays and holidays : 2.50F.*

Flattened domes and, to divide the nave from the aisles, a line of columns supporting a frieze, cornice and balustrade, were used by Soufflot instead of more orthodox elements. The great central dome was also intended to be supported on columns but Rondelet was apprehensive and substituted heavy masonry, so spoiling the effect. The dome's upper cupola has a fresco commissioned by Napoleon in 1811 from the artist, Gros, of *St. Genevieve's Apotheosis.* In 1849 Foucault took advantage of the dome's height to conduct an experiment proving the rotation of the earth *(see Conservatoire des Arts et Métiers, p 146).*

The Pantheon's walls are decorated with **paintings**★ dating from 1877 onward, the best known being those by Puvis de Chavannes of *Scenes from St. Genevieve's Life* (right wall), the *Saint watching over Paris and Bringing Food to the City* — left wall beyond the dome *(p 59).*

Crypt. — *Guided tours every 15 minutes from the back of the chancel, left side.* The crypt extends under the whole building and contains an urn with the heart of Gambetta and the tombs of great men in all walks of life throughout France's history : La Tour d'Auvergne, Voltaire, Rousseau, Victor Hugo, Émile Zola, Marcelin Berthelot, Louis Braille (inventor of a system of writing for the blind), Jean Jaurès, the explorer Bougainville...

ST-ÉTIENNE-DU-MONT CHURCH★★ □□ or □□ : L 15

It is in this church that St. Genevieve is venerated particularly. Both outside and inside, the church building is unique. It is also the only church in Paris to possess a roodscreen.

Construction. — Until 1220 the servants of the Abbey of St. Genevieve attended services in the church crypt then, their number becoming too great, a parish church, dedicated to St. Stephen, was built adjoining the abbey church. By the end of the 15C St. Stephen's had become too small. Rebuilding began in 1492 with the belfry tower and apse; in 1610 the foundation stone for the new façade was laid by Queen Margot, first wife of Henri IV, and in 1626 the new church was consecrated.

Exterior. — The **façade**★★ is highly original. Three superimposed pediments stand at the centre, their lines emphasized by the upward sweep of the belfry. The south aisle rises to a considerable height above the chapels. The chancel, the first part to be built, has Flamboyant style broken arch bays, the nave, the later, rounded windows of the Renaissance.

Interior. — The church is Gothic although it is 16C. The height of the arches over the nave and chancel, however, prevented the usual triforium being constructed and instead there is a line of windows. The walls along the aisles are also tall enabling wide, luminous bays to be hollowed out. An elegant balustrade course cuts the height of the tall pillars.

The Flamboyant vaulting above the transept catches the eye with its multiple ribbing and 5.50 m — 18 ft — intricately carved hanging keystone.

The 17C organ loft is highly ornate. Recitals are given regularly on the organ (92 stops).

The stained glass, which for the most part dates from the 16 and 17C is worth looking at in detail, particularly in the ambulatory and chancel.

The Roodscreen★★. — In the 15 and 16C all the major churches possessed roodscreens to illustrate the Epistles and the Gospels and so instruct their congregations. The screens' disadvantage, however, was that they hid all liturgical ceremony performed in the chancel from the faithful in the nave and in Paris they were, therefore, all removed apart from this one in which the wide arch gave a clear view.

The centre, with its Renaissance decoration, was constructed from 1521 to 1535; the twin side doors in the Classical style in 1609. Two lovely open spiral staircases lead to the rood loft and the course along the chancel pillars. Delightful feminine figures adorn the arch at either end.

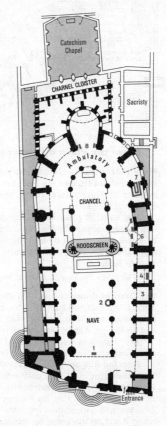

1) Marble slab marking the spot where an archbishop of Paris was stabbed to death by an unfrocked priest (3 January 1857).
2) 1650 **pulpit**★ supported by a figure of Samson.
3) **Stained glass window**★ of 1586 illustrating the parable of those invited to the feast.
4) 16C Entombment.
5) Over the arch, two ex-votos offered by the City of Paris : on the right, the City giving thanks to St. Genevieve, painted by de Troy in 1726 ; on the left, an earlier painting by Largillière (1696).
6) The epitaphs of Racine (by Boileau) and Pascal.
7) **St. Genevieve's shrine.** — St. Genevieve's relics, originally buried in the crypt of the neighbouring abbey *(p. 105)*, were exhumed and burnt upon the Place de Grève in 1793. When the abbey church was pulled down in 1802, the saint's sarcophagus stone was found and now serves as a support for the modern gilded copper shrine containing a few small relics.
8) Pascal (1623-1662) and Racine (1639-1699) lie buried near the pillars to the Lady Chapel. Racine was originally interred at Port-Royal-des-Champs and translated in 1711.

The Cloister. — It is sometimes called the Charnel House Cloister. At one time the church was bordered to the north and east by two small burial grounds in which lay the remains, notably, of Mirabeau and Marat after they had been removed from the Pantheon. The right side of the ambulatory opens onto the cloister which surrounded the burial ground at the church's east end and which, it is thought, may at one time have been used as a charnel house. The cloister's main gallery at the end and on the left was glazed early in the 17C with **stained glass**★, beautiful in vitality and colour. The small Catechism Chapel was added by Baltard in 1859.

POLICE MUSEUM (Musée de la Préfecture de Police) □□ or □□ : K 15

1 bis Rue des Carmes. Open Wednesdays and Thursdays, which do not fall on holidays, 2 to 5 pm.

The **Historical Collections of the Police Museum** display the evolution of the Paris police and firemen from the early Middle Ages to 1870. There are also legal documents such as *lettres de cachet* or royal warrants, prison registers and criminals' weapons.

Michelin plans ▥ or ▥ : H 14, H 15.
Distance : 4 km — 2 1/2 miles — Time : 3 1/2 hours. Start from the Louvre métro station.

This quarter, deprived of its active life, which the Halles — the former covered market — (which has since moved to Rungis) — attracted, is now undergoing a complete transformation. Although there has been a recent sprouting up of a large number of art galleries, boutiques, bookstores and antique stores, it is the future " Forum " *(p 107)* which will bring life back to the quarter.

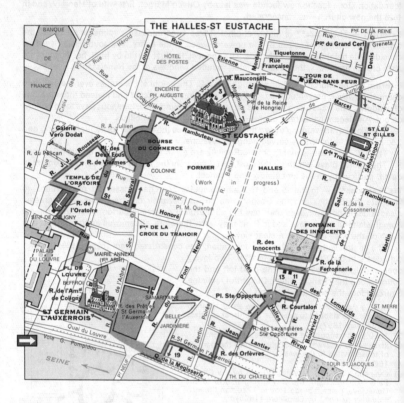

From the Place du Louvre to St-Eustache Church

Place du Louvre*. — This square was the site on which the Roman, Labienus, pitched his camp when he crushed the Parisii in 52 BC, and the Northmen when they besieged Paris in 885 *(p 59)*. The square's fine mansions *(map p 29)* including the Petit Bourbon, were demolished over the years.

Two hundred years later Haussmann transformed the narrow Rue des Poulies into the Rue du Louvre, demolishing in the process the last of the 17C houses. These were replaced by a Neo-Renaissance building by Hittorff and a Neo-Gothic belfry with a 38 bell carillon *(peals at 4.30 pm on the second Sunday and 8.30 pm on the following Tuesday in the month from April to September).*

Walk down the Rue de Rivoli to the Rue de l'Oratoire.

The Oratory Church. — In 1616 the Carmelite Oratorian Congregation, later to rival the Jesuits, had a church built by Le Mercier to which such preachers as Bossuet, Malebranche, Bourdaloue and Massillon attracted the royal family and court. The funerals of Louis XIII and his Queen, Anne of Austria, were held in the church.

The Oratorians were suppressed at the Revolution; the chapel became an arms depot, an opera storehouse and, in 1811, a Protestant church.

From the Rue de Rivoli and the church's east end, walk up the Rue de l'Oratoire to the 18C Jesuit style west face on the Rue St-Honoré. On the right is the Rue Jean-Jacques-Rousseau where the philosopher lived at the end of his life. On the left is the former street of easy virtue, the Rue du Pélican and, beyond the **Vero-Dodat arcade,** now deserted but crowded and garish when created in 1822 by two pork butchers who installed gas lighting aolng it and let the shops for fabulous rents. Also a relic from the past is the picturesque Place des Deux-Écus.

Take the Rue du Louvre to the Rue St-Honoré.

Rue St-Honoré. — This street, as of the 12C was one of the quarter's major arteries.

The site of No. 96 on the corner, the Rue Sauval, is where the poet and comedy writer, Regnard was born in 1655 and where some historians allege Molière was born in 1662. Wagner lived there in 1839.

Ahead is the **Croix-du-Trahoir Fountain**. The present monument (1775) by Soufflot, is a successor to the one erected by François I but in no way resembles it. The original stood in the middle of the road, raised on a flight of steps on which vegetables were spread out for sale. To one side stood the gallows from which the street on the left took its name of the Arbre Sec or Withered Tree.

It is said also that in 613 at these crossroads, on the orders of her enemy, Frédégonde, the old Queen Brunehaut of Austrasia was tied by her hair to a wild horse's tail and broken.

More than a thousand years later, on 26 August 1648, the arrest of the parliamentarian, Broussel, by Anne of Austria's forces in this same spot began a street row which, by the following morning, had developed into civil conflict : the Fronde had begun.

Turn left into the Rue Sauval, formerly known as the Rue des Étuves or Bath Boiler Street after the public baths once situated in it. These having become haunts of debauchery in the Middle Ages, were finally closed like all others in Paris, in 17C.

The Commercial Exchange (Bourse du Commerce). — This circular building is hemmed in to the west by a semicircle of tall porticoed mansions and to the east by a huge construction site — the former Halles market area.

It stands where for the past 800 years French history has been made : Blanche of Castille, mother of St. Louis died in the first building (Hôtel de Nesle) in 1252 on a bed of straw as a sign of humility; Philippe of Valois, John the Good, Charles V and Charles VI all lived there; Louis XII lost the mansion at cribbage to his chamberlain who converted it into a convent for repentant sinners. These were dislodged by Catherine dei Medici in 1572 when she had a mansion constructed by Delorme and Bullant. The queen lived in the Hôtel de la Reine until her death in 1589. The building subsequently became a luxurious brothel and was finally razed in 1748. A wheat market, built in Louis XVI's reign, was replaced in 1889 by the present rotunda, half encircled to the east by the market.

Inside, the vast circular hall is a central gallery reserved for accredited wheat, flour, sugar, wine and other brokers. Outside, abutting on the market side wall, is an ancient fluted column 30 m — 98 ft high, the only feature remaining of Catherine dei Medici's mansion and probably once a part of the observatory of her astrologer, Ruggieri.

Take the Rue Coquillière to St-Eustache Church.

THE HALLES   ⬛ or ⬛ : H 14

The Halles yesterday. — Paris' first central market was on the Ile de la Cité; the second on the Place de Grève now the Place de l'Hôtel-de-Ville; the third settled on the present site in about 1110. In 1183 under Philippe Auguste it was extended, permanent structures being erected and a surrounding wall built.

It was more a fair than a simple food market : everything made in Paris and outside and even abroad was sold there. The king levied site and sales taxes; city merchants and craftsmen were ordered to close their shops twice a week to encourage trade in the market where every street had its own special merchandise.

By the 16C, with a population of 300 000 in the capital, the food market assumed a paramount importance — eventually replacing all other types of selling in the market. Finally, even the wine and leather markets were squeezed out and on the orders of Napoleon, transferred to the Left Bank. The other shopkeepers moved to the ground-floors of neighbouring houses, each street being taken up by a particular trade.

Close to the nearby St-Eustache crossroads was the market **pillory** where dishonest traders were publicly exposed.

The Halles today. — By the 19C the great market, which had become a centre of insalubrity and insurrection, was in urgent need of reconstruction. As Rambuteau and Haussmann thrust wide main streets through the quarter (Rues de Rivoli, du Pont-Neuf, du Louvre, des Halles and Étienne-Marcel), a stone pavilion was built, designed by the architect **Baltard**, and, being unsuitable, razed. He then made plans of a hall of iron girders and skylight roofs, which was accepted and erected, reminiscent of the Gare de l'Est.

Ten halls in all were constructed between 1854 and 1866. These buildings, complete with vast underground storehouses and linked by roofed passages and alleys, became the model for covered markets throughout France and even abroad. Two further halls were opened in 1936.

The market space, however, eventually became totally inadequate and so operations have been transferred to **Rungis**, a vast open site near Orly Airport.

The Forum tomorrow. — The huge urban plan to be undertaken on the site of the former market has for objective to conserve the Halles' rich historic past (restauration of an outer area of some 22 ha — 54 acres) and investing the central area, at the crossroads of several of Paris' main thoroughfares, with a new and vital focal point. The underground area will contain a complex of key transport improvements — the final central section of the east-west section of the RER express métro and a line linking to the SNCF — and the Forum.

The **Forum**, a pedestrian concourse lying east of the Commercial Exchange, will be lined with boutiques and galleries, linked to the métro system, and communicate to cultural and sporting facilities as well as to the Beaubourg Centre.

The ground level, for environmental reasons, left as an open space, will be landscaped at different levels and arranged to include green areas, pools and paths providing a good view of the east end of St-Eustache.

Surrounding this 5 ha — 12 acre traffic-free oasis will be a hotel, café-restaurants, private flats and an antiques centre.

■ ST-EUSTACHE CHURCH** 🔟 or 🔟 : H 14

St-Eustache, Gothic in plan and outline, Renaissance in decoration, is one of Paris' most beautiful churches. Services and concerts held there maintain a long tradition of organ and choral music. Last century it was the setting for first performances of works by both Berlioz and Liszt.

Construction. — In 1214 a small chapel, dedicated to St. Agnes was built on this spot. A few years later, the chapel was rededicated to St. Eustace, a Roman general converted, like St. Hubert, by the vision of a cross between a stag's antlers. According to legend he was martyred together with his wife and two sons by being enclosed in a bronze bull which was heated white hot.

But the Halles parish, which had become the biggest in Paris, dreamed of a church worthy of its new status. Grandiose plans were made with Notre-Dame as the model.

The foundation stone was laid in 1532. Construction was slow, however, in spite of liberal gifts and the church was only consecrated a century later, in 1637. The original plan had been adhered to, although the west front had never been completed, when in 1754 it was decided to replace this Renaissance front by a Classical one with columns.

During the Revolution the church was renamed the Temple of Agriculture; in 1844 it was badly damaged by fire and subsequently reconstructed by Baltard.

St-Eustache, so close to the Louvre and the Palais-Royal, at the centre of everything going on in the capital and also the parish church of the Halles corporations, became a focal point of public ceremony — the baptisms of Armand du Plessis, the future Richelieu, of Jean-Baptiste Poquelin (Molière), the future Marquise de Pompadour, Louis XIV's first communion, the funerals of La Fontaine, Molière and the Revolutionary orator, Mirabeau.

The church was at one time paved with tombstones including those of Louis XIV's statesman, Colbert, Admiral de Tourville who beat the combined Anglo-Dutch fleets off Beachy Head in 1690 and was defeated, in turn, off La Hogue in 1692, and the composer Rameau.

Chevet. — On the right take the Rue Rambuteau, skirting the church. From the corner where the Rues Montorgueil and Montmartre meet at the St-Eustache crossroads you can see the church chevet and the final circular Lady Chapel.

The belfry spire above the transept was considerably lopped last century, to accomodate a semaphore station.

Retrace your steps.

Transept façade*. — This fine Renaissance composition is flanked by twin staircase turrets ending in pinnacles. Beneath the gable point is a stag's head with a Cross between the antlers recalling St. Eustace's conversion. The doorway covings have lost their statues; those at the arch shafts are modern. The pilasters, niches, mouldings, grotesques and rose windows are beautifully and delicately fashioned.

Interior. — St-Eustache measures 100 m long, 44 m wide and 34 m high — 328 × 144 × 112 ft. The church's majesty and the richness of decoration in its pillars and vaulting strike one immediately.

The plan is that of Notre-Dame with nave and chancel encircled by double aisles and flat transepts. The vaulting above the nave and chancel is Flamboyant, adorned with numerous ribs and richly carved hanging keystones particularly in the transept and chancel.

The elevation, however, is entirely different to the cathedral's. The aisles, devoid of galleries, rise very high, the arches being so tall that between them and the elongated windows there is only space for a small Renaissance style gallery.

The stained glass windows in the chancel are after cartoons by Philippe de Champaigne (1631) and recall the mediaeval skill in this craft. St. Eustace appears at the centre, surrounded by the Fathers of the Church and the Apostles.

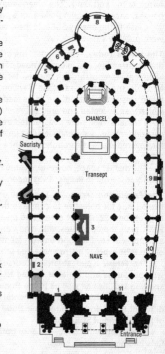

1) On the door tympanum : the *Martyrdom of St. Eustace* by Simon Vouet (17C).
2) *Adoration of the Magi,* a copy of a painting by Rubens.
3) Churchwarden's pew presented by the Regent, Philippe of Orleans in 1720.
4) *Tobias and the Angel,* by Santi di Tito (16C).
5) *The Ecstasy of Mary Magdalene,* painting by Manetti (17C).
6) *The Pilgrims at Emmaüs,* an early Rubens.
7) Colbert's tomb designed by Le Brun. Coysevox carved the statues of the minister and of Abundance ; Tuby that of Fidelity.
8) Statue of the Virgin by Pigalle. Chapel frescoes by Thomas Couture (19C).
9) 16C statue of St. John the Evangelist.
10) Bust of the composer Jean-Philippe Rameau who died in 1764.
11) Epitaph to 17C Lieutenant-General Chevert.

From St-Eustache to St-Germain-l'Auxerrois

Turn right into the narrow Rue du Jour from where opposite No. 4, there is a good **view*** of the flying buttresses and upper parts of the church. No. 4, once the Paris seat of Royaumont Abbey, passed to Montmorency-Bouteville, who was executed by Richelieu for contravening his regulations on duelling.

At No. 3 Rue Montmartre a blind alley ends at the beautiful north transept door.

Opposite, at No. 16, is the curious **Queen of Hungary Passage** — named after a market stall holder who presented a petition to Marie-Antoinette. The queen commented on the woman's likeness to the Hungarian queen and both she and the alley where she lived were renamed. The so-called queen, like her nominator, died in the Terror.

Bear left into the typical Rue Montorgueil, then into the Rue Mauconseil.

Rue Mauconseil. — The street was from the 16 to 18C the home of a series of theatrical companies. The first to occupy the theatre built on the Hôtel de Bourgogne land in 1548, like others of its time, had no women players (until 1634).

Racine first presented *Mithridate* and *Iphigénie* to the public in this theatre in 1673 and 1674. In 1680 the company, by royal command, combined with that of the Rue Mazarine (*p 137*). The Italians succeeded them with the improvised performances of Harlequin, Columbine, Isabella. Among the comedians was a clown, Scaramouche, who could still knock off his partner's hat with a high kick at the age of 83. The company was disbanded in 1697 after an attack on Mme de Maintenon. The last troupe to play the theatre before it disappeared was the Comic Opera (1716-1782).

John the Fearless' Tower* (Tour de Jean sans Peur). — Follow the Rue Française on the left. At No. 20 in the Rue Étienne-Marcel, in a schoolyard, is a square machicolated tower (*not open*) built by John the Fearless for his own protection in 1408 following the assassination, on his orders, of the Duke of Orleans. The tower formed part of the **Hôtel de Bourgogne,** the former Artois mansion abutting on the Philippe Auguste perimeter wall. Continue to the Rue Tiquetonne (old houses with attractively restored façades) on the right, and the Rue St-Denis.

Rue St-Denis. — The street, opened in the 7C to relieve the Rue St-Martin of excessive traffic, soon became the busiest and most prosperous in Paris.

Kings rode along it when making solemn entries to the capital and visiting Notre-Dame; royal funerals followed it on their way to St-Denis Abbey. The past forgotten, it is now renowned as a street of pleasure.

The progress of a new king was greeted with triumphal arches, porticoes and even fountains — the last much preferred as they played free wine or milk! One, much restored, remains from the time of Louis XI, the Queen's Fountain at No. 142 (corner of the Rue Grénéta).

Church of St-Leu-St-Gilles. — *92 bis Rue St-Denis.* Two 6C saints, Lupus (Leu in French), Bishop of Sens, and the Provençal hermit, Giles, are patrons of this church, built in 1320 and remodelled several times. A new east end and the north tower belfry were constructed in 1858 when the Sébastopol Boulevard was laid.

Inside, the nave's Gothic bays contrast with the taller Classical chancel. The keystones are interesting, also a 16C marble group by Jean Bullant of St. Anne and the Virgin, 15C alabaster low reliefs fragments of an altarpiece the former Innocents' Cemetery (*at the sacristy entrance*) and a stone Christ Entombed (*in the crypt beneath the chancel*).

Walk left down the Rue St-Denis, past the Rue de la Grande-Truanderie — Vagabonds' Row, contemporary with the mediaeval Court of Miracles (*p 118*).

Fountain of the Innocents*. — The 19C square stands on the site of the Cemetery and Church of the Holy Innocents which dated back to the 12C.

The cemetery with its series of communal graves was encircled by a charnel house about which horrific tales were told of bones being ground up for flour during the siege of Paris in 1590 by Henri of Navarre; at other times, however, in spite of a famous illustration of the Dance of Death, the area was a popular place for a stroll. In 1786 the cemetery became a market after some two million skeletons had been transferred to a quarry thereupon renamed the Catacombs (*p 154*).

This Renaissance fountain by Pierre Lescot, carved by Jean Goujon, stood in 1550, at the corner of Rue St-Denis. Backed against a wall, it had only three sides; when removed to its present site in the 18C, a fourth side was added; a new base was substituted in 1865 — the original low reliefs are in the Louvre.

Go through a passage beneath the Rue des Innocents houses to the **Rue de la Ferronnerie,** where you turn left. It was while riding in this street in his carriage that Henri IV was assassinated on 14 May 1610 in front of No. 11. The sign at No. 13 was a crowned heart pierced by an arrow — the witnesses to the murder felt this to be an omen. His assailant, Ravaillac, was later quartered on the Place de Grève.

Return to the Rue St-Denis and cross the **Rue des Lombards** — a reminder of the mediaeval Lombard moneylenders — to follow the map route to the Rue des Orfèvres with its gold and silversmiths' houses on the left. In the Rue St-Germain-l'Auxerrois on the right, which dates from 860, No. 19 was once an episcopal prison where intemperate playwrights, including Beaumarchais, were locked up.

From 1660 the Rue Bertin-Poirée housed the **Lottery,** originally a private Italian venture, but soon taken over as a source of revenue by the monarch — the Pantheon and Military Academy were built from the funds. It was proscribed by Louis-Philippe but restarted as the National Lottery in 1933.

■ ST-GERMAIN-L'AUXERROIS★★ ⅡⅡ or ⅡⅡ : H 14

The present church, on the site of an 8C sanctuary demolished by the Northmen and a later one built by Robert the Pious, combines five centuries of architectural design with a Romanesque belfry, radiant Gothic chancel, Flamboyant porch and nave and Renaissance doorway. The tympanum and pier and the magnificent roodscreen by Lescot were removed in the 18C to allow the passage of processions.

When the Valois moved into the Louvre in the 14C, St-Germain became the royal parish church and the receptacle for gifts and decoration.

It was from this tower that the bells rang on the night of 24 August 1572 giving the signal for the Massacre of St. Bartholomew when thousands of Huguenots, invited to celebrate the marriage of Henri of Navarre to his cousin, Marguerite of Valois, were slaughtered in accordance with a plan laid by the Cardinal Duke of Guise, Catherine dei Medici, Charles IX and the future Henri III.

During the Revolution, it became a barn; in 1831 it was further desecrated. Finally, however, it was restored (1838-1855).

Many poets : Jodelle, Malherbe; painters : Coypel, Boucher, Nattier, Chardin, Van Loo; sculptors : Coysevox, the two Coustous; architects : Le Vau, Robert de Cotte, Gabriel the Elder, Soufflot and others associated with the court, are buried in the church.

Since 1926, because of a wish by the painter and drawer Adolphe Willette (1857-1926) artists come to St. Germain on the first Sunday in Lent to receive ashes and to pray for those artists who will die in the year.

Exterior. — From the Samaritaine pavement you will get a good view of the east end and Romanesque belfry which abuts on the apse.

The chancel aisles are covered by a series of small attic-like structures in which the bones taken from tombs in the cloisters, which at one time surrounded the church, were heaped. The apsidal chapel given by the Tronson family is decorated with a frieze of carp. On the south wall of the church the gargoyles and supporting consoles are carved with delightful fantasy. The transept façade is lightened by a Flamboyant rose window.

The Porch★★. — The porch, which is the building's most original feature, was built between 1435 and 1439. The statues at the pillars are modern. The outer bays which are also the lowest, are surmounted by small chambers, covered with slate, in which the chapter placed the church archives and treasure.

The three central bays have multi-ribbed Flamboyant vaulting, while the other two are plain Gothic. The centre doorway, the most interesting, is 13C. The figure in the right embrasure is St. Genevieve with a candle which a small devil is trying to snuff out and an angel *(next niche)* stands ready to relight.

Interior. — The nave is flanked by double aisles which continue round the chancel to the flat apse. The restored 17C organ (1) comes from the Sainte-Chapelle *(p 68)*. The **churchwarden's pew★** (2), dating from 1684, is thought to have been used by successive kings and their families. At its back is a 15C polychrome carved wood triptych (3 — *light switch)* and, in the chapel opposite, a fine Flemish **altarpiece★** (4 — *light switch)* of the same period. The **stained glass★** in the transept, and the two rose windows are late 15C. The much compartimented vaulting above the transept is a good example of the Flamboyant style.

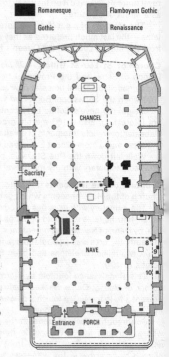

Romanesque Flamboyant Gothic
Gothic Renaissance

CHANCEL

Sacristy

NAVE

Entrance PORCH

The chancel is surrounded by an 18C grille before which stand 15C polychrome statues of St. Germanus (5) and St. Vincent (6). In the 18C, when the roodscreen was removed (the low reliefs are in the Louvre), the columns were fluted and their Gothic capitals transformed into garlanded torri.

The Chapel of the Holy Sacrament (7) contains a 14C polychrome stone statue of the Virgin; against a pillar (8), a 14C Cross; a Last Supper (9) by Theo Van Elsen (1954); one of the original statues (10) from the main doorway, St. Mary the Egyptian, and a 13C statue of St. Germanus (11).

Picturesque Halles

Imagine in the centre of Paris a scene of nightmare congestion, which existed from about 1110 to 1969 of food laden lorries — a rich variety of colour and smell so vividly described by Émile Zola as " the stomach of Paris ".

Nevertheless, inspite of the market's move to Rungis, the old Paris tradition still exists of eating onion soup, snails and grilled pig's trotters at 5am in cabarets and restaurants with colourful names :

Le Chien qui Fume — The Smoking Dog
Le Père Tranquille — The Quiet Father
Le Pied de Cochon — The Pig's Trotter.

BEAUBOURG - HÔTEL DE VILLE ★★

Michelin plans ▮▮ or ▮▮ : H 15, H 16 - J 15, J 16.
Distance : 3.5 km — 2 miles — Time : 5 hours. Start from the Châtelet métro station.

This walk between the Halles and the Marais reveals striking contrasts : taking you through a Paris with its dignified mansions, through a quarter where contemporary culture reigns and ending in a quarter which holds the City government building.

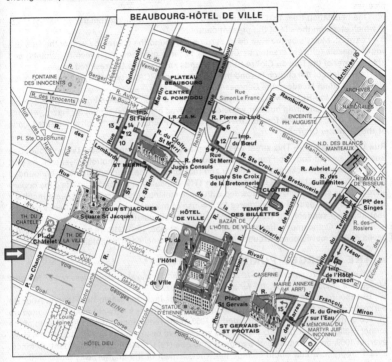

BEAUBOURG-HÔTEL DE VILLE

From the Place du Châtelet to the Georges Pompidou Centre

Place du Châtelet. — The square gets its name from the Grand Châtelet or Great Barbican which commanded the Pont au Change.

The Châtelet, or as it was known, Palm Fountain (1808) was erected to commemorate Napoleon's victories. The sphinx and statue decorated base dates from 1858.

The two theatres on either side were built by Davioud in 1862. The Châtelet, after the Palais de Congrès *(p 131),* has the largest auditorium in Paris seating 3 600 and usually plays light opera and musicals. Opposite, on the site where the writer Gérard de Nerval hanged himself in 1855, is the Théâtre de la Ville, a centre of popular culture.

The St-Jacques Tower★. — The tower is the old belfry of St-James-the-Butcher's, built in the 16C and one of the starting points for pilgrims making the journey to Santiago de Compostela in Spain. The church disappeared in 1802. A weather point *(not open to the public)* has been installed in the square and at the top of the 52 m — 171 ft — tower which had to be underpinned when the mound on which it abutted, was removed to make way for the Rue de Rivoli. The statue of the physicist and philosopher, Pascal, recalls the experiments which he began on the Puy de Dôme (Auvergne), into the weight of air in 1648.

Leaving the Square St-Jacques, cross the Rue de Rivoli and take the Rue St-Martin one of the oldest streets — it is treelined and offers a fine perspective. Its slight incline, like that of the steps of the neighbouring Rue St-Bon, gives an idea of the height of the old mound.

The St. Merry Quarter. — The quarter round the church has always been crowded with craftsmen. In the Middle Ages there were linen drapers, rivalling those of Flanders, haberdashers and hairdressers — Paris' taste and fashions had begun their influence throughout Europe.

At every political insurrection the barricades went up. In June 1832, a young boy and an old man, flourishing a tricolour, were killed near the Rue du Cloître-St-Merri — an event on which Victor Hugo based his description of the death of Gavroche in his novel *Les Misérables.*

Today the quarter is adjusting to its new role as the cultural center of contemporary art.

Turn right on Rue de la Verrerie. Still standing amidst surroundings evoking the past is the St. Merry presbytery (No. 76) with its fine 18C porch giving access to the church.

St. Merry Church★. — St. Merry or Medericus who died on this spot in the 7C used to be invoked for the release of captives. The building although begun in 1520 and completed in 1612, is curiously, in the 15C Flamboyant Gothic style. It was fomerly the rich parish church of the Lombard money lenders (who gave their name to the nearby street — p 100). The outside with the west face stands directly on the narrow Rue St-Martin, and small houses and shops crowd the south wall and chancel.

The Flamboyant interior was remodelled under Louis XV by the architect Boffrand and the Slodtz brothers. There remain, nevertheless, good 16C stained glass windows, in the first three bays of the chancel and transept, and fine ribbed vaulting at the transept crossing.

In addition to the majestic 17C organ loft — the organ itself was at one time played by Camille Saint-Saëns — and the beautiful woodwork by the Slodtz brothers in the pulpit, sacristy and the glory at the back of the choir, the church possesses a series of interesting pictures.

One bell dating from 1331, probably the oldest in Paris, remains from the mediaeval chapel which stood on the site of the present church.

Leave St. Merry's by the Rue de la Verrerie; go round the church by way of the Rue des Juges-Consuls (officers created by Charles IX to settle differences between merchants) and at the corner of the Rue du Cloître-St-Merri stands an attractive 18C restored house.

To the right of the church beyond the terrace where IRCAM (*see below*) is located there is a view of the south façade of the Georges Pompidou Centre.

Return to the Rue St-Martin. It was in the small and sordid alley, Impasse St. Fiacre, in the 17C that a man hiring out four wheeled cabs, lived beneath the sign of St. Fiacre, whence the name came to be used for cabs in France and also in England. To the left stands the façade of the St. Merry Church.

Rue Quincampoix. — This street was the scene of the Scots financier, **John Law's** " South Sea Buble. '' Law had come to France and, in due course, became Comptroller General. As part of his scheme for quickening commerce and reorganizing the country's finances he founded a bank which he established in the street, in 1719. Speculation began to run rife : the houses all round, the street itself, were crowded with those making fortunes overnight — a hunchback was said to have gained 150 000 *livres* for the use of his back as a desk. The frenzy lasted a year and then suddenly, in 1720, the bank failed, the speculators fled.

The Rue Quincampoix has several old houses at Nos. 10, 12, 13, 14 and 36 with unusual paved courts, mascaroons, wrought iron balconies and nailed or sculptured doors.

■ THE GEORGES POMPIDOU CENTRE★★

Open noon to 10 pm (10 am to 10 pm Saturdays and Sundays). Closed Tuesdays. 5F National Museum of Modern Art, only ; 10F for a pass valid all day.

Beaubourg is the name of an old village that was included within the Philippe Auguste perimeter wall at the end of the 12C. Situated in the heart of a very old quarter; cleaned up in 1936 of its decaying houses; included in 1968 in the redevelopment plan for the site of the former Halles market (*p 108*), the plateau was to have been the site of a public library. However, in 1969, on the initiative of Georges Pompidou (1911-1974), the then President of France, a vast program, which would change the whole aspect of the quarter, was envisioned — it was decided to create a multi-purpose cultural centre.

Architecture. — The architects Richard Rogers (British) and Renzo Piano (Italian), who took part in an international competition held in Autumn 1970, were selected by an international jury to create this multi-media cultural centre. They have archieved a building (1972-1977) totally futuristic in conception.

A gigantic parallelepiped unfolds its steel frame, glass walls and bright colours 166 m long, 60 m wide and 42 m high (545 × 197 × 138 ft). Devoid of any decoration, it stands a pile of steelwork a surrealistic sculpture confronting its onlooker. The façade is a tangle of pipes and tubes latticed along its glass skin, giving an effect of a solid yet pliant superstructure. Stuck on the façade the caterpillar-like clear tube envelopes the escalators.

The skeletal construction of the centre sheathed with tubes and funnels recalls a ship or factory — the past conception of a traditional museum is rejected in its entirety.

The elimination of all possible clutter brought on by the utilities — stairs, lifts, escalators, corridors, ventilation shafts, water and gas conduits — liberates 7 500 m² — 264 860 cubic feet of free space on each floor for research, animation and information.

A slightly inclined **Piazza** in front of the centre — the museum's outside reception area — is the playground of artists revealing their talents : whether it be the troubadour, fire-eater, poet, mime or juggler. On the right the Children's Workshop can be seen through the window.

On the ground floor, a large open area, the **Forum**, made up of several levels, contains temporary exhibits, a poster shop and book store. On the left is a large hexagonal portrait of *Georges Pompidou* by Vasarély.

Activities. — The Centre, contrary to preconceived ideas seeks to demonstrate to the public that there is a close correlation between art and daily activities. For both the specialists — artists, researchers — and the general public, this multi-purpose cultural centre offers an astonishing variety of activities and modern communication techniques encouraging curiosity and participation.

The Centre is divided into four departments :

The **Public Information Library** (BPI), encompassing three floors, offers to the public a wide variety of French and foreign books, slides, films, periodicals...

The **Industrial Design Centre** (CCI) on the ground floor, demonstrates the relationship between individuals and spaces, objects and signs through : architecture, urbanism, industrial design, visual communication and community services.

The **Institute for Acoustic and Musical Research** (IRCAM) (*located underground, between the Centre and St. Merry Church*) unites musicians, composers and scientists for the purpose of creating music with what modern technology has to offer (*studio closed to the public*).

The **National Museum of Modern Art** (MNAM) occupies the 3rd and 4th floors of the Centre and uses the 5th floor for its temporary exhibits.

National Museum of Modern Art★★★

The largest contemporary art museum in the world; this museum has gathered under one roof an exceptional quality and variety of painting and sculpture, permitting the visitor to follow the evolution of art beginning with Fauvism and Cubism and continuing through Constructivism, Hyperrealism, and the entire contemporary art scene.

The majority of the works were formerly in the Museum of Modern Art in the Tokyo Palace *(p 144)* complemented more recently by acquisitions and gifts.

VISIT

A quick tour of the museum (1 1/2 hours) can be done by keeping to the main aisles. To understand a certain movement or artist, the visitor can branch off into the side galleries (they are numbered or lettered).

Brancusi's Studio. — *Before taking the escalator to the 3rd floor; access every 15 minutes (same ticket can be used as that for the museum).* The reconstructed studio reveals where Constantin Brancusi (1876-1957), the pioneer of modern abstract sculpture, created.

Certain works of art cited below may have been removed and transferred to the reserve collection (for access, apply to a hostess). 3rd floor reserve collection deals with works of art from 1905 to 1920; on the 4th floor two different reserve collection sections : 1918-1945 and 1945 to contemporary.

3rd Floor. — The entrance area holds the Graphic Arts Room *(left on entering — temporary exhibits, free of charge);* the museum cinema *(in the extension of the Graphic Arts Room, free of charge)* and Kandinsky Salon *(free of charge).* Turn left after putting ticket in turnstile, following a clockwise pattern.

The art displayed on this floor deals with Fauvism beginnings of Cubism and early Abstract Expressionism. While Picasso was beginning his artistic career, dabbling in his Blue and Rose periods, with *Nu assis* (1905) and *Les trois Hollandaises* (1905), a reactionary art movement **Fauvism** *(fauve : wild beast in French)* was at its peak. These painters Derain *(Les deux péniches),* Dufy *(La rue pavoisée),* Vlaminck *(Paysage aux arbres rouges),* Marquet *(Portrait d'André Rouveyre; Rotterdam* — gal. 2) and Van Dongen *(Nini des Folies Bergères au sein nu)* were painting the same objects as their predecessors — landscapes, figures, still lifes and portraits — but applying thick colourful brushstrokes. Matisse *(Le luxe* — 1907; *Algérienne* — 1909) did not stop at Fauvism but continued experimenting.

At the same time, but considered apart, was Suzanne Valadon *(works hung on 4th floor)* and her son Utrillo, with his naive yet realistic canvases : *Impasse Cottin, Les jardins de Montmagny* (both in gal. 2).

The brilliant Fauve canvases were rejected by the early **Cubist** painters. These painters translated their pictoral vision by more or less geometrical lines depicting the volume or make-up of objects. Follow the evolution of Picasso *(Femme assise* — 1909; *Joueur de guitare* — 1910; *Arlequin* — 1925, 4th floor), and Braque *(Guéridon* — 1911; *Jeune fille à la guitare* — 1913; *Homme à la guitare* — 1914; *Guéridon noir* — 1919), the innovators of the movement. Sculpture was also influenced by Cubism as illustrated by Duchamp Villon's *Le grand cheval majeur* (1914). Others who belonged to the movement were Léger with *La Noce* (1910-11) and Gris *(Le petit déjeuner, Pierrot,* both in gal. E).

The Delaunays, Robert *(La ville de Paris* — 1911-12) and Sonia *(Marché au Minho* — 1915, *Les prismes electriques* — 1914; both in gal. 13), half-way between Cubist geometry and colourist research, show in their works how colour becomes form and content.

In Kandinsky's *Improvisations* (gal. 14) colours, shapes and lines are liberated and fly through the canvas.

Expressionism, in its early stages, mixed with fantasy can be seen in Chagall's *A la Russie, aux ânes et aux autres* (1911) and *Double portrait au verre de vin.*

4th Floor. — *Access by escalator.*

Cubism to Abstract Expressionism. — *South to central section.* Welcoming you off the escalator are Matisse's monumental *Nus de dos;* further on to the right is his *Le violoniste à la fenêtre.* After the escalator turn right, to the end, to admire Henri Laurens' bronze sculptures : *l'Adieu* and *La sirène* — so solid yet ethereal. Picasso demonstrates his constantly evolving style in *La femme aux pigeons* — 1930 (gal. 6). On the other side of the wall is the austere yet sensitive *Le tapis bleu* (1925) by Juan Gris. Another Cubist is the architect Le Corbusier *(Une nature morte aux nombreux objets* — gal. 6). Braque's Cubist works are shown in gallery 17 : *Le billiard, Une nature morte à la partition « Socrate » d'Eric Satie* (1921). The linear controlled canvases by Mondrian *(Composition)* can be seen beside the sculpture of Pevsner which develops movement in space. Paul Klee's mystical works (gal. 20) are created out of abstract elements. More fantasy is shown in Picabia's haunting sculpture.

Kandinsky's works (gal. 23) reveal a conflict between the lines, colours and shapes yet at the same time evoking a certain lyricism *(Ambiguïté, complexité simple* — 1939).

A sense of observation and love of texture is shown in Bonnard's *Un coin de table* (gal. 24). Chagall's mixture of Russian and Jewish folkore is depicted in his fairytale works (gal. 25) : *La guerre, Autour d'elle, l'Acrobate.* In gallery 26 Modigliani's *Le portrait de Dédie,* Soutine's Expressionistic portrait *The Groom* (1928) and Foujita's delicate *Mon intérieur* (1921) are hung. Both Dufy *(L'atelier de l'Impasse Guelma)* and Van Dongen *(L'artiste peint par lui-même en Neptune)* influenced by the Fauve palette, developped a style quite their own (gal. 28).

Contrary to the other Cubist artists, Léger (gal. I) worked the Cubist theories into a modern machine world : cones, cylinders and robot-like figures are depicted in his works : *Compositions aux deux perroquets, la Danseuse bleue* (1930), and *Cirque* (1918).

Dada and Surrealism. — *Eastern section*. Dadaism, born in Zurich during World War I, was originally a violent rebellion against a civilization apparently bent on self-destruction, shown by Arp in his painting *Danseuse* or by his biomorphic sculptures (seen throughout this floor). Surrealism tended to become abstract with Miro's sculpture *(Objet du couchant)* and representational with Dali's nightmare images (*La Vache Spectrale* — 1928) — nearby in a glasscase are wire sculptures by Calder. Also belonging to the movement is Ernst with his wierd and disturbing forms — sculpted and painted (gal. 29).

This section also contains Picasso's *Deux femmes sur la plage* (gal. 31), *La tristesse du roi* by Matisse and Léger's *Les loisirs*. Before leaving this section admire the monolithic yet graceful *Le phoque* by Brancusi.

Contemporary Art. — *Eastern section; behind the firewall*. Henry Moore's *Figure allongée* introduces you into this section which contains the diverse forms of expression making up modern art; contemporary, and international works of art are displayed in a variety of different mediums : Lyrical and Abstraction, Pop and Op Art, Action Painting, New Realism, Environmental, New Figurative Art and Hyperrealism.

The black paintings of Soulages and the energetic yet linear paintings by Hartung are hung beside sculptures by Germaine Richier and César (*Le diable*); Giacometti's elongated *Femme debout* is in gallery 34.

Action painting is exemplified in George Mathieu's large canvas. *Les Capétiens partout* (gal. M); Poliakoff's paintings tend to be more abstract.

George Segal's *La caissière* (1966) evokes a certain haunting loneliness (gal. 42) also note the Claes Oldenburg (*Banana splits and glaces en dégustation* — 1964).

Several rooms contain one particular work of art such as Edvard Kienholz's *Sugar plums dancing* — 1964 (gal. 43) or Eva Aeppu's *Groupe de 13* — 1968 (gal. 44). Amusing is Dubuffet's *Jardin d'hiver* (gal. 45) *(must take shoes off)*. Intriguing is *Ben's Store*, a store belonging to a certain Ben Vauter, who had created, with this store, a centre of creativity in Nice from 1958-1972. Haunting is Duane Hanson's *Bowery bums* (1969-1970).

As you leave do not miss the Warhol, Niki de Saint Phalle, Vasarely (*Boglar vert* — 1966) Lichtenstein (*Modular painting* — 1969) and, under the escalator, *Le carrefour de l'Odéon* by Raymond Masson.

Terraces. — Displayed on the terraces are among other sculptures : by Ernst (*Le Capricorne*) and Tinguely (*Une machine); mobiles and stabile by Calder.

5th Floor. — From the end of the escalators and terraces a beautiful **view*** of the rooftops of Paris can be seen — from right to left : hill of Montmartre and the Sacré-Cœur basilica, St-Eustache Church, the Eiffel Tower, Maine-Montparnasse Tower, Church of St-Merry (in the foreground) Notre-Dame (behind it is the cupola of the Pantheon) and Hôtel de Ville.

From the Georges Pompidou Centre to the Hôtel de Ville

To the right, the Rue Beaubourg runs along the façade of the Centre, which holds all the conduits used for the functionning of the building; colours designate these functions : white conduits : ventilation system; blue conduits : air conditioning system; green conduits : fire prevention system; yellow conduits : electrical system; red conduits : transportation system.
Turn left into the narrow Pierre au Lard Alley.

By No. 6, a passageway and some steps lead to a **courtyard,** which once belonged to the Aigle d'Or Inn, the starting point for the stage-coaches in former times. On the corner of Rue St-Merri there are two fine 17C houses (Nos. 12 and 9), and a little along on the left is the sordid Cul-de-Sac du Bœuf, one of the oldest blind alleys in Paris. The Rue St-Merri continues as the Rue Ste-Croix-de-la-Bretonnerie. Take the road to the right called Square Ste-Croix-de-la-Bretonnerie, which opens into Rue des Archives, opposite the Billettes Church.

The Billettes Church. — It is here, according to legend, that the miracle of the " boiled God " occured in 1290 : a usurer, Jonathan, cut a host and threw the pieces into a cooking pot; the water turned to blood and ran into the street attracting attention to the moneylender who was burned alive.

In the 14C a monastery was erected on the site by the Brothers of Charity known as the Billettes on account of the heraldic billet on their habits. They were succeeded by Carmelites who in 1756 built the present sanctuary which became a Lutheran church in 1812.

The Billettes Cloister. — *1st door to the left after the Church*. The only remaining mediaeval cloister in Paris gives onto a small courtyard. Note the simplicity of its architectural elements.

Continue right, along the Rue Ste-Croix-de-la-Bretonnerie passing by the Rue de Moussy, a former street of free love. The **Rue Aubriot,** dating from the 13C, with its old houses, some of which date from the Middle Ages, makes a delightful picture.

Turn into the Rue des Guillemites (another name for the 12C White Mantle order — *p 85*) where, leading out of No. 6, is the curious **Passage des Singes** (Monkey Passage), a series of old inner courts which progress, to the right, to the Rue Vieille-du-Temple.

On the left is the Rue du Trésor, so named in 1882 after a copper vase full of mediaeval gold coins had been unearthed. By No. 20, Rue Vieille-du-Temple is the now modernized Hôtel d'Argenson Alley named after the family from which have come many of France's ambassadors, police chiefs and ministers.

Take Rue du Grenier-sur-l'Eau on the right to reach the Rue des Barres : clear view of the east end of St-Gervais and its original buttresses. At No. 15 is the gallery of the former charnel house. Continue along the Rue François-Miron where the **precincts** of the church adorned by the elm tree, where everyone gathered and justice was dispensed; the façades and wrought iron balconies have an old world style.

Church of St-Gervais-St-Protais*. — The church stands on a low mound with steps leading up to it at either end. A basilica dedicated to the saints, Gervase and Protase, Roman officers martyred by Nero, has stood on the site since the 6C. The main part of the present building, in Flamboyant Gothic, was begun in 1494 and completed in 1657.

The church became famous for its sacred music due to eight members of the Couperin family, who successively, held the position of organist from 1656 to 1826.

The façade (1616-1621) with superimposed Doric, Ionic and Corinthian orders, was the first to be built in the Classical style in Paris.

In the interior, of the original construction, there remain the Flamboyant vaulting and several 16C windows and stalls. The organ built in 1601 and enlarged in the 18C is the oldest in Paris.

In the north aisle, near the font, is a model of the church façade carved by du Hancy, author of the large panels in the main door. The altar front in the third chapel is a 13C low relief of the Death of the Virgin : the Gilded Chapel is decorated with painted panels inlaid in gilded panelling. To the left of the transept crossing is a beautiful 16C Flemish Passion painted on wood and, left of the crossing, against a pillar, a Gothic polychrome stone Virgin and Child. A wooden Crucifix by Préault (1840) and a fine 17C wrought iron grille adorn the sacristy exterior. In the Lady Chapel there is a remakable Flamboyant keystone, hanging 1.5 m below the vault and forming a circlet 2.5 m in diameter — 5 ft and 8 ft.

HÔTEL DE VILLE   ▯▯ or ▯▯ : J 15

The Hôtel de Ville is Paris' official reception and city government building.

From the Middle Ages to the Revolution. — The present Place de l'Hôtel-de-Ville was known, until 1830, as the **Place de Grève.** It then formed part of the foreshore — *grève* — and became a meeting place for those out of work — hence the expression *" faire la grève ".*

(After Seals' Department photo, National Archives)

Seal of the Watermen's Guild (1210)

Municipal government began in Paris with the appointment by St. Louis in 1260 of leading men to administer the township. These men were members of the powerful watermen's guild from whose coat of arms the boat motif was incorporated in that of the city. In the 16C the device was complemented by the motto *Fluctuat nec mergitur* — she is buffetted by the waves but does not sink.

The municipal assembly, headed by a merchant provost and four aldermen moved from the Place du Châtelet to the Pillared House on the Place de Grève in 1357, at the instigation of Étienne Marcel, who became leader of the States General and raised the whole of France in revolt; he held Paris, let the English into the city, but failed and died by the hands of the Parisians in 1358, as he was about to give the city over to Charles the Bad, King of Navarre.

Under François I the Pillared House fell into ruin. The king, intent on building a large town hall, had plans drawn up by Il Boccador, and the first stone was laid in 1533. The building was completed, however, early in the 17C.

Until the Revolution the municipal authority was weak, the king making his own appointments, although those selected had to be citizens of Paris.

On 17 July 1789 Louis XVI appeared in the hall to kiss the newly adopted tricolour cockade. Throughout the Revolution the hall was in the hands of the Commune.

From the Consulate to the Third Republic. — In 1800 Napoleon Bonaparte reorganized the capital's administration, appointing a mayor and two assistants for each of the twelve districts and twenty-four additional councillors. As today the real power lay with the prefects of the Seine and the police.

In 1848 when Louis-Philippe was dismissed, it was in the Hôtel de Ville that the provisional government was set up and from there that the Second Republic was proclaimed on 24 February 1848. It was at this time that Baron Haussmann, as Prefect of the Seine, undertook the work replanning the capital.

On 4 September 1870, after the defeat of Sedan, Gambetta, Jules Favre and Jules Ferry proclaimed the Third Republic from the Hôtel de Ville and instituted a National Defence Government. The capitulation of Paris on 28 January 1871, however, roused the citizens and in their anger they removed the government, installing in its place the Paris Commune of 1871. In May during its final overthrow, the Hôtel de Ville, the Tuileries and several other buildings were set on fire by the Federalists.

For details on Paris administration today see p 19.

TOUR

Guided tours, Mondays 10.30 am. Apply Accueil de Paris, 29 Rue de Rivoli, ℡ 277.15.40.

The Hôtel de Ville was entirely rebuilt between 1874 and 1882 in the Neo-Renaissance style complete with 136 statues of the illustrious to adorn the building's façades.

Inside, the sumptuous main staircase leads to a state hall and reception rooms. Ornate decoration, part Renaissance, part *Belle Époque,* reveals the official style in the early years of the Third Republic. Amid the caryatids and statues, coffered ceilings and chandeliers, are a bust of the Republic by Rodin, frescoes by Laurens and Puvis de Chavannes and witty scenes of Parisian life by the caricaturist, Willette *(p 110).*

Michelin plans ⑩ or ⑪ : from F 13 to F 15 — from G 13 to G 17.

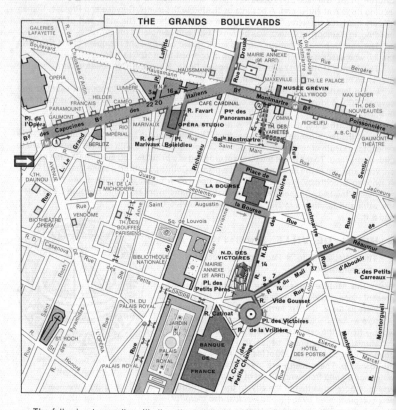

THE GRANDS BOULEVARDS

The following two walks will allow the tourist to see the varying aspects of this quarter one of the liveliest in Paris.

1 THE GRANDS BOULEVARDS   ⑩ or ⑪ : from F 13 to G 17

Distance : 3 km — 2 miles — Time : 1 1/2 hours (not including the visit to the Grévin Museum).
Start from the Opera métro station.

Well known buildings; long tree lined vistas; a tide of pedestrians moving earnestly on business or idling slowly; roads; wide café terraces with tables overflowing onto the pavement; cinemas, theatres, thousands of shops a plethora of lights and advertisements; in short the Boulevards — their prestige as high, their fame as great, as ever.

The ramparts transformed. — By 1660 Louis XIV had established himself firmly on the throne and the fortified perimeter walls around Paris had become obsolete and fallen into disrepair. The part of the Charles V wall between the Bastille and the St. Denis Gate, and the ramparts erected under Charles IX and Louis XIII *(p 18)*, were therefore knocked down, the moats filled in and a raised terrace thoroughfare constructed in their place. This fareway, sufficiently wide to allow four carriages to ride abreast, was bordered by side roads lined by a double avenue of trees. Triumphal arches replaced the fortified gates.

The project, when it was finally completed in 1705, was known as the Boulevard.

The place to take the air. — In about 1750 the Boulevard became fashionable : seated in the shade on straw-bottomed chairs Parisians watched horse carriages and riders pass by.

Gradually the west end became the area where the nobility and the rich built their private mansions; the east end, the Boulevard du Temple, almost a fairground, with crowds drawn to the theatres and dance halls, circuses, waxworks, puppets, dancers, acrobats, mechanical figures, cafés, restaurants, booths and barrows. For a hundred years the crowd rejoiced; by 1830 the local theatres had played violent melodrama for so long that the area was nicknamed the Criminal Boulevard.

The Boulevard des Italiens, opened under the Directory, acquired an elegance which spread to the Boulevard Montmartre and persisted until the middle of the 19C.

The roads were first paved in 1778 and about the same time street lights, burning animal fat, appeared and were declared altogether blinding; gas lamps were installed in the Passage des Panoramas *(p 118)* in 1817, and on the Boulevard in 1826. The first bus appeared on 30 January 1828 when it travelled from the Madeleine to the Bastille. Footpaths were surfaced.

The modern boulevard. — The creation by Haussmann of the Opera and Republic Squares and the wide highways leading to them, began the transformation which still goes on as crowds replace the fashionable; lights become more glaring; advertising depersonalizes; famous cafés disappear — and the only constant is the Parisian himself.

From the Opera to Richelieu-Drouot

Walk from the Opera Square *(p 73)* along the east end of the Boulevard des Capucines to the Boulevard des Italiens.

The old Boulevard des Italiens. — The street's history is linked with fads and fashions. *Muscadins* and *Merveilleuses* haunted it at the time of the Directory; *Gandins* during the Restoration, were succeeded by Dandies who also followed English fashion and, in 1835, were the first to smoke in public. Waxed moustaches, imperials and crinolines appeared during the Second Empire.

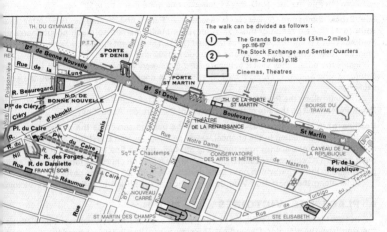

The walk can be divided as follows :
① The Grands Boulevards (3 km – 2 miles) pp. 116-117
② The Stock Exchange and Sentier Quarters (3 km – 2 miles) p. 118
▭ Cinemas, Theatres

The boulevard today. — The uninspired Palais Berlitz, at the corner of the Rue Louis-le-Grand, has replaced the Pavillon de Hanovre, the favourite ice-cream restaurant of the *Merveilleuses*; No. 22 is where the Café Tortoni stood; No. 20, the famous **Maison Dorée** restaurant, was once the meeting place for fashionable Paris; elegantly decorated façades line the boulevard and Rue Lafitte (go as far as No. 3); No. 16 is where the Café Riche received its patrons from 1791 until early this century.

The Opéra-Studio. — *Temporarily closed*. The theatre, formerly the Opéra-Comique, stands on the site of the theatre constructed by the Duke of Choiseul in 1782 in his own grounds for the Comic Opera company *(p 109)*, commonly called " the Italians ". The boulevard took its name from the company.

Choiseul opened the theatre to attract people to the area he had bought for development. The company gradually changed its repertoire from French to Italian light opera and ultimately, with Offenbach and Johann Strauss, included operettas.

Today young singers and musicians are trained at the Opéra-Studio where they also give occasional performances.

Richelieu-Drouot Crossroads. — The Café Cardinal, stands on the site of what was known, in the 17C, as the " modest and secluded " house of the poet, Regnard.

The **Auction Rooms** (Hôtel des Ventes Drouot, *9 Rue Drouot*), a little to the left of the road junction, are to be rebuilt, meanwhile the auctions will be held in Orsay station *(p 126)*.

From Richelieu-Drouot to the Place de la République

Boulevard Montmartre. — On the right at No. 11 is the **Passage des Panoramas** *(p 118)*. At No. 7 stands the **Théâtre des Variétés** built in 1807, the home of light comedy and operetta presenting the wit and gaiety of Meilhac and Halévy, Offenbach, Flers and Caillavet, Tristan Bernard and Sacha Guitry.

Grévin Museum★. — *10 Boulevard Montmartre. Open 2 to 7 pm; 1 to 8 pm Sundays, holidays and school holidays. 13F; children 9F.*

Grévin, a caricaturist, founded the museum in 1882. (The first waxworks were introduced in Paris in the 18C.) It contains historical scenes, distorting mirrors, conjuring sessions — amusement for one and all.

Continue along the Boulevards Poissonnière and Bonne-Nouvelle. The **Rue de la Lune,** to the right, forms a sharp angle with the Rue de Clery, typical of old Paris. Further on, these boulevards become the St-Denis and St-Martin Boulevards, each marked at its start by a monumental gate.

Porte St-Denis★. — The gate was erected by the City in 1672 in celebration of Louis XIV's victories on the Rhine — 40 strongholds captured in less than two months. On either side are carvings of the pyramids superimposed with trophies and on the boulevard side, in addition, allegorical figures representing Holland *(left)* and the Rhine *(right);* above the arch can be seen the crossing of the Rhine.

Porte St-Martin★. — The gate which is only 17 m high — 56 ft was erected by the dean and aldermen in 1674 to commemorate the capture of Besançon and defeat of the German, Spanish and Dutch armies. The carvings illustrate not only the taking of Besançon but also the breaking of the Triple Alliance, the capture of Limburg and the defeat of the Germans.

Two theatres stand near the gate : the Renaissance (1872) and the Porte St-Martin. Continue down the Boulevard to the Place de la République *(p 148)*.

2   THE STOCK EXCHANGE AND SENTIER QUARTERS

🔟 or 🔢 : G 14

*Distance : 3 km — 2 miles — Time : 2 hours (not including the visit to the Stock Exchange). Sta̶
from the Rue Montmartre métro station. Try to do this visit on a weekday.*

No. 11 Boulevard Montmartre is the **Passage des Panoramas** which was opened in 179̶
The name comes from the two vast panoramas of capital cities and historic scenes painte̶
and displayed in rotundas by the American, Henry Fulton. No. 47 has kept its old aspe̶

Turn left into the Rue N.-D. des Victoires to reach the Place de la Bourse.

The Stock Exchange (Palais de la Bourse). — Paris' first exchange was John Law̶
bank *(p 112)*. As a result of this bankruptcy, the public learned so much about shares ar̶
holdings that a public exchange was founded (1724). The present building was begun by Bro̶
gniart in 1808, completed in 1826 and enlarged in 1902 and 1907.

Inside the public may visit a gallery *(guided tours every 40 min. from 11 am to 1 pm, exce̶
Saturdays and Sundays; time : 1 1/2 hours; 5F)*. From another gallery one can see the actu̶
exchange.

Continue along the Rue Notre-Dame-des-Victoires (18C mansion at No. 14) to the Place d̶
Petits-Pères, built on the site of the Monastery of the Barefoot Augustins.

Basilica of Notre-Dame-des-Victoires. — The basilica served as the monastery chape̶
Inside are 17C panelling in the chancel, seven paintings by Van Loo *(Louis XIII dedicating t̶
church to the Virgin,* scenes from the *Life of St. Augustine)*, a fine 18C organ loft and a mon̶
ment to the 17C composer, Lulli *(2nd chapel on the left)*. The church is famous for its annu̶
pilgrimage to the Virgin which goes back to 1836; some 30 000 ex-votos cover the walls.

Walk along the short Rue Vide-Gousset (Pickpocket Street) to the Place des Victoire̶

■ PLACE DES VICTOIRES★   🔟 or 🔢 : G 14

In 1685 Marshal de la Feuillade, to curry favour with Louis XIV, commissioned a statue ̶
the king from the sculptor, Desjardins. The statue, unveiled in 1686, showed the king, crow̶
ed with the laurels of victory, standing on a pedestal adorned with six low reliefs and fo̶
captives representing the vanquished Spain, Holland, Prussia and Austria.

The statue was melted down in 1792; a new figure by Desaix replaced it in 1806 only to ̶
melted down in turn in 1815 (and reappear as Henri IV on the Pont Neuf!). The present eque̶
trian statue of the Sun King was sculpted by Bosio in 1822.

The side of the square with even numbers is the least damaged and gives some idea of t̶
intended 17C elegance.

One of the façades of the **Bank of France** can be seen on looking along the Rue Catin̶
from the entrance of Rue Aboukir. The Bank on the Rue de la Vrillière was founded at t̶
instigation of Napoleon in January 1800. First housed at No. 4 Rue d'Aboukir, it moved in 181̶
to the mansion *(not open)* built in 1635 by François Mansart and remodelled by Robert de Cott̶

From the Place des Victoires to the Boulevard Bonne-Nouvel̶

Walk out of the Place des Victoires along the Rue Vide-Gousset and turn into the Rue d̶
Mail. At Nos. 5 and 7 (both 17C) belonging to Colbert, are, on the upper capitals, a faun̶
mask and cornucopias and interlaced snakes (the snake — *coluber* in Latin — Colbert's emblem̶
respectively. At No. 14, an 18C hôtel, lived Madame Récamier. The newspaper *Le Figaro*
printed in the building located at No. 37 Rue du Mail.

The Sentier. — The Sentier quarter begins on the other side of the Rue Montmartre. It ̶
the centre of the wholesale trade for materials, trimmings, hosiery and ready-made clothe̶

After the Rue de Cléry, turn right into the Rue Réaumur (where *France-Soir* is printe̶
which you follow to the Rue St-Denis, which you turn left on to reach the Passage du Cair̶

Caire Passage and Square. — Napoleon's victorious campaign in Egypt in 1798 arous̶
great enthusiasm in Paris — architecture and fashion were greatly influenced and streets an̶
squares in this area were given names in memory of his successes.

Walk under the covered arcades of the strange Passage du Caire to the square (the hea̶
of the old Court of Miracles) where No. 2 has a façade decorated with Egyptian motifs.

The Court of Miracles. — A Court of Miracles was a place where, in the Middle Age̶
miscreants lived out of the reach of the authorities. During daylight, the lame, the blind and th̶
maimed went out to beg in town; at night they returned, shed their wooden legs and othe̶
props and indulged in the orgies described vividly by Victor Hugo in the *Hunchback of Notr̶
Dame*. It was this nightly miraculous cure from infirmity that gave the court its name.

Turn left onto the Rue des Forges which runs into the Rue de Damiette and the Rue d̶
Nil. The crowded Rue des Petits Carreaux leads to the Rue de Cléry.

The Rue de Cléry is the old counterscarp of the Charles V perimeter wall; the passag̶
of the same name, at No. 57, now crosses the houses by means of steps which once crosse̶
the ramparts. The whole quarter stands on **Mount Orgueil**, a natural mound used as a redout̶
and which, in the 16C, afforded a good viewpoint over the capital — hence the name of th̶
street, Beauregard, which you follow to **Notre-Dame de Bonne-Nouvelle**. The classical belfr̶
is all that remains of the church restored by Anne of Austria — the remainder of the buil̶
ing dates from 1828. Inside, two 17C pictures placed at the ends of the aisles, and attrib̶
uted to Mignard, show Henrietta of England and her three children before St. Francis ̶
Sales and Anne of Austria with Henrietta.

By taking the Rue de la Lune *(p 117)* on the right one arrives at the Boulevard Bonn̶
Nouvelle.

Michelin plans ▢▢ or ▢▢ : L 11 - M 10, M 11.
Distance : 5 km — 3 miles — Time : 4 hours. Start from the Montparnasse-Bienvenüe métro.

This crowded quarter, which traditionally belonged to artists and the working class is today the scene of one of the major urban renewal projects to be undertaken within the heart of Paris.

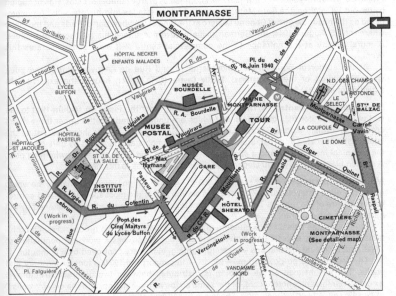

Mount Parnassus. — The debris from age-old quarries formed a heathlike grass covered mound. For students, chased away from the Pré-aux-Clercs by Queen Margot *(p 124)*, it became a favourite haunt to declaim poems away from the confines of the city — they nicknamed it Mount Parnassus after the mountain of Apollo and the muses.

In the 18C the mound was razed but the boulevard laid across its site, a fragment of the Farmers General perimeter wall, complete with toll-gates, kept the name alive.

A pleasure ground. — The Revolution saw the springing up of cafés and cabarets on the city outskirts and revellers enjoying the Montagnes-Suisses and Élysée-Montparnasse gardens and the dancing at the Arc-en-Ciel and Grande Chaumière. The polka and the can-can were first seen here before they became the rage of Paris. At the Observatory crossroads, where Marshal Ney was executed *(p 123)* were, first, the Bullier Hall, then, a few years later, the Closerie des Lilas café. Crowds gathered at the Constant Dance Hall and in the drinking houses in the village of Plaisance to dance the mazurka between sips of tart Suresnes wine.

As the quarter began to spread out, Haussmann intervened, he planned to create an entirely built up area which included the old villages of Plaisance, Vaugirard and Montrouge. He then proceeded to divide it up with the Rue de Rennes, the Boulevard Arago and the Boulevard d'Enfer (now Boulevard Raspail).

Bohemian Montparnasse. — At the turn of the century avant-garde artists, poets and writers, moved to the Left Bank of the Seine, particularly Montparnasse. The atmosphere had already been described by Henri Murger many years earlier in his *Scenes of Bohemian Life* on which Puccini had based his opera *La Bohème*.

Among the first to live in the quarter were the satirical writer Alfred Jarry and the artist Douanier Rousseau. They were joined by Apollinaire, Max Jacob, Jean Moréas and Paul Fort who, on Tuesdays, presided over noisy sessions at the Closerie des Lilas.

The 1900 Exhibition Wine Pavilion was reconstructed at No. 52 Rue de Dantzig, renamed the **Ruche** or Beehive, and replaced the Bateau-Lavoir of Montmartre *(p 76)*, providing lodging and studios for Modigliani, Soutine, Chagall, Zadkine and Léger. Talk went on for hours in the café-restaurants (le Dôme, la Rotonde, le Sélect and La Coupole) among the Russian political exiles — Lenin, Trotsky — musicians — Stravinsky, Satie and " the Six " — poets — Cocteau — and foreigners — Hemingway, Foujita, Picasso, Eisenstein, Ibanez... It was the golden age of the **Paris School** and it lasted into the mid-thirties, ending only with the outbreak of war in Spain and Western Europe.

Montparnasse today. — This former international Bohemian quarter is entirely Parisian. Anonymous crowds of revellers and artists attracted by the cafés, cinemas and nightclubs (around Rue de la Gaîté and neigbouring streets) rub shoulders with the local population of workers, shopkeepers and artisans.

Since redevelopment the physical aspect and character of the area has radically changed, the Maine-Montparnasse complex has become the nucleus of a business area while the Vandamme-Nord section has a mixture of offices, housing, sporting facilities and hotel accommodation. Added to this are the ghost streets (Rue Vercingétorix) and vacant lots awaiting redevelopment and the activity of the construction sites.

■ THE MAINE-MONTPARNASSE COMPLEX* 🔟 or 🔟 : L 11 - M 11

Dating from 1934 the original plan for this area was revised in 1958 when it became a major urban renewal project with the aim of creating a high density business area on the Left Bank. Work began in 1961.

Place du 18-Juin-1940. — Until 1967 this site, lined by a large number of cafés, was occupied by the old 19C station, the Gare Montparnasse, which as it fades into history, will be remembered as the headquarters of General Leclerc at the time of the liberation of Paris and the place where, on 25 August 1944, the German military governor signed his garrison's surrender. A mural plaque at the entrance to the commercial centre *(left side)* commemorates this event.

At the corner of Boulevard du Montparnasse and Rue de l'Arrivée, stands the cube shaped building of the **International Textile Centre** (CIT), which houses the export-action activities of over 200 firms.

The Commercial Centre. — The podium extending from the Place du 18-Juin-1940 to the foot of the tower consists of 8 levels, 6 of which are underground. On the upper three floors are the department stores, Galeries-Lafayette and C&A, 60 or so luxury shops presenting the latest fashions, cafés and restaurants. The remaining floors are occupied by parking space, the technical installations and a sports centre *(entrance Rue du Départ)* with swimming pool. A sunken plaza on the Rue du Départ side gives direct access to the métro.

Maine-Montparnasse Tower.** — This 200 m — 656 ft — high tower, dominating the whole quarter — adds a new landmark to the Paris skyline and is the most spectacular and controversial feature of the project. The strictly geometrical lines of the façades are softened by the harmonious curved form.

This tower, the tallest office building in Europe is the design of a group of French architects The building, with 52 floors given over to office space, has a working population of 7 000. The technical installations — heating, lighting, etc. — are controlled by a computer.

The foundations go down 70 m — 230 ft — to support the 120 000 tons of masonry and shafts. The weight load of the building is distributed between two different structures : a central reinforced concrete core, of the same shape as the building, and the outer " walls " of closely spaced vertical columns. These are linked by horizontal beams. The curtain walls are covered with bronze tinted glass.

The building is separated from the new railway station, by a parvis paved with pink Sardinian granite under which passes the Avenue du Maine.

Ascent. — *Open 1 April to 30 September 9.30 am to 11.30 pm; 1 November to 31 March 10 am to 10 pm; 8.50F (to the 56th floor); 10.50F (to the top, 58th floor).*

The 56 th floor observatory affords a magnificent **panorama***★ of Paris and its suburbs. A luminous frieze running round the top of the wall helps you to pick out the main landmarks : the Eiffel Tower with the skyscrapers of the new Défense quarter in the distance, the Louvre, the Sacré-Cœur, Notre-Dame, the Bois de Vincennes, Orly Airport and the Bois de Boulogne. On a clear day the view can extend as far as 40 km — 25 miles. By night Paris becomes a fairytale wonderland. There is also a bar and panoramic restaurant at this level.

The Station. — Trains from western France now run into a U shaped terminus surrounded on three sides by immense 18 storey glass, steel and concrete blocks. The station proper, on five levels, occupies the central area — a vast concourse connects with the métro and supplies every amenity, even a small chapel to St. Bernard *(entrance at No. 34)* — the lectern was carved from a railway sleeper.

The longer sides of the U, extending nearly 275 yds back along the track, are occupied by 1 000 flats and a major postal sorting office on the left and, on the right, the Air France and other offices, overlooking the Square Max Hymans and Boulevard de Vaugirard.

From Maine-Montparnasse to the Pasteur Institute

At No. 34 Boulevard de Vaugirard stands the **National Postal and Philatelic Centre**. The unusual façade has five decorative panels of light reflecting prisms to break the monotony of the windowless walls of the 5 exhibition floors.

Postal Museum.** — *Open 10 am to 5 pm; closed on Thursdays and holidays : 5F — Sundays 2.50F. Library, photographic library, stamps collector's workshop, lecture theatres, temporary exhibition galleries and a stamp counter.*

Recently opened in these new galleries, the museum presents an attractive account of the postal services through the ages. Start on the 5th floor where in Gallery I a short film gives a brief historical introduction. In Gallery 2 note the parchment scroll, used by religious orders in the Middle Ages as a means of communication between abbeys and the balloon used during the 1870-71 siege of Paris. Gallery 3 shows the development of the postal network in France, from the time of the early relay posts for mounted carriers to the 18 000 post offices of today. The next two galleries display models of different means of postal transport.

Galleries 10-13 are of special interest to the philatelist. Note the model of a present day stamp printing machine. Next comes a complete collection of French stamps since the first issue in 1849 and finally other national collections, usually displayed in rotation. The final two galleries show the present methods and machines for the sorting and franking of mail.

Follow the Boulevard de Vaugirard towards the Avenue du Maine which you take to the left, then left again into the Rue Antoine Bourdelle.

Bourdelle Museum*. — *No. 16. Open 10 am to 5.40 pm; closed on Mondays and holidays (except Easter Sunday and Whit Sunday); 3F — free on Sundays. The museum also has temporary exhibitions.*

Bourdelle's (1861-1929) house, garden and studio have been converted to display several hundred of the artist's sculptures, paintings and drawings — many of which may also be seen at the Champs-Élysées Theatre and in the Alma Quarter *(pp 144, 145).* The most outstanding items among his immense output are the huge bronzes, now in the garden, his portrait busts of his contemporaries, including his master, Rodin, the writer Anatole France, and the composer Vincent d'Indy and the spectacular series of **portraits of Beethoven*** of whom he made 21 different studies.

Continue along the Rue Antoine-Bourdelle to the Rue Falguière on the left. This brings you to the Boulevard Pasteur where you turn right and, shortly afterwards, left into the Rue du Docteur-Roux.

Pasteur Institute. — *No. 25.* This internationally famous Institute contains laboratories for pure and applied research (with an annexe at Garches — *p 173),* lecture theatres, a vaccination centre, a hospital for the treatment of infections, diseases and a serum and vaccination production plant (at Louviers-Incarville).

The Institute and its Lille, Lyons and 16 other auxiliary institutes abroad continue the work of Louis Pasteur (1822-1895), whose tomb is in the crypt and whose apartment has been converted into a museum *(open from Monday to Friday 2.30 to 5 pm; by appointment ☎ 541.52.66 extn. 523). A tour of the Institute can also be made by appointment, same hours, ☎ 541.52.66 extn. 586.*

From the Pasteur Institute to the Montparnasse Cemetery

Follow the Rue du Docteur-Roux; bear left into Rue Vigée-Lebrun and continue along Rue du Cotentin which takes you to the Cinq-Martyrs-du-Lycée-Buffon Bridge, from which there is an impressive **view*** of the new quarter. In the opposite direction is the Plaisance quarter at present undergoing redevelopment. In the mid-19C Plaisance was one of the villages surrounding Paris.

After the bridge turn left into the Rue du Commandant-René-Mouchotte, which passes one of the main postal sorting offices and on the right the elegant white building of the **Sheraton Hotel,** which contrasts with the surrounding buildings. The architect Pierre Dufau was also responsible for two of the towers at La Défense (the Septentrion and Assur towers). This hotel contains 1 000 rooms and conference hall; this complex also includes office and housing space, a commercial centre and skating rink with ice rinks (one for curling). Two overhead passageways link the Vandamme-Nord centre to the Modigliani Terrace.

Turn right into Avenue du Maine then left into Rue de la Gaîté.

Rue de la Gaîté. — This old country road has, since the 18C, been lined throughout by cabarets, dance halls, restaurants and other pleasure spots — hence its name. The street's tradition which began with the Mère Cadet, the Veau qui Tète and the Gigoteurs Dance Hall, is maintained today by the Mille Colonnes Restaurant (No. 20 bis), the Gaîté-Montparnasse (No. 26), the Bobino Music-Hall (No. 20) and the Montparnasse Theatre (No. 31). The theatre's reputation for popular drama was revived in the 1930's but has since faded.

Turn right into the Boulevard Edgar-Quinet for the entrance to the cemetery.

Montparnasse Cemetery

1) Soutine *(p 119),* painter.
2) Baudelaire, poet.
3) Bourdelle (no inscription), sculptor.
4) Tristan Tzara *(p 145),* Romanian Dadaist poet.
5) Zadkine *(p 145),* sculptor.
6) A. Jussieu *(p 139),* botanist.
7) Rude *(p 47),* sculptor.
8) Henri Poincaré, mathematician.
9) Le Verrier *(p 123),* astronomer.
10) Sainte-Beuve, writer-critic.
11) *The Kiss,* by Brancusi, Romanian sculptor.
12) André Citroën, engineer and industrialist.
13) Guy de Maupassant, writer.
14) César Franck, composer.
15) Saint-Saëns, composer.

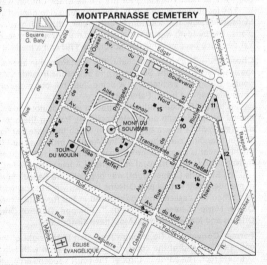

MONTPARNASSE CEMETERY

From the Montparnasse Cemetery to the Place du 18-Juin-1940

Make for the Boulevard Raspail and turn left towards the **Vavin Crossroads.** This crossroads, originally the summit of the Parnassus Mound, bustles with life and is now the heart of the old quarter. The famous statue of **Balzac** by Rodin stands on an island site in the Boulevard Raspail. Walk up the Boulevard Montparnasse which is lined with big café-restaurants and cinemas. Pass the Church of Notre-Dame-des-Champs (Our Lady of the Fields) whose name recalls a much older country church before reaching the Place du 18-Juin-1940.

Michelin plans ⑩ or ⑪ :
L 13, L 14 — M 13, M 14.
Distance : 3 km — 2 miles —
Time : 2 1/2 hours. Start from
Port-Royal métro station.

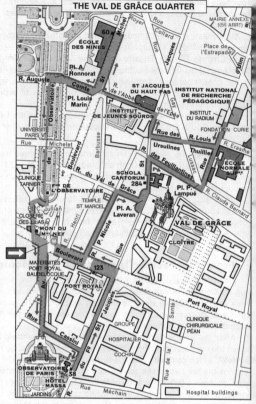

THE VAL DE GRÂCE QUARTER

This former " Valley of Grace " is now devoted to medical care and higher education. The first half of the 17C saw the establishment of religious communities : in 1605, the **Carmelites** (No. 284 Rue St-Jacques), Louise de la Vallière retreated to the convent when no longer favoured by Louis XIV; in 1612, the **Ursulines**; in 1622, the **Feuillantines** founded by Anne of Austria; in 1626, the **Visitandines.** The same year, Mother Angélique Arnaud ordered the construction of **Port-Royal,** the dependency of the Jansenist Port-Royal-des-Champs. Her tomb lies in the chancel of the church at No. 123 Boulevard de Port-Royal.

From the Boulevard de Port-Royal, turn left and walk up the Rue Pierre-Nicole to reach the Val-de-Grâce.

VAL-DE-GRÂCE★★

⑩ or ⑪ : M 14

All the 17C buildings of the former abbey remain. A few years after the foundation of the new Oratory congregation (*p 107*) in the Rue St-Jacques in 1611, Anne of Austria bought the mansion to establish in it a Benedictine community which took the same name as its provincial convent, Val-de-Grâce. Anne visited the community frequently to pray and discreetly to intrigue against Richelieu. At 37, Anne, who had been married twenty-three years, was still without a child. She promised the gift of a magnificent church if her prayers were answered and kept her vow on the birth of Louis XIV in 1638. The plans for the Val-de-Grâce Church were drawn by François Mansart.

The foundation stone was laid by the young king himself in 1645. Anne of Austria, finding Mansart too slow, replaced him by Le Mercier, who, until his death, executed his predecessor's plans. The building was at last completed (in 1667 and consecrated in 1710, Louis XIV was 72). Val-de-Grâce became a military hospital in 1793 and a medical school in 1850.

Church★★. — The church, probably the most Roman in appearance in France, was erected in the Jesuit style after the Sorbonne and before the Invalides. Above the two tier façade with a double triangular pediment is a dome, less tall but more ornate than its Paris rivals and obviously inspired by St. Peter's.

Inside, the Baroque influence appears in the sculptured vaulting over the nave, the monumental baldachin with six twisted columns framing the altar and the magnificent **cupola★★** decorated with a fresco by Mignard in which there are 200 figures each three times lifesize. The outstanding carvings are by the Anguier brothers and Philippe Buyster. The Nativity at the high altar is a copy of the original group by Michel Anguier which was given to St-Roch's by Napoleon (*p 91*). The royal monogram LA has been used as a decorative motif throughout.

The St. Louis Chapel (*right*) was originally the Benedictine chancel. From 1662 the hearts of members of the royal and Orleans families were deposited in the St. Anne Chapel, on the left. When the caskets were desecrated at the Revolution there were 45, including those of Queen Marie-Thérèse, " Monsieur " (Philippe, Duke of Orleans), the Regent, Philippe of Orleans and Marie Leczinska. Most have disappeared.

Former Convent. — Go through the porch to the right of the church. The **cloister★,** which opens off the end of the court, is Classical in style with two superimposed galleries and a Mansard roof. The gardens, through the court's second arch, give a good view of the convent's majestic rear façade, the pavilion in which Anne of Austria stayed, distinguished by a porch with ringed columns, and the rear of the church dome.

Museum. — *Open 10 am to noon and 2 to 4.45 pm (3.45 pm Fridays). Closed Saturdays, Sundays and holidays. Access beneath the first porch on the right, at the end of the arcade.*

Displays include documents and mementoes of the great military physicians (Parmentier, premier pharmacist during the Empire; Villemin, Roussin, Broussais, Vincent, Laveran, Nobel prizewinner, 1907) and the French Health Service. Models and equipment indicate treatment meted out to the wounded during the Empire and the First World War.

From the Val-de-Grâce to the Observatory

Schola Cantorum. — *269 Rue St-Jacques.* The conservatory was founded privately in 1894 by Ch. Bordes and the composer Vincent d'Indy, to restore church music. The buildings formerly belonged to a community of English Benedictines who sought refuge in Paris after the Anglican Schism of 1531; the body of James II, who died in exile at St-Germain-en-Laye in 1701, rested in the chapel (now secularised) until the Revolution when the building was desecrated.

Bear right in the Rue des Feuillantines then left into the Rue d'Ulm.

École Normale Supérieure. — *45 Rue d'Ulm.* The school of higher studies for those entering the teaching profession was created by the Convention in 1794. It transferred to these buildings in 1847. For many university and other learned men and politicians, the " Normale " has proved to be the springboard to a brilliant career.

The **French Office for Modern Methods of Teaching** is at No. 29 Rue d'Ulm. It houses a small historical museum *(ground floor : open weekdays only 9 am to 12 pm and 2 to 6 pm; closed holidays)* and temporary exhibitions.

Return to the Rue St-Jacques by way of the Rues Louis-Thuillier and des Ursulines.

National Institute for the Deaf (Jeunes Sourds). — A hospital was established on this site to succour pilgrims on their way to Compostella in Spain in the 14C by monks from Altopascio (High Pass) near Lucca in Italy. In 1790, one year after the death of the Abbot de l'Épée who had worked on the education of deaf mutes, the hospital took up his work.

Church of St. James of the High Pass (St-Jacques-du-Haut-Pas). — The church, built in the Classical style between 1630 and 1685, became a Jansenist centre. The astronomer, Cassini *(see below),* is buried inside. The Rue de l'Abbé-de-l'Épée leads to the Bd St-Michel.

School of Advanced Mining Engineering (École Supérieure des Mines). — *Enter through No. 60.* The school was founded in 1783 and moved to the present buildings, the former Hôtel de Vendôme, in 1815. The **mineralogical collection★★** is among the world's richest. *Open Tuesdays to Fridays 2.30 to 5 pm, Saturdays 2 to 4.30 pm; closed holidays and during 5 weeks in June-July.*

Avenue de l'Observatoire. — The wide avenue with its central flower borders is lined by the buildings of the Pharmacy Faculty and other institutions. The **Observatory Fountain★** (1873) by Davioud is known for its decoration of the four quarters of the globe by Carpeaux (Oceania was omitted for reasons of symmetry!). The view towards Montmartre is attractive.

Before the Closerie des Lilas café, so famous in the 1920's, stands the vigorous François Rude's **statue of Marshal Ney** (1853) — executed nearby in 1815 for his support of Napoleon.

THE OBSERVATORY★   ▢▢ or ▢▢ : N 13

The Observatory's construction, on orders from Colbert and to plans by Claude Perrault, was begun on 21 June 1667, the summer solstice, and was completed in 1672. The Cassini's a family of Italian astronomers, continued in succession as directors until the Revolution. The dome and wings were added under Louis-Philippe.

The research conducted at the Observatory has included the calculation of the true dimensions of the solar system (1672), of the meridians of longitude, until then more than a little exaggerated — Louis XIV commented that the Academicians' calculations had considerably reduced the extent of his kingdom! — the speed of light, the production of the first map of the moon, the discovery by mathematical deduction of the planet Neptune (Le Verrier, 1846), the classification of the stars by size...

The building. — The building's four walls are oriented to the cardinal points of the compass, the south face also determining the capital's latitude. The meridian of longitude, calculated in 1667, which passes through the building was known as the Paris Meridian, until 1884 when the Greenwich mean was adopted generally with the exception of France and Ireland, which only followed suit in 1911. Midday bearings are to be found elsewhere in Paris besides on the actual meridian *(see diagram).*

The Observatory has been the seat of the International Time Bureau which since its inauguration (1919) sets universal time. Timepieces, accurate to one millionth of a second, have been installed in cellars 28 m — 92 ft — below ground which remain at a constant temperature of 11.86 °C — 53 °F. The cellars also house the speaking clock (☏ INF. 84.00).

Guided tours : first Saturday in the month at 2.30 pm on written application to the Secrétariat, 61 Avenue de l'Observatoire 75014 Paris, enclosing S.A.E. : small museum of old instruments, modern equipment, large telescopes, revolving observatory dome.

Walk up the Rue du Faubourg St-Jacques to No. 38, the **Hôtel Massa** *(p 44* — the Men of Letters Society). Make for Port-Royal.

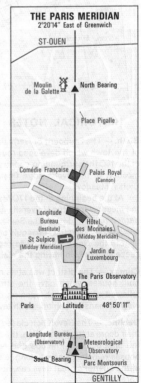

THE PARIS MERIDIAN
2°20'14" East of Greenwich

ST-OUEN

Moulin de la Galette   ▲ North Bearing

Place Pigalle

Comédie Française   Palais Royal (Cannon)

Longitude Bureau (Institute)   Hôtel des Monnaies (Midday Meridian)

St Sulpice (Midday Meridian)   Jardin du Luxembourg

The Paris Observatory

Paris   Latitude   48° 50' 11"

Longitude Bureau (Observatory)   Meteorological Observatory

South Bearing   Parc Montsouris

GENTILLY

Michelin **plans 10** or **11** : from H 10 to J 12.
Distance : 3 km — 2 miles — Time : 3 1/2 hours. Start from the Chambre-des-Députés métro.

The " noble faubourg " which lies off the far bank of the Seine from the Tuileries and east of the Invalides, includes many fine old 18C town houses and monuments.

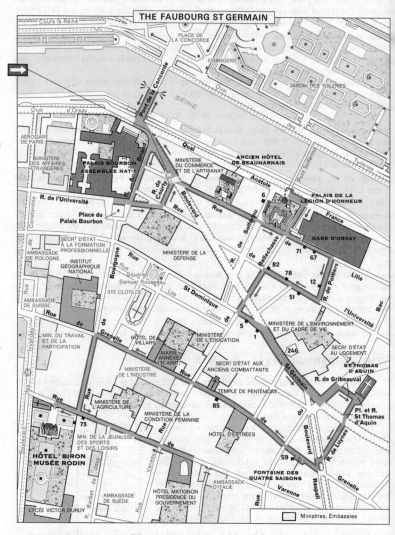

THE FAUBOURG ST GERMAIN

Ministries, Embassies

HISTORICAL NOTES

Birth. — The Faubourg St-Germain was originally, as its name implies, the suburb *(faubourg)* of the town which developed round the Abbey of St-Germain-des-Prés *(p 92)*. Until the end of the 16C the surrounding countryside was used for farming and hunting, except for a strip of meadow at the river's edge finally won from the abbey by the University and named the Clerks' Meadow.

At the beginning of the 17C Marguerite of Valois, first wife of Henri IV, took the east end of the meadow from the University as part of the grounds in which to build a vast mansion with a garden running down to the Seine. The acquisition was made so casually that the embankment came to be called the Malacquis or Misappropriated Quay. On the death of Queen Marguerite in 1615 the University tried to reclaim the land but, after twenty years of legal proceedings, succeeded only in having the main street of the new quarter named the Rue de l'Université.

Climax. — The district was at its most fashionable in the 18C. Noble lords and rich financiers built houses which gave the streets an individual character : one monumental entrance followed another, each opening on a courtyard closed at the far end by the façade of an elegant mansion behind which lay a large garden.

Decline. — The Revolution closed these sumptuous town houses and although they reopened their doors at the Restoration, the quarter never fully regained its status, as the fashionable, at the time of Louis-Philippe and Napoléon III, migrated to the Champs-Élysées. The finest houses remaining now belong to the state or serve as ambassadorial residences. Something of the quarter's great days can, however, still be recalled in the Rues de Lille, Grenelle and Varenne.

From the Concorde Bridge to the Legion of Honour Palace

The Pont de la Concorde. — The bridge was designed by the civil engineer, Perronet, in 1787 when he was 79. It was completed by 1791, the stones from the Bastille having been used in its construction so that, it was said, " the people could for ever trample the ruins of the old fortress ". During Louis-Philippe's reign the bridge was decorated with 12 colossal statues of famous men but the ornament was not liked and the figures were dispatched first to Versailles and subsequently dispersed to provincial towns!

Walk to the centre of the bridge, which was doubled in width in 1932, for remarkable **views★★** along the Seine and across the Place de la Concorde to the Madeleine.

■ THE PALAIS-BOURBON★ ▢▢ or ▢▢ : H 11

Construction. — In 1722 the Duchess of Bourbon, daughter of Louis XIV and Mme de Montespan, acquired land on which to build a house fronting on the Rue de l'Université. By 1728 the palace and terraced gardens running down to the Seine were complete.

Twenty-eight years later Louis XV bought the property so that it could be altered to form part of the general scheme of the Concorde Square; in 1784, however, Louis XVI sold it to the Prince of Condé who enlarged and embellished it. Finally, the adjoining **Hôtel de Lassay** was added and renamed the Petit or Little Bourbon.

Work was almost finished when the Revolution broke out. The palace was confiscated to serve as a chamber for the Council of the Five Hundred. Next it was used to house archives and Lassay House and its outbuildings as accommodation for the École Polytechnique.

In 1807 Napoleon commissioned Poyet to design the present façade overlooking the Place de la Concorde in harmony with the Greek plan of the Madeleine. At the Restoration the palace was returned to the Condés only to be bought back in 1827 and converted for use by the Legislative Assembly.

Exterior. — The Antique style façade with a portico is decorated with an allegorically carved pediment by Cortot (1842), statues, on high, of Minerva by Houdon and Themis by Roland, and below, among other figures, those of Henri IV and Louis XIV's ministers, Sully and Colbert. The allegorical low reliefs on the wings are by Rude *(right)* and Pradier *(left)*.

Take the Rue Aristide-Briand, on the left, to the Place du Palais-Bourbon from which you will get a good view of the 18C palace.

Interior. — *To visit apply in writing to the Quaestor's office, 126 Rue de l'Université, 75007 Paris.* Among the most impressive of the many rooms decorated with paintings and sculpture, are the lobby, with its ceiling by Horace Vernet, the Council Chamber and the **Library★★**. This is a fine room in itself and, in addition, magnificently decorated with a *History of Civilisation*, painted by Delacroix between 1838 and 1845. Houdon's portrait busts of Voltaire and Diderot are also in the library.

Apply in writing to the Quaestor's office to attend a debate in the National Assembly. Proceedings are conducted by the President of the **National Assembly** from the bureau formerly used for the Council of the Five Hundred *(see above).*

(Archives Photographiques, Paris)

Palais-Bourbon — Demosthenes haranguing the waves
(Delacroix fresco)

He faces the deputies — 491 when all are present — seated on benches arranged in a semicircle. Government members occupy the front bench below the speaker's stand (N. B. the political right and left are as viewed by the president and therefore the reverse as seen from the gallery).

Walk out of the Place du Palais-Bourbon, along the Rue de l'Université, down the Rue de Courty and across the Boulevard St-Germain to the Rue de Lille where you turn right. This street, named in honour of the town of Lille is typical of the old " noble faubourg ".

Nos. 80 and 78 were designed by the architect, Boffrand in 1714. The first, the **Hôtel de Seignelay,** occupied by the Ministry of Commerce, was owned originally by Colbert's grandson, then by the Duke of Charost, tutor to the young Louis XV and aristocrat philanthropist who was saved from the guillotine by his own peasants. By 1839 it had passed to Marshal Lauriston, a descendant of John Law, the Scots financier *(p 112).*

The **Hôtel de Beauharnais,** next door, received its name when Napoleon's son-in-law bought it in 1803 and redecorated it sumptuously for his own and his sister, Queen Hortense's, use. Since 1818 the house has been the seat of first the Prussian, and later, the German diplomatic missions to France.

The writer Jules Romain lived at No. 6 Rue Solférino from 1947 to his death (1972).

Continue to No. 64, the Palace of the Legion of Honour.

■ THE PALACE OF THE LEGION OF HONOUR ⑩ or ⑪ : H 11

The **Hôtel de Salm** was built in 1786 for the German Prince of Salm who, finding himself penniless after living in the house for only one year, sold it to his architect and rented it back. In 1795 the property was made the prize in a lottery. It was won by one, Lieuthrand, a former wigmaker who amassed a fortune as supplier to the army and pronounced himself a marquis. He was however, condemned for forgery, and put in prison where, not long after, he disappeared. Mme de Staël and her husband, the Swedish ambassador, the next owners in 1799, were succeeded by Napoleon who, two years after creating the order, made the mansion the Palace of the Legion of Honour. It was burnt down during the Commune of 1871 and rebuilt, in 1878, by the members of the Legion to the original plans. The only parts remaining of the early building are the low reliefs on the outside walls.

Turn left down to the Quai Anatole-France to look at the back of the palace where there is a delightful semicircular pavilion in complete contrast to the severe lines elsewhere.

The Legion of Honour Museum*. — *2 Rue de Bellechasse. Open 2 to 5 pm; closed Mondays, 1 January, 1 May, 15 August, 25 December; 5F.*

The museum presents in the Grand Chancellery galleries, original documents, decorations, pictures, uniforms and arms, the orders of chivalry and nobility of Pre-Revolutionary France (Malta, the Star, St. Michael, the Holy Spirit, St. Louis), and the creation of the Legion of Honour by Napoleon on 19 May 1802, its rapid expansion during the Empire (personal decorations of Bonaparte and his brothers), educational establishments and its subsequent history.

Further galleries show other French civil and military decorations (academic awards, the Military Medal, Military Cross, the Cross of the Liberation, Order of Merit) and foreign orders.

From the Legion of Honour Palace to the Four Seasons' Fountain

Across the Rue de Bellechasse, the former **Orsay Station** illustrates the popular steel architectural style of the late 19C. Built between 1898 and 1900 by Laloux, it was saved from demolition in 1973. The company Renaud-Barrault has installed a theatre, in the form of a circus, which can seat an audience of 900. The station houses the Auction Rooms, while awaiting the reconstruction of their former premises Rue Drouot (Hôtel des Ventes — *p 117*). They have a character all of their own and perhaps the oddest atmosphere in Paris with auctioneers, porters, collectors, dealers, amateurs, the purely curious, working their way through a surrealist collection of goods.

Continue down the Rue de Lille where No. 71, **Hôtel de Mouchy** dates from 1775 and No. 67, **President Duret's house**, from 1706. Turn right down the Rue de Poitiers where at No. 12, the **Hôtel de Poulpry** (1700), the monarchist group known as the Poitiers Street Committee used to meet in 1850.

Turn right in the Rue de l'Université, at one time the quarter's main street and still lined with interesting houses : No. 51, the **Hôtel de Soyécourt** was built in 1707; No. 78 in 1687; No. 82 is where the poet and politician Lamartine lived from 1837 to 1853 (inscription).

Turn left in the Rue de Bellechasse and, as it emerges on the Boulevard St-Germain, look right to see the more modern — 1877 — part of the Ministry of Defence. The old part overlooking the Rue St-Dominique consists of two houses and a former monastery. Cross the boulevard and continue down the Rue de Bellechasse before turning left in the Rue St-Dominique.

This street, which got its name from a former monastery for Dominican novices, was amongst the quarter's most interesting before a large part of it was swept away to make way for the Boulevard St-Germain. No. 5, the **Hôtel de Tavannes,** has a fine round arched doorway surmounted by a scallop and crowned by a triangular pediment. The artist, Gustave Doré, died in the house in 1883. No. 1, the **Hôtel de Gournay,** was erected in 1695.

The Rue St-Dominique ends on the Boulevard St-Germain on which you turn right. No. 246, now with No. 244 the Ministry of Works, was formerly the **Hôtel de Roquelaure,** the residence of the lawyer and statesman Cambacérès (1753-1824) and later the seat of the Council of State.

St. Thomas Aquinas Church. — The church, formerly the chapel of the Dominican novitiate monastery, was begun in 1682 in the Jesuit style to plans by Pierre Bullet. The façade was only completed in 1769. Inside are 17 and 18C paintings and a ceiling (absidal chapel) painted by Lemoyne in 1723 of the Transfiguration. The sacristy has Louis XV panelling.

Take the Rue St-Thomas-d'Aquin and, on the far side of the Boulevard St-Germain, the Rue de Luynes before crossing the Boulevard Raspail and turning right in the Rue de Grenelle.

Fountain of the Four Seasons* (Fontaine des Quatre-Saisons). — The beautiful Four Seasons' Fountain, carved by Bouchardon between 1739 and 1745 was commissioned by Turgot, the dean of the local merchants' guild and father of Louis XVI's minister. The commission was undertaken in answer to complaints that the stately quarter was almost totally without water!

A seated figure of Paris looking down on reclining personifications of the Seine and the Marne adorns the Ionic pillared fountain front. The sides are decorated with figures of the Seasons and low reliefs showing cherubs performing the seasons' labours.

The Romantic poet, Musset, lived at No. 59 Rue de Grenelle from 1824 to 1839, when he wrote most of his poetic dramas.

Fountain of the Four Seasons.—Winter

From the Fountain of the Four Seasons to the Hôtel Biron

Rue de Grenelle. — The stately private residences have been converted to government offices and embassies and it remains as difficult as ever to see the houses behind the monumental gateways; only through a half open door will you glimpse the beautiful façades erected by Delisle-Mansart, Boffrand or other 18C architects.

The Hôtel Bouchardon, at No. 59, decorated with the Fountain of the Four Seasons, will house a Maillol Museum.

At No. 79 stands the great **Hôtel d'Estrées** (1713); No. 85, is the **Hôtel d'Avaray** (1728), the Royal Netherlands Embassy. **Pentémont Temple** with its Ionic cupola of 1750 was at one time a convent chapel; then the nuns were replaced by the Imperial Guard and these, in turn, by the civil servants of the Ministry of War Veterans. No. 110, the **Hôtel de Courteilles** (1778), dominating the street with its massive façade, is now the Ministry of Education; No. 116 was built in 1709 for Marshal de Villars and considerably remodelled. No. 118, is the much smaller, **Hôtel de Villars,** built in 1712 and extremely elegant with twin garlanded, oval windows. Continue to Nos. 138-140, the **Hôtel de Noirmoutiers** (1722), at one time the army staff headquarters and the house in which Marshal Foch died on 20 March 1929. Today it is the office of the IGN — the National Geographical Institute.

Rue de Varenne. — The street was laid along a rabbit warren — *garenne* which became distorted, in time, to Varenne — belonging to the Abbey of St-Germain-des-Prés. There are attractive old houses in this street also : No. 73 the great **Hôtel de Broglie** (1735); No. 78, the **Hôtel de Villeroy** (1724), now the Ministry of Agriculture; No. 72, the large **Hôtel de Castries** (1700).

The most famous, of course, is the **Hôtel Matignon** at No. 57. The house was built by Courtonne in 1721 and has since been considerably remodelled. Talleyrand, diplomat and statesman to successive regimes, owned it from 1808 to 1811, then Madame Adelaïde, sister to Louis-Philippe. In 1935 it became the office of the President of the Council of State and in 1958 the Paris residence of the prime minister.

Turn back along the Rue de Varenne to No. 77, the Hôtel Biron (on the left).

HÔTEL BIRON★★ - RODIN MUSEUM★★   ⊞ or ⊞ : J 11

The house and garden enable one to see Rodin's sculptures in a perfect residential setting.

In 1728, one Abraham Peyrenc, a wigmaker who had accrued a fortune and agrandised his name to Peyrenc de Moras, commissioned Gabriel the Elder to build him a house in the Rue de Varenne. In time the beautiful building came into the hands of the Duchess of Maine, grand-daughter of the great Condé and wife of the son of Louis XIV and Madame de Montespan, and then of Marshal Biron, a general in the Revolutionary government who died, decapitaded, in 1793.

In 1797 the house was turned into a dance hall. Under the Empire it reverted to its role of residence, first of the papal legate then of the ambassador of the Tsar. In 1820 it was taken over by the Convent of the Sacred Heart as an educational establishment. Madame Sophie Barat, the mother superior (canonised : 1925), had the Neo-Gothic chapel constructed and the greater part of the residence's panelling ripped out, seeing in the wood carving a symbol of the vanities of the age — a few ornamented rooms, nevertheless, do still remain.

After the Congregation Law of 1904, under which many convents were dispersed, the educational part of the building and the gardens were converted into the Lycée Victor-Duruy and the house was made available to artists. Thus Auguste Rodin came to live in and enjoy the house until his death in 1917, presenting his work by way of rent. The house has since been converted into a museum and the gardens, restored to their original form.

The museum★★. — *Open 10 am to 5 pm (5 pm 1 October to 31 March); closed Tuesdays, 1 May, 1 November, 25 December; 5F — Sundays 2.50F. Turn left out of the hall.*

Rodin's sculpture, primarily in bronze and white marble, is immensely striking, vital, life-like. Creation in the guise of figures emerging from the living rock was a favourite theme **(Thought, The Hand of God)** although he excelled in studies of the nude **(St. John the Baptist).**

On the ground floor are some of the most expressive works : the bust of **Clemenceau, The Cathedral, The Kiss, The Walking Man.** At either end of the gallery, in corresponding rotundas which have kept their fine panelling, are **Eve** and the **Age of Bronze.**

Victor Hugo and the Muses
(Avenue Henri-Martin)

At the top of the beautiful 18C staircase, on the first floor, are the smaller works, the plasters for the large groups and for the statues of **Balzac** *(p 121)* and **Victor Hugo.**

Finally, in the garden, can be seen the sculptures which made Rodin's reputation during his lifetime, **The Thinker** (on the right), **The Burghers of Calais** and **The Gates of Hell** (on the left) and the **Ugolin group** (in the centre of the pool).

The personal collections of the artist (furniture, pictures, antique) are displayed in the house and in the former chapel *(temporary exhibitions).*

Michelin plans ⑩ : from E 1 to E 5 and K 1 to K 5 or ⑪ : detailed map.

This vast park of nearly 900 ha — 2 224 acres — is cut by wide shaded roads *(speed lim)* leading to ornamental lakes, flower gardens, two racecourses, cafés and restaurants.

The wood's past. — In Merovingian times the forest was hunted for bear, deer, wolves an wild boar; in 1308 local woodmen went in pilgrimage to Our Lady of Boulogne and, on the return, built a church which they called Our Lady of Boulogne the Lesser. In 1556 Henri II en closed the forest; in the 17C Colbert converted it into a Royal Hunt with straight rides marke

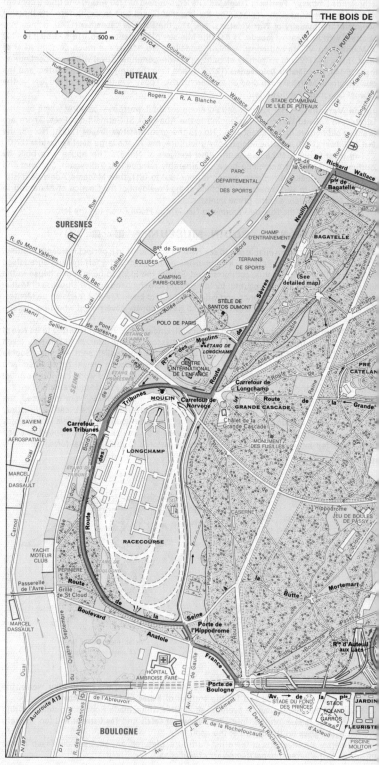

t their meeting points by Crosses, as at the Croix Catelan. Louis XIV opened the wood to
he public but it was not until the Regency that it became highly fashionable and great
ouses began to be built (Madrid, La Muette, Bagatelle, St. James' Folly).

During the Revolution the forest became the refuge of the pursued and the destitute.

he present. — When Napoleon III gave the forest to the capital, Haussmann demolished the
urrounding wall, landscaped the area after Hyde Park, built the Longchamp racecourse,
estaurants and much more. 1854 saw the opening of the Avenue de l'Impératrice (since 1929
he Avenue Foch); 1870, the Auteuil racecourse.

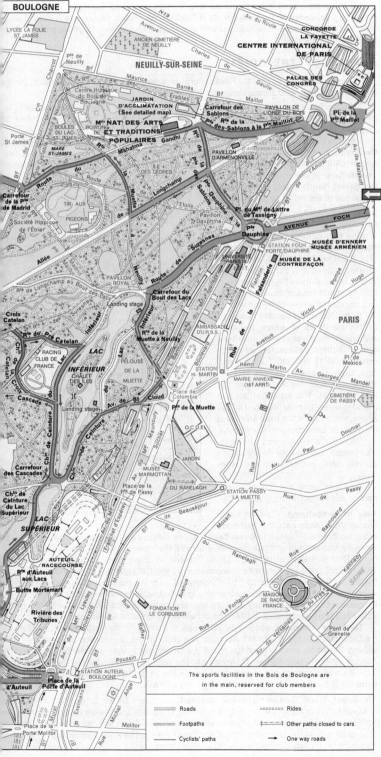

■ **AVENUE FOCH**★ ▥ or ▦ : from F 5 to F 7

The way to the Bois de Boulogne from the Étoile is along Haussmann's most magnificent roadway, the wide (120 m — 393 ft) Avenue Foch.

In 1968, beneath the outer roadways, a vast underground car park was opened, linked by a subway to the express *métro* and shopping centre.

No. 59 Avenue Foch houses two small museums *(open Sundays 1 to 5 pm — 4 pm in winter — closed in August);* the **Armenian Museum** with jewels, religious and folk art objects and the **Ennery Museum** with Chinese and Japanese furniture, ceramics, bronzes, lacquerwork, jade and several hundred netsuke (small carved ivory or bone belt ornaments).

Off the avenue, at 16 Rue de la Faisanderie, the Manufacturers' Syndicate have opened an interesting **Counterfeit Museum** (Musée de la Contrefaçon — *open Mondays to Fridays, 9 am to noon and 2 to 5.15 pm; closed holidays)* with examples of commercial forgeries and non-copyright publicity material.

■ **TOUR OF THE BOIS**★★

You may hire a bicycle near the Pavillon Royal everyday 1 May through 30 September; the rest of the year Saturdays and Sundays only.

Take the Porte Dauphine - Porte des Sablons road, then the Allée de Longchamp to the left and finally the Muette - Neuilly road to the right. Skirt the lake known as the Mare St James by the Mahatma Gandhi road.

Pass the Porte de Madrid crossroads once the site of François I's castle of 1531 **Château de Madrid** which was demolished in 1793, and the St. James area named after a Baron St. James who erected a folly in the park when the crown sold off plots for cash before the Revolution. The Richard Wallace Boulevard then the Sèvres-Neuilly road, on your left, brings you to the entrance to Bagatelle.

Bagatelle★. — *Admission : 1F — 2F for exhibitions.*

The first house to be built on the site was in 1720; it fell into ruin and in 1775 the Count of Artois, the future Charles X, bought it, betting his sister-in-law, Marie-Antoinette, and winning, that he would have a house designed and completed within three months.

By the 19C it had come to be owned by the Hertfords of whom the third and fourth marquesses and the latter's son, Sir Richard Wallace, formed a large collection of 17 and 18C French paintings, furniture, and art objects. The City of Paris bought the house from the family in 1905. The art collection had already been transferred to London where, since 1897, it has been on view as the Wallace Collection, Hertford House.

Bagatelle is well known for its beautiful garden, particularly its walled iris garden *(May)* water lilies and roses *(June)*.

Continue along the Sèvres-Neuilly road to the Longchamp crossroads.

Tour of Longchamp. — At the Longchamp crossroads note the manmade but nevertheless picturesque **Grande Cascade**★. The château to the right was given to Haussmann by Napoleon III and has since 1949 housed the International Children's Centre.

In 1256 St. Isabel, sister to St. Louis, founded an abbey nearby, Our Lady of Humility. This, in time, came to be known as Longchamp or Long Field after the original clearing beside the Seine. By the 18C austerity had disappeared from the nunnery. Services at the end of Holy Week were crowded by the fashionable and what came to be known as the Longchamp Procession took place regularly until the last days of the Second Empire — even though the abbey had been suppressed in 1789. The old **mill** on the left is the only abbey building to remain.

Longchamp Racecourse, opened by Napoleon III in 1857, is the setting each midsummer for the famous *Grand Prix (p 10)*. Amongst new installations is a panoramic restaurant overlooking the whole course. Continue round the racecourse to the Porte de Boulogne and the Avenue de la Porte d'Auteuil. On your right you pass the stadium where the French Open Tennis Championships are played every year in the spring *(p 10)*. At No. 3 you will find the entrance to the Floral Nursery Garden of the city of Paris.

Municipal Floral Garden★ (Fleuriste Municipal). — *Open 10 am to 6 pm (5 pm October to March), April to September 1F; 2F for exhibitions.* The plants and flowers on display are grown for Paris' municipal parks and to adorn official occasions. There are also a formal Garden, an arboretum and hothouses with tropical and exotic plants. The azalea *(latter half of April)* and chrysanthemum *(late October)* shows draw large crowds.

BAGATELLE

Continue to the Place d'Auteuil and take to the left the Route d'Auteuil aux Lacs which circles the Auteuil Racecourse famous for its jumps including a 8 m — 28 ft — water jump (p 7). The road then skirts the **Upper Lake*** (Lac Supérieur) before running alongside the left bank of the **Lower Lake**** (Lac Inférieur). Popular with Parisians on Sundays this lake has on the other bank a boat quay (hire charge : 11.70F an hour for 1 or 2 persons ; 13.40 for 3 or more persons ; deposit obligatory : 50F) and the stage for the boats to the islands (café-restaurant). Advance beyond the Cascades crossroads and bear left, past the Racing-Club, then right to the stone Catelan Cross.

Pré Catelan*. — This attractive well kept area (free entry) named after a court minstrel from Provence murdered there in the 14C, includes a luxurious café-restaurant and a cooper beech nearly two hundred years old with the most widespread branches of any tree in Paris — it shades nearly 500 m² — 600 sq yds. A **Shakespeare Garden** (tours 11 am, 3, 4.30 and 5.30 pm ; 1F) is planted with flowers, herbs and trees mentioned in his plays.

Continue, right, along the Pré-Catelan road to return to the Cascades crossroads.

Return to Porte Dauphine where you take once again the Porte Dauphine — Porte des Sablons road to reach the Sablons crossroads. Make for the modern buildings at No. 6 Mahatma Gandhi road.

National Museum of Popular Art and Traditions** (Musée National des Arts et Traditions Populaires). — Open 10 am to 5.15 pm ; closed Tuesdays and certain holidays ; 5F ; 2.50 Sundays and holidays. This museum gives a glimpse of day to day life in pre-industrial France. The **Cultural Gallery** (ground floor) evokes man's environment, the technical progress made by man to enable him to exploit the natural resources and the institutions he created for community living. The **Study Gallery** (basement) has displays concerning agriculture, husbandry, domestic life, crafts, local beliefs and customs, games, music and local folklore.

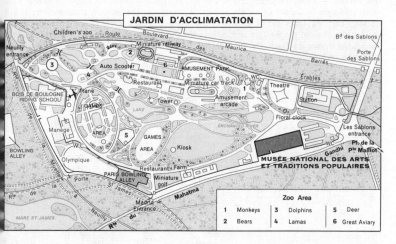

JARDIN D'ACCLIMATATION

Zoo Area					
1	Monkeys	3	Dolphins	5	Deer
2	Bears	4	Lamas	6	Great Aviary

Children's Amusement Park* (Jardin d'Acclimatation). — Open in summer 9 am to 6.30 pm (7.30 pm on Sundays and holidays) in winter 9 am to nightfall : 2.50F. Special attractions everyday (dolphin act). A miniature railway runs on Wednesdays, Saturdays and Sundays from 1.30 pm.

This park, primarily arranged as a children's amusement park, includes a small zoo (containing a typical Norman farm) and a Children's Museum (Musée en Herbe). A miniature railway runs from the entrance to the Maillot Gate.

At the Maillot Gate are, to right and left, the Armenonville and Orée du Bois Restaurants — two of the most elegant Second Empire buildings in the park.

■ CENTRE INTERNATIONAL DE PARIS - PALAIS DES CONGRÈS**
10 or 11 : E 6

The Paris Conference Centre **(CIP)**, situated near the Bois de Boulogne on the Champs-Élysées-Défense axis, provides a modern conference centre **(Palais des Congrès)** in addition to other business and recreational facilities and hotel accommodation.

The **Main Conference Hall***** (to see the inside you must go to a performance) within the centre is unique in Europe. This dual purpose hall for conferences and entertainment has a convertible stage and a seating capacity of 4 300. It is the home of the Paris Symphony Orchestra and every care has been given to the acoustics of the auditorium : the decorative forms of the walls and the roof ensure acoustic uniformity.

On several floors around the main conference hall there are exhibition halls (1st floor), other smaller conference and meeting rooms, business suites and offices and around 80 shops lining the Rue Basse and the Rue Haute. In addition there are restaurants, cinemas, a discotheque, an air terminal, parking space and on the seventh floor spacious kitchens restaurants and function rooms can cater for over 4 000 guests at a time.

Dominating the centre is the 42 storey hotel, **Concorde-La Fayette.** This 1 000 room hotel communicates directly on the ground and seventh floors with the conference centre. On the top floor there is a panoramic bar (open 11 am to 2 am, access is reserved for customers only) which affords an extensive **view*** of Paris, the Bois de Boulogne and at the far right La Défense.

Michelin plan 🗺 : detailed map and map 🗺 27.

Vincennes — a fortress, the focal point of many events in French history, picturesque lakes, scattered wood, the largest zoo in France, a delightful floral garden — takes a day to discover and enjoy fully, whether by car or on foot.

THE CHÂTEAU★★ map 🗺 17, 27

This " mediaeval Versailles " has two distinct aspects within its walls where a tall forbidding keep stands close to a majestic group of 17C buildings.

The manorhouse. — In the 11C the crown acquired Vincennes Forest from St. Maur Abbey; in the 12C Philippe Auguste built a manorhouse within its confines to which St. Louis added a Holy Chapel. This king also forbade anyone to hunt the animals of the forest while, seated at the foot of an oak, he received his subjects without let or hindrance of ushers.

The castle. — The castle was constructed by the Valois : Philippe VI, John the Good and finally Charles V who completed it in 1370. Charles further invited the members of his court to build themselves houses within the walls to create a royal city, but it was not until the reign of Louis XIV that the nobility sought to live in the king's shadow.

The classical château. — Mazarin, appointed governor of Vincennes in 1652, had symmetrical royal pavilions designed by Le Vau and built to frame the main courtyard which faced south overlooking the forest. In 1660, one year after the pavilions' completion, the young Louis XIV spent his honeymoon in the King's Pavilion but subsequently preferred other royal domains.

The prison. — From the beginning of the 16C to 1784, the keep, no longer in favour as a royal residence, was used as a state prison. Supporters of the League, of Jansenism, of the Fronde, libertines, lords and philosophers were held; the disgrace of detention in Vincennes was far less than at the Bastille and, among the many held, the famous included the Great Condé, the Prince de Conti, Cardinal de Retz, Fouquet (guarded by d'Artagnan), the Duke of Lauzun *(p 71)*, Diderot, Mirabeau...

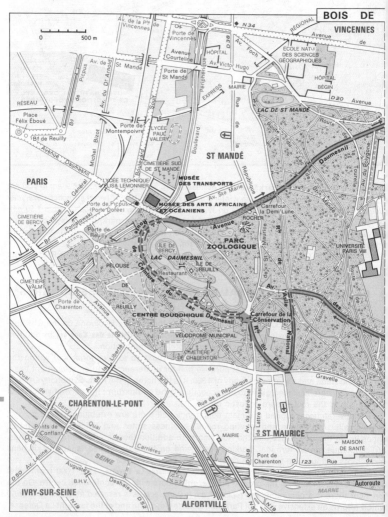

The porcelain factory. — In 1738, quite by chance, the château became a porcelain factory when two craftsmen, dismissed from Chantilly, sought refuge at Vincennes and began to practise their skill.

A company was formed which produced painted objects in soft paste, including sprigged flowers in natural colours. Porcelain bouquets and even " gardens " became highly fashionable before the factory was transferred to Sèvres in 1756 *(p 173)*.

The arsenal. — Under Napoleon the château was converted into a formidable arsenal. The towers were lopped to the height of the perimeter wall and mounted with cannon, the rampart crenelations removed, and the keep once more converted to a prison.

Daumesnil's Refusals. — In 1814 when the Allies called for the surrender of Vincennes, the governor, General Daumesnil, known as Peg Leg since the loss of his leg at the Battle of Wagram, retorted " Give me back my leg and I'll give you Vincennes " *(p 56)*.

At the end of the Hundred Days, the castle was again invested and there came a second refusal to surrender. Five months later, however, the doors were opened to Louis XVIII.

1830 found Daumesnil still governor and insurgents attempting to attack Charles X's ministers detained in the keep. The governor refused them entry, announcing that before giving in he would blow himself and the castle sky high.

The military establishment. — Under Louis-Philippe, Vincennes was incorporated in the Paris defence system; a fort was built beside it, outer openings were blocked up, the ramparts reinforced with massive casemates and the complex virtually interred by glacis.

On 24 August 1944 the Germans, in the half hour before their departure from the castle, shot 26 resistance fighters, exploded three mines, breaching the ramparts in two places and damaging the King's Pavilion, and set fire to the Queen's Pavilion.

Restoration. — The restoration of Vincennes was begun by Napoleon III who commanded Viollet-le-Duc to begin the work which, lasted a century, and is now completed.

The main courtyard looks again much as it did in the 17C since the moat round the keep has been redug, the 19C casemates removed and the pavilions restored. The château, in fact, is being revealed, once more, as one of the great historic royal houses of France.

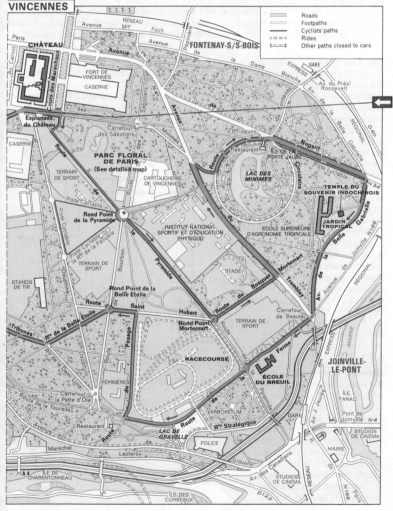

TOUR OF THE CHÂTEAU

We suggest you begin by walking right round the outside of the château.

The Keep★★ (**Donjon** — exterior). — This magnificent construction epitomizes the greatness of 14C military architecture. The 52 m tall — 170 ft — tower, quartered by turrets, with a spur to the north for latrines, a tiring room and a small oratory, was encircled by a sentry path protected by now vanished battlements and machicolations.

The keep proper was surrounded by a fortified wall and a separate moat. The base of the wall was protected against sappers by massive stonework, corner turrets and a covered watch path, complete with battlements, machicolations and gun embrasures.

The Tour du Bois and the Colonne du Duc d'Enghien. — The arcades of the Classical Vincennes portico overlooking the forest and closing the perimeter wall on the south side, come into view as you arrive on the Château Esplanade. The Bois Tower at the centre was reduced by Le Vau in the 17C when he transformed the gate into a state entrance (it appears as a triumphal arch from inside).

From the bridge over the moat can be seen, at the foot of the Tour de la Reine (Queen's Tower) on the right, the column marking the spot where the **Duke of Enghien**, Prince of Condé, accused of plotting against Napoleon, was executed by firing squad on 21 March 1804. (His body was exhumed on the orders of Louis XVIII and reinterred in the north oratory in the Holy Chapel).

The Cours des Maréchaux. — It was in the penultimate of the five truncated towers of the east wall, the Devil's Tower (Tour du Diable), that the porcelain factory was established. The avenue is modern.

Guided tours of the keep and chapel : 10 to 11.15 am and 1.30 to 5.15 pm (4.30 pm 1 October to 31 March); closed Tuesdays, 1 January, 1 May, 1 November, 25 December; 4F — 2F Sundays and holidays.

Tour du Village★. — This massive tower 42 m high — 138 ft — the only one beside the keep not to have been lopped in the 19C, served as the governor's residence in the Middle Ages.

Sainte-Chapelle★. — The Holy Chapel, modelled on the Sainte-Chapelle *(p 68)* and begun by Charles V in the 14C in place of the one built by St. Louis, was only completed in the 16C in the reign of Henri II. The building, apart from the windows and some decoration, is pure Gothic; the façade with its beautiful stone rose windows is Flamboyant. The interior consists of a single elegant aisle with highly decorative consoles and a frieze running beneath the windows which, in the chancel, are filled with unusually coloured mid-16C **stained glass**★.

The Keep★★. — The keep interior now serves as the château museum.

Pass across the drawbridge, protected by a barbican, to a court, then through two gates, the second being that of the Temple Tower brought here after the demolition of the prison in which Louis XVI and his family were held *(p 148)*. From the inner courtyard enter the great south hall where there is a well 17 m deep — 56 ft.

Each of the keep's floors, except the topmost one, is the same with a main chamber with vaulting resting on a central pillar and four small dependent rooms in the turrets. These were later converted into prison cells (graffiti on the walls). The first floor, originally a royal reception room hung with fine tapestries, was subsequently also used as a prison. A wide spiral staircase leads to what was once the royal bedchamber (Henry V of England died of dysentery in this room in 1422).

Stairs (150) continue to the terrace, commanding the château, the wood and the southeast suburbs of Paris.

Classical Vincennes★. — With the main courtyard as Le Vau intended, once more closed to the north by a portico, the **Queen's** and **King's Pavilions** (naval and military archives) now restored and his triumphal arch and colonnades overlooking the wood being rebuilt, this part of the Château of Vincennes has returned to its former Classical glory.

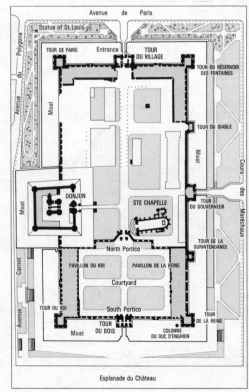

THE BOIS★★   plan ⅠⅠ : detailed map

The Royal Forest. — Philippe Auguste enclosed the wood as a royal hunt with a wall 12 km long — 7 miles; Charles V built the small Beauté Château within it on a low hill overlooking the Marne. In the 17C it became a fashionable place to take the air.

The Bois in Modern Times. — Napoleon III ceded Vincennes in 1860 — except the château and military installations — to the City of Paris to be made into an English style park.

In 1931 a Colonial Exhibition was held in the wood round Lake Daumesnil where the African and Oceanian Art Museum and several monuments in the Tropical Garden remain as souvenirs. Nowadays the 1 000 year old **Throne** or **Gingerbread Fair** is held each spring on the Reuilly Lawn recalling the concession obtained in 957 by the monks of St. Anthony's Abbey to sell a rye, honey and aniseed bread in memory of their saint in Holy Week.

Paris Floral Garden★★. — *Open daily 9.30 am to 6 pm; 1.50F — 4F during shows (Sundays and holidays from 1st Sunday in March to 14 July and 1st Sunday in September to 11 November).*

The setting created for the 1969 Flower Show has since been established as a garden; flowers, a lake and water garden, a restaurant and special display pavilions (not floral). An **exotarium★** *(5F)* contains a wide variety of tropical fishes and reptiles.

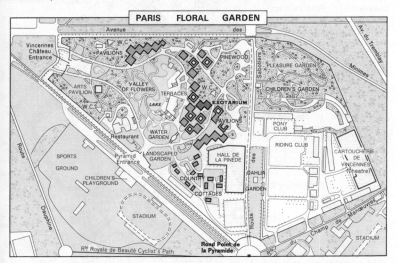

The Minimes Lake. — The lake, named after a former monastery on the same site, includes three islands, of which one, the Porte Jaune, is accessible across a bridge (café, boats).

Indochinese Memorial Temple and Tropical Garden. — *Open Sundays 2 to 4 pm*. The garden, in which stand the Institute of Tropical Agronomic Research and the Tropical Forestry Centre *(No. 45 bis, Avenue de la Belle Gabrielle)*, has a Chinese gate by the main entrance and, on the far side of the garden, a Temple to the Memory of the Indochinese killed in the 1914-1918 War. Beside the temple is an alley inspired by the famous avenue at Angkor Watt.

Breuil School of Horticulture. — Horticulture and landscape design. Beautiful gardens. *Tour of the Arboretum, 1 to 5 pm Mondays, Wednesdays and Fridays; other expositions can be visited on written application to the director*. On the left is the small Gravelle Lake and on the right the Vincennes **trotting track** *(p 10)*. Next are the " Experimental University Centre ", (1968), and the Vincennes cycle track.

Lake Daumesnil★. — A great many people flock to the lake shore, its two islands (café on Reuilly Island) and to hire its rowing boats *(9F an hour)*.

Buddhist Centre (Centre bouddhique du Bois de Vincennes). — *Scheduled opening date : Spring 1979*. South of the Lake Daumesnil is the Buddhist Temple of Paris, where the 180 000 roof tiles were carved out of a chestnut tree with an axe. Inside is a monumental statue of Buddha (9 m — 30 ft), in gold leaf.

African and Oceanian Art Museum★. — *Open 9.45 am to noon and 1.30 to 5.15 pm; closed Tuesdays and holidays; 5F — Sundays 2.50F.*

The principal themes of African art (life and death) are evoked in the entrance hall. On the first floor is a collection of headdresses and masks from West Africa. Examples of Oceanian art *(ground floor)* include bask and painted stone sculpture (Australia), masks (New Guinea) and strange funerary figures (New Hebrides). The North African countries *(second floor)* are represented by Tunisian pottery, embroidery from Fez and fine **jewellery★**. A tropical fish aquarium and whale fishing equipment are on display in the basement.

Transport Museum (Musée des transports). — *60 Avenue Ste-Marie, at St. Mandé. Open Saturdays and Sundays May to October 2.30 to 6 pm. 5F.* Collection of horsedrawn carriages since Louis XIV, trams, trolleybuses, buses and métro cars.

Zoological Garden★★. — *Open 15 February to 31 October, 9 am to 6 pm (7 pm Sundays and holidays); 9 am to 5.30 pm the rest of the year; 6F.* 600 mammals and 700 birds of some 200 different species live in natural surroundings. At the centre is an artificial rock 72 m — 236 ft high — inhabited by wild mountain sheep. **View★** from the top *(lift : 2F; stairs : 1F)*.

Michelin plans ⑩ or ⑪ : J 13, J 14 — K 13, K 14.
Distance : 2 km — 1 mile — Time : 2 1/2 hours. Start from the Odéon métro station.

On this walk the Institute and Mint are the main monuments; the Conti and Grands-Augustins Quays the vantage points, the Rohan Courtyard an example of Renaissance architecture.

From the Carrefour de l'Odéon to the Institute

Cross the Boulevard St-Germain and opposite Danton's statue, by No. 130, cut into the Commerce-St-André Court, opened in 1776 on the site of a tennis court built in the former ditch at the foot of the Philippe Auguste perimeter.

It was in this passage that a Dr. Guillotin perfected, on some sheep in 1790, his " philanthropic decapitating machine " and at a small printers, No. 8, that Marat produced his paper, *The People's Friend*. From No. 4, now a locksmith's workshop, can be seen one of the towers which formed part of the Philippe Auguste wall.

Rohan Courtyard*. — Turn right after No. 4 into Rohan Courtyard — a series of three courts and once part of the 15C mansion of the Archbishops of Rouen (Rohan is a deformation of Rouen). In the second, of these typically provincial style courtyards, stands a Renaissance building, the last trace of what was once the home of Diane de Poitiers, mistress of Henri II.

Continue along the peaceful Rue du Jardinet into the Rue de l'Éperon where the Lycée Fénelon stands, the first girls' school to be opened in Paris, (1893). Bear right *(Rue St-André-des-Arts)* then left into the Rue Séguier, dating back, under the name Pavée d'Andouilles, to 1179 and lined still by old houses.

The quays. — The **Quai des Grands-Augustins,** built in 1313, is the oldest in Paris. It got its name from the Great Augustine Monastery established by St. Louis in the 13C on the site which extended along the waterfront to the Rue Dauphine. Glance, as you pass, at the new and second-hand book and antique shops, at No. 35, a 17C mansion and at No. 51, also a 17C house and now the famous Lapérouse Restaurant.

The **Quai de Conti** begins at the Rue Dauphine. Running off just beyond, beneath an arcade, is the curious **Rue de Nevers,** a blind alleyway hollowed out in the 13C and remaining mediaeval in character. It ends abruptly at what once was part of the Philippe Auguste wall. On the corner of the Rue Guénégaud stands the Mint.

■ THE MINT* (Hôtel des Monnaies) ⑩ or ⑪ : J 13

Construction. — A succession of buildings have stood between the Rue Dauphine and the Philippe Auguste wall since the Nesle Mansion was first erected on the site in the 13C. The house was rebuilt by Louis of Gonzague, Prince of Nevers, in 1572, remodelled in 1641 and renamed by the Princess de Conti when she came to live there in 1670. In the 18C Louis XV transferred the Mint to the mansion, selecting a hitherto unknown architect, **Antoine,** to design the workshops and make any other alterations necessary. The simplicity of line, sober bossage and decoration of the lower parts of the building and the arrangement of the frontage pleased the public after the surfeit of Classical orders and colonnades. The architect himself became so attached to it that he lived in the building until he died in 1801.

Tour. — A staircase rising from the beautiful coffered entrance, circles twice before reaching the suite of panelled rooms overlooking the quay *(displays on view : 11 am to 5 pm; closed Sundays and holidays)*. Medals are on sale in the far wing *(9 am to 5.30 pm, noon on Saturdays; closed Sundays)*. The pressing of blanks into French and other coins, and the production of telephone discs and dies for the Assay and Weights and Measures offices now take place in Pessac (Gironde). The Mint also produces medals and decorations *(guided tours, Sundays and Wednesdays, 2 to 3.30 pm, closed during the summer holidays)*.

A pyramid in the second court on the left is a former meridian bearing *(map p 123)*.

THE INSTITUTE QUARTER

■ THE INSTITUTE OF FRANCE★ 🔟 or 🔟 : J 13

The Academy dome marks the building from afar.

Long before the present building, the site formed part of the Philippe Auguste perimeter which at its end on the Seine was defended by the **Nesle Tower,** standing where the left wing of the Institute has since been erected (the Mint side).

The tower's history became widely known when Alexandre Dumas dramatized it in a play.

In 1661, three days before he died, Cardinal Mazarin, when making final bequests from his immense wealth, left 2 million *livres* for the foundation of a college of sixty scholars from the provinces acquired by France under his ministry. The College of Four Nations — Piedmont, Alsace, Artois and Roussillon — was opened in 1688 and closed in 1790 when the building became successively a prison, civil engineering school and museum.

The building next became the home of the Institute, a body founded by the Convention and transferred from the Louvre by Napoleon in 1806. It incorporates the French Academy, founded by Richelieu in 1635 and the Academies of Inscriptions and Belles Lettres (1663) Science (1666), Fine Arts (1795) and Moral and Political Sciences (1832).

The French Academy (l'Académie Française). — Membership of the French Academy is limited to forty and is exclusively masculine. The admission ceremony, following election and approval by the head of state, the Academy's patron, is made a great Paris occasion. Members are commonly known as " immortals " although the wearing of a green robe at solemn meetings and collaboration in the production of the Dictionary of the French Language have not saved the majority from total obscurity — whereas those refused admission include : Descartes, Pascal, Molière, La Rochefoucauld, Rousseau, Vauvenargues, Diderot, Beaumarchais, Balzac, Maupassant, Proust, Zola...

The majority of present academicians are writers — Julien Green, Ionesco, Joseph Kessel, Paul Morand — but also represented are the Church, the army, diplomacy, medicine, the cinema (René Clair) and technology.

Tour of the Institute. — The rounded wings ending in square pavilions and framing the Jesuit style chapel at the centre, were designed by Le Vau to harmonize with the Louvre, of which he was also an architect, on the far bank of the Seine. The courtyard through the left gate beneath the cupola, is lined on either side by twin porticoes which precede respectively, left, the Mazarin Library, originally the cardinal's own collection and, right, the ceremonial hall.

A tour of the interior *(reserved to cultural associations)* includes the academy council chambers and the former Mazarin Chapel beneath the dome which, since 1806, has been the ceremonial hall. Outstanding among the statuary, pictures and tapestries are Mazarin's tomb by Coysevox and Philippe de Champaigne's painting of *Richelieu on his Deathbed*.

From the Institute to the Carrefour de l'Odéon

Walk round the right wing of the Institute, behind the chapel, to the Rue Mazarine.

Rue Mazarine. — **Molière's** first appearance as an actor was made in 1643 at the theatre which stood at No. 12. He had joined the company which lodged next door, at No. 10, and included the Béjart family of two brothers and two sisters, on inheriting some money from his mother. He was 21, had always been stagestruck and gladly abandoned the legal career chosen for him by his father. Symbolically he changed his name from Poquelin to Molière.

The company leased the indoor tennis court at No. 12 and built a theatre inside it which Molière and his companions, with youthful audacity, named the Illustrious Theatre.

The first Paris **fire station,** home of the capital's first fire brigade which was created in 1722, was at No. 30. It was mustered by François Dumouriez du Perrier, onetime valet to Molière, member of the Comédie-Française and father of 32 children.

No. 42, again an indoor tennis court converted into the **Guénégaud theatre,** was where in 1671, opera was presented for the first time in France. The work, *Pomone* by Perrin and Cambert, played for eight months before the rival composer, Lulli, jealous of its success, had the theatre closed. After Molière's death in 1673, his company, evicted from the Palais-Royal by Lulli again, made the theatre their home until 1689 *(see below)*.

Carrefour de Buci. — By the 18C the Buci crossroads had become the focal point of the Left Bank with bustling pedestrians, wheeled traffic and a sedan chair rank, a guard post, a gibet and a pillar to which miscreants were attached by an iron collar. Today the junction is the scene of a colourful daily market *(not on Sundays)*.

Rue de l'Ancienne-Comédie. — The street got its present name in 1770, the date the Comédie-Française left.

When the Four Nations College opened in 1688, the austere Sorbonne teachers at its head disapproved of the proximity of the Comédie-Française and forced the company to leave the Rue Mazarine *(see above)*. The players, amongst whom was Molière's widow, Armande Béjart, sought another tennis court and finally found one at No. 14 — the façade between the 2nd and 3rd floors is adorned with a reclining figure of *Minerva* by Le Hongre. The theatre opened in 1689 with *Phèdre* by Racine and Molière's *Le Médecin Malgré Lui*. Eighty-one years later, in 1770, the company, by this time once more in low financial waters, left for the Tuileries Palace Theatre before finally moving to the Odéon.

The old **Café Procope,** at No. 13 goes back to 1685 when it was founded by a Sicilian of that name. The establishment's popularity knew no bounds : it was the centre for all the wits of the time, for news, scandal and serious debate.

137

Michelin plans ⑩ or ⑪ : E 9, E 10.
Distance : 1.5 km — 1 mile — Time : 2 hours. Start from the Monceau métro station.

This elegant quarter includes one of Paris' rare green open spaces and also fine oriental and decorative art museums.

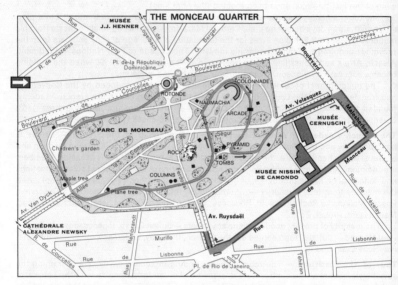

THE MONCEAU QUARTER

Monceau Park*. — In 1778 the Duke of Orleans, the future Philippe-Égalité, commissioned the painter-writer Carmontelle to design a garden on the Monceau Plain, then rich in game.
The artist produced a land of dreams, scattered with follies and landscaped after the fashion of the English and German gardens of the time. He constructed a pyramid and a pagoda, a Roman temple, feudal ruins, Dutch windmills, a Swiss farm, naumachia and mounds linked by a network of rising and falling paths. Some still remain.
At the Revolution, Monceau Park — in which Garnerin, the first parachutist, had landed on 22 October 1797 — passed to the lawyer and statesman Cambacérès. It returned briefly to the Orleans before, in 1852, the financier, Pereire, sold part of the park for the building of luxurious houses. In 1862, the engineer Alphand, creator of the Buttes-Chaumont, laid out a further area after the style of an English park.
The suggested itinerary includes the most picturesque parts. The rotunda at the entrance, known as the Chartres Pavilion, was originally a tollhouse in the Farmers-General perimeter wall and has fine wrought iron gates. The many statues in the park take second place to the trees. The oval naumachia basin is modelled on the Roman pools constructed for the simulation of naval battles; the colonnade brought to adorn it was from the never completed mausoleum of Henri II at St-Denis while the nearby Renaissance arcade stood before the Pre-Commune Hôtel de Ville.
Leave the park by the Velasquez Avenue where at No. 7 you will find the Cernuschi Museum.

Cernuschi Museum*. — *Open 10 am to 5.40 pm. Closed Mondays and holidays; 3F, Sundays free (except during expositions).*
The banker Cernuschi left the City of Paris on his death in 1896, his house and extensive collection of Oriental art. The museum is devoted to ancient Chinese art and includes neolithic terracottas, bronzes, jade and ancient ceramics as well as ink drawings and a series of handsome funerary statuettes. A 5C stone Bodhisattva and an 8C Tang painting on silk, *Horses and their Grooms,* are outstanding. On the first floor there is a collection of contemporary Chinese paintings and galleries for temporary exhibitions.
On leaving the museum, walk round the houses to the right to No. 63 Rue de Monceau.

Nissim-de-Camondo Museum*. — *Open 10 am to noon and 2 to 5 pm. Closed Mondays, Tuesdays, and holidays; 5F.*
In 1936 Count de Camondo presented his house and 18C art collection to the nation in memory of his son Nissim, who had died in the 1914-1918 War.
The mansion presents an elegant Louis XVI interior with panelled salons, furniture made by the greatest cabinet-makers, Savonnerie carpets and Beauvais tapestries *(p 154),* paintings by Guardi and Hubert Robert and gold and silver ornaments. Among the outstanding pieces are tapestries of the Fables of La Fontaine after cartoons by Oudry and a splendid Sèvres porcelain service, known as the Buffon service, in which every piece is decorated with the design of a different bird.
Nearby is **St. Alexander Nevsky Cathedral** *(12 Rue Daru)* the Russian Orthodox Church of Paris. The cathedral was erected in 1860 in the Russian Neo-Byzantine style and is decorated inside entirely with frescoes, gilding and icons. The services are magnificently sung in the tradition of Holy Russia.

J.-J.-Henner Museum. — *43 Avenue de Villiers. Open 2 to 5 pm, except Mondays and holidays; 3F.* Portraits and drawings by the Alsatian artist, Jean-Jacques Henner (1829-1905).

Michelin plans ⑩ or ⑪ : L 16 — M 16, M 17.
Distance : 3.5 km — 2 miles — Time : 4 1/2 hours. Start from Jussieu métro station.

This very varied walk contains : an ancient arena, the Salpêtrière Hospital, a mosque with its minaret, and a menagerie.

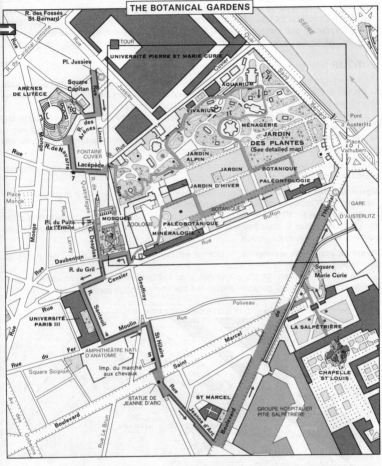

THE BOTANICAL GARDENS

The Place Jussieu is lined by the modern façades of the **Pierre and Marie Curie University** buildings (Paris VI and Paris VII) built on the site of the former wine market. Inside is a **mineralogy museum★★** *(5 Rue des Fossés-St-Bernard, Tower 15; open Wednesdays and Saturdays 3 to 5 pm; closed during university vacations)* which has a display of sparkling crystals and multicoloured rocks.

Walk first along the Rue Linné then the Rue des Arènes and enter the Capitan Square.

The Lutetia Arena (Arènes de Lutèce). — The exact date of the Gallo-Roman arena remains unknown. It was destroyed in 280 by the Barbarians; buried for fifteen hundred years; rediscovered by accident when the Rue Monge was being laid in 1869; used as a bus depot. Only since the beginning of this century has the site been methodically excavated and restored.

The arena was constructed for circus and theatrical presentations, although many of its stone tiers have now vanished and the arena is somewhat overgrown, the stage and wings remain.

Make for the Botanical Gardens by way of the Rue de Navarre and Rue Lacépède (No. 7 is a 18C mansion).

■ THE BOTANICAL GARDENS★★ (Jardin des Plantes) ⑩ or ⑪ : L 16

In 1626 Hérouard and Guy de la Brosse, physicians to Louis XIII, obtained permission, firstly, to establish in the St. Victor suburb, the Royal Medicinal Herb Garden which had previously been on the Ile de la Cité *(p 70)* and subsequently, to found a school of botany, natural history and pharmacy. In 1650 the garden was opened to the public.

After Fagon, Louis XIV's first physician, the botanist Tournefort, and the three Jussieu brothers journeyed widely to enrich the Paris collection.

It was during the curatorship of Buffon from 1739-1788, assisted by Daubenton and Antoine-Laurent de Jussieu, nephew of the earlier brothers, that the garden was at its greatest. Buffon's 36 volume *Natural History* was equalled by his expansion of the garden to the banks of the Seine, planting of lime trees along the avenues, creation of the maze, amphitheatre and museum galleries... so great indeed, was his prestige that a statue was erected to him in his lifetime.

The National Natural History Institute. — At the Revolution the garden's name was changed to that of Natural History Institute and a menagerie was created by transporting the royal animals from Versailles. This enabled Parisians to see for the first time such wild animals as elephants (brought from Holland in 1795), bears (all the animals which have occupied the pit have been called after the first one which was known as Martin), giraffes (1827) etc. In 1870, however, when Paris came under siege, the citizens' hunger exceeded their curiosity and most of the animals were slaughtered for food. With Geoffroy-St-Hilaire, Lamarck, Lacépède, Cuvier, Becquerel and many other great names, the institute won international recognition in the 19C which it maintains today through its teaching and research.

TOUR (open daily 9 am to 6 pm or 5 pm in winter).

In the 17C a tall mound built up from public waste was converted by Buffon into a **maze**. At the summit is a small kiosk overlooking the rest of the garden and the mosque. A column nearby marks the grave of Daubenton, naturalist and Buffon's collaborator.

The famous cedar of Lebanon, planted by Bernard de Jussieu in 1734 on the hillside facing the Seine was brought back, so the story goes, by the scientist from Syria on a sailing ship — he was said to have kept it in his hat, moistening it daily from his water ration. In fact, he was given it by Kew Gardens and only carried it across the Channel!

Winter Garden (Jardin d'Hiver). — *Open 2 to 5 pm; closed Tuesdays; 2F.* The garden contains a large collection of tropical and desert plants.

Alpine Garden (Jardin Alpin). — *Open 10 am to noon and 2 to 5 pm April to October; closed Tuesdays; 2F.* It includes plants from mountains and polar regions.

Beyond several 18C buildings, near Cuvier's house, can be seen a cross-section of the trunk of an American sequoia tree more than 2 000 years old. It is inlaid with tablets describing events contemporary to its growth.

Vivarium, aquarium, menagerie. — *Open 9 am to noon and 2 to 6 pm; 5F; see panels for feeding and photographing the animals.*

Big reptiles, birds and beasts are shown in an old fashioned setting in which they nevertheless appear contented and their presence adds interest to the gardens.

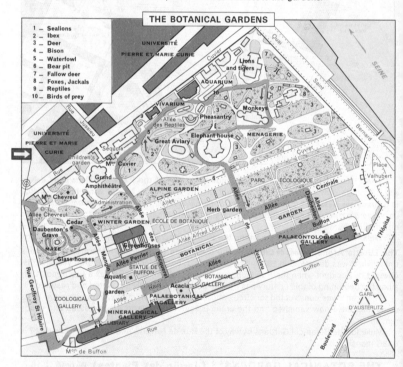

Botanical Garden (Jardin Botanique). — Paths divide the formal flowerbeds which make a magnificent show. More technically, the Botanical School Garden contains more than 10,000 classified plants and the oldest tree in Paris, a Robinia or false acacia, planted in 1636, can be seen close by near the Becquerel Alley.

Galleries

Palaeontology. — *Visit by appointment :* ☏ 707-06-04; *3F.*
Models of prehistoric and earlier animals, fossils, etc.

Palaeobotany. — *Open 1.30 to 5 pm; closed Tuesdays; 3F.*
Evolutionary trends and specimens of fossil plants.

Mineralogy*. — *Open 10 am to 5 pm; closed Tuesdays; 5F.*
Minerals, meteorites and precious stones.

By way of the Rues Daubenton and Georges-Desplas, make for the Mohammedan Institute
f Paris, on the right, and its commercial annexes; a Moorish café, an Arab restaurant, the
ouks and *hammam*.

▪ THE MOSQUE★ ▢▢ or ▢▢ : M 16

*Entrance : Place du Puits-de-l'Ermite. Guided tours 10 am to noon and 2 to 6.30 pm (6 pm the
est of the year); last tour 30 mins. before closing time; closed Fridays and Moslem holidays; 5F.*

The white buildings overlooked by a minaret, making one feel far from home, were erec-
ed between 1922 and 1925.

Three holy men supervise the enclave : the *muphti,* lawyer, administrator and judge; the
man who looks after the mosque; the *muezzin* or cantor who calls the faithful to prayer twice
a day from high up in the minaret.

Native craftsmen from the Mohammedan countries have contributed to the decoration of
he halls and courts with Persian carpets, copper from North Africa, cedarwood from Lebanon,
a dais from Egypt, matting from Morocco, etc.

A Hispano-Moorish style courtyard has a garden at its centre surrounded by arcades — a
ymbol of the Muslim Paradise. At the heart of the religious buildings is a *patio,* inspired by
hat of the Alhambra in Granada. The prayer chamber is outstanding for its decoration and
magnificent carpets.

From the Mosque to the Salpêtrière Hospital

Turn left on leaving and until you reach the Rue Censier, right into the Rue de Santeuil,
ined along its full length since 1966 are the steel and glass buildings of the **Arts Faculty**
Université Paris III). The site was, until the Revolution that of the Hospital of the Hundred
Girls, an orphanage founded by Louis XIII for legitimate children. From 1865 until quite
ecently, whilst a leather market stood on the site, the air reeked of the smell of leather and
anning.

Turn left in the Rue du Fer-à-Moulin which skirted the former cemetery for the executed
and those who had died in the Hôtel-Dieu hospital.

On the right the Rue Geoffroy-St-Hilaire leads to the Boulevard St-Marcel. On the left
before the boulevard is the place where, in the 18C, deserters from the army were tortured to
death by strappado — a method by which, with his hands bound behind his back, a man was
repeatedly thrown from a great height until his body virtually disintegrated. Louis XVI put an
end to such punishment in 1776. The place was then turned into a horsemarket (now in the
Rue Brancion, XV *arrondissement*) at which pigs and dogs were also sold — a blind alley recalls
the market by its name : Marché-aux-Chevaux.

Cross the Boulevard St-Marcel, which was constructed in 1857, and walk round the statue
of Joan of Arc, to continue down the street of the same name which was at one time the main
street of the local village of Austerlitz.

Turn left up the Boulevard de l'Hôpital where at No. 76 stands the modern **Church of
St-Marcel.** The building, constructed in 1966 of concrete, pine and metal with stained glass by
sabelle Rouault, presents a pleasing harmony of materials and colours.

Continue left along the boulevard, lined on one side by the modern University Centre
Hospital buildings, to the Marie-Curie Square beneath the overhead railway.

▪ THE SALPÊTRIÈRE HOSPITAL★ ▢▢ or ▢▢ : M 17

The hospital has all the grandeur of the Grand Siècle.

Historical notes. — In the time of Louis XIII a small arsenal on the site manufactured
gun powder from saltpetre. In 1656 Louis XIV established a General Hospital for the Poor of
Paris in the saltpetre works in the hope of clearing the capital's streets of beggars and the
more vicious characters — fifty-five thousand beggars were known to exist in Paris at the
time.

By 1662, 10 000 pensioners had been taken in, but following the cleaning up of the Courts
of Miracles *(p 118)* in 1667, the buildings had to be enlarged — a project undertaken by Le Vau
and Le Muet. In 1670, a chapel was added, designed by Libéral Bruand at the same time as
he was building the Invalides *(p 55)*.

Gradually the hospital began to take in indiscriminately the mad, the infirm, the orphaned
and prostitutes — the hospital, in fact, became a prison with all subject to the same harsh
regime. At last, at the end of the 18C, one of the doctors, Philippe Pinel (1745-1826) began the
work on a reformed treatment for the insane which was to win him and the hospital wide
acclaim, a century later Professor Charcot, under whom Freud came to study, was to further
the hospital's reputation with research and treatment in advanced neuro-psychiatry.

Tour. — A formal garden precedes the central wing of the immense, austere and majestic
edifice which has a certain family resemblance to the Invalides.

At the centre is the octagonal dome of the **St. Louis Chapel** surmounted by a lantern. The
chapel ground plan is unusual with a rotunda encircled by four aisles forming a Greek cross
and four chapels at the angles of the crossing. Eight areas were thus formed in which the
inmates could be placed separately : women, girls, the infectious, etc.

The old Salpêtrière Hospital and the Pitié Hospital together now form the University
Hospital Centre, a small town on its own covering an area of 30 ha — 74 acres.

The Gare d'Orléans-Austerlitz métro station is on the right.

Look at the maps on pp 4-7 for an idea for your next walk.

Michelin plans ⒑ or ⒒ : E 10, E 11 - F 11.
Distance : 3.5 km — 2 miles — Time : 3 1/2
hours. Start from the Madeleine métro station.

The Faubourg St-Honoré quarter, with its former town houses and luxury shops comes as a complete contrast after the quarter to the west laid out by Haussmann.

Starting from the Madeleine *(p 72)* walk up the Rue Tronchet, lined by attractive shops, left along the Boulevard Haussmann, past the Printemps department store, until you come to the Louis XVI Square and the Expiatory Chapel.

Expiatory Chapel. — A small cemetery, opened in 1722, was used as burial ground first for the Swiss Guards killed at the Tuileries on the 10 August 1792 *(p 40)* and then for the victims of the guillotine which stood in the Place de la Concorde *(p 43)*. These last numbered 1 343 and included Louis XVI and Marie-Antoinette. Immediately on his return to Paris, Louis XVIII had the remains of his brother and sister-in-law disinterred and transported to the royal necropolis at St-Denis (21 January 1815 — *p 168*).

Tour. — *1 February to 31 March and October, 10 am to noon and 1.30 to 5 pm (6 pm 1 April to 30 September; 4 pm 1 November to 31 January); closed Tuesdays; 3F.*

The cloister occupies the site of the old burial ground. Charlotte Corday, who stabbed Marat in his bath to avenge the Girondins, and Philippe-Égalité are buried on either side of the steps leading to the chapel in which two marble groups show Louis XVI and an angel (by Bosio) and Marie-Antoinette supported by Religion symbolized by a figure with the features of Mme Elisabeth, the king's sister (by Cortot). The crypt altar marks the place where Louis XVI's and Marie-Antoinette's bodies were found.

Continue along, the Bd Haussmann to the Place St-Augustin where, facing the Cercle Militaire, stands a replica of the statue of Joan of Arc by Paul Dubois. The original is in Reims.

St. Augustine's. — Baltard, the architect of the old covered market (the Halles), who designed this church in 1860, employed for the first time in such a building a metal girder construction which enabled him to dispense with the usual buttressing. The triangular shape of the site demanded an edifice widening out from the porch to the chancel which he capped with a vast dome.

Walk left up the Avenue César-Caire and the Rue Portalis to No. 14 Rue de Madrid.

Conservatoire National de Musique : musical instruments' museum*. — *Open Wednesdays and Saturdays 2 to 4.30 pm; may be closed in August, phone : 292.15.20.*

In addition to the hundreds of stringed, wind and percussion instruments, there are such historical items as Marie-Antoinette's harp, Berlioz' and Paganini's guitars, Beethoven's clavichord and the piano on which Rouget de Lisle, on arriving in Paris, played his own composition which came to be known as the *Marseillaise*.

Return to the Place St-Augustin by way of the Rue de Lisbonne and the Boulevard Malesherbes. Continue down the Rue La-Boétie, on the right. The Avenue Percier, again on the right brings you out in the Boulevard Haussmann at No. 158.

Jacquemart-André Museum**. — *Open 1.30 to 5.30 pm; closed Mondays, Tuesdays, holidays and in August; 3F.*

This late 19C house contains outstanding 18C European and Italian Renaissance art.

On the ground floor the times of Louis XV are vividly recalled with paintings and drawings by Boucher, Greuze, Chardin and Watteau; sculpture by Pigalle and Houdon; Beauvais tapestries and signed pieces of furniture and art objects. Foreign schools of painting of the 17 and 18C are represented by Rembrandt, Canaletto, Reynolds, Murillo and frescoes by Tiepolo (ceilings in rooms 4, 5, 13 and over the stairs). There are also beautiful 16C Limoges enamels and Palissy ceramics.

Tuscan Primitives, the Florentine Quattrocento (Botticelli paintings, Della Robbia terra cottas, Donatello sculpture), the Venetian Renaissance (Mantegna, Tintoretto, Titian). Uccello's famous *St. George Slaying the Dragon* (room 9) and a fine bronze bust by Bernini (room 7) furnish the Italian Rooms.

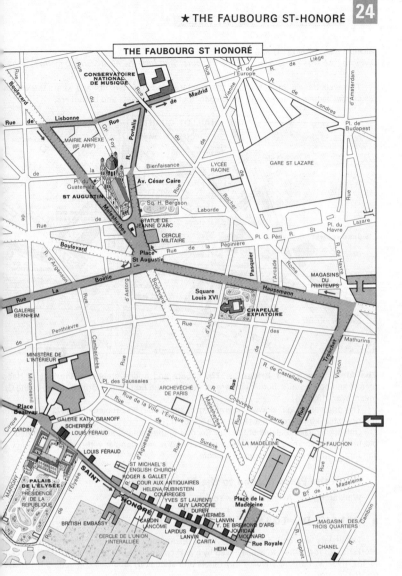

THE FAUBOURG ST HONORÉ

Follow the map route to the Place Chassaigne-Goyon.

Church of St-Philippe-du-Roule.—The church, designed in imitation of a Roman basilica was erected between 1774 and 1784. The semicircular chancel was added in 1845. Outstanding are the Ionic columns and a fresco over the chancel of the *Descent from the Cross* by Chassériau.

Rue du Faubourg St-Honoré**. — Turn left down the Rue du Faubourg-St-Honoré, which dates back to the 13C when it was known as the Chemin du Roule. The superstitious Empress Eugénie had No. 13 suppressed which it remains to this day. The street imparts a leisured elegance with its luxury shops, particularly near the Rue Royale and the Rue de l'Élysée.

Somewhat before, in the Place Beauvau, created in 1836, a fine wrought iron gate marks the entrance to the Ministry of Home Affairs installed since 1861 in this 18C mansion.

Opposite is the **Élysée Palace** and at the back an extensive garden, forming a large green island in the heart of Paris. The mansion was constructed in 1718 for the Count of Evreux. It was acquired for a short time by the Marquise de Pompadour and then by the financier Beaujon who enlarged it; during the Revolution it became a dance hall. Caroline Murat, Napoleon's sister, then the Empress Josephine both lived in and redecorated it. It was in this palace, after Waterloo, that Napoleon signed his second abdication of 22 June 1815 and that the future Napoleon III lived and planned his successful *coup d'état* of December 1851.

Since 1873 the Élysée Palace has been the Paris home of France's twenty successive presidents. The Council of Ministers meets each Wednesday in the Murat Salon. *Not open to the public.*

Among the 18C mansions on the same side of the street is the **British Embassy.** The Hôtel de Chárost at No. 35 had been purchased by Pauline Bonaparte in 1800 but, on Napoleon's banishment to Elba, came into the market again. Wellington heard of it and in August 1814 purchased it for a total sum, including its contents, of 870,000 francs. Within a week of its acquisition, the general had moved in, delighted both with the mansion and its garden running down to the " Elysian Fields ".

Turn left into the Rue Royale, to return to the Madeleine.

Michelin plans **10** or **11** : G 8, G 9.
Distance : 2.5 km — 1 1/2 miles — Time : 4 hours. Start from the Alma-Marceau métro station.

This walk travels through one of the most luxurious quarters of Paris where the wealth residential section mingles with the elegance of the couturiers and perfumers.

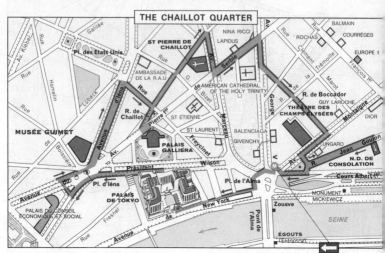

The Alma Square and Bridge. — The square and bridge created in the time of Napoleon III and now a traffic bottleneck, are named after the first Franco-British victory in the Crimean War (1854).

The original bridge, slowly undermined by the Seine, was replaced in 1972 by an asymmetrical steel structure with a 110 m span — 361 ft.

Only the Zouave remains of the four Second Empire soldier statues which decorated the old bridge; he serves as a high water marker and is very popular with Parisians — once in January 1910, the water came up to his chin.

From the Place d'Alma to the Place d'Iéna

Walk along the Avenue of New York.

■ PALAIS DE TOKYO★ **10** or **11** : G 8 - H 8

The Palais was built for the 1937 World Exhibition, formerly the Savonnerie Tapestry Workshop *(p 154)*. The two wings linked by a portico, line a series of terraces, which descend to the river and are adorned by low reliefs and statues by Bourdelle, including his **France**★ *(in the centre)*.

Museum of Modern Art of the City of Paris (Musée d'Art Moderne de la Ville de Paris). — *Enter on Alma side. Open 10 am to 5.40 pm, 8.30 pm Wednesdays; closed Mondays and holidays. 5F (free on Sundays).*

The collection underlines the importance of the **Paris School** in painting and sculpture since the beginning of the 20C (Utrillo, Derain, Soutine, Modigliani, Rouault, Dufy, Gromaire...). It is dominated particularly by the biggest picture in the world 600 m² — 6 095 sq ft Dufy's *The Good Fairy Electricity,* representing the scientists and thinkers, who mastered this form of energy. Several rooms display works illustrating the trends of contemporary art one of which contains the tapestries of Jean Lurçat.

Museum of Modern Art★ (Musée d'Art Moderne). — *Entrance : Avenue du Président Wilson Trocadero side. Open 9.45 am to 5.15 pm; closed Tuesdays and holidays; combined ticket : 8F.*

This museum, the branch museum of the Georges Pompidou Centre *(p 112)*, exhibits works by Braque, Dunoyer de Segonzac, Laurens, Rouault, Victor Brauner and Post-Impressionists born before 1870. *Scheduled to move to Orsay (p 126)*. Revolving exhibitions permit the public to discover the works belonging to the Louvre's reserve collection.

Upper ground floor. — *To the right on entering.* The Post-Impressionist works exposed concentrate especially on the Pointillism of Seurat, the Pont-Aven School, Gauguin being one of its leaders and the Nabis movement (1890-1900).

The Pointillists, who believed that the juxtaposition or superimposition of primary colours in dots conveyed the fugitive shimmering of light, are represented here by Signac (*l'Entrée du Port de Marseille*), Seurat (*Port-en-Bessin, Le Cirque* — his last work), and Cross (*l'Après-midi à Pardigon*). Pissarro dabbled in Impressionism (*l'Église du Gisors*). Maillol's works (*la Maison en Roussillon, la Femme à l'Ombrelle*) show his talents as an artist as well as a sculptor. Vuillard (*la Nature morte à la Salade*), Vallaton (*le Dîner*), and their leader Bonnard (*la Maison de Messia, le Jour d'Hiver*) belonged to the Nabis movement born of a common admiration for Gauguin (*le Paysage de Bretagne, la Belle Angèle*). Note also *Bretonnes aux Ombrelles,* a hieratic work done by Émile Bernard.

Lower Galleries. — Presented here are **gifts**. Among the works are Dunoyer de Segonzac *(l'Étang de Ville-d'Avray, les Buveurs* — 1910, *le Massif des Maures, le Golfe de St-Tropez* — 1938), Rouault's works of individual pathos *(Un Christ aux Outrages, le Tribunal, Une Sainte Face* — 1933, *Satan, Miserere)* and the cubist, Braque *(l'Estaque, Une Composition au Violon* — 1910, *Vanitas*, and a sculpted horse's head). The Symbolist galleries display works by Eugène Burnand *(les Disciples Pierre et Jean Courant au Sépulcre)*, Victor Brauner *(Mandragore)* and the sculpted women by Laurens.

Go up Avenue du Président Wilson to the Place d'Iéna; giving onto the Place is the concrete Economic and Social Council building (Palais du Conseil Économique et Social) désigned by Auguste Perret (1937) and the Guimet Museum.

■ **GUIMET MUSEUM**★★ ▢▢ or ▢▢ : G 7

Open 9.45 am to noon and 1.30 to 5.15 pm. Closed Tuesdays and holidays. 5F (2.50F Sundays).
The museum, founded by Émile Guimet, a 19C collector from Lyons contains Oriental works of art.

The ground floor is reserved for Far Eastern art : Khmer art (Cambodia), is well represented by intricately carved temple pediments and a series of **heads of Buddha** in the typical pose with eyes half-closed and a meditative smile. The seated Shiva with ten arms is an example of central Vietnamese art.

The Lamaist section includes a remarkable collection of Tibetan and Nepalese banners *(thanka)* as well as ceremonial objects and gilded bronzes of the latter the most noteworthy is the graceful **dancing Dakini**.

The first floor shows the evolution of Indian art from the 3rd century BC to the 19C. There are the carved low reliefs from Northern India and the Hindu sculpture and bronzes originating from the southeast. Outstanding among the sculpture is the beautiful **Cosmic Dance by Shiva**. The art of both Pakistan (represented here by the famous Bodhisattva from Shabaz-Garhi) and Afghanistan (the Begrâm treasure : sculptured ivories of Indian origin and Hellenistic plasters), note in particular the draped garments of the Bodhisattva. Note also a collection of Chinese bronzes (2000-207 BC).

On the second floor *(closed : under reconstruction)* are the exceptional displays of **Chinese ceramics** from the Calmann and Grandidier collections and exquisite lacquerwork. There is also the series of Buddhist banners which was discovered in a cave of Touen-Houang. The jewels from Korea include a funerary crown.

From Japan can be seen 18C wooden dance masks *(gigaku)* and the " Portuguese Screen " (16C), composed of six panels depicting the arrival of a dignitary, who is being greeted by Saint Francis Xavier.

From the Place d'Iéna to the Place d'Alma

In this residential quarter of private mansions (hôtels) and luxurious apartment houses live many foreigners.

Palais Galliéra. — *10 Avenue Pierre-I*'-*de-Serbie*. The Duchess of Galliéra, wife of the Italian financeer and philanthropist, had this building built (1878-1888) in the Italian Renaissance style.

Housed in the mansion is the **Costume Museum** *(open 10 am to 5.40 pm; closed Mondays and between each exhibition, 5F)*. Revolving exhibitions present men, women and children's fashion and dress from 1735 to the present.

Follow — on the left — the Rue du Chaillot, the main street of the old village of Chaillot, to Avenue Marceau, one of the twelve avenues radiating from the Étoile.

Church of St. Peter of Chaillot. — The church was rebuilt in the neo-Romanesque style in 1937. Overlooking its façade, on which the life of St. Peter has been carved by Bouchard, is a 65 m high — 213 ft — belfry.

Cross Avenue Marceau, and take Avenue Pierre-I''-de-Serbie entering an animated quarter dotted with banks, art galleries, luxury boutiques, couturiers and perfumers. By the Avenue de Boccador you will arrive at the elegant Avenue de Montaigne.

Champs-Elysées Theatre. — *13 Avenue Montaigne*. The theatre, the work of the Perret brothers was in 1912 one of the first large reinforced concrete buildings to be erected in Paris. The high reliefs on the façade are by Bourdelle; the decoration on the ceiling is by Maurice Denis. At times, Diaghilev and his Russian ballet company, the Marquis de Cuevas and his dancers, and the actor Louis Jouvet all starred at the theatre.

Church of Notre-Dame de Consolation. — *23 Rue Jean-Goujon*. A fire at a charity bazaar in 1897 killed 117 people on the site on which this memorial chapel, designed by Guilbert, was erected (1901).

The decoration is Neo-Baroque : note the handsome marble columns at the entrance to the side chapels. Niches contain urns and cenotaphs. It is the Italian church in Paris.

The statue on the Cours Albert-1 is of the Polish poet and patriot, Mickiewicz (1795-1855) by Bourdelle.

Sewers (Egouts). — *Open Mondays, Wednesdays and last Saturday in the month 2 to 5 pm. Closed on public holidays, the day before and after holidays, during a storm or heavy rain and when the Seine floods (☎ 551.10.29); 3F. Access : corner Branly Quay-Alma Bridge.*
Historical exhibitions, film shows, recorded commentaries available for the visit of some of the underground galleries.

Michelin plans ⑩ or ⑪ : from G 15 to G 17.
Distance : 2.5 km — 1 1/2 miles — Time : 2 1/2 hours. Start from the République métro station.

This quarter was the domain of Knights Templar and Benedictines from St. Martin's.

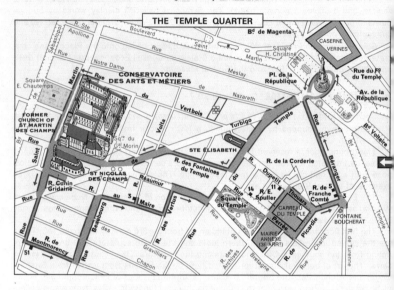

Place de la République to the Conservatoire des Arts et Métiers

At 195 Rue du Temple stands **St. Elizabeth's**, a 17C convent chapel now the Church of the Knights of St. John of Malta and outstanding for the hundred 16C Flemish **low reliefs★** of biblical scenes round the ambulatory.

Turn left in the Rue Turbigo to approach the former **St-Martin-des-Champs★** with its Romanesque east end (1130-restored), fine capitals, belfry of the same period and Gothic nave.

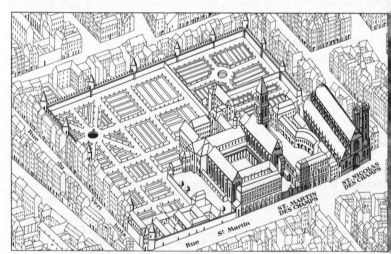

The Priory of St-Martin-des-Champs in 1734 (Turgot drawing)

■ CONSERVATOIRE NATIONAL DES ARTS ET MÉTIERS★★
⑩ or ⑪ : G 16

The Conservatory, an institution for technical instruction, a considerable industrial museum and a laboratory for industrial experiment, has incorporated in its present buildings the old church and refectory of the St. Martin in the Fields priory which once stood on the site. This Benedictine priory had developed around the original Chapel to St. Martin erected in the 4C. In 1273 the precincts were enclosed by a fortified wall, parts of which can still be seen if you continue round to the Rue Vertbois (watch tower). The Conservatory, created by the Convention in 1794, was installed five years later in the priory.

Refectory★★. — *Open in the morning only, apply in writing to the Head of the Conservatory, 292 Rue St-Martin, 75003 Paris.* Enter the courtyard where on the right is the former monks' refectory by Pierre of Montreuil (13C), now the library. The interior is true Gothic with pure lines, perfect proportions and seven slender columns down the room's centre. On the right is a beautiful door with delightful carvings on its outer panels.

NATIONAL TECHNICAL MUSEUM** (Musée National des Techniques)

Open noon to 5.45 pm, Sundays 10 am to 5.30 pm. Closed holidays; 2F (free Sundays).
The museum displays technical progress in industry and science.
Mount the steps at the end of the courtyard. The double flight staircase is by the 18C architect of the Mint, Antoine.

The following galleries are of particular interest :

Ground floor : 2 — the Echo Room with apparatus and mementoes of the 18C chemist, Lavoisier; **4 to 9** — metallurgy, steel making and foundry work;
10 — the former **Church of St. Martin in the Fields*** (St-Martin-des-Champs — *exterior : p 146*) where, below the early 12C vaulting in the ambulatory showing clearly the transition from Romanesque to Gothic — are exhibits on locomotion — cycles, cars, aircraft, etc. and, suspended from the roof, Foucault's pendulum which demonstrated the rotation of the earth (19C); **11** — agricultural machinery; — **12** — *temporary exhibition hall;*
13 — topography and geodesy dating back to the 16C; **15** — automata (Marie-Antoinette's clockwork dulcimer-playing puppet of 1784); **16 to 20** — astronomy and horology; — **21** — railways;

First floor : 23 — in the stateroom — models based on the Encyclopaedia (late 18C) and two specimens of Pascal's arithmetic machine; **24** — energy (mills to turbines, etc); **26-27** — physics and electricity; **28-29** — glass from the greatest European glassworks; **30 to 32** — acoustics, optics, mechanics; **33 to 37** — radio, television, electronic acoustics; **38 to 40** — photography and films; **46** — graphic arts (printing) and technology of everyday life (heating, elevation, lighting, domestic equipment); **47 to 49** — spinning and weaving, sewing machines.

On leaving bear left in the Rue St-Martin to St. Nicholas'.

■ ST. NICHOLAS IN THE FIELDS* (St-Nicolas-des-Champs)
🚇 or 🚇 : G 15

The church, built in the 12C by the priory of St. Martin in the Fields for the monastery servants and neighbouring peasants, was dedicated to one of the most popular mediaeval saints, Nicholas, 4C Bishop of Myra in Asia Minor and patron of children, sailors and travellers. It was rebuilt in the 15C and enlarged in the 16 and 17C. The Revolution rededicated it to Hymen and Fidelity.
The façade and belfry are Flamboyant Gothic, the south **door*** Renaissance (1581).
Inside, the nave is divided into five by a double line of pillars; the first five bays are 15C; the vaulting in the aisles beyond the pulpit rises in height, semicircular arcs succeed pointed arches; the sides of the pillars towards the nave have been fluted. The chancel and chapels contain a considerable number of mostly French 17, 18 and 19C paintings; the twin sided high altar is adorned with a retable painted by Simon Vouet (16C) and four angels by the 17C sculptor, Sarrazin. The best point from which to see the forest of pillars and double ambulatory is the Lady Chapel (Adoration of the Shepherds by Coypel).
The typically Parisian organ is 18C; the organist was for a time Louis Braille (*p 105*).

From St. Nicholas to the Temple Square

Continue left down the Rue St-Martin and along to the Temple Square. On the way you pass No. 51 Rue de Montmorency, the oldest house (1407) in Paris, once the **house of Nicolas Flamel**, legal draughtsman to the university and bookseller who made a fortune copying and selling manuscripts. He used the proceeds in good works, including setting up above his shop (now a restaurant) an " almshouse " in which the high rent charged for the lower floors allowed the upper rooms to be given rent free to the poor who were asked, in an inscription above the old shop fronts, to say a prayer for their benefactor.
Turn left in the Rue Beaubourg, scene of street fighting in 1834, and right into the old Rue au Maire. Off this, at No. 3 Rue Volta, is a **house***, dating from the 17C, which reveals a timbered façade (gable now gone).
Continue along the Rue au Maire before turning left into the narrow Rue des Vertus. This, in turn, leads to the Rue Réaumur and the Square du Temple.

No. 3 Rue Volta

■ THE FORMER TEMPLAR DOMAIN

Monks, knights and bankers. — In 1140 the religious and military order, founded in 1118 in the Holy Land by nine knights to protect pilgrims and known as the Order of Knights Templar, established a house in Paris. By the 13C the order had achieved great power with 9 000 commanderies throughout Europe and an unrivalled international banking system. In France the knights had become independent of the crown and had acquired possession of one quarter of the land area of Paris — including all the Marais.

The Templars fortified their domain and its keep became a refuge for local peasants and those fleeing royal jurisdiction. Craftsmen also congregated, exempt from guild taxes, until there were 4 000 within the walls where even kings were known to seek shelter.

Philip the Fair decided to suppress this state within a state and one day in 1307 had all the Templars in France arrested; the order dissolved; the leader and fifty-four followers *(p 70)* burnt at the stake and the property divided between the crown and the Knights of St. John of Jerusalem, later known as the Knights of Malta.

The Templar Prison. — The Knights of Malta were suppressed in their turn at the Revolution and the Temple Tower, as it is known, was used as a prison for Louis XVI, Marie-Antoinette, the king's sister Mme Elisabeth, the seven year old Dauphin and his sister, on their arrest on 13 August 1792 *(see Carnavalet Museum, p 82).*

The king was held in the tower and it was from here, therefore, that he went to the guillotine on 21 January 1793 following his trial and conviction by the Convention. The following July the Dauphin was separated from his mother, who, in August, was transferred with her sister-in-law to the Conciergerie *(p 66)* which she was to leave only to go to the guillotine on 16 October. Two years later, on 8 June 1795, a young man in the Temple Tower died and the mystery arose which has never been solved, of whether he was Louis XVII, the son of Louis XVI or who he was. In 1808 the tower was razed to prevent Royalist pilgrimages and the domain converted into an open air old clothes market known as the Carreau du Temple or Temple Stones. In 1857 Haussmann laid out the covered market, the town hall, on the other side of Rue Perrée, and the present square.

The Temple Tower during the Revolution

■ SQUARE AND CARREAU DU TEMPLE ▥ or ▥ : G 16 - H 16

Cross the square where, on the left at No. 14, is the Assay Office (Hôtel de la Garantie) for precious metals. At the far end, left of the town hall, is the Carreau, still lined, like the surrounding Picardie, Corderie and Dupetit-Thouars streets, with clothes, costume and fancy clothes shops and stalls *(market except Mondays : 9 am to noon, 1 pm Sundays).* At No. 11 Rue Dupetit-Thouars is the Lycée Duperré.

From the Temple to the Place de la République

Continue along the Rue de Franche-Comté and, leaving the 1699 Boucherat Fountain on your right at the end of the street, turn left up the Rue Béranger (At Nos. 3 and 5 there is an 18C hôtel where in 1857 the poet and writer of popular songs, Béranger, died.) into the Rue du Temple to the Place de la République.

■ PLACE DE LA RÉPUBLIQUE ▥ or ▥ : G 17

The original square was named Place du Château-d'Eau. On it stood the Théâtre Historique, built in 1847, by Alexandre Dumas as a setting for his historical dramas — it opened with his *Queen Margot* for which crowds queued for seats for two days and nights.

In 1854 Haussmann decided to replace the small square with the present vast expanse as part of his anti-revolutionary street planning scheme. The diorama built in 1822 by Daguerre, of daguerreotype fame, was knocked down in favour of a barracks for 2 000 men and wide avenues cut through turbulent areas — the Boulevard Magenta, Avenue de la République, Boulevard Voltaire and Rue de Turbigo. The Boulevard du Crime was razed.

The square was completed by 1862 with the **Statue to the Republic** by Morice erected in 1883. The best part is the base by Dalou on which are bronze low reliefs of the great events in the history of the Republic from its inception to 1880 when the 14 July was celebrated as a national holiday for the first time in the Place de la Nation.

Paris was not built in a day...

Unlike Rome and New York but like London, no one knows when Paris was founded. Julius Caesar sighted Lutetia in 53 BC and made the first written reference to the town in his Commentaries.

In 1951 Paris officially celebrated its second millenium.

Michelin plans 🔟 or 🔢 : J 17 - K 16, K 17.
Distance : 2 km — 1 1/4 miles — Time : 1 1/2 hours. Start from the Bastille métro station.

■ THE PLACE DE LA BASTILLE 🔟 or 🔢 : J 17 - K 17

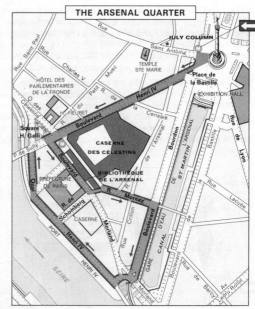

THE ARSENAL QUARTER

The vast crossroads, scene of the historic events of 1789, is dominated by the July Column.

Construction of the Bastille. — The first stone of the Bastille, which was intended to provide Charles V with a fortified residence, was laid in 1370 and the last in 1382. Its history is far from heroic : besieged seven times in periods of civil strife it surrendered six times.

The prison regime. — Prisoners were usually detained under the notorious *lettre de cachet* or royal warrant, and included the enigmatic Man in the Iron Mask and Voltaire. In 1784 *lettres de cachet* were abolished : the Bastille was cleared and its demolition planned.

The Taking of the Bastille. — In July 1789 trouble broke : the popular minister, Necker, was dismissed by the king; the Exchange closed and the militant crowd, marched first on the Invalides to capture arms *(p 54)*, then on the Bastille. By late afternoon the Bastille had been seized and the prisoners — only seven in number — symbolically freed.

Demolition. — The fortress was immediately demolished, 83 of its stones being carved into replicas and sent as dire reminders of the evil of despotism to the provinces.

THE SQUARE TODAY

Paving stones mark out the ground plan of the Bastille on the square which was modified in appearance by the opening of the Rue de Lyon in 1847, the Boulevard Henri-IV in 1866 and the building of the station in 1859 (since 1970 converted into an exhibition hall, in January-February there is the International Fair of Contemporary Art).

The July Column. — The bronze column 52 m high — 171 ft — crowned by the figure of Liberty, stands in memory of Parisians killed in July 1830 and 1848.

Walk to the Arsenal from the square by way of the Boulevard Henri-IV, passing on your right Henri-Galli Square *(p 61)* and the Hôtel Fieubet *(p 79)*.

■ THE ARSENAL
🔟 or 🔢 : K 17

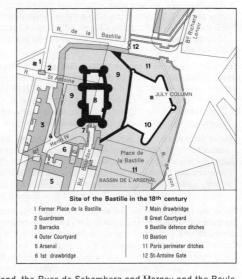

The royal arsenal, founded in the 16C by Henri II, was disbanded by Louis XIII and the building converted into a court where Fouquet was tried for embezzlement. The **library**, created in 1757, was established as a public library in what remained of the Arsenal building in 1797. In the 19C it became the early meeting place of the Romantics. It possesses more than a million and a half volumes, 15 000 MSS, 120 000 prints and a large collection on the history of the theatre. The building also includes rooms and an oratory with fine 17C paintings and ceilings and 18C salons. *Open Wednesdays 2 to 4 pm; closed 1 to 15 September; apply 1st floor; 2F.*

Site of the Bastille in the 18th century

1 Former Place de la Bastille	7 Main drawbridge
2 Guardroom	8 Great Courtyard
3 Barracks	9 Bastille defence ditches
4 Outer Courtyard	10 Bastion
5 Arsenal	11 Paris perimeter ditches
6 1st drawbridge	12 St-Antoine Gate

Walk along the Boulevard Morland, the Rues de Schomberg and Mornay and the Boulevard Bourdon beside the St. Martin's Canal *(p 155)* to the Henri-IV Quay.

Michelin plans ▨▨ or ▨▨ : from K 18 to K 21.
Distance : 4 km — 2 1/2 miles — Time : 3 hours. Start from the Bastille métro station.

The crowded streets of the Faubourg St-Antoine between the Bastille and Nation Squares, for centuries the centre of French cabinet-making, were closely associated with the Revolution.

Origin and Artisan Franchise. — The community grew up round the fortified Royal Abbey of St. Anthony, founded in 1198. Louis XI added to the abbey's privileges by giving it power to dispense justice locally and allowing the craftsmen in the vicinity to work outside the established powerful and highly restrictive guilds. The cabinet-makers of St-Antoine thus became free to design furniture and, from the 17C, copied or adapted pieces from the royal workshops and began to employ mahogany, ebony, bronze and produce marquetry.

The industrial period. — By the time of the Revolution, workshops had developed in size, in the case of Réveillon, populariser of painted wallpapers, to 400 employees.

The Revolution abolished the guilds thereby reducing the local craftsmen's advantage which suffered further with 19C mechanisation. Small workshops, nevertheless, abound.

In October 1783 **Pilâtre de Rozier** made the first aerial ascent from Réveillon's factory yard in a balloon of paper made on the spot, inflated with hot air and secured by a cable.

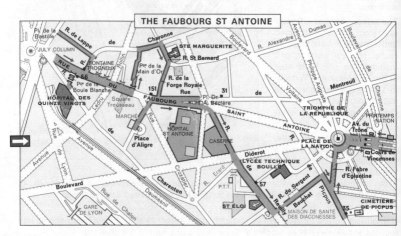

THE FAUBOURG ST ANTOINE

Rue du Faubourg St-Antoine*. — The street is lined with furniture shops and honeycombed with courts and passages, often with picturesque names, where timber is matured and carpenters and cabinet-makers can be seen at work — there is a pungent smell of sawn wood and varnish.

There follow the **Quinze-Vingts Hospital** founded by St. Louis for 300 (15 × 20) blind persons and later transferred to these 18C buildings — onetime barracks — on the Rue de Charenton; the Trogneux Fountain (1710); the picturesque **Rue de Lappe** (wrought iron and Auvergne shops); the Main-d'Or Passage, typical of the old quarter with timber stores and saw-mills, which comes out on the Rue de Charonne off which you turn right into the Rue St-Bernard.

St. Margaret's Church. — Built in the 17C and enlarged in the 18C, the interior is disparate in style, the nave low and plain with basket handle arching, the chancel tall and light. The marble *pietà* (1705) behind the high altar is by Girardon; the unusual false relief frescoes (1765) in the Souls in Purgatory Chapel, left of the chancel, are by Brunetti.

The cemetery contains a tomb presumed to be that of Louis XVII who is said to have died in the Temple in 1795 *(p 148 — apply to the sacristan).*

From St. Margaret's to the Picpus Cemetery. — Return to Rue du Faubourg-St-Antoine where at No. 184 is the St. Anthony Hospital (on the site of an old abbey) and next door, the modern building, work of the architect Wogenscky (1965). *Not open.*

Beyond the Boulevard Diderot, amidst the old and ill paved passages, are the **Boulle** Lycée of Cabinet-Making (No. 57) and, opposite, the tall belfry of the **Church of St-Éloi** (1967).

Turn left into the Rue du Sergent-Bauchat and right into the Rue de Picpus.

Picpus Cemetery. — *35 Rue de Picpus. Guided tours 2 to 6 pm, 15 April to 1 October (4 pm 1 September to 14 April); closed Mondays and August.* In 1794 the guillotine on the Place de la Nation fell on the heads of 1 306 people including 16 Carmelite nuns whose bodies were thrown into two communal graves. The ground was later enclosed by a wall and an adjoining cemetery opened in which relatives of those guillotined on the square could be buried.

Walk, right, up the Rue de Picpus and Rue Fabre-d'Églantine.

Place de la Nation*. — The square was originally named the Throne Square in honour of the state entry made by Louis XIV and his bride, the Infanta Maria-Theresa, on 26 August 1660, when a throne was erected at which the king received due hommage. It was renamed, by the Convention in 1794, the Square of the Overturned Throne when they placed a guillotine upon it and renamed a third time, on 14 July 1880, during the first anniversary celebrations of the Revolution. The bronze group by Dalou illustrates the **Triumph of the Republic*.**

The Throne or Gingerbread Fair *(p 135)*, was formerly held on the nearby Cours de Vincennes.

Michelin plans ⬜ or ⬜ : L 15 - M 15.
Distance : 2.5 km — 1 1/2 miles — Time : 2 hours. Start *from Censier-Daubenton métro station.*

The beautiful Church of St. Medard marks the opening of the unique Rue Mouffetard.

■ ST. MEDARD'S CHURCH
⬜ or ⬜ : M 15

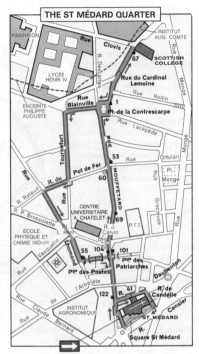

THE ST MÉDARD QUARTER

Construction. — St. Medard's was originally the parish church of a small market town on the River Bièvre. Its patron, Saint Medard, counsellor to the Merovingian kings of the 6C, was also the author of the delightful custom of giving a wreath of roses to maidens of virtuous conduct. The church, starting with the nave in the mid 15C, was completed in 1655.

The " Convulsionnaires ". — In 1727 a Jansenist deacon with a saintly reputation died at the age of 36 of mortification of the flesh and was buried in the St. Medard churchyard beneath an upraised black marble stone. Sick Jansenists came to pray before the tomb, to lie upon and underneath it, giving rise to a belief in miraculous cures which led to massive scenes of collective hysteria.

In 1732, Louis XV decreed an end to the demonstrations; the cemetery was closed; an inscription nailed to the gate :

By order of the King, let God
No miracle perform in this place!

Tour. — The exterior is interesting. From the front with the great Flamboyant window overlooking the Rue Mouffetard, continue right, along the narrow and picturesque Rue Daubenton where at No. 41 a gate and passage lead to a small side entrance to the church. The famous cemetery surrounded the apse.

Return to the façade by way of the Rues de Candolle and Censier and the square.

The Flamboyant Gothic nave has modern stained glass; the unusually wide chancel is Renaissance influenced with unsymmetrical semicircular arches and rounded windows. In 1784 the pillars were transformed into fluted Doric columns. There are paintings of the French School, a remarkable 16C triptych *(behind the pulpit)* and, in the second chapel to the right of the chancel, a *Dead Christ* attributed to Philippe de Champaigne.

■ RUE MOUFFETARD★   ⬜ or ⬜ : L 15 - M 15

The Rue Mouffetard, downhill, winding, lined with old houses and crowded with life, is one of Paris' most original streets.

The bustle is greatest in the morning particularly at the lower end where the street climbs between small domestic shops distinguished by painted signs which date from far back and are sometimes picturesque as " At the clear Spring " at No. 122 where a well has been carved on the façade, and No. 69 where a tree in relief surmounted the now vanished sign of the Old Oak.

Nos. 104 and 101, on opposite sides of the street, mark the entrances to quiet passages — Posts and Patriarchs — far removed from the noise and scurry of the capital. The Iron Pot Fountain — Pot-de-Fer — at No. 60 runs like others in the district, with the surplus water from the Arcueil Aqueduct which Marie dei Medici had constructed to bring water to the Luxembourg Palace. Its Italian style bossages are reminiscent of the Medici Fountain *(p 96).*

When No. 53 was demolished in 1938, a cache was discovered in the ruins of 3 350 gold coins bearing the head of Louis XV, placed there by Louis Nivelle, the king's bearer and counsellor.

An inscription at No. 1 Contrescarpe Square recalls the Pinecone cabaret — Pomme-de-Pin — described by Rabelais. Pascal died in 1662 where No. 67 now stands in the Rue du Cardinal-Lemoine while No. 65 is the **Scottish College,** a building with a noble façade which has belonged to the Roman Catholic Church of Scotland since the 14C. Inside, a magnificent staircase leads to the Classical style Chapel, where a royal relic (the brain) was deposited in 1701 on James II's death in exile at St-Germain-en-Laye *(p 171).* The building is now a girls' hostel, the Foyer Ste-Geneviève. *Apply at the porter's lodge in advance (☎ 033.11.41) to visit the chapel.*

Return to Contrescarpe Square.

Continue along the Rue Blainville (glance to the right at the Pantheon dome) and left down the old and quiet Rue Tournefort. Turn right out of the Rue du Pot-de-Fer into the Rue Lhomond which descends the Montagne Ste-Geneviève (the steps beside the road indicate the mound's original height). On your left is the modern Albert-Châtelet University Centre. Turn up by No. 55, into the Passage des Postes, to return to the Rue Mouffetard and St. Medard's Church.

Michelin plans 🔟 or 🔟 :
H 6 - J 6.
*Distance : 2.5 km — 1 1/2 miles
— Time : 2 1/2 hours. Start from
the Trocadéro métro station.*

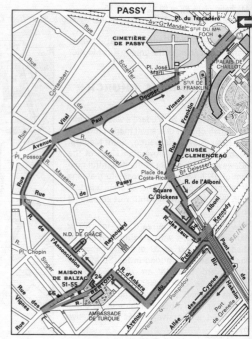

In the 13C Passy was a
woodcutters' hamlet; in the
18C it became known for its
ferruginous waters and in 1859
it was incorporated in the city
of Paris.

The " Fellows of Chaillot "
or *bonshommes* was the familiar name by which the Minim
Friars, whose monastery stood
on the hill until the Revolution,
were known, presumably because of the red wine produced by the community and still
recalled in the names of the
Rue Vineuse and Rue des
Vignes.

Today the houses in their
own gardens that used to make
up the peaceful residential
quarter are giving place to
large blocks of flats.

Make your way from the
Place du Trocadéro *(p 49)*
along the Rue Franklin.

Clemenceau Museum. — *8 Rue Franklin. Open Tuesdays, Thursdays, Saturdays, Sundays and holidays 2 to 5 pm; closed August; 3F.*

The great man's apartment is as it was on the day of his death in 1929. Mementoes in a gallery on the first floor recall his career as a journalist and statesman : the Montmartre mayoralty, the Treaty of Versailles and the premiership.

Continue down the Rue de l'Alboni, to the right of the high level métro station, and, hearing right, turn into the Rue des Eaux, at the end of which are a small street and square named after Charles Dickens. No. 5 Rue des Eaux, originally the site of a quarry, was converted under the Empire, into the first sugar beet refinery in France.

Allée des Cygnes. — Continue along the Rue des Eaux and over Bir-Hakeim Bridge to the islet which divides the Seine at this point. The Allée des Cygnes, or Swans' Walk, which was built up on the riverbed at the time of the Restoration, makes a pleasant stroll with a good view of the Radio-France House *(p 155)* on the right and of the new residential and office towers on the left. The figure of *France Renaissante* at the upstream end of the island is by the Danish sculptor, Wederkinch (1958).

Return to Avenue du Président Kennedy, turn left to Rue d'Ankara.

Rue d'Ankara. — The former château park of Marie-Antoinette's devoted friend, the Princess of Lamballe, at the end on the left, is now occupied by the Turkish Embassy and private houses In the 19C it belonged to Doctor Blanche, a specialist in mental illnesses who converted it into a home for the insane. Among his patients were Gérard de Nerval and Guy de Maupassant, two famous writers of that time.

Rue Berton*. — The Rue Berton, on the left, is one of the most unexpected in Paris — its ivy covered walls and gas brackets giving it an old country town atmosphere. No. 24 was the back entrance to Balzac's house *(see below)*.

Rue Raynouard. — This street is full of historical interest. Many famous people have lived in this street named after an obscure academician of the Restoration : Louis XIV's powerful financier, Samuel Bernard, the Duke of Lauzun, Jean-Jacques Rousseau, the song writer, Béranger and Benjamin Franklin, when in France negotiating an alliance for the new republic of the United States with Louis XVI. It was at this time also that he erected over his house, No. 66, the first lightning conductor in France. The modern blocks of flats at Nos. 51 to 55 are by Auguste Perret (d. 1954).

Finally No. 47, half-hidden in its garden, was **Balzac's house** from 1840 to 1847 *(open daily; closed Mondays and holidays; 10 am to 5.40 pm; 3F, free Sundays)*. Manuscripts, caricatures and engravings in the house reflect the Human Comedy described in his novels which can be seen in an adjoining museum-library.

Turn left into the Rue de l'Annonciation, the former name of the 17C chapel, much rest-
ored and now known as Our Lady of Grace. Cross the Rue de Passy, the old village main street, to go along the Rue Vital and Avenue Paul-Doumer, on the right.

Passy Cemetery. — The cemetery above Trocadero Square, contains, amidst burgeoning greenery, the remains of many who have died since 1850 from the world of literature (de Croisset, Tristan Bernard, Giraudoux), painting (Manet, Berthe Morisot), music (Debussy, Fauré) and aviation (Henry Farman).

■ MARMOTTAN MUSEUM★★ ▣ or ▣ : J 5.

Métro Station : Muette

2 Rue Louis-Boilly. Open daily except Mondays, 10 am to 6 pm; 5F.

In 1971 the Marmottan Museum was transformed by an outstanding bequest by Michel Monet of 65 paintings by his father. The museum had developed from the bequest in 1932 by the art historian, Paul Marmottan, of his house and Renaissance, Consular and First Empire collections to the Academy of Fine Arts. The Donop de Monchy legacy in 1950 added works by Claude Monet including the famous *Impression — Sunrise* which gave the Impressionist Movement its name.

The majority of the Monet paintings, acquired in 1971 and for which a special underground gallery has been built, were painted at the artist's Normandy home at Giverny. They form a dazzling series of water lily, wistaria and garden scenes and with canvases by Renoir, Sisley, Pissarro, make a perfect complement to the Jeu de Paume and Orangery Museums *(p 42)*.

The **Ranelagh Gardens,** on the far side of the Avenue Raphaël, date from 1860 when they were laid out on the site of an earlier, similarly named garden and café of high revelry. This had been established in 1774 and called in the spirit of Anglomania of the time, after the then equally gay London pleasure gardens established by Lord Ranelagh.

■ THE PÈRE-LACHAISE CEMETERY★★ ▣ or ▣ : H 20, H 21.

Métro Station : Père-Lachaise

Open 7.30 am to 6 pm, 16 March to 5 November; 8.30 am to 5 pm, 6 November to 15 January; 8 am to 5.30 pm, 16 January to 15 March; Sundays and holidays open from 9 am, closing time established according to the season.

In 1626 the Jesuits bought in this country area, a site on which to build a house of retreat. This became a frequent visiting place of Louis XIV's confessor, Father La Chaise, who gave generously to the house's reconstruction in 1682. The Jesuits were expelled in 1763. Forty years later, the city acquired the property for conversion to a cemetery.

The cemetery was the scene of the Paris Commune's final and bloody stand on 28 May 1871. The last insurgents were cornered and attacked on the night of the 27th, fierce fighting taking place among the graves. At dawn the 147 survivors were stood against the wall in the northeast corner — the **Federalists' Wall** (Mur des Fédérés) — and shot. They were buried where they fell in a communal grave which remains an annual political pilgrimage for many.

Paris' largest cemetery, designed by Brongniart, is on rising and falling ground.

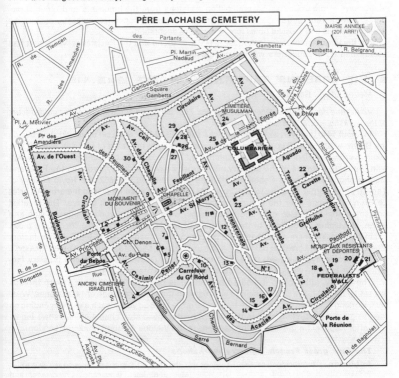

PÈRE LACHAISE CEMETERY

1) Colette	11) Corot	21) 1871 Commune victims
2) Rossini (cenotaph)	12) Molière and La Fontaine	22) Oscar Wilde
3) Baron Haussmann	13) Hugo family	23) Sarah Bernhardt
4) Abelard and Heloïse	14) Marshal Ney	24) Marcel Proust
5) Chopin	15) Beaumarchais	25) Guillaume Apollinaire
6) Cherubini	16) Marshal Masséna	26) Delacroix
7) Bellini	17) Murat and C. Bonaparte	27) Michelet
8) Thiers	18) Modigliani	28) Gérard de Nerval
9) David	19) Edith Piaf	29) Balzac
10) Auguste Comte	20) Paul Éluard and M. Thorez	30) Bizet

■ BUTTES-CHAUMONT PARK★   ⅠⅠ or ⅠⅠ : D 19, D 20 - E 19, E 20.

Métro Station : Buttes-Chaumont

Until 1864-1867 when Napoleon III and Haussmann converted the area into a park, Paris' first open space to the north, Chaumont, the bare or bald *(chauve)* mound, was a sinister area of quarries and rubbish dumps.

Haussmann took full advantage of the differences in ground level and of the quarries to dig a lake, fed by the St. Martin's Canal, in which he massed part natural, part artificial rocks 50 m — 150 ft — high. Two bridges lead to the island which he crowned with a temple commanding an extensive view of Montmartre and St-Denis.

■ FORMER CARMELITE CONVENT★   ⅠⅠ or ⅠⅠ : K 12.

Métro Station : St-Placide

Open 2.30 to 4.30 pm, Sundays 5 to 6 pm. Closed Tuesdays, 1 January 14 July, 1 November, 25 December and in August.

A monastery for Barefoot Carmelites, founded on the site in 1613, survived until the Revolution. On 30 August 1792, 116 priests had their throats cut; during the Terror, 120 of the 700 prisoners, by now held in the monastery, were guillotined. In 1797 it was returned privately to the Carmelites and, in 1841, became the Catholic Institute, where, in 1890, Branly was to discover the principle of radio.

The Church of St. Joseph of the Carmelites, built between 1613 and 1620, was the first example of the Jesuit style in Paris and the first church to be built in the capital with a dome. Several of the chapels have preserved an interesting Louis XIII decoration. There is a beautiful Bernini **Virgin★** to the left of the transept.

The garden, where many priests met their death, retains its conventual character.

■ THE CATACOMBS★   ⅠⅠ or ⅠⅠ : N 12, N 13.

Métro Station : Denfert-Rochereau

Open only 1st and 3rd Saturdays in the month at 2 pm, 16 October to 30 June; every Saturday at 2 pm, 1 July to 15 October; closed holiday Saturdays and day before holiday; 5F. Entrance 2 bis Place Denfert-Rochereau (southwest side). It is recommended to take a torch.

In 1785 it was decided to turn the disused parts of the quarries formed by excavation since Gallo-Roman times at the bases of the three " mountains " — Montparnasse, Montrouge and Montsouris — into ossuaries. Several million skeletons from the Innocents' and other cemeteries were thereupon transported to Montrouge where the bones were stacked against the walls, the skulls and crossed tibias form a macabre decoration.

On the liberation of Paris in August 1944 it was found that the Resistance Movement had established its headquarters within the catacombs.

■ THE GOBELINS' TAPESTRY FACTORY★   ⅠⅠ or ⅠⅠ : N 15.

Métro Station : Gobelins

42 Avenue des Gobelins. Open Wednesdays, Thursdays and Fridays, 2 to 4 pm; guided tours of the workshops 2.15, 2.45 and 3.30 pm; 5F.

In about 1440 the dyer, Jean Gobelin, who specialised in scarlet, set up a workshop beside the Bièvre which was to be used by his descendants until the reign of Henri IV when it was taken over by two Flemish craftsmen, summoned by the king. Colbert, charged by Louis XIV with the reorganisation of the tapestry and carpet weaving industry, grouped the Paris and Maincy shops around the Gobelin workshops thus creating, in 1662, the Royal Factory of Tapestry and Carpet Weavers to the Crown. At the group's head he placed the artist, Charles Le Brun. Five years later the group was joined by the Royal Cabinet-Makers. The greatest craftsmen, including also gold and silversmiths, were therefore working side by side and in an atmosphere propitious to the evolution of the Louis XIV style *(see the Louvre p 39)*.

In the last 300 years more than 5 000 tapestries have been woven at the Gobelins factory after cartoons by the greatest painters — Le Brun, Poussin, Mignard, Boucher, Lurçat, Picasso...

The former royal **Savonnerie** (1604-1826) and **Beauvais** (1664-1940) carpet and tapestry factories have, over the years, been incorporated to form the present single unit.

The factory, although in a modern building, has retained 17C methods : warp threads are set by daylight, the colours being selected from the factory's range of 14 000 tones. Weavers, working from mirrors, complete from 1 to 8 m² — 1 to 8 sq yds — each a year depending on the design. All production goes to the state. The deconsecrated chapel contains two tapestries after Raphaël (in the style of the cartoons in the Victoria & Albert Museum, London).

The four great French Tapestry workshops

Aubusson : producing less fine hangings for the lesser 17 and 18C aristocracy and bourgeoisie; floral and plant, animal, Classical fable and, later, landscape, *Chinoiseries* and pastoral scenes (after Huet) were the most used motifs.

Beauvais : very finely woven in the 18C often with vividly dyed silks which, unfortunately, have faded. Motifs include grotesques, Fables after La Fontaine (by Oudry), Boucher's Italian Comedy, Loves of the Gods, *Chinoiseries*, and pastoral scenes (after Huet). 18C designs continued into 19C.

Felletin : coarser weave hangings with rustic motifs.

Gobelins : sumptuous quality hangings often with gold interwoven. Renowned for originality, series include The Life of the King, The Seasons and Elements, Royal Residences, Louis XV at the Chase. Motifs also after Oudry and Boucher (Loves of the Gods — *p 39*). Neilson, a Scot, became the most influential weaver in late 18C.

■ **MONTSOURIS PARK★** ⑩ or ⑪ : R 13.

Métro Station : Cité Universitaire

Haussmann began work on this nondescript area, undermined by quarries and capped by dozens of windmills on either side of the RER B line and lesser Paris Ring Road in 1868. By 1878 he had turned it into a park : the 16 ha — 50 acres — had been landscaped and paths constructed to climb the mounds and circle the cascades and large artificial lake (the engineer personally involved in the construction committed suicide, on the lake's suddenly drying out on opening day).

The park is dominated by the south bearing of the old Paris meridian *(plan p 123)* and even more emphatically by a reproduction of the Bardo (the Bey of Tunis' palace) made for the 1867 Exhibition and offered to the city by the Bey. The municipal meteorologircal observatory is in a nearby building.

Painters, attracted by the park's peace and proximity to Montparnasse at the beginning of the century, left their mark on the area, as, for instance, the Douanier Rousseau and Georges Braque who had a studio (west of the park) in a street, which now carries his name.

■ **RADIO-FRANCE HOUSE★** ⑩ or ⑪ : K 5.

Métro Station : Ranelagh
116 Avenue du Président-Kennedy.

Guided tours daily 10 am to noon and 2 to 5 pm; closed Mondays; 4F. Public admitted to concerts and to certain broadcasts.

One concentric building 547 m — 500 yds — in circumference and a tower 70 m tall — 230 ft — covering in all 2 ha — 5 acres — go to make up Radio-France House. It was designed and erected by Henry Bernard in 1963 and is the biggest single construction in France. It is here in the 62 studios and the main auditorium (studio 104) that the programmes of France-Inter, France-Culture, F I P 514 and Radio-France-Internationale (programmes in 18 languages broadcast all over the world) are produced.

The Statue of Liberty, on the far side of the new Grenelle Bridge, is a reduced copy of the one by Bartholdi which stands at the entrance to New York harbour.

On the opposite bank, a new urbanization project is being realized. The quarter, known as the **Front de Seine★** will include sixteen residential and office towers as well as cultural and sports facilities. A concrete podium will be built 5.5 m — 18 ft — above the ground, creating a traffic free zone which will be given over to gardens, offices and commercial premises. The planned completion date for the entire project is 1980.

■ **PARADISE STREET★** ⑩ or ⑪ : E 15 - F 15.

Métro Station : Gare de l'Est

The street is known today for its shops of beautiful tableware, the chief points of sale of the Lorraine glass, china and porcelain factories. No. 30 *bis* is **Baccarat,** the glassmakers. Adjoining it is a magnificent **museum★★** *(open 9 am to 5.30 pm; Saturdays 10 am to noon and 2 to 5 pm; closed Sundays),* in which are displayed pieces of equal beauty to those which have adorned royal palaces and state residences throughout the world for the last hundred and fifty years.

Poster Museum (Musée de l'Affiche). — *No. 18. Open noon to 6 pm. Closed Tuesdays; 5F.*

This small museum is located in the former Choisy-le-Roi China and Porcelain house. Go through the small courtyard decorated with pictorial multicoloured tiles in relief and up the stairs to the museum where, by changing exhibitions, some 50 000 posters are exposed.

■ **ST. LOUIS HOSPITAL★** ⑩ or ⑪ : F 17.

Métro Station : République

Open 1.30 to 3.30 pm and 6.30 to 8 pm. One of the oldest hospitals in Paris.

In 1606 Paris was decimated by the plague; great fires were lit in the streets to purify the air; trumpet and drum processions were made to restore morale; but the scourge continued.

Henri IV therefore decided to build a hospital where the sick could be cared for in isolation and to call the establishment after the King, St. Louis, who had died of plague in Tunisia. The establishment has remained a hospital specializing in skin diseases, throughout its history.

The brick and stone buildings, reminiscent of the Place Royale (des Vosges) and Place Dauphine with their steeply pitched roofs and dormer windows are divided by flower lined courts.

■ **ST. MARTIN'S CANAL★** ⑩ or ⑪ : E 17 - F 17

Métro Station : Jaurès

The peaceful, old-fashioned reaches of the 4.5 km — 2 3/4 mile — canal, dug at the time of the Restoration to link the Ourcq Canal with the Seine, are navigated by some 4 000 barges a year. The embankments, where the water course is above the surrounding plain, the nine locks and bordering trees, make the landscape very reminiscent of Holland.

The canal disappears in Frédéric-Lemaître Square (beyond the Quai Valmy) to flow underground and reappear at the Place de la Bastille.

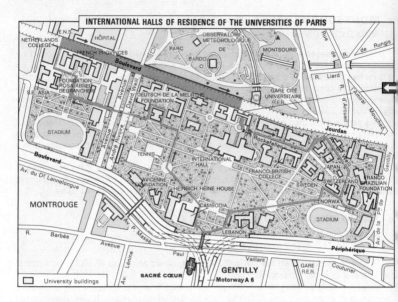

■ INTERNATIONAL HALLS OF RESIDENCE OF THE UNIVERSITIES OF PARIS* (Cité Internationale Universitaire de Paris)

10 or **11** : R 13 - S 13, S 14.

Métro Station : Cité Universitaire

Main Entrance : 19-21 Boulevard Jourdan. The " city " on the edge of Montsouris Park, spreads over an area of 40 ha — 100 acres — housing 6 500 students from 116 different countries in its 37 halls of residence. Each hall forms an independant community, reflecting in its architecture an individual character, frequently inspired by the country which founded it. The first hall, the E.-and-L.-Deutsch-de-la-Meurthe Foundation was opened in 1925 and, apart from a long gap from 1937 to 1949, a new one has been opened every year. The International Hall (1936) with a swimming pool, theatre and vast rooms was presented by John D. Rockefeller Jr; the Swiss and Brazilian Halls were designed by Le Corbusier. The Persian Hall, one of the latest (1968), is interestingly modern.

The **Sacred Heart Church** (Sacré-Cœur), the community's parish church, stands on the far side of the ring road and is reached by a footbridge from which you can see traffic speeding along the A6 motorway. Built between 1931 and 1936 in Neo-Romanesque style, it is plain with preponderant blue stained glass windows.

■ FLEA MARKET (Marché aux Puces) **10** or **11** : A 14.

Métro Station : Porte de Clignancourt

Open Saturdays, Sundays and Mondays.

The market developed from the casual offering of their wares by hawkers to the curious at the end of the 19C, to an established trading centre in the 1920's. A lucky few picked up masterpieces from the then unknowing sellers; now more than 2 000 stalls attract a motley throng to pick over every imaginable type of object.

The stalls are grouped :

Vernaison : period furniture, ornaments.
Malik : secondhand clothes, spectacles, records.
Biron : antiques and valuables.
Paul-Bert : oddments, ironwork, china.
Jules-Vallès : country furniture, curios.
Cambo : furniture, paintings.

■ ST-NICOLAS-DU-CHARDONNET CHURCH **10** or **11** : K 15.

Métro Station : Maubert

A chapel was constructed on this site in a field planted with thistles *(chardons)* in the 13C; in 1656 it was replaced by the present north to south oriented building apart from the façade which was completed only in 1934.

The **side door*** (Rue des Bernardins), with remarkable wood carving after designs by Le Brun, a parishioner, is the best exterior feature. The Jesuit style interior is liberally decorated with paintings including works by Claude, Corot and Le Brun (his funeral monument, by Coysevox, stands in an ambulatory chapel on the left near Le Brun's own monument to his mother). The 18C organ loft is from the former Innocents' Church *(p 110)*.

Michelin map **101** 22.
Access also by train : Gare des Invalides to Versailles Rive-Gauche.

The French monarchy reached its zenith in Versailles — to build a Versailles became the ambition of every king and princeling in Europe and echoes, therefore, of the château architecture and style, the gardens, the Trianons, are to be found in palaces and mansions in almost every country in the West whether they were friendly or opposed to Louis XIV.

The town grew up in the shadow of the palace, never emerging in its own right and, like the palace, remains much as it was in the 17 and 18C.

HISTORICAL NOTES

Louis XIII's Château. — At the beginning of the 17C, Versailles was a village surrounded by marsh and woodland. Game abounded and Louis XIII, who enjoyed hunting, bought a local manor farm which, in due course, he had reconstructed by Philibert le Roy (1631-1634). The resulting small rose brick and stone château consisting of a main building and two wings can still be seen with the Marble Court at its centre. Gardens surrounded the château.

The palace enlarged. — Louis XIV came to the throne at five and achieved majority at twenty-three in 1661. In the intervening years he had grown attached to his father's château and determined to enlarge it and also to outstrip in grandeur the country mansion at Vaux-Le-Vicomte of Fouquet, his finance minister. To this end he commissioned the three who had been working for Fouquet — Le Vau as architect, Le Brun as decorator, Le Nôtre as garden designer, to reconceive the château at Versailles.

Louis XIII's construction was too small to be enlarged; the land was too wet to grow plants satisfactorily and there was insufficient water for the fountains which were an integral part of any 17C garden. Such details meant little to the king! Soil was shifted, land was drained, building began — and although construction was to continue for a further half century, by 1664 the first of the many celebrations that one associates with Versailles were being held there to the satisfaction of king and court.

The palace of palaces. — In 1678, Jules Hardouin-Mansart, then aged 31, took over as project architect — a post he was to occupy until his death thirty years later. By 1685, 36 000 workmen with 6 000 horses were engaged on the palace site under the direction of Mansart, Le Brun and Le Nôtre. Such numbers are understood when it is appreciated that the installation of 1 400 fountains (today 600), necessitated the diversion of the River Bièvre and 16 000 ha — 37 000 acres — of land being drained; bedding plants numbered 150 000 a year; there were 3 000 orange, pomegranate, myrtle and rose-laurel trees to be moved seasonally into the orangery. 100 statues were commissionned by Le Brun for the gardens alone.

Life at Court. — The court numbered 20 000. Included in these were 9 000 soldiers billetted in the town and 5 000 servants housed in the palace annexes. A thousand nobles and their 4 000 servants lived in the palace itself and at least 1 000 lesser nobility frequented the precincts in the hope of recognition by the king from whom favours, riches, position, everything depended. Louis encouraged this attraction as a means of keeping his nobles under his eye and control, encouraged also their rivalries in place-seeking, fashion, gambling to distract their attention from political dissension. All was gaiety until 1684 when the influence of Mme de Maintenon became paramount.

On the death of the Sun King in 1715, the court returned to Paris. In 1722, however, Louis XV moved back to Versailles though not to live in the public style of Louis XIV — it was during his reign that certain palace rooms were converted into private apartments.

Since 1789, Versailles has ceased to be a royal residence.

To the glory of France. — The execution of Louis XVI on 21 January 1793 marked the start of Versailles' spoliation : the furniture was auctioned, the fine art removed to the Louvre, the palace itself allowed to fall into disrepair, the gardens were abandoned.

The rot was only stopped by Louis-Philippe who gave 23 million francs from his personal fortune towards the palace's rehabilitation and conversion into a museum " to the glory of France ". Restoration has continued ever since, particularly after the 1914-1918 war with the assistance of a munificent gift by John D. Rockefeller and since 1950.

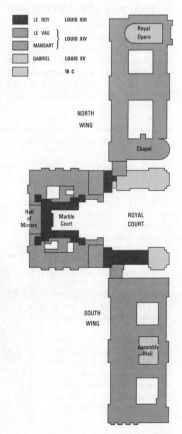

LE ROY — LOUIS XIII
LE VAU — LOUIS XIV
MANSART — LOUIS XIV
GABRIEL — LOUIS XV
— 19 C

Royal Opera

NORTH WING

Chapel

Hall of Mirrors

Marble Court

ROYAL COURT

SOUTH WING

Assembly Hall

THE PALACE

Versailles that is to say the **Palace, Gardens** and **Trianons** cannot be seen in a single tour. Aim at a general impression on your first visit and the return, possibly after a lapse of several years, to pick out special items to look at and enjoy in detail.

There are official guided tours in French and English (Easter holidays, July and August) of the major parts of the palace. For exact times and full details, write to Service des Visites, Château de Versailles, 78000 Versailles. There is a restaurant for light meals by the ticket office (documentation in English available).

	FREE VISIT	GUIDED TOURS	
State Apartments★★★	Daily 10 am to 5 pm - *6F*		
Museum of French History★★	Some galleries may be closed : ☎ 950-58-32 ext. 316 - *6F*		
Grand Trianon★★	Daily 10 am to 6 pm (4.30 pm in winter) - *6F*	11 am and noon Saturdays and Sundays - *6F*	
Petit Trianon★★	Daily 2 to 6 pm (4.30 pm in winter) - *4F*	4 pm (3 pm in winter) including French Pavilion and Queen's Theatre - *12F*	CLOSED MONDAYS and some holidays (2)
Gardens★★★ and Park *(1)*	Dawn to dusk - (by car - *4F*)		
Chapel★★★			
King's Private Apartments★★★			
Queen's Private Apartments★★			
Royal Opera★★	For exact time and full details : ☎ 950-38-32 ext. 320 - *6F*	1 April to 30 September at 11 am, noon, 1 and 2 pm (11 am, noon and 2 pm the rest of the year) - *9F*	
Mme de Maintenon's Suite★			
Mme de Pompadour's Suite			
Mme du Barry's Suite			

(1) Open everyday. Fountains and illuminations p 165. - 5F.
(2) 1 January, 1 May, 1 November, 25 December.

■ THE PALACE EXTERIOR★★★

Place d'Armes Façade. — The square, as vast as the Place de la Concorde and the meeting point of three avenues each wider than the Champs-Élysées — the Avenue de St-Cloud, Avenue de Paris and Avenue de Sceaux — serves as a forecourt to the magnificent **royal stables★** (now a barracks) designed by Jules Hardouin-Mansart to house Louis XIV's 2 500 horses and 200 carriages, and simultaneously to emphasize Versailles' massive expanse.

Beyond the wrought iron gates are three courts : the **Ministers' Court,** lined by wings of the palace formerly occupied by ministers and government officials; the **Royal Court,** beginning where the equestrian statue of Louis XIV erected in 1837 now stands and formerly separated from the outer court by a grille through which none but the royal family, princes and peers, might pass; and, finally, the **Marble Court★★,** surrounded on three sides by the old Louis XIII Château and originally upraised, ornamented with a fountain and paved in black and white marble.

Garden Façade★★★. — Pass through the façade, decorated with columns and statues, to the gardens and park. This façade — 680 m long — 733 yds — overall, is divided into three, the centre being well in advance of the north and south wings on either side. Monotony has been avoided by the lines of windows, uniform at each of three levels, and the horizontal lines of balcony balustrade, cornice and roof balustrade being broken respectively by projecting pilasters, columns and, at the higher levels, by ornamental vases and great trophies.

Marking the royal apartments at the centre of the main façade and the focal point from the gardens, are statues of Apollo and Diana, symbolizing the king and queen, surrounded by the months of the year.

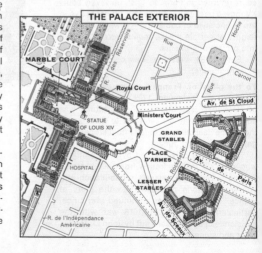

THE PALACE EXTERIOR

■ THE APARTMENTS★★★

1. - The Chapel and The State Apartments

The state apartments and reception rooms and the royal apartments occupy the north and west areas of the first floor of the central wing.

The Chapel★★★. — Go through from the ground floor entrance to the vestibule where a low relief by Coustou shows Louis XVI crossing the Rhine. Continue up the circular stairway to the upper vestibule where superbly carved wooden doors open on to the royal gallery.

The Chapel, dedicated to St. Louis, harmoniously ornate in its white and gold decoration, remains one of Hardouin-Mansart's masterpieces although it was only completed in 1710 after his death, by his brother-in-law, Robert de Cotte. The pillar and arcade sculpture are by Van Cleve, Robert Le Lorrain and G. Coustou; the organ loft is by Robert de Cotte; the marble altar with bronze gilt ornament by Van Cleve and the Resurrection in the apse by La Fosse.

Louis XIV attended mass daily and, although still surrounded by the court, it was while the Sun King was in chapel that any subject had the right to petition him.

The Chapel was the setting for all the religious occasions of the Court : baptisms, weddings. The marriage of the Dauphin (the future Louis XVI) and Marie-Antoinette, daughter of Francis I and Maria-Theresa of Austria, was celebrated here on 16 May 1770.

The court circulated in the Hercules Salon, the State Apartments and the Hall of Mirrors and these, therefore, reflect the style of Louis XIV in all its sumptuous magnificence — only the finest multicoloured marble from the Pyrenees was used, bronze was everywhere sculptured and gilded, craftsmen from none but the most reputed workshops were employed.

Go up the former Ambassadors' Staircase to the reception rooms.

The Hercules Salon★★. — The salon, on the site of an earlier chapel, was created in 1712 and was named after the huge fresco of Hercules, 315 m² in area — 3 390 sq ft — painted on the ceiling between 1733 and 1736 by François Lemoyne. (The artist committed suicide not long after completing this work). The room's original rich decoration was enhanced by the two Veronese paintings, *Eliezer and Rebecca* over the marble mantlepiece and *Christ at the House of Simon the Pharisee,* the latter given by the Venetian Republic to Louis XIV.

The Grand Apartment★★★. — The Grand Apartment, a suite of six salons by Le Vau (1668), decorated by Le Brun and each named after the paintings decorating the ceilings, were where Louis XIV held court between 6 and 10 pm on three evenings each week.

The **Abundance Salon (1)** was at one time hung with pictures from the royal collection by Veronese, Titian and Rubens. *(see the Louvre pp 27-39).*

The **Venus Salon** (2), the first of the planetary salons, was decorated by René Antoine Houasse with a Venus Triumphant. The heavy gilt stucco, dividing the ceiling panels, is offset by *trompe-l'œil* paintings on the walls.

The marble statue of the young Louis XIV as a Roman Emperor is by Jean Warin.

The **Diana Salon** (3) contains the famous bust of Louis XIV by Bernini. In the time of the Sun King, it served as the billiard room.

The **Mars Salon** (4), formerly where the musicians played, is decorated with tapestries *(temporarily)*. The carpet is a Savonnerie; on the walls (hung where they were originally) *Louis XV* by Rigaud and *Marie Leczinska* by Van Loo.

The **Mercury Salon** (5) *(restoration in progress)* with further tapestries in the series, also contains the astronomical clock made for the king in 1706. The salon was used for gaming on those evenings Louis was not holding court. It was also where Louis XIV lay in state for one week after his death.

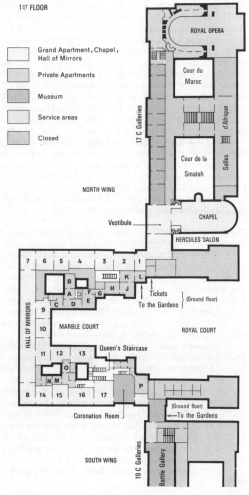

1ST FLOOR

☐ Grand Apartment, Chapel, Hall of Mirrors

Private Apartments

Museum

Service areas

Closed

ROYAL OPERA

Cour du Maroc

Cour de la Smalah

17 C Galleries

d'Afrique

Salles

NORTH WING

Vestibule

CHAPEL

HERCULES'SALON

7 6 5 4 3 2 1

B K L

A F

C D E H J

G

Tickets
To the Gardens } (Ground floor)

9

10 MARBLE COURT

ROYAL COURT

11 12 13 Queen's Staircase

O

N M

8 14 15 16 17 P

(Ground floor)
←To the Gardens

Coronation Room

HALL OF MIRRORS

19 C Galleries

SOUTH WING

Battle Gallery

The **Apollo Salon** (6), the former throne room, is the most sumptuous of the planetary series. Louis XIV saw Apollo as his ideal, the god of wisdom and prophecy, of light and the arts — and took as his personal symbol Apollo's attribute, the sun. This motif is everywhere in the palace : on the ceiling of this salon La Fosse painted *Apollo in a Sun Chariot attended by the Seasons*. At the end were the silver throne and canopy at which Louis received ambassadors. Today there remain the painted ceiling, the early commodes by Boulle and the magnificent gilded sconces.

The **War Salon** (7) is decorated with a great oval medallion, carved in relief by Coysevox, of the king riding in triumph over his enemies and being crowned by the goddess of war.

The **Peace Salon** (8) which contains a painting by Lemoyne of *Louis XV bringing peace to Europe* and a small replica of *Ariadne Asleep* (original in the Vatican), served as a music room in the time of Marie Leczinska and Marie-Antoinette.

The Hall of Mirrors*. — The most famous hall in the palace and perhaps even in the world, must have been fantastic when the king and queen in full dress moved among their court beneath lighted chandeliers. It is 75 m long by 10 m wide — 246 × 33 ft; light from the 17 windows is reflected in the 17 mirrors of equal size on the wall opposite. Le Brun painted the ceiling in glorification of the Sun King's early reign from 1661-1678, although he reigned until his death in 1715.

The hall was the setting for the greatest occasions : princely marriages such as that of Marie-Antoinette and the future Louis XVI, receptions and splendid festivals...

Then the 32 silver chandeliers would be lit, flowers and orange trees in silver tubs disposed, Savonnerie carpets laid and all would appear in their finery. Ten of the original twenty-four gilded candelabras ordered by Louis XV now stand in the hall, as well as 20 crystal chandeliers.

Stripped of furnishings the hall became the scene in 1871 of Bismarck's proclamation of the King of Prussia as Emperor of Germany and on 28 June 1919 of the signing of the Versailles Treaty which ended the First World War.

The King's Suite*. — *(Closed temporarily for reorganization; scheduled opening date 1980).* Between 1684 and 1701 Jules Hardouin-Mansart redesigned for the king the apartments in the Louis XIII château overlooking the Marble Court. The decoration epitomised the Louis XIV style : ceilings, no longer compartmented, are surrounded by heavy friezes, panelling has replaced marble on the walls, large mirrors surmount the fireplaces.

The **Council Chamber** (9) was transformed by Louis XV in 1755 when it was given its present dimensions and decoration of gold and white Rococo panelling and blue silk hangings. The table was used for the signing of the 1919 Versailles Treaty.

The **King's Bedchamber** (10) is as it was under Louis XIV. The royal bed, in the exact centre of the palace and turned towards the east, was the centrepiece of the morning and evening ceremonies which took place daily at 8 am and midnight from 1701 to 1789 when the reigning monarch rose and retired before the assembled members of his court. It was also amid these sumptuous surroundings, which date structurally from 1689, and in this same bed, that at 77, Louis XIV, still surrounded by courtiers, died of gangrene poisoning on 1 September 1715.

On the right mantelpiece is a very realistic bust of *Louis XIV* by Coysevox, on the left mantelpiece Louis XIV's clock by Thuret.

The **Œil-de-Bœuf** or **Bull's Eye Salon** (or Second Antechamber) (11), is so called after the false window in the form of a bull's eye over the chimneypiece.

A delightful freize of children at play surmounts the entablature along its entire length in this courtiers' antechamber. Three busts decorate the salon, *Louis XIV* by Coysevox, *Louis XV* by Gois and *Louis XVI* by Houdon.

The **First Antechamber** (12); the **King's Guards' Room** (13), are the last two rooms, beside the Queen's staircase precede the King's apartments.

The Queen's Suite*. — This suite of rooms overlooking the flowerbeds of the south garden (Parterres du Midi) form the counterpart of the king's state apartments.

The **Queen's bedchamber** (14) restored as it was in 1787, was designed for the Infanta Maria Theresa, bride of Louis XIV. She was succeeded by her daughter-in-law, Maria-Anna of Bavaria, wife of the Grand Dauphin, then Marie-Adélaïde of Savoy, Duchess of Burgundy and mother of Louis XV, Louis XV's wife Maria Leczinska, and finally by Marie-Antoinette. It was in this room that the queen spent her last night at Versailles before escaping from the mob on the morning of 6 October 1789. In all nineteen royal children were born in the room.

The four monotone ceiling paintings are by François Boucher; the silk has been rewoven to patterns originally chosen by Marie-Antoinette.

Tha **Queen's Salon** (15) has been reconstituted to look exactly as it did in 1789 with matching chimneypiece and furniture and almond green furnishings. The queen received ambassadors and held her circle in this salon, also known as the Peer's Salon.

The **Antechamber** (16) was the room in which the queen ate alone but in public as did the king in his bedroom. The room is decorated with two screens covered with Gobelins tapestries (17C) and a portrait of Marie-Antoinette and her children (1787) by Madame Vigée-Lebrun.

The **Queen's Guards' Room** (17) is pure Louis XIV in style with a painting on the ceiling by Coypel of Jupiter in his silver chariot. It was into this room that the revolutionaries burst on 6 October 1789 and stabbed to death one of Marie-Antoinette's bodyguards.

The **Queen's Staircase** was the formal palace approach to the royal apartments, it is a wide multicoloured marble staircase.

The **Coronation Room** and the **Battle Gallery** are parts of the Museum of French History (p 162).

2. - The Private Apartments *(Guided tours only, p 158).*

The State Apartments which were entirely public, were duplicated, from the time of Louis XV, by the Private Apartments.

The King's Private Suite★★★. — The suite was used by Louis XIV to display his personal art collection but was transformed by Gabriel for Louis XV into an informal suite in 1738.

The **Dogs' Antechamber** (A) has Louis XIV wooden panelling which was designed by Mansart

The **Hunters' Dining Room** (B) was, as of 1750, where the King dined with courtiers after the hunt. Note the beautiful Sèvres porcelain plaques representing hunting scenes, ordered by Louis XVI.

The **King's Bedchamber** (C) is the room where Louis XV died of smallpox on 10 May 1774. The bed was similar to the one now in the room. Although the king had continued the ritual rising and retiring in the state bedroom throughout his reign, he used to slip away to this warmer and more comfortable room!

The **Pendule** or **Clock Cabinet** (D) is so called after the astronomic clock made by Passement in 1754 which marks the hours, the days of the week, the date in the month, the months, the years and the phases of the moon.

The **Corner Room** (E) was completely transformed for Louis XV by Gabriel in 1753. On the Savonnerie carpet stands a precious Oeben and Riesener bureau. Gay cherubs surround the shell ornament on the walls. On the chest-medal cabinet, the candelabra which commemorates the role played by France during the American War of Independence, is flanked by two porcelain vases.

Louis XV's Inner Cabinet (F) was where the king kept his secret political and diplomatic documents.

Madame Adélaïde's Cabinet (G), formerly Mme de Montespan's room, was redecorated with rich panelling with musical, fishing and gardening motifs in 1753 by Louis XV for his favourite daughter. It was in this room that Mozart at the age of seven, in 1763, is said to have played the clavichord before the royal family.

Louis XVI's Library (H) originally contained Louis XIV's most precious paintings. In 1752 Louis XV divided off the Ambassadors' Staircase Gallery and used the remaining area as a gaming saloon.

Louis XVI again transformed it, getting Gabriel to convert it in 1774 to the library it is now, complete with the round Riesener table and tall Roentgen secretaire.

The **China Salon** (J) which is now being restored, was used by Louis XV to display his collection of Sèvres porcelain pieces. The next room was known as the **Billiard Room** (K).

Louis XVI's Gaming Room (L), known as the Rare Objects Cabinet under Louis XIV, has corner cupboards by Riesener, carved and gilded chairs by Boulard and fine crimson and gold brocade curtains which were woven in Lyon.

The Queen's Private Suite★★. — The rooms still have their Marie-Antoinette decoration.

The **Library** (M) contains the greater part of Marie-Antoinette's personal collection of books.

The **South Room** (N) is a small octagonal *boudoir* with attractive blue silk covered furniture. The clock was given to the queen by the city of Paris.

The **Gold Cabinet** (O) was used by the queen to receive friends, to pose for portraits and as a music room.

Mme de Maintenon's Suite★. — Mme de Maintenon, Louis XIV's morganatic wife, lived in this suite of four rooms during the last 33 years of his reign.

The two smaller rooms which were used as antechambers, are covered with crimson damask. The collection of 16C paintings on display was given to Louis XIV in 1711. They include scenes and portraits of historical figures.

The former bedchamber decorated with apple-green wall hangings, displays 17C works of art. Note the series of 12 *gouaches* by Jean Cotelle depicting the gardens of Versailles as they were in 1693, a magnificent lapis lazuli (Triumph of Louis XIII) and two gilded bronze clocks.

A narrow passage leads to the Grand Cabinet where Mme de Maintenon entertained the members of the royal family and where Racine declaimed his latest tragedies. The room is adorned with fine pieces of furniture and portraits of outstanding beauties of the time.

Mme du Barry's Suite. — *Second floor.* This suite installed all around the Stag Court and Marble Court, includes a bathroom, a dining-room, a bedchamber (*gouache* by Gauthier-Dagoty representing Mme du Barry being waited on by her little black boy Zamore), a corner salon from which Louis XV used to admire the view over the town and surrounding hillsides and a library. The woodwork has been restored to its original aspect.

Mme de Pompadour's Suite. — *Third floor (closed : restoration in progress).* Louis XV's mistress lived in these apartments for five years between 1745 and 1750. Carved woodwork and delicate 18C furniture constitute the sumptuousness of the Grand Cabinet.

3. - The Royal Opera★★ *(Guided tours only, p 158).*

In 1768 Jacques-Ange Gabriel began to construct the opera-house which was opened two years later at the wedding of the Dauphin, the future Louis XVI, and Marie-Antoinette. The interior was built of wood — with excellent acoustic results — and painted to look like green and rose marble. Ornament lies in the gilded low reliefs and medallions and vases coloured blue to pick up the colour of the sky on the ceiling painting, the deep blue seating and light blue curtain scattered with gold *fleurs de lys*. It took five years to restore the Opera to its present splendour. In 1957 the opening performance was attended by Queen Elizabeth II and Prince Philip.

■ THE MUSEUM OF FRENCH HISTORY★★

Some departments may be closed; for information see chart p 158.

The outstanding feature of this Museum of French History from the 16 to the 19C, is tha the thousands of portraits are seen in their contemporary settings and, in most cases, are o people who were associated with the palace.

16C Galleries. — *See Mme de Maintenon's Suite (p 161).*

17C Galleries. — These occupy most of the ground floor and first floor of the north wing Of the eleven ground floor galleries, one is devoted to Henri IV, the first to discover Versailles and to Louis XIII, who built the first château. The Louis XIII and early Louis XIV reigns are portrayed by Vouet, Philippe de Champaigne, Deruet and Le Brun. The kings and queens their children and favourites are shown on great state occasions and also informally. The Versailles Gallery shows the palace in construction.

On the first floor the portraits include members of the royal family, Louis XIV's successfu generals, the favourites, Mme de Montespan and Mme de Maintenon, portraits of Louis XIV's children, legitimate and illegitimate, and such great men of the time as Racine, Molière, La Fontaine, Le Nôtre, Couperin, Colbert...

18C Galleries★★★. — The galleries occupy the ground floor of the central wing and start historically, from the Queen's Staircase. Pictures in the **Dauphine's suite** *(closed temporarily* show Louis XIV's immediate successors : the Regent and Louis XV, at the age of five, b Rigaud. Next come a six-panel Savonnerie screen, pictures of the marriage of Louis XV and Marie Leczinska, a portrait of Mme de Pompadour, delightful allegorical portraits by Nattie of Louis XV's daughters, Mme Adélaïde as Diana and Mme Henriette as Flora. The furniture fine commodes and carved, silk upholstered chairs, contribute to the original atmosphere.

In the **Dauphin's suite** the former library is still beautifully panelled. The Grand Çorne Room is hung with further pictures by Nattier of Marie Leczinska and her daughters. The decoration of the Dauphin's bedroom dates from 1747, the chimney-piece being one of the finest in the palace.

The antechamber to the **gallery** below the Hall of Mirrors, is filled with portraits of the members of the royal family.

The antechamber to **Mme Victoire's suite,** *(reorganization and restoration in progress* fourth daughter of Louis XV, was previously Louis XIV's bathroom and was then equippe with a marble piscina and two baths.

The Nobles' Salon decorated with wood panelling contains furniture by Tilliard and com modes by Leleu.

The former bedroom of Mme Victoire will have furniture of an exceptional quality (lacquer work) and summer wall hangings. The final galleries document the great festivals and politica occasions of the century. The heavy Ambassador's Staircase, removed by Louis XV in 1752 led formerly to the **Ambassadors' Salon,** a room of impressive architectural proportions, fals relief painting and marble paving, where the most precious item is a clock designed b Claude Siméon Passement in 1754 illustrating the creation of the world. A model of th Ambassadors' Staircase can be seen in the antechamber.

The next gallery is devoted entirely to the American War of Independence and the Treat of Versailles of 1783 under which the independence of the 13 States was recognised.

The final galleries illustrate the last days of the monarchy and the approach of the Revo lution with such pictures as a study by David for his painting, *The Oath* in the Jeu de Paum and *Marat's Assassination*. Also displayed is the carpet that Marie-Antoinette and Mme Éli sabeth completed in the Templar Prison.

Empire Galleries. — The Consulate and Empire periods are evoked on the first floor of th south wing (Coronation Room and Battle Gallery) and in the vast attic above, as well as i the Chimay Attic above the Queen's Suite.

To visit the first floor galleries start from the Queen's Suite or the Queen's Staircase Documents, drawings, engravings, furniture and furnishings bring the Napoleonic era t life once more : in the **Coronation Room,** the former Guardroom, hang David's famous pair tings : *Napoleon's Coronation* and *The Distribution by Napoleon of Eagle Standards on th Champ-de-Mars in 1804* as well as Antoine-Jean Gros' *Battle of Aboukir*. Between the win dows looking on to the gardens, there are two portraits of Napoleon, each is surmounted by medallion of his wife at the time. On the ceiling is Callet's painting, *The Allegory of 18 Bru maire,* commemorating the overthrow of the Directory. The medallions round the paintin depict the glorious episodes in the life of Napoleon.

The **Battle Gallery★** was created in the former princes' suites in 1836. The gallery take its name from the 33 paintings representing the great French victories from Tolbiac (496 to Wagram (1809). The series was commissioned by Louis-Philippe and includes works b Horace Vernet (Bouvines, Friedland), Eugène Delacroix (Taillebourg) and Antoine-Jean Gro (Austerlitz). A collection of 80 busts and 16 mural bronze panels evokes the memories of hig dignitaries and officers who were killed at war.

The second floor galleries *(access : Escalier de Stuc)* evoke the First Italian campaign (Ba getti's *gouaches*, Gros' *Bonaparte on the Bridge at Arcole* — 174) the Egyptian and secon Italian campaigns. Portraits present notable people of the period by Gérard (181-183); th Imperial family (171) and artists and writers (168). The last rooms show the marriage of Napo leon to Marie-Louise (166) the Russian campaign (156) and the end of the Empire (Battl of Waterloo).

Restoration and Second Empire Galleries. — *Second floor. North attic, scheduled openin date : 1980.*

THE GARDENS*** AND GRAND CANAL**

The gardens at Versailles, extending over some 100 ha — 250 acres — provide not so much a setting to the palace as an open-air architectural extension the gardens were planned architecturally first by Le Vau, Le Brun and Le Nôtre and later by Mansart; axes, vistas, viewpoints were designed always with an architectural or statuesque point of focus and trees, shrubs and plants were used to provide background, mass and sometimes colour to pavilions, pools, fountains and statues. There is a remarkable sense of pattern and formality.

The garden's style evolved over the years from Baroque to Classical and on to the picturesque in statuary, fountains and buildings.

A lot of the colour disappeared with the reduction in bedding plants from the 150 000 a year of Louis XIV's time to the more modest quantities under later monarchs. Mass and silhouette changed as trees grew to majestic heights.

The basic idea from which the garden design evolved, however, has never been altered — this is that there should be two axes, one north to south extending the line of the palace terrace in either direction, the other due west from the same terrace centre. Symmetry, and therefore monotony, is avoided — in its place is balance.

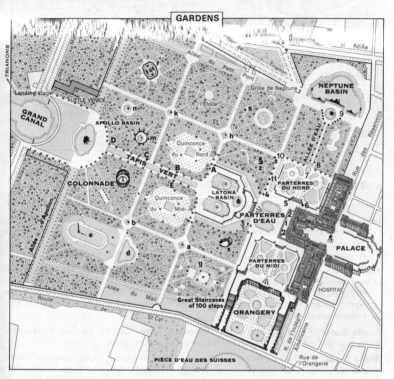

THE PARTERRES (1-11)

Parterres d'Eau*. — Just beneath the centre of the palace **terrace (1)**, itself the major viewpoint of the gardens and adorned with grand **vases*** (2) by Coysevox and Tuby, on War and Peace respectively, are the Parterres d'Eau. They are composed of vast basins decorated with bronze allegorical statues of the rivers of France with, at the end, two fountains, **Dawn (3)** and **Diana (4)**.

Parterres du Nord. — At the north end of the terrace, the Parterres du Nord serve as the setting for two superb bronzes, **Venus on a Tortoise (5)** by Coysevox (original in the Louvre) and the **Knifegrinder*** (6) a copy after the antique by Foggini (original in Florence). Close by is the **Pyramid Fountain*** (7) where, in a group by Girardon, tritons, dolphins and crabs support shells. The **Basin of the Nymphs of Diana (8)** with 17C **low reliefs***, follows, and then the **Allée d'Eau** or **Allée des Marmousets*** — the Water or, more commonly, Children's Alley, from the statues which line the long pool. Beyond the **Dragon Basin (9)** lies the **Neptune Basin*** **, the largest in the park, with an elaborate lead group of the Sea God, dragons and cherubs.

Not far away are the **Philosophers' Crossroads (10)** and the **Alley of the Three Fountains (11)** lined by a beautiful series of statues.

Parterres du Midi. — In line south of the palace terrace are the Parterres du Midi, formal box edged flowerbeds. From these there is a **view** ** over the **Orangery** ** down to the **Pièce d'Eau des Suisses** (Swiss Lake) and the Bernini equestrian statue of Louis XIV in the distance. Mansart took advantage of this downward slope when designing the Orangery : the roof of the central building is level with the parterres, the projecting wings on either side of the court, in which stand orange and palm trees in summer, end in the **Great Staircases of 100 Steps** (Escaliers des Cent-Marches).

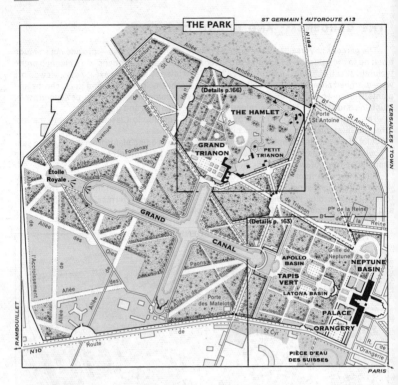

THE PARK

(Details p.166)
(Details p. 163)

■ THE GRAND PERSPECTIVE (A-E)

The theme of this East-West axis is based on the myth of the Sun and the legend of Apollo.

Latona Basin*. — This group of Latona and her children, Diana and Apollo is by Marsy. Latona who was insulted by the Lycian peasants demanded justice from Jupiter who turned them into lizards and frogs.

At the bottom of the steps is the delightful **Nymph with a Shell*** (A) by Coysevox.

Tapis Vert**. — This long avenue (translation : Green Carpet), offers fine perspectives of the Palace and Grand Canal.

It is lined wit vases and statues such as the Antique style Juno (B), a copy of the Venus dei Medici (C) and Artemis by Desjardins. Opposite stands another statue of Venus (E), after an Antique sculpture by Le Gros.

Apollo Basin*. — In the middle a massive group by Tuby shows the Sun God in his chariot rising from the sea among monsters of the deep, to light the world.

Grand Canal**. — *Boats for hire at the end on the right.* The Grand Canal measures 1 650 m long by 62 m wide — 1850 × 68 yds, the Petit or Small Canal 1 070 m — 1 170 yds. In Louis XIV's time the waters were alive and gay with brilliantly decorated gondolas manœuvred by gondoliers who lived in the Little Venice (Petite Venise), nearby.

The **Petit Parc**, a hunting reserve formerly surrounded by the Grand Parc which extended to Marly, encircles the Grand Canal. From the end of the Grand Canal, the Étoile Royale (Royal Star), there is an incredible **view***** back to the palace nearly two miles away.

■ THE GROVES

South. — **Bacchus** (a), by Marsy, at the centre of a group of Satyrs with grapes and vine leaves, represents autumn (in a basin at the juncture of two alleys); **Saturn** (b), a winged god surrounded by cherubs amidst ice flows and shells by Girardon, represents winter. The **Bosquet de la Reine** (g) or Queen's Grove *(closed in winter)* was created in 1775 on the site of the former Maze, it is now decorated with busts and statues (Aphrodite, the Fighting Gladiator). The **Water Mirror Basin** (d) was one of a pair. The **Jardin du Roi*** (e) or King's Garden should be seen in summer when it is in full flower and a mass of colour. To the right of the Green Carpet lies the circular **Colonnade****, erected by Mansart in 1685, it is composed of 24 Pyrenees marble columns.

North. — **Flora** (k) or Spring by Tuby and **Ceres** (h) or Summer by Regnaudin, are the remaining pair in the four statues of the seasons which mark alley meeting points. Through the railings surrounding the **Dôme Grove*** (m) can be seen different marbles and statues. In the **Enceladus Basin*** (n) by Marsy, only Enceladus' head and shoulders are visible amidst engulfing rocks. The **Obelisk Basin** (r) was designed by Mansart and only shows to advantage when the fountain is full on and the water rises in the shape of an obelisk. The **Ile des Enfants** (s) or Children's Island contains the delightful groups designed by Hardy in 1710 from what was originally the quadriga ornament of the Porcelain Trianon.

■ FOUNTAINS*** AND ILLUMINATIONS***

The fountains play — the Grandes Eaux — by daylight (1st and 3rd Sunday from 1 May to 30 September, 4 to 5 pm) and floodlight — Fêtes de Nuit — Phone : 950.36.22 for full details, reserved tickets (imperative for the night performances) etc. 5F.

The fountains are in operation for only a limited time; arrive promptly and keep walking or they may end before you have completed the tour!

The Neptune Basin is closed in the early part of the day when the fountains are due to play. The **Ballroom*** (x) and **Apollo's Bath*** (z) (built during the reign of Louis XVI and designed by Hubert Robert) groves are only open on fountain playing days.

THE TRIANONS**

Access : on foot, from the Neptune grille, straight along the Avenue de Trianon or from the far end of the Grand Canal, along the Allée de Bailly by car — *see map p 166; 4F.*

■ THE GRAND TRIANON**

Guided tours in the morning, see p 158.

From 1670 to 1687 there existed on the site a small château known as the Porcelain Trianon from its facing both outside and in with Delft blue and white tiles. Louis XIV enjoyed retiring to the peace of the small domain with his intimates, particularly Mme de Montespan. With time, however, she lost the king's favour and the château fell into disrepair! In due course the king replaced the earlier building with a pink marble and stone one designed by Mansart to which he returned with the new favourite, Mme de Maintenon. On the king's death, this second Trianon gradually fell into disuse, his successors preferring the Petit Trianon when this was built.

Finally at the Revolution the furniture was dispersed and all seemed at an end until Napoleon, after his marriage to Marie-Louise of Austria, decided to refurnish it. Louis-Philippe had it restored.

The château.** — Well proportioned wings with multicoloured pink marble pilasters border the main courtyard and are linked at their far end by a peristyle of predominantly rose-coloured marble columns through which can be seen the gardens beyond. At the roof edge, above the single storey, is a regular balustrade.

All the rooms which are open to visitors, are on the ground floor; they all open onto the gardens or courtyard by French windows.

The Apartments. — The rooms have been restored to their Louis XIV decor although the furniture throughout dates from the First Empire and the Restoration.

In one of the salons, in the left wing, is a gilded bronze table (dating from the time of Charles X, Louis XV's grandson) with an Italian mosaic of Achilles Shield as described by Homer and in the Seigneurs' Salon a teakwood table of which the top is made from a single piece of wood. The carpets nearly everywhere are Aubusson. The bed is the one ordered by Napoleon for the Tuileries and which Louis-Philippe later had modified.

The attractive Mirror Room was formerly the Council Chamber. The carved woodwork dates back to Louis XIV's time.

Louis-Philippe rearranged the right wing as reception rooms and gave the Emperors' Apartments, now hung with Gobelins tapestries, to his daughters. Further reminders of the princesses appear in the Grand Salon where the table drawers are marked to indicate where each kept her embroidery.

The Malachite Salon is named after the green malachite candelabra and other pieces presented by the Tsar Alexander I to Napoleon.

The **gallery*** lit by four massive Empire chandeliers, contains 24 illustrations commissioned by Louis XIV of the Versailles and Trianons gardens in the 17C.

The wing known as the Trianon-sous-Bois, which comes next, is now reserved for the French President *(not open)*. Beyond are a series of small rooms restored to look as they did when occupied by Napoleon : bedroom, bathroom...

Park*. — Surrounding the Trianons is a delightful park which Louis XIV began by planting with Mediterranean species, particularly those brilliant in colour or heavily perfumed. Louis XVI simplified the arrangement. From the terrace before the garden flowerbeds (1), overlooking the steps and Horseshoe pool (2), you get a good view across the canals. In the opposite direction, in line with the centre of the Trianon, is the Plat-Fond (3) and a little further right, the round Rond d'Eau (4), the **Buffet d'Eau*** (5), and the chestnut grove, the **Bosquet des Marronniers*** (6).

On the far side of the château are the King's Garden and further on by a bridge, the Petit Trianon.

Queen Elizabeth II is the only British monarch in the 20C to have made two State Visits to France (April 1957, May 1972). On the second visit, she stayed like her great great grandmother, Victoria, before her in the Grand Trianon, now the château that France has restored to receive visiting heads of state. First Secretary of the Central Committee of the Communist Party of the USSR, Brejnev, stayed there in October 1971.

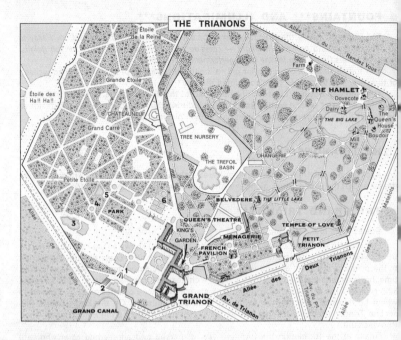

■ THE PETIT TRIANON★★

Louis XV, who enjoyed looking at both animals and flowers, established a menagerie and a botanical garden, directed by Jussieu, in the Trianon domain. Both were later dispersed. The king also commissioned Gabriel to design him a summerhouse, the French Pavilion and, at the end of his reign, the Petit Trianon.

The Petit Trianon was given by his successor, Louis XVI, to Marie-Antoinette who delighted in it, visiting it frequently, accompanied by her children and sister-in-law, Mme Elisabeth. There, the queen, who already felt free from the stifling etiquette of the 18C court, increased the feeling of informality even further, by ordering her architect, Richard Mique, and the painter, Hubert Robert, to modify the gardens and, in imitation of the countryside of her native Austria, build the celebrated Hamlet. It was when Marie-Antoinette was at the Petit Trianon that a page approached her on 5 October 1789 with the news that the Revolutionaries were marching on Versailles. The queen left immediately never to return.

Neither Pauline Bonaparte, Napoleon's sister, nor his wife, Marie-Louise, paid more than fleeting visits to the Petit Trianon and it was only with the Empress Eugénie, who felt considerable sympathy for Marie-Antoinette, that interest revived. The Empress' enthusiasm was such that by 1867 the château had returned, in part, to its former appearance and been largely refurnished with period pieces, including some which had belonged to the former queen.

Château. — The façade overlooking the entrance courtyard is sober, but that on the garden reflects all Gabriel's mastery of the 18C Neo-Classical style. Four colossal columns on either side of three tall windows, rise from ground level to the cornice over the first floor; above is a low balustrade matching that of the terrace fronting the façade and the central double stairway leading to the former gardens. Inside a stone staircase decorated with a wrought iron banister in which Marie-Antoinette's initials are used as a decorative motif, leads to a series of rooms. In the dining-room the paintings represent pastoral scenes, on the mantlepiece is a bust of the Emperor of Austria, Joseph II, Marie-Antoinette's brother. Remarkable decoration and pieces of furniture can be seen in the small dining-room and company salon. *Other rooms are still under restoration.*

The gardens★★. — *Walk along a path to the right to the lake.* There, on a small island, is the **Temple of Love** with, at its centre, Bouchardon's statue of Cupid cutting his Bow from the Club of Hercules (original in the Louvre). Beyond, past the informal garden and scattered round a second lake, the Big Lake (Grand Lac), are ten of the twelve thatched cottages designed by Mique for the peasants, shepherds and miller who lived in Marie-Antoinette's **Hamlet★★**. The cottages were used by Marie-Antoinette and her friends in the day time when they came and in the phrase of the time " played at being peasants ", making their own butter, minding the sheep and eating in the open air.

The **Belvedere** or **Music Room** overlooking the Little Lake (Petit Lac) was designed by Mique in Neo-Classical style. Inside are marble pavements, stucco ornament, arabesques and painted ceilings. The **French Pavilion★** (Pavillon Français), between the Grand and Petit Trianons, is considered Gabriel's greatest masterpiece of the small scale. Eight Corinthian columns ornament the round salon which is decorated with white and gold panelling and a frieze of animals above the entablature.

The **Queen's Theatre** *(guided tours p 158)* was where Marie-Antoinette could indulge her personal enjoyment of acting in plays and light opera before her friends.

Michelin map **101** 14
Access also by the RER or bus No. 73 from the Gare d'Orsay, Concorde or Étoile.

LA DÉFENSE★★   detailed map

The quarter gets its name from a monument (now on the parvis) commemorating the defence of Paris of 1871. The aim of this town planning project is to create a new business centre in **Courbevoie, Puteaux** and **Nanterre**. This area is divided into zones : A and B.

Zone A. — This zone of 130 ha — 321 acres — has as a centrepiece, a vast concrete **podium**, which rises in steps from the Seine. It is 1 200 m — 1 312 yds — long and varies in width from 70 to 250 m — 77 to 273 yds — and is a continuation of the Champs-Elysées-Pont de Neuilly axis. The originality of the plan lies underneath the podium where a complex network of communications exist : the A 14 motorway, two national roads, the La Défense's own ring road plus local access and link roads the RER express métro, suburban line and bus stations.

From the commercial centre, above the spacious RER station take the way out marked parvis. Standing on the podium, the skyline all around is broken by towers in a variety of architectural styles and a forest of cranes. Of the 30 towers planned to rise above the open spaces of the podium 18 are at present finished and they house the offices of important French and foreign companies, the National Gas, Electricity and General Maritime Companies, Banks and Insurance companies, IBM, Esso, Mobil Oil and Fiat.

From the end of the podium there is, on a clear day, a fine **perspective★** down the corridor between the towers, in the direction of Étoile. The first building to strike the eye is the **CNIT★** Exhibition Hall (National Centre for Industry and Technology) a concrete building in the form of an inverted shell with only 3 points of support. This is the venue for great commercial exhibitions. On the left is the polished granite and black tinted glass façade of the elegant **Fiat Tower★★** which with its 45 storeys is the tallest building. Note how the windows have been widened near the top to avoid a tapering effect. The red stabile (15 m — 49 ft — high) by Calder, his last work, is closeby. The Information Centre run by EPAD the coordinating body for the entire project, has maps and models of the La Défense quarter when finished. To the right stand a group of sombre office buildings which contrast with the rounded form of the residential tower, Eve in the background, and the decorative aluminium façade of the Générale Tower. In front of the Esso building the underground Galerie has temporary exhibitions. Note also a work by Agam. The fountains play with music and illuminations *(Wednesdays 1 to 2 pm; Saturdays and Sundays 3 to 4 pm)*. Passing Place des Corolles (whorl of petals) — named after the sculpture in the fountain by Louis Leygue — continue to Place des Reflets, bordered by the unusual form of the Aurore Tower with alternating bands of bronze tinted glass and concrete. Beyond, the original shape of the **Manhattan Tower★★★** attracts the eye. This building was recently bought by Kuwait. In the middle distance is the coloured green **GAN Tower★★** in the form of a Greek cross and to the right, the first tower to be built at La Défense, the **Roussel-Nobel Tower★**.

Zone B. — The area further to the west, will include housing, the university complex, **Paris X,** a **School of Architecture,** the **Préfecture** of the Hauts-de-Seine, sports facilities and open spaces including a 24 ha — 59 acre park *(parts already opened)*.

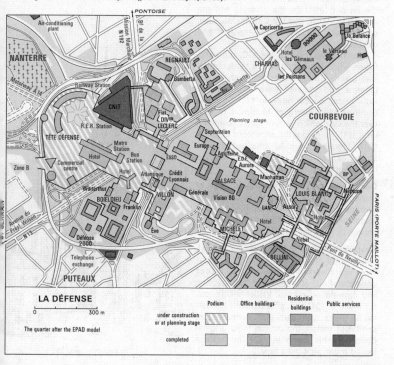

Michelin map **101** 16.
Métro station : St-Denis Basilique (line 13).

St-Denis, a dormitory town of more than 100,000 has but one tourist interest for a foreigner, the famous basilica, necropolis of the kings and queens of France. Every year a musical festival is given in the summer.

" Monsieur St. Denis ". — St. Denis, 3C evangelist and first bishop of Lutetia, continued on his way after having been decapitated in Montmartre *(p 75),* bearing his head in his hands. He was finally buried where he fell by a pious woman. In due course an abbey was erected over the tomb of this man, commonly known as Monsieur (Monseigneur) St. Denis. Such is the legend. Fact, at least, is that a Roman town, Catolacus, commanding both the Paris— Beauvais road and the river, stood on the site from 1C; that it was in a nearby field that Denis and his two companions would appear to have been martyred and that a popular pilgrimage chapel has existed in the area from the time of Constantine.

The first large church was built in 475, possibly at the instigation of St. Genevieve; this was pillaged in 570; rebuilt by Dagobert I and the bodies of the martyrs interred within it on 24 February 636. Finally a Benedictine community was established to look after the ever more popular pilgrimage. In about 750 Pepin the Short rebuilt the church.

Abbot Suger. — The basilica we see today is essentially the edifice erected by Suger, Abbot of St-Denis in the 12C, and of Pierre of Montreuil, architect to St. Louis in the 13C.

Suger, the son of poor parents, was " given " at the age of 10, to the abbey where his gifts greatly influenced his fellow novice, the future Louis VII. In 1122 Suger, by now one of the most learned men of his time, was elected Abbot of St-Denis. Louis VII appointed him minister and regent during his absence on the 2nd Crusade when the abbot's wisdom and care for the public good made the king, on his return, name him " father of the nation ".

Suger's personal flag, a red and gold oriflamme, became the military standard of France.

The Lendit Fair. — The fair, inaugurated by the abbey in 1109, attracted merchants and crowds from all parts of France and many countries abroad for the 600 years during which it flourished on the St-Denis plain. The University of Paris used to purchase from among the 1,200 stallholders the parchment required by the scholars on Mount St. Genevieve *(p 102).*

The Royal Necropolis. — For twelve centuries, from Dagobert to Louis XVIII, all French kings, apart from three Merovingians and a few Capetians, were buried at St-Denis. In 1793 the Convention decreed the destruction of the mausoleums; the coffins were exhumed, the bodies thrown pel-mel into unnamed graves; the tombs, however, were saved as the archaeologist Alexandre Lenoir, had removed them some time previously and placed them in a specially created museum. The tombs were returned to the basilica under Louis XVIII.

■ THE BASILICA★★

The church is a landmark in French architecture : as the first great Gothic edifice it became the inspiring prototype for late 12C cathedral architecture, notably Chartres.

Construction. — Under Suger, construction took place of the façade and the first two bays of the nave (1136-1140), the chancel and the crypt (1140-1144), and the Carolingian nave, provisionally conserved, was repaired and refaced (1145-1147).

At the beginning of the 13C, the north tower, which had been struck by lightning, was given a magnificent stone spire; the chancel and transept were enlarged and work begun on the nave. In 1247 St. Louis commissioned Pierre of Montreuil to take over the task which was, in fact, to continue until 1281, long after the architect's death in 1267. Immense wealth, amassed by the abbey, can be seen, in part, at the Louvre in the Apollo Gallery *(p 39).*

Decadence. — There followed centuries of neglect and, finally, depredation during the Revolution when the lead roofing was stolen. Napoleon ordered repairs and restored the church to worship in 1806.

Restoration. — In 1813 the architect, Debret, took charge of the building and for thirty-three years worked on it with a total lack of understanding of mediaeval architecture and devastating results. Viollet-le-Duc took his place in 1847 and, after patiently collecting all the relevant early documents, began, in 1858, to restore the church to its original design. By his death in 1879 the basilica looked much as it does now.

The basilica — early 19C

Exterior

The basilica has a strangely fortified appearance with crenelations and four massive buttresses and a general air of dissymmetry, lacking, as it does, a north tower and with both pointed Gothic and rounded Romanesque arches included in the main façade. Above the round arched doors are stained glass windows, blind arcades, a gallery of statues and a rose window — the first in any church and a feature which was, from the 13C, to form an integral element in the design of every Gothic cathedral. The tympana over the central, right and left doorways (restored and recarved respectively) illustrate the Last Judgment, St. Denis' last communion, the death of the saint and his two companions. At the doorway shafts are the Wise and Foolish Virgins, the labours of the months and the signs of the zodiac.

Interior

The northern of two bays is still supported on massive pillars and pointed arches, dating from Abbot Suger's time. Further within, Pierre of Montreuil has given the nave and adjoining aisles, the chancel, an architectural lift and lightness that are almost ethereal. The transept triforium, even at this date, was glazed with stained glass.

Tour : *Guided tours 1 April to 30 September, 10 am to noon and 1.30 to 6 pm (1 to 4 pm in winter). Closed Sunday mornings, 1 January, 1 May, 25 December; 5F — Sundays, 2,50F. The last tour 40 min before closing time.*

The Tombs***. — The kings of France, their queens, the royal children and a few great servants of the crown — Du Guesclin (1) — lay in St-Denis, 79 figures in all, until the Revolution. Now the tombs are empty and the statuary is therefore, virtually, a great museum of funerary sculpture.

The Effigies. — Until the Renaissance, tombal sculptures consisted only of effigies — among such are the 12C copper filleted cloisonnéd mosaics of Clovis (2) and Frédégonde (3) from St-Germain-des-Prés *(p 93)*. In about 1260 St. Louis had effigies carved of all his ancestors going back to the 7C. These are purely symbolic and of little interest except for King Dagobert (4) founding the basilica, Charles Martel (5), Pepin the Short (6) and a recumbent figure in Tournai marble (7). From the death of Philippe III, the Bold (8), in 1285, likenesses were produced from death masks — thus Charles V (9), Charles VI and Isabela of Bavaria (10) are true portraits.

The Mausoleums. — At the Renaissance funerary stones were replaced by mausoleums — their two tiers presenting a pathetic contrast : above the king and queen appear kneeling in full regalia; below as naked cadavers. Outstandingly ornate are Louis XII and Anne of Brittany (11), François I and Claude of France (12) by Philibert Delorme and Pierre Bontemps. Catherine dei Medici, who died thirty years after Henri II, had time to erect her husband's tomb but when she saw her own traditional style effigy, she fainted in horror and substituted a figure asleep — the visitor can compare the two versions, the first by Il Primaticcio (13) the second by Germain Pilon (14).

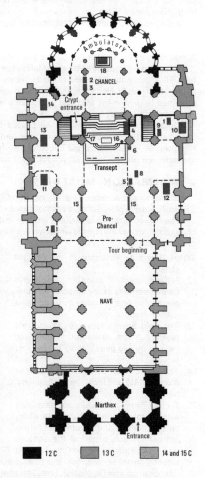

The Chancel. — The beautiful pre-Renaissance stalls (15) carved with biblical scenes are from the Normandy castle of Gaillon; the polychrome Romanesque **Virgin*** on her throne (16) is 12C and from St-Martin-des-Champs *(p 146)*; the episcopal seat (17) is a reproduction of Dagobert's throne *(original : p 89)*. A modern shrine, behind the chancel, contains relics of St. Denis, St. Rusticus and St. Eleutherius (18). The early Gothic **ambulatory*** dates from the time of Abbot Suger and forms a striking contrast to the high 13C nave and chancel.

The Crypt**. — The lower ambulatory, built in the Romanesque style by Suger in the 12C, was greatly restored by Viollet-le-Duc. In the centre, is the vaulted chapel of Pepin the Short, where a stone covers the tomb of the Bourbons, in which are buried Louis XVI, Marie-Antoinette *(p 142)* and Louis XVIII, and in the north transept, a communal grave excavated in 1817, which received the bodies of some 800 Merovingians, Capetians, Orleans and Valois.

Excavations beneath the high altar and nave have uncovered walls of the Carolingian martyrium, a rich late 6C Merovingian tomb, the foundations of five earlier sanctuaries as well as magnificent sarcophagi and jewels.

MALMAISON★★

Michelin map ▨▨▨ 13.
RER station : La Défense, then take bus 158 to Danielle Casanova.

Rueil-Malmaison lies encircled by a bend in the Seine to the west of Paris. The town's only claim to fame is the Malmaison Château Museum, treasure house of Napoleonic souvenirs.

Malmaison in Napoleon Bonaparte's time. — Josephine Tascher de la Pagerie, born in 1763, widow of General de Beauharnais, beheaded during the Terror, married General Bonaparte in 1796. Three years later she bought the château and 260 ha — 640 acre park — of Malmaison where she was to pass the happiest years of her married life with Napoleon. As First Consul, Bonaparte was already residing officially at the Tuileries but he paid frequent visits to the château, built in 1622, where he could live completely informally and Josephine was gay, elegant, extravagant and capricious.

Josephine alone at Malmaison. — After his coronation as Emperor, Napoleon frequented only the official residences of the Tuileries, St-Cloud and Fontainebleau but Josephine kept her affection for Malmaison and whenever possible, hastened to her own château and its glorious rose garden.

After the divorce Josephine returned to Malmaison which Napoleon had given her together with the Élysée Palace, a château near Évreux and a small fortune. She continued to receive guests such as the King of Prussia. She caught cold during the reception given for the Tsar Alexander I at the Château of St-Leu and died a few days later on 29 May 1814.

Napoleon returned three times to Malmaison after Josephine's death : firstly on his escape from Elba, secondly at the end of the Hundred Days when he sought refuge with his sister-in-law, the beautiful Hortense, and her young son, the future Napoleon III, and finally, when he remained largely in his personal apartments on the first floor, during the period between Waterloo and his departure for St. Helena.

On Josephine's death, the château passed to her son, Prince Eugène de Beauharnais. but when he died it was sold, passing from hand to hand until it returned to the family under Napoleon III. His wife, Empress Eugénie, then had the idea of converting Malmaison into a museum — a project, however, not fully realized until 1906.

■ MALMAISON MUSEUM★★

Guided tours : summer, 10 am to noon and 1.30 to 5.30 pm; winter to 5 pm; time : 1 hour. Closed Tuesdays; 5F — Sundays and holidays 2.50F.

The museum, which is devoted entirely to Josephine and Napoleon Bonaparte, consists of items donated or purchased which were originally in the château or at the Tuileries, St-Cloud or Fontainebleau.

Ground Floor : 1) Vestibule in the Antique style.

2) Billiard room : beautiful Savonnerie carpet, portraits of the Emperor and Empress in coronation robes by Gérard and Lefèvre respectively.

3) The Gold Salon : furniture, Josephine's tapestry frame. Beautiful mantelpiece flanked by two paintings by Gérard and Girodet.

4) The Music Room : the room is exactly as it was in 1812 and includes the Empress' harp.

5) Dining Room : the walls are decorated with mural paintings of dancers while, on the table is the magnificent silver-gilt centerpiece, a part of the banqueting service offered by the City of Paris to Napoleon at his coronation.

6) Council chamber : the room has been decorated to make it appear as though it were the interior of an army campaign tent. The chairs are from St-Cloud.

7) The Library : furniture, books and maps from the Malmaison and the Tuileries.

1st Floor : 8) The Emperor's Drawing Room : portraits by Gérard of the imperial family. In the centre, note the fine marble table.

9) Napoleon's Bedroom : the canopied bed and personal objects are from the Tuileries. It was in this set of rooms that the Emperor spent most of his time after Waterloo, before going to St. Helena.

10) Marengo Room : paintings of Napoleon's victories in the field by Gérard and Gros. On display are the personal belongings which he took on campaign.

11-12) Exhibition Galleries further illustrating the Emperor's life-style and character with paintings, uniforms, busts of Napoleon and Josephine, a mural frieze in the Antique style from the First Consul's house in the Rue de la Victoire, coronation mementoes and finally a precious porcelain table showing the Emperor surrounded by the victorious generals of the Battle of Austerlitz, 1805.

13-15) Josephine's Apartments : portraits and personal objects in profusion including her jewels, perfumes and her huge dress bills — at her death she had debts amounting to three million francs!

2nd Floor : 16) Queen Hortense's bedroom : furniture and personal mementoes.
17) Gallery devoted to Napoleon's exile on St. Helena from 1815 to his death (1821) and the return of his body to the Invalides (p 54).
18) Some of Napoleon's personal belongings, mementoes of his close friends and a collection of medals and coins.

Bois-Préau Château*. — Same times as Malmaison; 3F — Sundays, 1.50F.

The château, bought by Josephine in 1810, and bequeathed the following century by the Americans, Mr. and Mrs. Edward Tuck to the French, for use as a Napoleonic museum, contains mementoes of St. Helena, and one of his famous black cocked hats.

MOUNT VALÉRIEN

Michelin map ▓▓▓ 14.
Bus No. 175 from the Porte St-Cloud.

Mount Valérien was a sacred place as far back as the Gallo-Roman epoch. By the 17C it had acquired a path with Stations of the Cross leading to a popular pilgrimage chapel.
Later centuries have involved the mound in war : in 1870-71 it became part of the Paris fortification perimeter; between 1940 and 1944, 4 500 men of the Resistance were taken out and shot on its slopes. A **Memorial to Fighting France** decorated across its wide façade with a stone frieze showing the Cross of Lorraine and the struggle for liberty, was opened on 18 June 1960. In the crypt are the tombs of 16 soldiers and an urn containing the ashes of unknown victims. *Guided tours daily every half hour from 10 to 11.30 am and 2 to 6.30 pm — 4.30 pm 1 October to 31 March.* There is also an American Military Cemetery on the slopes of Mount Valérien with the dead from both World Wars.
To the right of the road, a terrace affords a wide panoramic view of Paris beyond the Bois de Boulogne.

ST-GERMAIN-EN-LAYE★★

Michelin map ▓▓▓ 12.
RER station : St-Germain-en-Laye.

The lovely old town, with its Renaissance château, park, great terrace and nearby St-Germain and Marly woods, is a most attractive excursion.

The Old Castle. — Louis VI, in the 12C, erected a castle commanding the Seine on St-Germain Hill to which St. Louis added a chapel in 1230. The castle, but not the chapel, was destroyed by the Black Prince in the Hundred Years War, and rebuilt by Charles V in 1368. François I, influenced by his travels in Italy, rebuilt the castle entirely in 1539 with the exceptions of the chapel and Charles V keep.

The New Château. — Henri II, son of François I and born in the castle, found the place stark and commissioned Philibert Delorme to erect him a country seat. It was completed by Henri IV. The royal diversions of the time — dancing, theatrical performances and recitals — were given added spice by the construction of fountains in the grounds which Henri IV delighted to turn on his guests. Louis XIV, who appreciated the joke, had similar fountains at Versailles (p 157). Like Henri II, Charles IX and Louis XIV were born at St-Germain — the birthdate, cradle and Bourbon lily of the latter being incorporated in the town's arms. Louis XIII died there.

Last Years. — The Old Castle and New Château were both used by the court — Louis XIV getting Jules Hardouin-Mansart to convert the five towers into living pavilions, Le Nôtre to lay out the park and terrace, before he finally left for Versailles in 1682.
The New Château passed to the future Charles X who demolished and never rebuilt it. Such parts as remained and the Old Castle furnishings were destroyed by the Revolution. Finally the Old Castle was converted into the museum of National Antiquities by Napoleon III in 1867. The treaty of peace concluded between the Allies and Austria was signed in the château in 1919.

Associations with Britain. — St-Germain's royal associations with Britain, besides the Black Prince, are several. Mary Stuart, later Mary Queen of Scots, lived in the castle from the age of six to her marriage ten years later in 1558 with the Dauphin, the future, shortlived, François II, son of Henri II. The wife of Charles I, Henrietta, daughter of Henri IV, lived there from 1645-1648 with her daughter during part of the Civil War and in 1689, James II, deposed from the throne, arrived to live in moody retirement until his death in 1701.

■ THE CHÂTEAU★

The château, an irregular pentagon in which the feudal substructure, watchpath and machicolations can be clearly seen even now, is given an added military aspect by the towers at each of its five corners. That to the left of the main entrance on the Place du Château is the Charles V keep which François I had capped by a turret which Louis XIV, in turn, had converted into an observatory where he installed Cassini (p 123).
The flat roofs, the first in France, are edged by a vase ornamented stone balustrade.
Go over a bridge and through the gate to the inner court; in the entrance hall are illustrations of the châteaux of St-Germain-en-Laye, through the ages.

Sainte-Chapelle*. — The chapel, built in 1230 by St. Louis, ten years before the Sainte-Chapelle in Paris (p 68), is undoubtedly by the same architect, Pierre of Montreuil. The tall windows, however, were too early to be glazed with the brilliant glass which makes the Paris chapel a mediaeval jewel and the beautiful rose window has been blinded by other constructions. On the arch keystones are carved heads which may well be portraits of St. Louis, his mother Blanche of Castille, his wife and other close associates.

Parterres. — An iron grille opens onto the gardens from the château which in this façade includes a loggia approached by a formal staircase. The moat now contains reconstituted megaliths and copies of Roman monuments such as Trajan's and Nero's columns. (The gardens are presently being filled up.)

Terrace★★**. — The Grande Terrasse — beyond the Petite Terrasse on which there is a viewing table — is one of Le Nôtre's masterpieces. It is

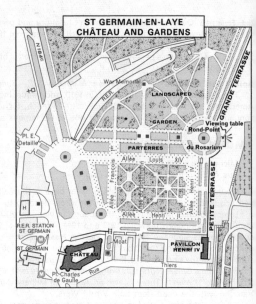

ST GERMAIN-EN-LAYE
CHÂTEAU AND GARDENS

2 400 m long — 2 500 yds — bordered with time trees and took four years to lay out, being completed in 1673. Beyond lies a **landscaped garden★**.

■ MUSEUM OF NATIONAL ANTIQUITIES★★

Open 9.45 am to noon and 1.30 to 5.15 pm; closed Tuesdays. 6F; 3F Sundays and holidays.
This museum contains rich archaeological collections — attractively displayed, from France's earliest inhabitants (Palaeolithic) to the Merovingian Period (8C).

Stone Age. — *Mezzanine floor.* The world map at the entrance will help you to situate the various cultures, geological periods and prehistoric sites, which are mentioned in the museum. There is also a large illuminated tableau which illustrates, chronologically, man's knowledge in prehistory.

During the **Lower Palaeolithic** (1 000 000-150 000 BC) man's earliest implements ranged from the most primitive pebble-tool to the bifacially flaked flints.

Gradually through the **Middle Palaeolithic** (to 40 000 BC), other materials such as bone, quartz crystals and rock crystal were also used to make primitive tools.

In the **Upper Palaeolithic** (40 000-10 000 BC) the nomadic hunters who sheltered in caves were undoubtedly members of *Homo Sapiens* and they were capable of making more intricate tools (harpoon points, flints and blades) and produced the earliest examples of art (engraved or relief carving). The figurine of the Brassempouy Woman (ca 25 000 BC) is the oldest known sculpture of the human form.

In the **Mesolithic** Period (ca 8 000 BC), an intermediate age (separating Palaeolithic from the Neolithic Period) tools are perfected; man is less concerned with artistic expression.

During the **Neolithic** Period, concentrated especially in the Near East (8 000 BC), man lived in settled communities and turned to crop growing and stock raising, made pottery and wove. The working of hard stones (jadeite) through polishing produced arms, and tools of great esthetic quality — more religious (votive objects) than utilitarian in content. Flint knapping continues.

Bronze Age (1800-750 BC). — With the gradual dominance of metals over stone there appeared a variety of small objects in copper then bronze (mixture of copper and tin) : daggers (case on the right), curved axes, bracelets decorated with geometric motifs, twisted torque-necklaces, sickles and fibulas. Note *(in case)* jewellery in solid gold or sheaths of beaten gold.

Iron Age. — Characteristic of the early Iron Age are the richly furnished graves of the **Hallstatt** (ca 750-450 BC) culture, called after a famous Austrian site. The graves of princes were distinguished by the presence of a large iron sword. Also included (in the graves) were fibulas (clasps or brooches) pottery and furniture as in the tomb at Magny-Lambert in the Côte-d'Or or even a four-wheeled wagon and harness. The **La Tene** culture which followed has left evidence of trade contacts between the civilized Mediterranean world and Champagne : a variety of fibulas, amber necklaces, glass and enamel pendants, Greco-Italian pottery and Celtic arms. The Gallic tribes still places two-wheeled chariots in the graves (see the reconstruction of such graves from Berru and La Gorge-Meillet), worked with leather and gold (case of jewellery) and struck coins. The arrival of Caesar in 52 BC and the taking of Alesia (note the model of the camp) marked the end of this culture.

Gallo-Roman Period (52 BC-3C). — *First floor.* The long *Pax Romana* and the tolerance of the invaders, allowed the expression of an original art which is well illustrated here through funerary and mythological statues, everyday objects (dishes, glassware and red pottery) and decorative features (mosaic showing the Work of the Months).

Merovingian Art (3-8C). — The turmoil of this period, marked by the invasions, has left few remains other than graves rich in objects of all sorts : swords and battle-axes, *cloisonné* jewellery, S-shaped fibulas and bronze buckles with fantastic decoration.

SÈVRES   Michelin map 🔟 24

The name of this small town is known all the world over for its brilliant multicoloured porcelain; it is also known, to the knowledgeable, as the seat of the International Weights and Measures Bureau and to historians for the treaty of Sèvres signed on 10 August 1920 between the Allies and Turkey.

SÈVRES PORCELAIN

Porcelain is a ceramic material, which when fired in the piece undergoes vitrification, emerging as an extremely hard, translucent product when finally moulded (as opposed to the opacity of china).

It was first produced in France in 1738 at Vincennes, the factory receiving a royal warrant in 1753. This was nearly half a century after the first man to make porcelain in Europe, Johann Friedrich Bottger, had established his factory in Dresden (1708).

The secret of the manufacturing process leaked from Saxony to France but until 1769, when a deposit of kaolin was discovered in the Limousin, only soft paste ware, consisting of marl and glass vitrifield in combination, could be produced. The new product, including kaolin and fired at a high temperature, had remarkable strength although it was more difficult to decorate.

In 1756 the factory at Vincennes was transferred to Sèvres and three years later became the king's exclusive property. As of 1758 a yearly sale of Sèvres products was held at Versailles and courtiers were expected to buy. The royal cypher of interlaced L's (Louis) was used from this period as the factory mark.

Sèvres soft porcelain was known for its natural sprigged flowers, statuettes and tableware, its wonderful ground colours (*bleu-roi* or royal, or Sèvres blue, as it came to be known, rose-red, turquoise, yellow, pea-green) and panel decoration of gallant scenes. Even jewels were made with gold and pearls inlaid in paste and fired. The pieces were magnificent; the prices prohibitive.

The finest Sèvres' designers were J.B. Pigalle (1714-1785) and E.M. Falconet (1716-1791).

Sèvres National Porcelain Factory★★. — *Guided tours 1st and 3rd Thursdays in the month at 2 and 3.30 pm. Closed July and August. No children under 16.*

Turning, firing, moulding are shown; one can follow the different stages in the decoration of porcelain — which passes through the hands of 20 craftsmen. If it does not pass the test of perfection it is destroyed.

The sales rooms contain traditional and modern pieces (*open 9 am to noon and 1.30 to 6 pm; closed Saturdays and Sundays*).

National Porcelain Museum★★. — *Open 9.30 am to noon and 1.30 to 5.45 pm; closed holidays; 5F — Sundays, 2.50F.*

The museum, founded in 1824, contains china and porcelain from all parts of the world including the Orient and the Middle East, and all the major factories of Europe from Sèvres itself and all other centres in France to Meissen, Berlin, Copenhagen Delft, Vienna, St. Petersburg, England (Wedgwood)...

ST-CLOUD PARK★★   Michelin map 🔟 23, 24

Open March, April, September and October 7 am to 9 pm; May to August 7 am to 10 pm; November to February 7 am to 8 pm; pedestrians free; cars : 4F. Restricted parking.

The park, which extends some 450 ha — 1 100 acres — over a hillside dominating the Seine, was landscaped by Le Nôtre and contains fine vistas, viewpoints, expanses of water, woods and shrubberies. It originally depended on a 17C château, designed by Mansart. This later became Napoleon's favourite residence, the scene of subsequent monarchs' visits and of Napoleon III's sumptuous receptions. It was burned down by the Prussians in 1870 and razed in 1891.

From the **Trocadero Garden★** and the **Rond-Point de la Balustrade** in the park, there is a splendid **panorama★★** of Paris from the Bois de Boulogne right across to the Bois de Meudon. The **Grande Cascade★** is a typical, elaborate 17C fountain with allegories of the Seine and the Marne and a second basin designed by Jules Hardouin-Mansart. The **fountains★★** only play the second and fourth Sundays from June to September (*4 and 5 pm*).

■ THE LA-FAYETTE MEMORIAL   Michelin map 🔟 north of 23

The La-Fayette Memorial in the park, was raised by an American foundation in honour of the 209 American voluntary aviators who joined the La-Fayette squadron in the First World War.

The monument consists of an arch and a colonnade reflected in a pool. The crypt beneath the terrace contains the bodies of the 67 pilots killed in action including the fighter ace, Lufbery.

Nearby is the Pasteur Institute (*p 121*) where Pasteur himself died in 1895 (*to visit, phone 970.07.15*).

If you are only staying a few days in Paris,
the map on p 11 shows you how to see
the capital's unique sights in four days.

INDEX

MUSEUMS BY SUBJECT

Army : 56.

Art : Louvre, 30; African and Oceanian, 135; Antique, 32, 88; Armenian, 130; Contemporary, 114; Decorative (historic artefacts), 91, 99; European Periods – Mediaeval, 45, 91 – Renaissance, 45, 142 –18C, 45, 73, 138, 142 – 19C and Impressionists, 42, 45, 153 – 20C and Paris School, 45, 144; Jewish, 78; Monuments, 50; Oriental, 130, 138,145; Popular, 131; Tapestries, 92,154,160; temporary exhibition halls, 42, 45,144.

Artists : Bourdelle, 121; Delacroix, 93; Henner, 138; G. Moreau, 76; Rodin, 127.

Books, MSS, Prints, Maps : 88.

Coins, Medals, Orders : 56, 88, 126, 136.

Counterfeit : 130.

Education : 123.

Glass, Porcelain : 155, 173.

History : of Paris 78, 82, 99; of France 84, 162, 172.

Hunting : 84.

Maritime : 50.

Music : 73, 142.

Personalities : Balzac, 152; Clemenceau, 152; Victor Hugo, 80; Napoleon, 170; Pasteur, 121.

Police : 105.

Post : 120.

Science : Anthropology and pre-history, 50, 172; Astronomy, 46, 123; Medicine, 122; Mineralogy, 123, 139, 140; Natural History, 140; Technology, 46, 147, 154.

Transport : 135.

Waxworks : 76, 117.

MANUFACTURE FRANÇAISE DES PNEUMATIQUES MICHELIN
© Michelin et Cie, propriétaires-éditeurs, 1979
Société en commandite par actions au capital de 700 millions de francs
R. C. Clermont-Fd B 855 200 507 - Siège social : Clermont-Fd (France)
ISBN 2 06 013 540 - 0

Composition et impression : TARDY QUERCY S.A. Bourges — Printed in France. 6.79.90 — Dépôt légal, 3e trim. 1979 (9321)